4/17

Philosophical Writing

Philosophical Writing:

Locke, Berkeley, Hume

John J. Richetti

Harvard University Press

Cambridge, Massachusetts, and London, England   1983

Publication of this book has been aided by a grant from the Andrew W. Mellon Foundation

Library of Congress Cataloging in Publication Data

Richetti, John J.
  Philosophical writing.

  Includes index.
  1. English prose literature — 18th century — History
and criticism. 2. Locke, John, 1632–1704.
3. Berkeley, George, 1685–1753. 4. Hume, David,
1711–1776. I. Title.
PR769.R5 1983 828'.508'09 82–23220
ISBN 0-674-66482-5

Acknowledgments

I wish to thank the American Council of Learned Societies for a fellowship that enabled me to begin work on this subject, and the Rutgers University Faculty Academic Study Program for a sabbatical year in which to complete this book. The Rutgers Research Council provided a welcome typing grant. Paul Fussell, Richard Poirier, Edward Said, and James Sutherland supported the project in its earliest stages, and I owe a great deal to them for their generous enthusiasm. Various friends and colleagues offered essential encouragement along the way: Joe Cady, Arthur Cash, Maurice Charney, the late James Clifford, Sheila Emerson, Dustin Griffin, Myra Jehlen, William Keach, Fred Keener, John Middendorf, Ruth Perry, Barry Qualls, and Elaine Showalter. Camille Smith, my copy editor at Harvard University Press, saved me from numerous embarrassments and by her skill and tact made this a better book. I am grateful to Joan Garrett-Goodyear for letting me use her splendid office for a semester. I am more than grateful to Deirdre David, whose wit, good sense, and affection have long sustained me.

Contents

Philosophical Writing

Introduction

Mildness, amid the neo-Nietzschean clatter . . .
—Ezra Pound, "The Age Demanded"

Literary critics have enlarged their territorial claims in the last twenty years, not simply from an imperial urge to invade other disciplines but from the conviction that "literature" as traditionally understood creates a falsifying dichotomy separating scientific and philosophical works from writing that is overtly imaginative and rhetorical. As Northrop Frye put it at the conclusion of the *Anatomy of Criticism,* "all structures in words are partly rhetorical, and hence literary," and "the notion of a scientific or philosophical verbal structure free of rhetorical elements is an illusion."[1] Frye's extension of the literary universe to include all discourse is, in Frank Lentricchia's keenly skeptical rendering, "the highest of all aestheticisms . . . in which every act of making is glorified as art."[2] For Frye, literary discourse is primal, and other modes of writing are enriched by lingering, vitalizing traces of rhetoric and imagination. For recent critics, this distant kinship Frye celebrates is writing's original sin, a neglected scandal which compromises all discourse. Disappointed, apparently, by literature, disgusted by ambiguity and indeterminacy their predecessors found delightful, many critics of a theoretical bent are now neo-Nietzschean revisionists, stripping all discourse down to the primal deceptiveness of literary language. The opportunities for criticism in an expanded literary order have largely given way to the grimly efficient exposé of all writing as rhetorical in a deep and damaging sense.

Everything written is indeed more or less literary, and critics who set out to deal with economics, philosophy, or science can lean on a sturdy platitude. But overt rhetorical elements in such books may be negligible or trivial. At first, a critic may find precious little practical work to do on the surfaces of such texts; he may be tempted to dive to the deepest, ultimate implications of the text in order to burst to the surface, gasping for air but clutching triumphantly the dark pearls of instability and self-referentiality. Critics are thus transformed into subversive antimetaphysicians, insisting like Paul de Man that "rhetoric radically suspends logic and opens up vertiginous possibilities of referential aberration."[3]

In this book I try to steer a middle course between de Man's subversive negations and Frye's affirming inclusiveness. The boundary between literature (or rhetoric) and writing is properly, I think, a historical issue, for "literature" is meaningless except as a historical category, a variable notion. Locke, Berkeley, and Hume provide a unique opportunity for an extraterritorial literary criticism precisely because for them that boundary was still uncertain and shifting. Their works are richly rhetorical and self-consciously persuasive, and yet the nature of philosophical writing is for them an unresolved issue, a recurring theme within their writing itself. They are powerful writers fully aware of the problematic nature of language, struggling not only to represent their thought persuasively but to defer to the authority of logic and rational demonstration, suppressing to some extent their own rhetorical force and movement. Situated historically as writers between the despised jargon of the Schools and an emerging professionalized scientific discourse, they are committed to stylish clarity in order to be understood by a broadly defined, thoughtful audience. In the pursuit of experiential simplicity, they share a deep distrust of language and make rhetorical control a moral issue. In short, their work is self-consciously concerned with its status as writing. Their texts are locally active, agitated specifically by the problem of writing about thinking. The search for a suitable rhetorical mode for philosophy is at the center of their thought.

But Locke, Berkeley, and Hume do not thereby subvert philosophy. They do not license literary criticism to appropriate philosophical discourse by revealing it as a covert imaginative projection of the world or as a persuasive vision of it disguised by a logical surface. Their works invite literary criticism, not to expose philosophy's unwitting dependence on the stabilizing assumptions hidden within language itself, but rather to evaluate philosophical writing as a deliberate and delicate effort to balance logic and rational demonstration against rhetoric or persuasion of any kind. I propose in this book to read their works in this spirit. It seems to me essential, in fact inevitable, to grant their writing a measure of stability and referentiality, or at least to allow them as writers a sufficient awareness of the ultimate trickiness of language. The issue is not so much what language will always do as what they attempt to do as writers, how they manage to be writers as well as philosophers. My reading is extended and detailed, concerned to appreciate their achievements as writers, to describe the pleasures their writing affords and to analyze the difficulties and even the contradictions they face in the process.

Chapter 1

Rhetoric, Style, and Philosophical Writing

How charming is divine philosophy!
Not harsh, and crabbed as dull fools suppose,
But musical as is Apollo's lute,
And a perpetual feast of nectar'd sweets,
Where no crude surfet raigns.

—Milton, *Comus*

"Since Wit and Fancy finds easier entertainment in the World, than dry Truth and real Knowledge, *figurative Speeches*, and allusion in Language, will hardly be admitted, as *an* imperfection or *abuse* of it. I confess, in Discourses, where we seek rather Pleasure and Delight, than Information and Improvement, such Ornaments as are borrowed from them, can scarce pass for Faults. But yet, if we would speak of Things as they are, we must allow, that all the Art of Rhetorick, besides Order and Clearness, all the artificial and figurative application of Words Eloquence hath invented, are for nothing else but to insinuate wrong *Ideas*, move the Passions, and thereby mislead the Judgment; and so indeed are perfect cheat: And therefore however laudable or allowable Oratory may render them in Harangues and popular Addresses, they are certainly, in all Discourses that pretend to inform or instruct, wholly to be avoided; and where Truth and Knowledge are concerned, cannot but be thought a great fault, either of the Language or Person that makes use of them. What, and how various they are, will be superfluous here to take notice; the Books of Rhetorick which abound in the world, will instruct those, who want to be informed: Only I cannot but observe, how little the preservation and improvement of Truth and Knowledge, is the Care and Concern of Mankind; since the Arts of Fallacy are endow'd and preferred. 'Tis evident how much Men love to deceive, and be deceived, since Rhetorick, that powerful instrument of Error and Deceit, has its established Professors, is publickly taught, and has always been had in great Reputation: And, I doubt not, but it will be thought great boldness, if not brutality in me, to have said thus much against it. *Eloquence*, like the fair Sex, has too prevailing Beauties in it, to suffer it self ever to be spoken against. And 'tis in vain to find fault with those Arts of Deceiving, wherein Men find pleasure to be Deceived."[1]

Locke's rhetorical complaint is part of a long tradition. Philosophers have regularly denounced rhetoric and drawn a line between their pursuit of truth and virtue and the arts of mere persuasion. Plato's analysis of rhetoric in the *Gorgias*, for example, identifies it as a minor art; something like cookery is his malicious comparison, a pure and therefore dangerous instrumentality seducing us from truthful nourishment to linguistic gastronomy. What does the Sophist make a man eloquent about? asks Socrates in the *Protagoras*, and what does the Sophist know and enable his disciples to learn? There is no intelligible answer, Plato insists. The wisdom he attributes to Protagoras or Gorgias is essentially a set of techniques for persuasion without any particular moral content or even direction. Rhetoric's relationship to truth and virtue, in Plato's reckoning, is necessarily careless, often uncomprehending, and perhaps destructive of them in the end.

Aristotle, of course, thought otherwise and argued that rhetoric is properly a branch of dialectic, even though its forensic and emotional side had been overemphasized by rhetoricians. Rhetorical example is a form of induction, and the enthymemes rhetoric uses are really syllogisms. "Every one who effects persuasion through proof does in fact use either enthymemes or examples: there is no other way."[2] Aristotle thus makes it clear that for him rhetoric is a practical art, an inevitability in any discourse that seeks to persuade. He does, perhaps, condescend to it slightly as a tool for popular communication restricted to matters not susceptible of systematic treatment, questions that "seem to present us with alternative possibilities," matters that "we deliberate upon without arts or systems to guide us, in the hearing of persons who cannot take in at a glance a complicated argument or follow a long chain of reasoning."[3]

The relationship between philosophy (or logic or dialectic) and various sorts of rhetorical theory is immensely complicated. Plato's representation of the Sophists as muddle-headed technicians of eloquence is only his influential simplification. Much philosophy until modern times inclines to a more tolerant attitude in which eloquence or expressive power of some sort is part of thought, at least a noble adjunct or persuasive enrichment for truth. But Platonic hostility and Aristotelian condescension seem to be perennial or even inevitable. Behind these attitudes there lurks a persistent, narrowly defined notion of the ontological status of language and thereby of its uses and limits. Even at its most eloquent, language is treated by many sorts of philosophy as a nearly transparent medium that directs us to truth if employed according to the rules of logic or within a supervising dialectic. Moreover, even the speaker tends to disappear in the ideal philosophical situation, to become in some sense merely a medium if he is true to the rules of philosophical discourse. He effaces himself, and it is truth not Socrates who speaks. Aristotle describes three kinds of persuasion furnished by the spoken word: "The first kind depends on the personal character of the speaker; the second on putting the audience into a certain frame of mind; the third on the proof, or apparent proof, provided by the words of the speech itself."[4] Much philosophy claims, in effect, to suppress the first two (*ethos* and *pathos*) and to offer a purified kind of nonrhetorical presentation, which does not persuade but commands assent or is awarded validity by a special kind of learned audience who can "take in at a glance a complicated argument or follow a long chain of reasoning."

In practice, what philosophy has offered is a controlled rhetoric that often begins with the old rhetorical turn of denying rhetoric and then goes on to establish its own forms of persuasion within its logical structures. Plato's dialogues are a powerful model for that procedure. Richard Lanham has argued wittily that Plato's profoundly antirhetorical version of truth is served by developing Socrates as "the great master of rhetorical, sophistic dialectic." In the *Symposium*, says Lanham, Plato's characters exhaust the rhetorical possibilities for locating truth, and even Socrates' heavenly ladder is dramatized in context as merely another verbal trick. We are left with Socrates himself, "divinely inspired," to lead us by the force of his personality and ineffable experience of truth and beauty "out of the magic circle of rhetoric which surrounds him in the *Symposium*."[5] Lanham's clever point is that Socrates disguises the essentially rhetorical nature of his personality, the role and dramatic context at its center, its defining ludic and agonistic elements.

To some extent, philosophical activity always involves those rhetorical elements Lanham describes with such verve. Plato's dialogues are again exemplary. Social events that become athletic contests, a series of logical (and rhetorical) wrestling matches, they sometimes turn nasty and are deadly in the end. It is easy to imagine Socrates as a well-preserved athlete, sexually vigorous and eager for the quasi-erotic intellectual encounter. Ingres' muscular figure about to toss back his hemlock is more an undaunted, bright-eyed battler than a weepy intellectual martyr or Erasmus' humanist saint. The origins of philosophy, Johan Huizinga remarked, are in riddles and in "problems," and the latter are literally "what is thrown before you." The philosopher is a champion who challenges others and "in style and form the earliest samples of philosophy are polemical and agonistic."[6]

These are neglected truisms, although the oral tradition of antiquity and the *quaestiones* and verbal disputation associated with medieval thought are reminders of the inevitable rhetorical adjuncts of philosophy. The philosophical "problem" as a challenge is less obvious, the dramatic occasion much more muted if we think about post-Renaissance modern thought and consider the philosophical text, thought whose medium is a printed book rather than the spoken word. A profound transformation of what might be called the dominant literary genres of philosophy marks the emergence of modern thought, as the autobiographical meditation, the essay, and the treatise succeed older forms such as the medieval commentary with its catechetical and interrogatory structure that is a form of dialogue.[7] In the process the rhetorical and polemical features of philosophy are transformed, as a new dramatic scene for thought is developed and enforced by those genres. The modern philosopher-writer is a man alone, a sort of voluntary Robinson Crusoe or self-appointed philosophical Adam whose thought tends to represent itself as a new beginning rather than a continuation and modification of older thought. This philosopher often claims not simply to have thought but to have established conditions that make authentic thought possible and truth available at last. The dialogue, polemic, commentary, and disputation of ancient and medieval thought have a communal context. They require, continually add to, and redefine a preexisting philosophy. Such thought has visible social location as well as overt ethical and political concerns. The radical epistemologizing of thought after, say, Descartes requires the denial or at least the functional dismissal of context. Society and its concerns become effects of consciousness rather than its cause or it accompaniment. What emerges as the genres of philosophical expression shift is a redramatization of thought as private in a new and radical sense, not only nonrhetorical but somehow preverbal in its solitary location and origins.

Father Ong has suggested that the erosion of the oral-aural culture of the dialogue and disputation by the typographical revolution led to a redefinition of knowledge whereby cognition became a matter of seeing rather than hearing and the reality to be known turned into a matter of contact between objects in a visual field rather than communication between men.[8] In that cultural situation, philosophic writing tends to be understood (perhaps by analogy with the experimental sciences) as a report of experience, a record of what has been observed or viewed rather than a verbal process whereby truth is articulated and a text engages other texts. Philosophical writers thus seek a new and radical transparency, which involves much more than the traditional denial of rhetoric. If philosophy is purely a sort of observation, then philosophic writing inevitably aspires to the condition of neutral scientific notation and comes in time to see itself as sets of diagrams, symbols, or formulae.

Recently, Jacques Derrida and his followers have made much of philosophy's denial of what they call its "textuality." Derrida's claim seems to be that philosophy conceives of itself as fundamentally a kind of unmediated speech that seeks access to a mythical fullness beyond language called "being." Derrida's project involves redefining philosophic utterance as a special sort of writing, a play of signifiers that seeks vainly to fulfill the promise of such a language and to deliver the signified in all its concrete fullness or "presence." As Richard Rorty puts it, for Derrida philosophy since Kant "is a kind of writing" and what philosophers really want to do is "not to write, but just to show."[9]

Now, it was one thing for some philosophy to make a great show of driving out rhetoric and to claim a purer kind of discourse for itself, for the rhetorical mode could exist as an energizing opposite to thought, a deluding oratorical practice that provided a storehouse of commonplaces and tropes for thought to exploit and to correct in the name of truth. But the implicit tendency of modern thought toward solitary and self-canceling discourse and its aspiration to radical transparency severs philosophy from other forms of writing, creates the untenable textual paradox Derrida plays with, and leaves philosophical writing at an impasse from which it has, perhaps, never quite recovered.

Indeed, philosophical writing has in large measure ceased to exist as writing for most modern commentators and historians. The philosophic tradition is now read anachronistically. What James Collins calls "the descriptive metaphysician" finds in the philosophic past "a sphere of invariant meanings which are only extrinsically affected by language and historical conditions."[10] For reasons that are themselves cultural and historical, philosophical commentators and academic philosophers rigorously and systematically exclude the cultural and historical (and thereby the rhetorical and the textual) dimension from their analyses of classical philosophical texts. Academic specialization, envious mimicry of the physical sciences, the emergence of mathematical logic, the decline of literary and historical education—all of these contribute to philosophy's perception of its past.

Philosophical writing has been treated for the last hundred years or so as if it formed part of a consecutive conversation and running debate among philosophers, a dialogue between the living and the dead, a group project or grand institute stretching from Plato to the present that has as its purpose the establishment of the transhistorical truth of things, the facts in the case. But this dialogue with the philosophical dead is a strange one, since the dead are in effect not allowed to speak their own language. Their writings are treated as if they were submissions to a modern journal of philosophy.[11] The only history such commentary acknowledges is philosophical history; that is, each thinker inherits the problems and corrects the answers of his predecessors, takes them up and continues to work on them. The activity of writing as a shifting historical variable, as a shaping network of conventions for the expression and dramatization of thought, is ignored or treated as a hindrance to philosophical rigor. Normally, reading involves a knowledge of the generic connections that as E. D. Hirsch reminds us, "determine in large part the implied author's intentions."[12] Philosophical writing is treated as if it were beyond genre, untouched by any literary conventionality. The work of academic philosophers consists in examining past systems with a fiercely unsentimental clarity that excludes any literary dimension or generic conventions and that separates truth from illusion or fallacy in, say, Descartes or Berkeley.

In a way, this is exactly as it should be, simply a more efficient and informed version of what philosophers have always done. But some academic philosophers are uneasy with the situation and see it as a potential distortion of the past. There is some stirring in the direction of an intellectual history of philosophical works that avoids the reductive circularity of the sociology of knowledge. A. W. Levi, notably, has set out to redirect contemporary understanding of the origins of philosophical systems by urging consideration of their historical and cultural context and function. Levi finds much that is valuable in this direction, for example, in a recent book by Stephen Toulmin and Alan Janik, *Wittgenstein's Vienna*, which locates that strange genius in the social and cultural context of the last days of the Austro-Hungarian empire.[13] They argue that Wittgenstein's thought is not simply or purely a revision of the philosophical problems defined by his predecessors, Frege and Bertrand Russell. The *Tractatus* is also Wittgenstein's attempt to solve ethical and linguistic problems that were his cultural inheritance from birth and residence among the cultivated middle class of Vienna at the turn of the century. The problem of the relationship between language and reality was a concern Wittgenstein shared with his intellectual contemporaries in the other arts and sciences. The special urgency of that problem for them was bound up with a situation in which political and social institutions were in the process of revealing their instability and even unreality. Everything that marks Wittgenstein as an extraordinary figure—the odd intensity of his personality, the eccentricity of his philosophic career, the oracular form of his writing and teaching—is made more coherent (and less singular) by attention to these historical circumstances.

In his own book, *Philosophy as Social Expression*, Levi looks at the careers of Plato, Aquinas, Descartes, and G. E. Moore and finds similar origins, determinants, and social functions for their thought. Plato's system, for example, Levi sees as rooted in what he calls the "aristocratic vision of the world," and the theory of ideas is partly the establishment of a separate and inviolable realm where politicians and unruly mobs cannot tamper. More suggestively perhaps, Levi points out that Descartes' radicalizing of epistemology is possible only within the special conditions of leisure-class existence, with its "idleness, tranquility, and economic independence." For the cool fraternal debate among philosophical equals that is the normal academic version of the history of philosophy, Levi substitutes the teeming family life of cultural paternity in which ideas are part of a complex of social and historical factors. Levi's effort is to return to a Hegelian wholeness whereby, as he puts it, "social, economic, and political development, the advance of the arts and sciences, deep personal and psychological attitudes, and philosophical theory causally interpenetrate, and by their participation in a common zeitgeist or possession of a common weltbild form one seamless web."[14]

But Levi avoids reductionism only by repeating the broadest platitudes of the history of ideas. His project makes nearly impossible demands on the historian of thought, and his own work promises much more than it can ever deliver. That vast network of causal relationships is a dream of reason, and a sociology of thought seems doomed to heroic aspiration rather than realization. However, Levi's protest against the hermetic ahistoricism of philosophical commentary provides an opening for a related, more modest historical and cultural understanding of philosophy that operates primarily on what is manifest or clearly implicit in the text of philosophy itself rather than on the enormous historical problematic of its context. Perhaps the philosophical text can be treated, like any other text, as an artifact; perhaps the language and literary strategies that are a part of thought can be placed in history, partly in the history of writing and partly in a larger historical network. Finally, perhaps there are important affinities or similarities between those intensely realized projections of the imagination called literature and those intensely realized constructions of the intellect called philosophy.

Here again some attention has recently been paid to one of these possibilities by an academic philosopher. Richard Kuhns finds that literature (poetry, at its purest) is language as perfomance (a "showing language") and philosophy is language as argument (a "saying language"). Philosophy, says Kuhns, tells us something about the world; literature shows us itself. And literary language reveals itself by what Kuhns calls style: "There is only in a remote sense a 'style' of logical affirmations, but there is in an immediate, qualitatively definite and identifiable sense a style of literary language. In fact, that language is literary reveals itself to us in style." Kuhns's purpose is to show that philosophical language is "peripherally a showing language" and that philosophical works can exist in some sense as self-contained projections of the imagination and thereby resemble works of literature.[15] This generous insight contains various interesting and limiting assumptions about style and literature.

Kuhns's notion of literature is essentially postsymbolist, and the pure nonreferentiality he identifies with literary language is surely a historical phase of critical theory rather than the defining feature of literature. Such an aesthetic may be congenial to the ahistoricism Kuhns shares with other philosophical commentators. When he reads literary works, Kuhns inhabits that timeless realm where academic philosophers interrogate the past; only now he is relaxed and ready for the pleasures of performance rather than braced for the analytic struggle. Literary language is like a Balanchine ballet, pure and exalting form purged of mine and plot. Kuhns argues, in effect, that philosophy can be like a modern production of Shakespeare, meaty with tragic argument but accompanied by the stylish touches of the latest director-genius. The form with which imaginative directors endow plays is supplementary to meaning, an enforcement of meaning that operates by implication and suggestion and is thus in part a subversion of the limited clarity of overt meaning. Kuhns suggests that when a philosopher manages to make his work literary, he operates like the clever theatrical director. He adds a style that accompanies meaning, as all style must, but that may also assume an independence and imaginative quickness of its own. Such style, says Kuhns, is immediately visible and consists of a text's calling attention to itself and to that extent becoming "literature." Literature, then, is a special, quite explosive condition of language where ordinary meaning and reference give way to exhilarating instabilities caused by that play of language called style. In the sense Kuhns gives it, style is self-conscious rhetoric, writing that performs within the privileged (or irrelevant) space of figurative language. Most philosophy would seem to represent a radical stabilizing of language in which style in that sense is minimized, or at least rigidly subordinated to meaning.

Now, there are certain figures who belong by those standards as much to the history of literature as to that of thought, unabashedly stylish and personal thinkers like Rousseau and Nietzsche. But style for them may indicate an uncertainty about meaning or it may represent a substitute for a missing stability in meaning. Something like that seems to be Paul de Man's difficult point in *Allegories of Reading*, where he says that Nietzsche's works exemplify an interplay between rhetoric and representation in which the intrinsic instability of language is dramatized. De Man finds Nietzsche balanced between the rhetorical or even oratorical cast of some of his works and the "deconstructive" insight of his thought as a whole. Rhetoric for Nietzsche is a matter of allowing the unresolvable contradictions between "performative" and "constative" language to emerge. De Man tells us that Nietzsche manages matters so that rhetoric "deconstructs its own performance," undermining meaning and representation in the process of revealing its own insubstantiality.[16]

A critic like de Man is deeply suspicious of the authorial control of language and meaning summed up in a term like "style." So, he refers us to an authoritative, objective category like rhetoric, which as he renders it is a set of confusions and contradictions bound to emerge in language itself. His purpose in reading some stylish philosophical texts is, in fact, to extend the instabilities of language clearly visible in literature into philosophy, where they are usually obscured. Although he never uses the word "style," the authorial choice and purpose it normally represents would be for him simply a writer's decision to enter the labyrinth of verbal expression, a preliminary commitment to be more or less rhetorical. A writer who attempts to possess what Kuhns calls style rushes into the vortex of contradictions de Man finds in language, a vortex spinning with visible force in the rhetorical operations of any text but paralyzing in texts that make rhetoric overt or central. Is it possible to find a writer operating between the extremes Kuhns and de Man describe? Does "style" commit us to the godlike primacy of the writer as artist-technician of language? Or do we have to see "style" as a writer's suicidal immersion in the deconstructive whirlpool of language?

Traditionally, style is simply a stable accompaniment to meaning. A definition like Michael Riffaterre's excludes language as pure performance or unstabilizing element: "Style is understood as an emphasis (expressive, affective or aesthetic) added to the information conveyed by the linguistic structure, without alteration of meaning. Which is to say that language expresses and that style stresses."[17] The mechanical implications of this view are manifest; style is added to the information the text could provide without style. There are necessarily moments (either in the text itself or somewhere else, perhaps in the writer's thought before it becomes a text) of pure information, devoid of style. Style is easily seen as an epiphenomenon of language, merely a set of expressive, affective, or aesthetic techniques, a rhetorical grab bag such as Plato said the Greek Sophists offered for sale.

That is a bit unfair to Riffaterre, but an understanding of style seems to require more delicate treatment of it as an integral feature of language. The rhetorical aspects Riffaterre isolates are parts that do not add up to a whole. In one obvious sense, stylistics presupposes a meaning that style promotes; style is always an adjunct to a preexisting sense. As E. D. Hirsch says, "we cannot say what the importance of style is to meaning until we know what the meaning is." But as Hirsch admits, the problem is that style may encompass a wide variety of linguistic traits— "lexical choices, clause types, word order, phonemic patterns, rhythm, word length, etymology, sentence length, norm deviation, and others"—so that it becomes difficult to say whether a trait is "a form or a content." Hirsch attempts to resolve matters by introducing a suprameaning that the reader can see linguistic or stylistic traits pointing to and lesser, lower-order meanings that those same traits express in themselves.[18] Hirsch's position is a moderate one, for it allows style a minor reverberation of its own while preserving the dominance of a "meaning" that writing moves toward and that is in some sense apart from it or precedes it.

Stanley Fish has challenged both moderate and conventional views of style by insisting that writing is never inert or quiescent and that something, as he puts it, is always happening in a text. For Fish, Riffaterre's neutral language that merely "expresses" is an analytical myth.

Style is more than local rhetorical effects, and the object of study for a stylistic criticism is the movement of the entire text through the reader's mind.[19] Edward Said turns to less totalitarian rhetorical analysis when he contends that style is an occasional achievement, "really a comparatively privileged *moment* in the life of a text." Said calls style the achievement of a voice; style actually occurs when a "writer's subjectivity has fully appropriated to itself an entire textual language in which the 'I' of the writer/speaker designates an ego functioning in a reality created by that language."[20] That is, style is the cumulative process whereby a writer aspires to establish his singularity and identity. Very few writers, it goes without saying, actually manage such an identity.

Style obviously includes those rhetorical devices Riffaterre speaks of, but they are part of the potential self-defining activity marking all texts that are neither diagrams nor scientific-mathematical notation. At the same time, it is impossible to chart every single movement in the stylistic totality of a text, or as Hirsch reminds us to settle clearly the priority of form or meaning at every given moment in the life of a text. Fish's claims are overstated, since some stylistic effects are either hopelessly minor or particles of much larger effects. We are left with what Said elsewhere calls the paradox that "something as impersonal as a text . . . can nevertheless deliver an imprint or a trace of something as lively, immediate, and transitory as a 'voice.'"[21]

Writing in the context of recent notions that turn the author into a sort of ghostly absence, Said insists that style is precisely the force that seeks to overcome the neutrality and "the silent, seemingly uncircumstanced existence of a solitary text."[22] Style, let us say, involves a shifting complex of external forces and motives that uses the text but is not exactly equivalent to it. Style is not quite an imponderable, even though as Dr. Johnson said of poetry it is much easier to say what it is not. By worrying and complicating the notion of style, we remind ourselves that it is not simply a number of qualities a text possesses but an author's activity visible in a text. Style is not just the man but a reminder that there is a person operating on the linguistic or rhetorical forms with which all writers work, attempting to sign those materials in a particular way. Philosophical writers, depending on custom or temperament, may choose to be more or less stylish, or they may allow the institutional identity of philosophic discourse in their time to speak for them. A philosopher may simply borrow the odd color of rhetoric for a forceful touch here or there, or some philosophical works may be permeated by a self-conscious rhetoric that approaches the self-referentiality modern literary criticism favors. What matters in any case and what constitutes style are the author's movements through the extent of his text, his presence or studied absence within the unfolding of his text as it is actually read.

Style thus rivals the static formulations of truth to which philosophy, at least implicitly, aspires. Style is a property of the text as it is experienced, something that cannot be adequately represented by paraphrase or summary, a performance that argues the presence of an enacting self in a dramatic situation. Style belongs to what Richard Lanham calls *homo rhetoricus*, who is necessarily skeptical and drawn to the play and pleasure of language, an actor whose identity "depends on the reassurance of daily histrionic reenactment" and who is "thus centered in time and concrete local event." Lanham contrasts rhetorical man with *homo seriosus*, who thinks of himself as "central" rather than social or dramatic and who views language as an imperfect means of expressing ontological stability.[23]

The philosopher is nothing if not serious, but language is his enveloping element, the precondition for his thought. The inhibiting or enriching format of thought is a speaking at length, a textual unfolding in which style (or the issue of style) is inevitable. Even phenomenology cannot simply "bracket" language. As Maurice Merleau-Ponty put it, "the philosopher is first and foremost the one who realizes that he is situated in language, that he is *speaking*; and phenomenological reflection can no longer be limited to a completely lucid enumeration of the 'conditions without which' there would be no language."[24]

Speculation like this this leads to technical philosophic issues about the nature of language that have preoccupied modern thought since the seventeenth century. I dare not wander into those depths. I rehearse these notions in order to approach the rhetorical and stylistic issues raised by some seventeenth- and eighteenth-century English philosophical texts. Philosophical writing in this period is self-conscious about the difficult relationship between thought and the expository necessity whereby thought acquires style and becomes persuasive by extralogical or rhetorical means. The old quarrel between rhetoric and dialectic grew more complicated as post-Cartesian thought tended to realize that dialectic itself might be as unstable as rhetoric. Given the troubling possibility of a complete rupture between language and a shadowy order of things, dialectic could perhaps no longer claim immunity from the problematic of language. Philosophical writing begins to tread carefully as it seeks simultaneously to repudiate rhetoric and to retain the authority of dialectic, even as it tends to redefine dialectic as implicitly rhetorical or merely verbal. Seeking to persuade, such writing disavows persuasiveness even as it tends to promote the view that logic depends upon the persuasions of subjective experience.

English philosophic prose from the seventeenth century through the mid-eighteenth century is caught within this paradox and struggles to purify itself of the rhetorical adjuncts so strongly at work in it. Whatever one makes of the scholarly dispute over the origins of this tendency, the literary identity of philosophy is discernibly flattened, as the stylistic ideal moves away from the reformed but still oratorical habits of Bacon and Hobbes to understatement, relative looseness, and plainness such as Locke cultivates.[25] Placed next to the writing of Bacon and Hobbes, the work of Locke and his successors has an understated manner by which syntax is simplified, diction pruned, and what Richard Lanham calls "density of ornament" severely reduced.[26] To be sure, such a manner inevitably bears its own stylistic identity and, as we shall see, gives Locke's *Essay* a controversial literary signature. These shifts in stylistic preference sustained an interest in the problem of writing. Such thinkers participated in a literary culture and habit of mind that made them aware, in practice anyway, of the situation Merleau-Ponty describes.

This discussion of style and philosophical writing returns us to the history of thought. A new approach to language and various revisions of the speaking voice (or its transformation) mark a stage in the history of philosophy. Modern thought can be outlined in very broadly conceived stylistic terms, as Levi points out, by considering the differences between Descartes and Hume, for example, and Kant. Both the *Discourse on Method* and the *Enquiry Concerning Human Understanding* belong to what Levi calls the Age of the Gentleman, and each in different ways employs an intimate and graceful personal style that aspires to be generally intelligible and accessible to readers of sense and moderate learning. *The Critique of Pure Reason* initiates what Levi calls the Age of the Professional, and its style and manner resist "all gracefulness, geniality, or stylistic charm. It has all the uncompromising difficulty and stiff professionalism of the learned journal and the advanced philosophical seminar."[27]

Whatever the validity of Levi's historical categories, the difference between these works as pieces of writing is striking. It allows us to say that the seventeenth and eighteenth centuries constitute a historical moment when the rhetorical nullity of philosophical writing has not yet been settled, when the textual paradox potentially at work in all philosophical writing is still visible. Kant's text is dense with special terminology and stripped of anecdote and concrete illustration; it is an antitext, in a sense, and demands study rather than mere reading from its audience. Its voice is impersonal and rigorously professional, just as the thought it delivers is purified of common or ordinary experience. In Descartes and Hume there is more than a residue of persuasiveness and ingratiation. The voices heard in their texts are often deliberately personal and nonprofessional, sometimes indeed antiprofessional. In his elegant little book on philosophical style, Brand Blanshard tells an amusing story. Macaulay received a translation of Kant and tried to read it, "but found it utterly unintelligible, just as if it had been written in Sanscrit." Macaulay was outraged rather than ashamed. His remarks illustrate an older expectation for philosophical writing: "It seems to me that it ought to be possible to explain a true theory of metaphysics in words that I can understand. I can understand Locke, and Berkeley, and Hume, and Reid, and Stewart. I can understand Cicero's Academics, and most of Plato; and it seems odd that in a book on the elements of metaphysics . . . I should not be able to comprehend a word." [28]

Most readers of philosophy are now professional students of philosophy, and their training is partly a matter of learning to ignore those clarifying voices and to translate the philosophers Macaulay thought he understood into the precise and technical terms of their trade. Contemporary philosophical readers separate the chaff of persuasive tone and manner from the logical kernel. They read Descartes and Hume as if they were Kant.

The task that remains, it seems to me, is to reread some of these texts as writing, thereby attempting a reconstruction of the interplay in them between writing (and whatever that may imply in particular cases) and thought. It seems to me worthwhile to mark the ways in which thought manages to unfold in writing without negating itself, making itself available both to Macaulay (and me) and to trained philosophical readers. In a brilliant essay on Hume, Raymond Williams remarks that we treat literature as writing that can be "*represented*" by summary or paraphrase "only for the agreed and limited purposes of particular discussions" but can "only be *found* in a particular structure and sequence of words." [29] I propose to try to find, in Williams' special sense, the unfolding literary structures and sequences of the three preeminent British philosophical writers whose works span what Levi identifies as a crucial period for philosophic style. In different ways, the works of Locke, Berkeley, and Hume deserve this finding as a necessary addition to the representation of their ideas.

In their separate ways, each of them exemplifies the psychological and sociological situations Levi identifies with the age of the gentleman in philosophy. Each had a profession distinct from his role as a philosopher, or more accurately each was a versatile writer and thinker whose work encompassed a number of subjects (not disciplines in the modern sense). Isaac Newton identified himself as a man of letters. So, too, all three philosophers were literary men in various public and effective ways, all were self-conscious and stylish writers attuned to audience and occasion. Each of them achieves a distinctive voice as a writer. Each in his work engages the problem of style by seeking to reconcile that voice with the projects of his thought. To borrow some terms from J. M. Cameron but to quarrel with some of his distinctions, the difference between sage and thinker had not yet been established. There is a clear line separating nineteenth-century sages like Carlyle and Emerson from thinkers like Mill, Hegel and Peirce, as Cameron says, "a plain difference, worth paying attention to, between the work of a thinker whose credit rests upon the force of his argument rather than upon the truth of his conclusions, and one whose structures of language, even when they are argumentative, are evaluated by the use of other than logical criteria."[30] Cameron's absolute distinction simply does not apply to the philosophical writing of the English seventeenth and eighteenth centuries. Locke and Berkeley, for example, have an obstrusive moral purpose embedded in their philosophical programs; so for that matter does Hume, who is a sort of inverted Pascal. These writers are out to be both logically valid and morally effective, although the two purposes are not always congruent. The lingering hope of such philosopher-writers is to close the emerging gap between technical or philosophic truth and a wisdom embodied in literary practice. Truth and correct understanding have always been moral issues, and it is only lately that the cool professionalism of philosophy has distracted from that urgency. Locke, Berkeley, and Hume are philosophers of great technical proficiency, but their works are moral essays as well as analytic discourse, edging consistently into human thematics and away from strictly abstract considerations.

Hume had an illustrious career as essayist, popular historian, man of letters, and diplomat. His career as a philosopher took shape around the maturing process and worldly experience that led him to revise the *Treatise of Human Nature* into the *Enquiries*. Berkeley's irrepressible literary talent allowed him to range from technical philosophical and physical treatises to popular essays, bristling religious polemics, and mystical aphorisms. He was also a public man, acquainted with literary-political figures like Swift and Pope, a sort of court philosopher during the 1720s when he debated in front of Queen Caroline once or twice a week with Clarke, Hoadly, and Sherlock.[31] Locke's *Essay* became the most widely read (or at least the best known) philosophical book of the eighteenth century. His writings on economics, religious controversy, and especially politics and education reached an enormous audience and had great effect and influence. Many of the works of this trio retain a clarity and readability that surprise and charm a modern reader.

And yet all three repeatedly express suspicions about language, partly from the traditional antirhetorical posture of philosophy but also out of the sense each clearly has that his thought represents a renovation of philosophic discourse, a renewal by linguistic purgation of its original directness and pertinence. It is sometimes difficult for us to imagine the sort of audience these thinkers thus have in mind, since each aims to address a nonprofessional audience that is neither learned nor vulgar in the traditional senses of those words. With some extravagance, Berkeley claims to "side in all things with the Mob,"[32] and each of these men in some way promotes "vulgar" notions or reconstitutes them in the face of learned distortions. Their clarity is often explicitly a matter not simply of rejecting rhetorical colors but of exposing the mere verbalism of an older philosophy or of current bogus pretenders to wisdom. Each one restores "experience" and actual perception to their rightful primacy through a language that is somehow not merely words and terms of art.

Locke's attack on rhetoric in the *Essay* is steady and consistent, his opposition implicit throughout in his rambling manner and on occasion strongly (and rhetorically) explicit. Even while ridiculing syllogistic reasoning, he concedes that it may have some use "to discover a Fallacy hid in a rhetorical Flourish, or cunningly wrapp'd up in a smooth Period; and stripping an Absurdity of the Cover of Wit, and good Language, shew it in its naked Deformity" (IV.xvii.4). Antiquated philosophical method or jargon such as the syllogism perpetuates is easily swept away, but the seductive power of wit and good language is a perennial danger whose force Locke dramatizes in his concluding image. The vivid opposition he promotes between such language and naked truth is a sustaining theme of the *Essay*, fully articulated in the last two chapters of Book III, "Of the Abuse of Words," and "Of the Remedies of the foregoing Imperfections and Abuses."

Berkeley literalizes matters when he concludes his introduction to the *Principles of Human Knowledge* by urging us to see ideas without the words needed to describe them: "It were therefore to be wished that every one would use his utmost endeavours, to obtain a clear view of the ideas he would consider, separating from them all that dress and encumbrance of words which so much contribute to blind the judgment and divide the attention" (II,40). Since what follows is nothing if not words, Berkeley issues directions to his reader for transforming his text and making it in effect a pretext for that reader's own thought:

> Whoever therefore designs to read the following sheets, I entreat him to make my words the occasion of his own thinking, and endeavour to attain the same train of thoughts in reading, that I had in writing them. By this means it will be easy for him to discover the truth or falsity of what I say. He will be out of all danger of being deceived by my words, and I do not see how he can be led into an error by considering his own naked, undisguised ideas. (II,40)

Hume is cagier than moderate Locke or brash Berkeley. His stylish manner bespeaks a profound respect for rhetoric, although he too is forced to claim that philosophical writing leads us to things that cannot be spoken about. For example, at the end of Section VII of the *Enquiry concerning Human Understanding*, Hume concludes his demolition of the notion of a force that propels matter and moves bodies by declining any more talk and saying very eloquently that eloquence would obscure matters:

> I know not whether the reader will readily apprehend this reasoning. I am afraid that, should I multiply words about it, or throw it into a greater variety of lights, it would only become more obscure and intricate. In all abstract reasonings there is one point of view which, if we can happily hit, we shall go farther towards illustrating the subject than by all the eloquence and copious expression in the world. This point of view we should endeavour to reach, and reserve the flowers of rhetoric for subjects which are more adapted to them.[33]

For Locke and Hume the stylistic ideal is a philosophical *mot juste*, for Berkeley a word within the philosophical word. All three make the philosophical text a special kind of event that calls attention to its own inadequacy and lack of transparency. The disavowal of language turns the occasion into a potentially comic circle. We are asked to read and then to turn away from reading, to pause awhile from letters and be wise. All this is hardly surprising, since each in his way attacks traditional ontology and asserts the primacy of epistemology. Their thought warns us not to be deceived by words, not to endow language with being, but to remember constantly that being is a matter of perception or of phenomenalist participation. All three may be said to argue that reality is a matter of experienced relationships and that philosophy has to return its readers to the dynamics of "ideas" and away from the static delusions of substances and essences. The relationship closest to hand for them as writers is that provided by their text, that which obtains between ideas and words, between writer and writing, and between reader and writing. What this leads to in literary terms is an active text. The text busily disavows normal rhetoric even while reintroducing modified and understated rhetorical forms; it is drawn to a recurring dramatization of textual inadequacy, its own or more often that of rival descriptions of the world. The antiessentialist drive of these thinkers prevents their claiming substance of a final kind for their statements; their thought is a continual return to the act of discovery, the uncovering of inadequacy in traditional formulations. Their writing is thereby committed to perform for us, to match in some way the movements of intellect and to stage dramatically (and frequently ironically) those failures and evasions of reason that the new and enlightened reason sees.

In so doing, all three seem to involve themselves in the breakdown of discourse that empiricism implies. For empiricism, as Derrida has put it, is "the opposition of philosophy and nonphilosophy" and "an inability to sustain on one's own and to the limit the coherence of one's discourse." Derrida considers this inability a scandal and complains that empiricism produces something "as truth at the moment when the value of truth is shattered." He points out that "the philosophical text, although it is in fact always written, includes, precisely as its philosophical specificity, the project of effacing itself in the face of the signified content which it transports and in general teaches."[34]

This somewhat self-righteous description of a kind of empiricist philosophical writing can be put to other uses. In the hands of Locke, Berkeley, and Hume and in the cultural context in which their writing takes place, that collection of paradoxes and contradictions surrounding the philosophical text as such is controlled and manipulated to specific ends. In different ways that constitute a coherent sequence and development in British philosophical writing, each of them arranges a confrontation and interaction between language and the experiences and objects it seeks to describe. What Derrida identifies as the secret duplicity of philosophy, these writers exploit as an inherent irony and a literary pleasure in empirical philosophizing.

Elsewhere, Derrida finds that philosophy attempts to control and analyze plurality of meaning and that philosophy is the ambition to make language "univocal."[35] Philosophy, he says, admits a plurality of meaning but seeks to render it finite, resembling in this Swift's projector in the School of Languages at Lagado who substituted things for words and carried them on his back. Gulliver describes "two of those Sages almost sinking under the Weight of their Packs, like Pedlars among us; who when they met in the Streets would lay down their Loads, open their Sacks, and hold Conversation for an Hour together, then put up their Implements, help each other to resume their Burthens, and take their Leave."[36] Derrida's deconstruction of philosophy is anticipated, to some extent, by the richly absurd implications of philosophy's ironic self-portrait. Socrates' irony extends to himself. When he describes the difference between the lawyer and the philosopher in the *Theaetetus*, the latter's abstraction from the normal course of life leads Socrates to tell the story of Thales and to admire "the clever, witty Thracian handmaid," who said to the philosopher after he fell into a well as he looked at the stars "that he was so eager to know what was going on in heaven that he could not see what was before his feet. This is a jest which is equally applicable to all philosophers."[37]

In the literary tradition stretching back to Socrates and Aristophanes, philosophizing is a rich source of comic material, and the philosopher, foolish and self-absorbed, is a recognizable comic type, a character like the *senex amans* or the *miles gloriosus*. Swift, again, summarizes this set of comic stereotypes when he remarks at the very end of "A Discourse Concerning the Mechanical Operation of the Spirit" that "too intense a Contemplation is not the Business of Flesh and Blood; it must by the necessary Course of Things, in a little Time, let go its Hold, and fall into *Matter*." Philosophers are like deluded lovers, "*Platonicks*, who pretend to see Stars and Heaven in Ladies Eyes, and to look or think no lower." Both ignore reality and are bound to fall into the same Swiftian pit. The philosopher's eyes are "fixed upon the *Constellations*," but he finds "himself seduced by his *lower Parts* into a Ditch."[38]

Empiricism is a project for avoiding that absurdity, a sort of controlled "fall into *Matter*." In different ways, Locke, Berkeley, and Hume take steps to control the potential moral absurdity of their enterprise. Their philosophy is founded on a moral and social fable in which the philosopher is an alert and inquisitive narrator, surprised by his discoveries and amused by the history of delusion he uncovers. The reader is asked to see that he has in some way originally known the truth of things but that he has allowed himself to be deceived by false theories or been content to dwell in unexamined ignorance or vagueness, out of either self-interest or mere laziness. There are even moments when the philosopher claims mainly to remind us of simple truths and sadly (more often comically) neglected facts of common perception. The prevailing tone in such philosophical talk is amused amazement at the inability of many people to admit simple truth or their readiness to believe what turn out upon examination to be fantastic theories supporting common notions. Such a tone assumes a world of recurrent moral and psychological situations and borrows its structure from literary satire. There is a revived Socratic irony and an implicit comic scene that serves these writers as means of exploiting those instabilities of empiricist discourse which so trouble Derrida.

Their works frequently bear out R. G. Collingwood's point that "every piece of philosophical writing is primarily addressed by the author to himself." For Collingwood philosophical method always involves a self-critical and self-questioning format in which the philosopher, unlike the historian or the physicist, is always "confessing his difficulties."[39] All three of these writers seem to obey Collingwood's principle; they are all aggressively antisystematic and claim to welcome disruptions and inconsistencies. Up to a point, all three illustrate what Arthur Danto says about empiricism, that it is properly understood as a theory of how we learn rather than a judgment of how we understand.[40] That is to say, empiricism is a project for rendering in all its fullness the process whereby the mind comes to possess the materials needed to go on to understanding. In their different ways, Locke, Berkeley, and Hume are ready to do justice to what Hannah Arendt complained is "hardly ever mentioned" by philosophy, the appearances of the world, "the sheer entertainment value of its views, sounds, and smells."[41] Their thought seeks to reconstruct the locales and reenact the scenes of perception. It tends therefore toward dramatic and narrative modes of presentation, and in this way it is part of the shifting of philosophical genres Marías describes.[42]

This literary tendency has caused some commentators to suppose that in Locke's case, for example, the mind is passive, since his account of the mind's activities is so massively circumstantial, so full a story of the adventures and possibilities of perception. All three philosophers are reluctant to simplify the subject-object dichotomy, unwilling to draw back from the ironic reciprocities necessary to represent perception. But at the same time, they tend to combine the powers of the imagination and the intellect, or to dramatize the intellect as a capacity for vivid formulation. Consider an entry from Locke's journal for 1676:

[March] 27th Rain. Imaginary space seems to me no more any thing
than an imaginary world; for if a man and his soul remained, and the
whole world were annihilated, there is left him the power of imagining
either the world, or the extension it had, which is all one with the space

it filled; but it proves not that the imaginary space is any thing real or positive. For space or extension, separated in our thoughts from matter or body, seems to have no more real existence, than number has (sine enumeration) without any thing to be numbered; and one may as well say, the number of the sea sand does really exist, and is something, the world being annihilated, as that the space or extension of the sea does exist, or is any thing after such annihilation. These are only affections of real existences; the one, of any being whatsoever; the other only of material beings, which the mind has a power not only to conceive abstractedly, but increase by repetition, or adding one to another, and to enlarge which, it hath not any other ideas but those of quantity, which amounts at last but to the faculty of imagining and repeating, adding units, or numbering. But if the world were annihilated, one had no more reason to think space any thing, than the darkness that will certainly be in it.[43]

Locke rejects imaginary worlds but conjures up the mind's power to im- agine and vividly recreate the world in the face of its annihilation. True, the mind is inserted in matter and cannot imagine space without matter in it or imagine an authentically new world, but that mind is still a con- siderable power, able to abstract and to enlarge the number of things in the world. Locke's meditation seems to be about the limits of conception but winds up vividly demonstrating the range and vivacity of imagination even as it renders those limits.

"I find," says Berkeley in the *Principles of Human Knowledge*, "I can excite ideas in my mind at pleasure, and vary and shift the scene as oft as I think fit. It is no more than willing, and straightway this or that idea arises in my fancy: and by the same power it is obliterated, and makes way for another" (II,53). Jonathan Bennett complains with some justice that such imaging "is not essential to the human condition, and some people lack it entirely." For modern commentators like Bennett, one of the scandalous weaknesses of this trio is their tendency to assimilate "the sensory far too closely to the intellectual."[44] The "ideas" and "images" all three speak of are irreducibly mixed, with the essentially visual reconstructions of the imagination dominating their version of mental ac- tivity. Memory, for example, cannot be pure images, according to A. J. Ayer. "Not everybody is a good visualizer: and even the images obtained by those who are will tend to be schematic; they will rarely, if ever, reproduce in every detail the forms and colours of the remembered scene."[45] But in their accounts of mental experience, Locke, Berkeley, and Hume tend to rely on visualization, even though they seem well aware of the limitations of memory. They are I think drawn to the dramatic moment of perception in which intellect and visual imagination are inseparable and in which the imperfections of the literal imagination Ayer speaks of are less important than the power and necessity of such activity for perceiving the world and especially for narrating that perception.

Intelligent but unimaginative commentators like Bennett and Ayer do not admit that the mental habit of visualization may have been sharper (or more necessary and less literal) in an age lacking the technology of visual reproduction that informs our view of the world. Photography and other aggressively reproductive visual media look at things for us, as it were, and rhetorical representation may strike us as merely verbal and woefully inadequate. The literary culture of the late seventeenth and eighteenth centuries depends upon the evocation of a visual panorama not restricted by the literalizing demands of photographic reproduction. The sensory and visual reconstructions of philosophical exposition, it should be clear to any reader, partake of that latitude. What is at stake is best understood in terms of assumptions that seem to govern the thought and, equally important, to facilitate the writing of Locke, Berkeley, and Hume. Commentators like Bennett are naturally unwilling to grant those assumptions, as they are bent upon resolving particular philosophical problems rather than upon submitting themselves to the persuasive dramatizations of philosophical writing.

In that dramatization, an inevitable, perennial impasse emerges with great clarity. To have knowledge of the world, as Arthur Danto formulates the problem, is to be outside the world in a special sense, "for the world is what we have knowledge of, and between us and the world there is then a relationship which is not a relationship internal to the world itself."[46] The mind, obviously, is never passive, and all philosophy involves a struggle with the subject-object dilemma. These writers approach that dilemma by means of a relatively stable visual world, which is often in fact a world of literary and moral conventions, of shared visualizations of experience. They treat the mind (and the sensory apparatus that is part and parcel of mind and yet not the same thing as mind) in a frequently paradoxical sense as both spectator and spectacle. The moral-literary tradition helps to sustain that paradox, as it makes philosophizing itself an activity in which it is essential to keep an eye on yourself lest you wander into comic solipsism or find yourself betrayed, in Swift's phrase, by your lower parts into a ditch.

Near the end of the *Treatise of Human Nature* Hume stresses that our compassion is contradicted and our moral judgments varied by our psychological and social relationships. The pleasure or pain we perceive in others leads to its opposite in us because we inevitably compare those states to our own. "The direct survey of another's pleasure naturally gives us pleasure; and therefore produces pain, when compar'd with our own. His pain, consider'd in itself, is painful; but augments the idea of our own happiness, and gives us pleasure."[47] Generalization is tested by narrative illustration, an anecdote in which Hume observes himself observing:

Suppose I am now in safety at land, and would willingly reap some pleasure from this consideration: I must think on the miserable condition of those who are at sea in a storm, and must endeavour to render this idea as strong and as lively as possible, in order to make me more sensible of my own happiness. But whatever pains I may take, the comparison will never have an equal efficacy, as if I were really on the shore, and saw a ship at a distance, tost by a tempest, and in danger every moment of perishing on a rock or sand-bank. But suppose this idea to become still more lively. Suppose the ship to be driven so near me, that I can perceive distinctly the horror, painted on the countenance of the seamen and passengers, hear their lamentable cries, see the dearest friends give their last adieu, or embrace with a resolution to perish in each others arms: No man has so savage a heart as to reap any pleasure from such a spectacle, or withstand the motions of the tenderest compassion and sympathy. 'Tis evident, therefore, there is a medium in this case; and that if the idea be too feint, it has no influence by comparision; and on the other hand, if it be too strong, it operates on us entirely by sympathy, which is the contrary to comparison. Sympathy being the conversion of an idea into an impression, demands a greater force and vivacity in the idea than is requisite to comparison. (Pp. 594–595)

Hume's initial generalization is revised by a vividly rendered but ironic tableau of self-discovery. Thought is first confirmed by personal experience and then modified by an extension of experience into more exactly observed social and moral circumstances. The experience Hume depicts is filtered by literary conventionality. As his footnote points out, the shipwreck scene is a paraphrase of the opening lines of the second book of Lucretius, but the spectator here will find himself moved in ways that the ancient Epicurean denies. The musing moral philosopher who examines his own emotions in secure soliloquy and then sees himself moved irresistibly from complacency to tears as the wrecked ship moves nearer is related to any number of stock characters in the moral literature of the age who find themselves surprised by an actual world and their relationship to it and have to revise their theories and abandon preconceptions.

Hannah Arendt quotes the same lines from Lucretius to mark the change of what she identifies as a Greek philosophical stance in the world whereby the spectator is positioned for knowledge in a privileged, self-conscious, but still participating sense. In Lucretius, the spectator claims to be aloof, safe from experience rather than stationed in it.[48] That aloofness is exploited for ironic effect in Hume's philosophical narrative. Observation exists in a sort of double regress in which the thinker looks at the normal link between experience and understanding and then looks again at the very scene of perception from a longer perspective, shifts the scene and the focus, varies the tempo of experience and understanding to come through to other conclusions. So, too, in Locke and Berkeley philosophical narrative is often a matter of reflexive observation, accomplished by slowing the tempo of experience, enlarging and isolating moments of perception, dramatizing conventional understanding and explanation in order to examine them in a new light and to break down, incidentally, any traces of aloofness. Of course, something like this is part of many philosophic methods, but Locke, Berkeley, and Hume share a suspicion of the vulgar aloofness Arendt describes as a moral danger for philosophy. Aloofness is the persistent moral and intellectual error against which their thought operates. Their writing habitually stages a turn from logic and demonstration to anecdote and example, thus placing them and their readers in the center of a reality fraught with uncertainty and confusion.

A mixture of diffidence and deliberately outrageous assertion in their writing matches the ambiguous position of their thought in relation to the world. Although their thought is rooted in Cartesian notions of the mind and the world, all three, as Leslie Stephen noted, can be called anti-Cartesians in that they set out to confound metaphysics and the rational simplicity and neatness of the *cogito*.[49] "Knowledge," as Theodor Adorno put it in attacking the falseness of Cartesian clarity, "comes to us through a network of prejudices, opinions, innervations, self-corrections, presuppositions and exaggerations, in short through the dense, firmly founded but by no means uniformly transparent medium of experience."[50] In general, Locke, Berkeley, and Hume promote a version of experience that resembles the complicated network Adorno describes.

Modern philosophical commentators tend toward ahistorical impatience with such an ambiguous position, or to look at it another way, with such a rich dramatic presentation. An exception who can help us to understand exactly why this should be the case is Ian Hacking, who points out that seventeenth- and eighteenth-century thought is governed by assumptions that cause modern perplexity over certain classical empiricist notions, stretching back to Bacon and Hobbes and extending through Locke and Berkeley. Hacking notes that "idea" is a bewilderingly versatile term in these writers. For them an idea was simply a principle of classification different from our arrangement of mental phenomena, a principle whereby "an idea is any object that can be contemplated by a thinking being without existential commitment to anything except that being." In that philosophical tradition, what we mean by ideas, impressions, sensations, and perceptions is all included in the term "idea." Hacking argues further that the empiricists lacked a "theory of meaning" such as has powerfully emerged since the nineteenth century whereby private mental discourse is located in and inseparable from a public discourse, an objective world of language and phenomena where things make sense. Instead of distinguishing among the possibilities of meaning in which a word may refer either to an idea in my mind or to an actual object in the world, or in which a word's meaning may be what its speaker wants people to do or what they do when they hear it, the empiricist, says Hacking, concentrated meaning in the private mental operations of particular speakers.[51]

Hacking's summary is philosophically accurate but strangely indifferent to moral-literary surroundings. In the writings of Locke, Berkeley, and Hume there is obviously a clear dramatic occasion in which some kind of larger context is provided for the isolated "existential commitment" Hacking speaks of, in which "ideas" are brought out of their privacy and submitted to public judgment. The thought of all three depends upon the narrative of the mental history of an individual, the philosophic speaker. But that mental history has in some way to be accommodated to the parallel mental histories of readers; the philosopher uses himself as an example and presents himself as the ideal ordinary man, sometimes unreflective, sometimes sharply thoughtful, but never the possessor of a professionally trained insight or perspective. In different ways, each of these thinkers exists within the problematic of individuality explored by Michel Foucault. They operate in what Foucault calls a historical moment in which individuality is formed not by status, ancestry, nor in "historico-ritual mechanisms" but by norms that substitute "for the individuality of the memorable man that of the calculable man."[52] The philosophical text depends to some extent upon such a measurable man, a purified and deindividualized version of the philosopher, and to that extent what he presents is a generalized humanity that enforces inescapable norms. Moreover, a moral ideology cooperates with the special sort of redefined individuality Foucault describes. The cultural context in which these three thinkers exist is suspicious of that privacy and individualism Hacking identifies as the core of their thought.

Their problem as writers, then, is to balance a profoundly individualistic epistemology with a cultural and literary habit of mind that suspects individuality and self-definition and insists upon the presence of an audience for meaningful discourse. The situation is exceedingly delicate at every level, since the pressure of wayward individualism upon society and tradition is perhaps the most urgent moral theme of the period. The political and economic corollary of the epistemology Hacking summarizes is the "possessive individualism" C. B. Macpherson has called the paradoxical core of English political ideology after Hobbes, whereby "the individual is essentially the proprietor of his own person and capacities, for which he owes nothing to society."[53]

Martin Battestin has argued that there is a lingering Pythagorean natural order expressed in Augustan arts and letters, supported by the physico-theologians and deists alike but subverted by the arguments of the philosophers.[54] Battestin surely overstates the case, for such order seems present in Augustan literature mainly as a shattered ideal rather than a supervising norm. Nevertheless, philosophy is consistently wary and apologetic about its own implications and the subversive possibility of philosophical investigation is a recurrent theme, for example, in Locke. He uncovers a confused and limited world in which our perceptions are fleeting, in which there is great potential for disturbing uncertainty, in which even the notion of personal identity is in some danger. As John Dussinger suggests, Locke's *Essay* suppresses its discovery that "existence is only a psychological fiction."[55] Why, asks W. B. Carnochan, was there no cultural crisis in the late seventeenth and early eighteenth centuries? Locke either "did not understand or admit the radically skeptical consequences of his epistemology" because "he wanted to have a new world and yet not to taste of its bitterness."[56] Literary critics like Dussinger and Carnochan are willfully ahistorical and neglect the ideological underpinnings that preserved Locke from those consequences. God provides Lockean man with reason that, if properly managed, leads to freedom and understanding rather than confusion.[57]

But perhaps the defining qualities of the literary practice of the time represent an intrinsic defense against what Carnochan calls imminent cultural crisis. The extreme implications of skeptical epistemology and individualistic ideology, whether psychological, political, religious, or economic, are consistently attacked by most writers of the time, and not only by those we identify as conservatives. What Paul Fussell calls the "rhetorical world of Augustan humanism" is by virtue of its commitment to "rhetoric" the bearer of a conservative, reassuring, and anti-individualistic ideology. Those recurring topoi and common places, those dominant tropes of irony and understatement which constitute the rhetorical world Fussell speaks of work to undermine claims of extreme and independent selfhood. The writer establishes connection with a tradition of forceful examples and images, of limiting, recurrent human situations. Skillful presentation by the writer and the reader's practiced recognition of that rhetoric involve both of them in a relationship that excludes extreme skepticism and unruly individualism by making recognition and implicit communication the defining parts of reading and writing. Augustan rhetoric can be playful in Lanham's sense, and it does encourage a dramatic sense of self as a role. But it also invokes a tradition and an inevitability whereby the self is limited to certain roles and rhetoric expresses a cultural and moral order. Such a rhetorical mode discourages the purely expressive private utterance (or the notion of such) that is the extreme literary implication of an individualistic epistemology; in this rhetorical world, the private speech needed to do full justice to the implications of private experience can be only a deluded or inarticulate solipsism.

We have come full circle, in a way, to the point where style is a writer's means of responding to a cultural problematic, and rhetoric more than simply the persuasive adjunct of philosophical expression. Although naturally less given to trope and image and commonplace than the essayistic manner proper to literary criticism, politics, or history, Augustan philosophical writing needs the voice established by style as a way of stabilizing the disorderly possibilities and implications of thought. Perhaps what can be called a moral and social ideology is expressed by an interplay between the radical tendencies of thought and the conservative drift of particular kinds of writing and habits of expression. There is, I think, a continuity between the recurring philosophic scene in the writing of Locke, Berkeley, and Hume and the thematic and stylistic arrangements of a good deal of the literature that extends from Dryden to Johnson.

Much Augustan writing establishes order by traveling through disorder, organizing disparate and contradictory materials, holding them for example in the tensions of the couplet or in antithetical balance of another formal sort and then watching as they are eroded or dispersed by the pressures of what is labeled as experience or reality. But often (and this strikes me as the signature of the period's style) a reassertion of ultimate formal control or authority is at least attempted, as for example in mock-heroic and the near-parody of Fielding's novels. A formal order is both proposed and undermined; generality and the coherence it provides are challenged by a particularity and individuality that are respected but disavowed.

Philosophical writing confronts a similar paradox. A strongly held and polemically asserted view of the world acquires coloration and distinctiveness from a voice as well as from argument; a style begins to found an imaginative world even as the writer seeks to elaborate an objective world rather than his particularity as a writer. The object pursued by a strong-willed and powerfully intellectual subject tends to become a version of the subject, who in turn struggles to restore his world to an objective order, to refound that order by negating to some extent his own powerful subjectivity. Such order is elusive, hopelessly compromised by empiricist intervention. In its pursuit, philosophical writing does not have the overt formal ordering of literary genres but struggles to acquire its own literary identity within its own ambiguous and shifting arrangements. It cultivates literary tonalities like irony, urbanity, humility, nostalgia; it speaks to an audience it conjures up and thus tries to locate philosophical discourse in an actual social and moral world. At times, it seems to stress continuities of a fragile and temporal sort, making its own language a provisional and delicate instrument rather than an enforcer of a shared culture. In this regard, such writing may reveal what Murray Cohen suggests is the dominant temporal pattern of early eighteenth-century literary language. Cohen finds the spatial stability traditionally assumed behind Augustan literature contradicted by the practice of writers like Swift and Fielding, in whose works "individual schemes, particular images and completed representations give way to arts of contrast, disruption, change, and transformation."[58]

In one sense, much eighteenth-century writing is dominated by a preference for aphoristic generality, an aim for the pithy, the memorable, and the summarizing. This ambition is both a strength and a weakness, for such discourse drives toward compressed presentation of that which is extensive and more or less sprawling or unmanageable. The shapeless or less shapely alternative is neglected or perhaps not perceived as clearly as it should be. Irvin Ehrenpreis argues convincingly that the best Augustan writing is aware of the dangers of epigram, and he says that in Dryden and Pope, for example, "one can observe the language rising deliberately from a relaxed flow to an epigram and sinking back again."[59] And Fielding and Swift, to use Cohen's examples, are writers who specialize in disrupting the world implied by the aphoristic, one by the force of satiric transformation, the other by the ironic juxtapositions of comic fiction. Such writing calls attention to its capacities for recasting conventional formulations, but at the same time by its stylistic energy and wit it tends to promote experience and to undercut the possibility of final formulation of any sort. This is, I realize, an extreme way to interpret the stylistic vigor or ironic writers, but I think these are the possibilities philosophical writing consistently stirs up. Such writing is drawn to the elegance, point, and summary of literary arrangement but is committed to elaborate a reality defined as emerging and more or less unpredictable as individuals experience it. Thought extracts experience that constantly challenges the shapeliness of literary formulation. For Locke, Berkeley, and Hume in their various ways, philosophical writing involves achieving a style and asserting a thematic organization that defer at once to a moral-literary tradition and to the series of radical revisions of the world their thought represents. At their most extreme, those revisions lead to soliloquy and solipsism, stylistic and ideological absurdities their literary-moral manner tries to neutralize.

Locke is the clearest example of a powerful writer who tried to make deference and modesty his literary signature. From the first, the *Essay* was recognized as an attempt to establish a new way of writing philosophy. Not everyone was enthusiastic about the innovation. Timothy Goodwin, the biographer of Locke's most bitter opponent, Bishop Stillingfleet, characterized the book as modish popularizing:

This Essay abounding with a Set of new Philosophical Terms, as if some wonderful Improvement of Knowledge was to have been hoped for from it, and being written with a graceful Air, and liveliness of Spirit, and elegancy of Style and politeness of Expression, a smoothness in Reasoning, and an ingenious improvement of his Arguments to the best Advantage, by a closeness of Reference, and patness of Similitudes and Allusions, no wonder true Understanding, and a right Apprehension of Things, set off with these uncommon Advantages, should easily recommend it self to the Affections of the Studious, especially the younger part of them.[60]

That is in fact a good description of the *Essay*, which is ingratiating and persuasive in just those ways. Later readers have come to take Locke at his word as merely a modest and plain speaker. Indeed, simplicity and downright drabness as a writer are what some critics have granted him. George Saintsbury singled out Locke's style as the lowest moment in the history of English prose and found that his literary innovation consisted in making that prose "positively mean in every point of style."[61] A less exquisite judge, Locke's modern commentator R. I. Aaron, concluded that his style reflected his genuine directness and simplicitly.[62]

Locke himself said he was surprised by his literary success. When his friend Molyneux urged him to have the *Essay* translated into Latin so that foreigners might see this new kind of philosophizing and be liberated from the old disputatious manner, Locke hesitated. Molyneux reported that Locke's authorship of an essay on the coinage had been quickly detected by knowledgeable persons.[63] Locke replied in modest and self-effacing terms, granting himself only a special lack of style:

I know too well the deficiency of my stile, to think it deserves the commendations you give it. That which makes my writings tolerable, if any thing, is only this, that I never write for any thing but truth, and never publish anything to others, which I am not fully persuaded of my self, and do not think that I understand. So that I never have need of false colours to set off the weak parts of an hypothesis, or of obscure expressions, or the assistance of artificial jargon, to cover an error of my system, or party . . . I think there wants nothing but such a preference of truth to party, interest and vain glory, to make any body out-doe me, in what you seem so much to admire.[64]

Locke's claims are moral rather than stylistic, although stylistic self-definition is always a moral question. Style is overtly a matter here of moral will and involves the ascetic denial of the temptations and allurements of style. And yet, one might ask maliciously, what greater gratification than to be the writer of the *Essay* and to have one's "style" recognized by the learned world and by gentlemen, politicians, and persons of leisure? The transparent vanity of authors is not the issue. Rather, the recurring diffidence Locke displays in his letters and insists upon in the *Essay* itself is central to his position as a thinker, disingenuous in actual fact but a necessary part of his thought.

When John Wynne of Jesus College, Oxford asked him to write an English epitome of the *Essay* for the use of undergraduates, Locke replied at first with quiet irony that he had not expected such a request, since he wrote "in a plain and popular stile, which haveing in it noething of the aire of learning nor soe much as the language of the schools was litle suited to the use or relish of those who as teachers or learners applyd them selves to the mysterys of scholastique knowledge."[65] All of Locke's rather coy modesty in these examples is an ironic counterstatement to scholastic "mysterys" and a positive example of how to write philosophy without becoming merely a propagator of philosophical language.

The tradition of plain talk in philosophy that Locke represents (and thinks of himself as renewing) resembles in a secular sense an old rhetorical-theological strategy that Stanley Fish reminds us was articulated by another professor of rhetoric, St. Augustine: "The teaching of the truth need not be accompanied by pleasing words or forceful exhortations, because the truth itself, if it is understood, both delights and moves."[66] Such a paradox returns us for a moment to Derrida's analysis of empiricism as the juncture of what he calls philosophy and nonphilosophy.[67] For Augustine divine truth was nearly ineffable; for Derrida what truth there is seems to reside in the writing out of the notion of truth. For Locke truth lies in the process of investigation, in the arrangements whereby writing narrates as clearly and simply as possible the movements of mind through its ideas and through the sensations and perceptions of the mind-body organization. But that is as difficult to manage as it is easy and instinctive for the mind to do. It seems fair to say that for Locke in the *Essay* writing is not so much a transparent or neutral discourse as it is a semiopaque medium within which a difficult truth may be enacted.

Rosalie Colie has placed Locke's *Essay* very clearly in the essayistic tradition founded by Montaigne and has emphasized Locke's control of literary tone and occasion, which allows him freedom of organization. She sees his logical looseness as licensed by this essayistic tradition in which dialectic and scholastic logic are played down and exchanged for simplified or personal argument. "Crisp and aphoristic or loose and rambling, the essayist spoke directly and personally to his readers; in exchange for the frankness with which the essayist appeared to present his thinking self, he was allowed certain liberties from logical rigour." But in spite of Locke's fluency and cunning ease as an "essayist," there are times, Colie notes, when "his thinking overrode his need to express that process clearly to his readers, and certainly overcame his pretensions to prose style."[68] Locke's failures of clarity, his defining and notorious ambiguity as a thinker, are further evidence that the *Essay* passes from the ironic literary control Colie describes to the depiction and even at times the enactment of difficulty and obscurity. To read Locke as I shall in the next chapter is to listen to a voice that makes its audience aware of a *process* of signification and of the difficulties of representation. In that awareness, the *Essay* earns its diffidence, becoming on occasion an ironic narrative in which the narrator discovers his own limitations and his implication in what he describes. It becomes difficult to defer to the truth because the cumulative effect of the *Essay* is to complicate the notion of truth, to query its status and location.

Derrida provides an interesting objection at this point and an analytic indictment of the duplicity of what he calls western metaphysics. He sees a hidden "onto-theological" basis in western thought whereby "experience is always the relationship with a plenitude, whether it be sensory simplicity or the infinite presence of God." Derrida reads the history of philosophy from Descartes to Hegel as built on the notion that such a plenitude is available to a thought that hears itself speak and understands itself: "the subject takes from itself into itself, does not borrow outside of itself the signifier that it emits and that affects it at the same time." Such a bias, he says, excludes "writing," and by that he means "the invoking of an 'exterior,' 'sensible,' 'spatial' signifier interrupting self-presence."[69] If I understand Derrida correctly, then at least at the level of literary performance, Locke's thought attempts to include writing by dramatizing the difficulties of knowing a plenitude whose stability is consistently interrupted, to echo Derrida's terms, by a "signifier" that is shifting and uncertain. The "self-presence" of the speaker in the *Essay* is interrupted, or at the least, the idea of self-presence or the fundamental stability Derrida associates with it is precisely the narrative issue in Locke's *Essay*.

Locke's speaker hears himself speak and wonders often enough how he came to say or know what he says; he discovers and indeed exposes his own (and others') delusions of centrality. His diffidence is the prelude to a recurring and moving thematics of loss, in which thought discovers that sensory simplicity is immensely complicated and tragically evanescent. At its expressive best, Locke's writing approaches what Raymond Williams calls the present tense that art substitutes for the "habitual past tense" of thought, which is something "so different in its explicit and finished forms, from much or even anything that we can presently recognize as thinking, that we set against it more active, more flexible, less singular terms—consciousness, experience, feeling—and then watch even these drawn towards fixed, finite, receding forms."[70] At moments, Locke attempts to watch consciousness, experience, and feeling as they are drawn toward or driven toward fixed forms; the effort and the force of his writing take the reader back again toward those other active and unfixed states.[71]

It is hardly a paradox to say that Locke's suspicion of rhetoric, his claim to "speak of things as they are," is a sign of his acute interest in writing. The reader of the *Essay* is instructed to be alert, to check his own words and the ideas appropriate to them against Locke's. Berkeley seems to be another kind of writer, a philosopher who treats words with the contempt some philosophy says they deserve. The introduction to the *Principles of Human Knowledge* promises to deliver certain ideas in as few words as possible. Locke's *Essay* is a long conversation with a reader in which the understanding is itself a sort of reader of signs as it wonders about representations of its own experience. For Berkeley, thought is wordless, a matter of turning refined and revised perception or vision upon the world and constituting it by thinking about it. Words, he concedes, are "of excellent use" but they have been misused.

> But at the same time it must be owned that most parts of knowledge
> have been [so] strangely perplexed and darkened by the abuse of words,
> and general ways of speech wherein they are delivered [, that it may
> almost be made a question whether language, has contributed more to
> the hindrance or advancement of the sciences]. Since therefore words are
> so apt to impose on the understanding, [I am resolv'd in my inquiries to
> make as little use of them as possibly I can:] whatever ideas I consider, I
> shall endeavour to take them bare and naked into my view, keeping out
> of my thoughts, so far as I am able, those names which long and con-
> stant use hath so strictly united with them. (II, 38–39)

Berkeley modified this declaration and omitted the words in brackets from the second edition of the *Principles*, but he never retreated from disparagement of the merely verbal. The *Principles* finds language corrupt, encrusted with prejudice. Berkeley asks the reader repeatedly to turn away from the text and to consider his own notions. "It is but looking into your own thoughts, and so trying whether you can conceive it possible for a sound, or figure, or motion, or colour to exist without the mind, or unperceived. This easy trial may make you see, that what you contend for, is a downright contradiction" (II,50). Berkeley's book is a prod to philosophic action, a guide to experiment by which an "easy trial" makes actual seeing a substitute for mere propositions ("what you contend for").

Berkeley's charming bluntness and bravado mask, however, a literary exuberance, a persuasive clarity of expression, and even a careful rhetorical strategy. As he explains in a letter to a friend in 1710, the *Principles* was written so as to present to its audience a falsely soothing and conventional appearance. Berkeley reserved the notion of the nonexistence of matter, wishing it to emerge dramatically in the course of the work: "I imagine whatever doctrine contradicts vulgar and settled opinion had need been introduced with great caution into the world. For this reason it was I omitted all mention of the non-existence of matter in the title-page, dedication, preface, and introduction, that so the notion might steal unawares on the reader, who possibly would never have meddled with a book that he had known contained such paradoxes" (VIII,36).

Despite his philosophical contempt for mere language, Berkeley briefly develops in the Introduction a shrewd analysis of how words actually work. He notes that they do much more than simply communicate ideas, "as is commonly supposed." Rather, words have a persuasive and affective function that is often quite to the side of their meaning. Berkeley appeals to the reader for the truth of his associationism:

I entreat the reader to reflect with himself, and see if it doth not often
happen either in hearing or reading a discourse, that the passions of
fear, love, hatred, admiration, disdain, and the like arise, immediately
in his mind upon the perception of certain words, without any ideas
coming between. At first, indeed, the words might have occasioned
ideas that were fit to produce those emotions; but, if I mistake not, it
will be found that when language is once grown familiar, the hearing of
the sounds or sight of the characters is oft immediately attended with
those passions, which at first were wont to be produced by the intervention of ideas, that are now quite omitted. (II,37)

Berkeley sees very clearly how language becomes absorbed by individuals and appropriated for private emphasis and even for other meanings. Language is a sort of gesture each man makes, just as speech is "metaphorical more than we imagine," as Berkeley remarked in the *Philosophical Commentaries*. (I,24,#176).

Such a close interest in actual language is appropriate for the author of *Alciphron* (1732) and *Three Dialogues between Hylas and Philonous* (1713), among the finest philosophical dialogues in the language. The *Principles* and its predecessor, *An Essay towards a New Theory of Vision* (1709), make the reader conscious of being addressed directly, of taking part in an implicit dialogue. A sense of audience and a striving for the tone and quality of engagement or conversation with it are features of Berkeley's writing I think every reader must notice. If we consider Berkeley's self-consciousness about the manifest outrage to common sense in his central doctrine, then that quality is another aspect of his rhetorical strategy, a reassuring balance for his strange and disturbing assertions.

Hume, as we shall see, is especially good at that kind of balancing of reassuring style and radical substance. Berkeley for his part tends to move from ingratiation to an almost Johnsonian assertiveness. A passage from the *Principles*, for example, is a bit of a near-dialogue whose tone is reminiscent of some of the gambits in the *Life of Johnson*:

But let us examine a little the received opinion. It is said extension is a
mode or accident of matter, and that matter is the *substratum* that sup-

ports it. Now I desire that you would explain what is meant by matter's *supporting* extension: say you, I have no idea of matter, and therefore cannot explain it. I answer, though you have no positive, yet if you have any meaning at all, you must at least have a relative idea of matter; though you know not what it is, yet you must be supposed to know what relation it bears to accidents, and what is meant by its supporting them. It is evident *support* cannot here be taken in its usual or literal sense, as when we say that pillars support a building: in what sense therefore must it be taken? [For my part I am not able to discover any sense at all that can be applicable to it.] (II,47)

Locke's diffidence is exchanged for assertiveness. Berkeley cultivates a voice and a logical manner designed to reduce his interlocutor to a silence we are instructed to imagine. The abruptness of the rapid interrogative constructions points to that silence, as if Berkeley is waiting for the reply he knows is not possible. He then supplies and refutes the absurd literal answer to his question. "It is evident *support* cannot be taken in its usual or literal sense" is what the interlocutor is too embarrassed to say. Berkeley's writing frequently speaks in this way, suggesting a distinctive voice engaged in a sort of rough dialogue.

In large part, that implicit dialogue serves Berkeley's paradoxical doctrines, which require that the usual and ordinary view of things be presented in order to preserve the quality of those doctrines as paradoxical and neglected truth. Where Locke tends to use himself and his own experiences as a *dramatis persona* and *mise en scène* for staging the difficulties of understanding, Berkeley constructs scenes in which his voice eventually reduces rivals to silent, embarrassed confusion. Their defeat is necessary to dramatize the irrefutable simplicity of the correct view of things, which is how Berkeley identifies his conclusions. "So long as I confine my thoughts to my own ideas divested of words," he says in the Introduction to the *Principles*, "I do not see how I can easily be mistaken . . . To discern the agreements or disagreements there are between my ideas, to see what ideas are included in any compound idea, and what not, there is nothing more requisite than an attentive perception of what passes in my own understanding" (II,39).

The brash challenge in that statement is partly owing, I think, to Berkeley's precocious philosophical development; he was twenty-six when the *Principles* was published. With the *Theory of Vision* and *Three Dialogues*, it forms what Berkeley's late-nineteenth-century editor, Alexander Fraser, called "his *reductio ad absurdum* of Abstract Matter."[72] The hero of these books and master of that almost absurdly confident style reconstitutes the strange and the unusual as the neglected obvious and vanquishes scientists, mathematicians, and abstract philosophers in the name of a literal and concretely personal perception. His statements are always strong counterstatements; they depend upon a recurring dramatic enactment that pits him and his brilliant simplicities of formulation against incredulous opponents who can only counter with falsifying verbalism.

The vigorous and well-defined personae found in the writings of Locke and Berkeley may have something to do with the nature of English as well as with the stylistic conventions of the time and the nature of their philosophical projects. Hugh Kenner has suggested in a brilliant aside that different languages enforce different styles of thought and that it is somehow fitting that "Locke in a language where *large* and *red* precede *apple* should have arrived at the thing after sorting out its sensory qualities, whereas Descartes in a language where *grosse et rouge* follows *pomme* should have come to the attributes after the distinct idea."[73] French is an instructive contrast. Some French writers have either admired or deplored the dense, concrete quality they perceive in English. When Gide told St.-John Perse he was studying English to give his own writing the "weight and mass in the language of Newton," the latter objected that French was a superior instrument, able "to signify rather than represent the meaning" and to use "words only as fiduciary symbols like coins as values of monetary exchange."[74]

These are sensitive impressions rather than valid distinctions between the two languages, but they may help to account for the massive abstractions now favored by French critics, the solidity and objectivity they seem inclined to grant to the fetish they call the "text," a thing that speaks without a human voice if we are to believe them. Many English texts by comparison seem to be signed by an author and modified in various ways by a distinctive speaking voice. At the least, since these are impressions, English philosophical writing like Locke's and Berkeley's is committed to projects and inquiries that require a disturbed or agitated textual surface in which, to return to Raymond Williams' point, the present tense that evokes thought as a process of consciousness, experience, and feeling is the dominant or the recurring tense.

Of course, neither Locke nor Berkeley is interested in representing rather than signifying his thought, neither presents his books with the possibility that they are as much persuasive enactment as compelling argument. Rather, those tendencies are inevitable adjuncts of their writing, perhaps in part because of the nature of English but more clearly because of the nature of their philosophical projects. The polemical urgency of their thought, the positive and reforming side of each of their systems, gives way to some extent as they proceed to a set of disturbing moral and ideological thematics summed up in the radical epistemology each develops. Their distinctive styles are means of preserving the quality of ordinary experience in the context of the subversive possibilities of their expositions. Writing as the communication of a distinctive style and self helps to preserve them and their audience from the implications of those expositions. The "textuality" they achieve is precisely the opposite of that objective and compelling monumentality some critics find in a text after it is let loose in the world.

Hume has an equally strong sense of audience and tends toward the same kind of implicit dialogue and humanizing intimacy. He is set apart by the awareness he displays of writing's rhetorical and persuasive qualities, an awareness that is often a question of exploiting the radical soliloquizing mode natural to philosophical discourse. Hume seems to me (and the point is a commonplace of the history of philosophy) to be the most aware of the three of the reflexive and circular implications of the Cartesian epistemology all of them investigate. Hume takes the fictions of the understanding, the mental discourse of the individual uncovered if not quite admitted as fictions by Locke and Berkeley, and faces them with a rhetorically and dramatically controlled self-consciousness. Hume's thought returns again and again to a balancing within his philosophical narrative of the self-centered discoveries of the inquiring mind against the social and moral situations that are the context of those discoveries. The soliloquizing philosophic voice discovers its own limitations and dramatizes for ironic effect its own instability as it fashions the fictions of understanding and communicates Hume's awareness of their fictionality. Norman Kemp Smith began his classic study of Hume by pointing to the central issue: for Hume, commonsense notions such as the existence of bodies, the reality and stability of the self, and belief in causes are just not accounted for in the systems of Locke and Berkeley. Such notions, Kemp Smith notes, cannot be proved but must nevertheless be believed,[75] a stance that makes Hume's world remarkably like a literary universe in its mixture of falsity and necessity and its exploration of fictionality. Hume's task as a writer is to stage that paradox, to bring together for ironic effect the philosopher's world of learning and reasoning and the "conversable world" of "company and conversation," opening up in that conjunction new literary possibilities for the dramatization of thought as an activity in the world.[76]

Hume's *Treatise of Human Nature* is a youthful, even an astonishingly precocious work, at times brash and roughly paradoxical in manner, Baconian in ambition, and quite as impolite occasionally in its interrogations as Berkeley's early works. Here is a challenge to rivals near the beginning of volume one:

I wou'd fain ask those philosophers, who found so much of their reasonings on the distinction of substance and accident, and imagine we have clear ideas of each, whether the idea of *substance* be deriv'd from the impressions of sensation or reflexion? If it be convey'd to us by our senses, I ask, which of them; and after what manner? If it be perceiv'd by the eyes, it must be a colour . . . But I believe none will assert, that substance is either a colour, or a sound, or a taste. The idea of substance must therefore be deriv'd from an impression of reflexion, if it really exist. But the impressions of reflexion resolve themselves into our passions and emotions; none of which can possibly represent a substance. We have therefore no idea of substance, distinct from that of a collection of particular qualities, nor have we any other meaning when we talk or reason concerning it. (Pp. 15–16)

Other philosophers "imagine"; the young Hume examines and sees that "talk" and "reason" are usually the same, that reasoning about such philosophical chimeras as substance is just "talk." But the persona in the *Treatise* is not merely assertive and brashly interrogative; rather, Hume's voice is consistently self-depreciating and ironic as well, pretending often to retreat from the outrageous and paradoxical implications of argument. At his wittiest, Hume carries on a mock-rigorous self-examination, which declares that philosophy must present as many proofs as possible if it is to challenge received notions. After asserting, for example, that ideas we believe in are simply livelier and more forceful than others, he steps back and tells us elaborately that careful proof is required here:

However convincing the foregoing arguments may appear, we must not rest contented with them, but must turn the subject on every side, in order to find some new points of view, from which we may illustrate and confirm such extraordinary, and such fundamental principles. A scrupulous hesitation to receive any new hypothesis is so laudable a disposition in philosophers, and so necessary to the examination of truth, that it deserves to be comply'd with. (Pp. 106–107)

In the context of the *Treatise*, with its quite self-conscious spirit of innovation and even of philosophical revolution, that seems disingenuous in the extreme. And yet there is a justice in the tone and in the demand for proof that it half undermines, since Hume is at once philosophizing and dramatizing the comic inadequacy of philosophic activity of a certain kind. The speaker of the *Treatise* loves to pretend he is discovering difficulties as he writes, and the book is sometimes a comically overt record of the process of thought rather than simply the systematic exposition of the results of thought. There is an implicit historical joke in Hume's praise of the "scrupulous hesitation" of philosophers to accept any new hypothesis, since the *Treatise* is out to challenge the stubborn, self-interested blindness of philosophy as it has been traditionally practiced. The *Treatise* is thereby comically active, disrupted by a series of mock-serious surprises when the speaker seems overcome for a moment, trapped as he pretends to be within the inherently comic limitations of a philosophy that claims to be scrupulous but is simply impervious to new or, better, to a scandalously neglected truth.

Here is a key passage from Book I:

Having thus given an account of all the systems both popular and philosophical, with regard to external existences, I cannot forbear giving vent to a certain sentiment, which arises upon reviewing those systems. I begun this subject with premising, that we ought to have an implicit faith in our senses, and that this wou'd be the conclusion, I shou'd draw from the whole of my reasoning. But to be ingenuous, I feel myself *at present* of a quite contrary sentiment, and am more inclin'd to repose no faith at all in my senses, or rather imagination, than to place in it such an implicit confidence. I cannot conceive how such trivial qualities of the fancy, conducted by such false suppositions, can ever lead to any solid and rational system. (P. 217)

Hume seems to control such ironic reversals, and the persona in the *Treatise* is often truly a visible mask, a personality manipulated for effect. From the very beginning of the book, that is, the "I" who tells us about his experiences is implicitly ambitious, eager to do great things. Such a revolutionary mood is part of the implicit dramatic scene of modern thought, as each thinker necessarily sets out to revive philosophy. But Hume's "I" routinely discovers that his experiences illustrate the limitations of experience and the fallibility of unconsidered impressions, ideas, and perceptions. Hume is out to make such limitations and fallibility the dramatic center of his thought. Even more than Locke or Berkeley and with a much greater spirit of fun, he loves to ground his arguments in personal anecdote in which the process of thinking is dramatized and thereby redefined into a combination of perception and intellectual formulation after the fact of sense impressions.

Thus, at the beginning of the *Treatise*, the narrator remembers a mental experiment or, rather, performs it on the spot for his readers:

When I shut my eyes and think of my chamber, the ideas I form
are exact representations of the impressions I felt; nor is there any
circumstance of the one, which is not to be found in the other. In running over my other perceptions, I find still the same resemblance and
representation. Ideas and impressions appear always to correspond to
each other. This circumstance seems to me remarkable, and engages
my attention for a moment. (P. 3)

But "a more accurate survey" reveals that the "I" has been "carried away
too far from the first appearance," and the climax of this vignette is his
retraction, as the scene shifts from his chamber to the outside world:

I observe, that many of our complex ideas never had impressions, that
corresponded to them, and that many of our complex impressions never
are exactly copied in ideas. I can imagine to myself such a city as the
New Jerusalem, whose pavement is gold and walls are rubies, tho' I
never saw any such. I have seen *Paris*; but shall I affirm I can form such
an idea of that city, as will perfectly represent all its streets and houses
in their real and just proportions? (P. 3)

Such remarks were, in part, calculated to excite the angry murmurs of
zealots, and the equation of the New Jerusalem and the speaker's
chamber is an amusingly malicious touch. But the participant-observer
that Hume devises as the main character in his narrative allows a situation
that is primarily and ironically self-regulatory rather than satirical or
polemical. Hume's literary procedure is only incidentally the attack on
older philosophical notions and terms; his main technique as a writer is
the enactment of a controlled uncertainty in which thinking is consistently qualified by experience and experience in turn is redefined by further reflection. Such double irony in the presentation of mental-physical
process makes Hume, even in the *Treatise*, a rather more interesting
writer than Berkeley or Locke.

The *Treatise* has a scenic richness that Hume chose to modify and
abridge in the two *Enquiries* he carved out of it. His revision was also accompanied by a noticeable refinement of style, a literary manner perfected
in the *Essays Moral and Political* he published in the 1740s. The writing has a poise and a balance in its constructions and in its attitudes that
blunt the polemical edge and simplify the ostentatiously intricate arguments of the *Treatise*. The revision is partly a shift in tone from an imper-
tinent to a polite and insinuating persona, as the *Enquiries* seek to establish a reassuring and pointedly civilized manner in which writer and reader
are united as sensible and discerning equals. Hume shifts from a broadly
dramatic and ironic employment of scenes to a more narrowly focused

manner that consistently turns to aphorism and epigram. Hume's mature style communicates implicitly by its tendency to aphorism the crucial notion that truth is a sharp insight that acquires its edge in a social context.

An epigram requires a knowing audience, one able to understand and value the compression of large, complicated issues into neat and often paradoxical formulations that command assent and give pleasure through such arrangement. Consider, for example, this sequence from the opening section of the *Enquiry Concerning the Principles of Morals*:

It must be acknowledged, that both sides of the question are susceptible of specious arguments. Moral distinctions, it may be said, are discernible by pure *reason*: else, whence the many disputes that reign in common life, as well as in philosophy, with regard to this subject: the long chain of proofs often produced on both sides; the examples cited, the authorities appealed to, the analogies employed, the fallacies detected, the inferences drawn, and the several conclusions adjusted to their proper principles. Truth is disputable; not taste: what exists in the nature of things is the standard of our judgement; what each man feels within himself is the standard of sentiment. Propositions in geometry may be proved, systems in physics may be controverted; but the harmony of verse, the tenderness of passion, the brilliancy of wit, must give immediate pleasure. No man reasons concerning another's beauty; but frequently concerning the justice or injustice of his actions. In every criminal trial the first object of the prisoner is to disprove the facts alleged, and deny the actions imputed to him: the second to prove, that, even if these actions were real, they might be justified, as innocent and lawful. It is confessedly by deductions of the understanding, that the first point is ascertained: how can we suppose that a different faculty of the mind is employed in fixing the other? (P. 171)

Now, this is a "specious argument," Hume's brilliant and eminently fair paraphrase of a position he rejects. His imagined opponent shares many of Hume's views, however, and argues with a smoothness that matches him at his best. Sounding like Hume, this speaker evokes a discordant world of wrangling in "common life, as well as in philosophy." He concedes and indeed prefers the directness of aesthetic perception to ordinary thinking. Controversy in other matters is summarized; the confusions inherent in the intellectual world are rendered and in effect dismissed as tedious by a series of marching participial phrases. The maxim that seems to resolve matters is irrefutable in it pointed brevity: "Truth is disputable, not taste." The elaboration that follows is a balance ending with the triumphant simplicity of good taste in an elegant and easy setting. The verbal symmetry and simple opposition of these two sentences rescue the reader from the potentially endless and shapeless sequence that is the history of this old question. But then the scene shifts from the coffee-house or salon to the courtroom. A similar brevity informs this scene, and the irrefutable simplicity attached to aesthetic experience passes over into moral and legal experience. The argument turns on a sharp rhetorical contrast between a demonstrable lack of argument in one area and a necessary fullness of it in the other, a witty swing from *de gustibus non disputandum* to our own equally indisputable habits of rational self-justification. That justice deals with matters of fact is something we must admit. Given that admission, it seems to follow that morality is also available to the same "faculty" that determines those matters.

Hume follows with a paraphrase, equally skillful, of the opposing position. This speaker concedes the intellectual force of the understanding but builds a rebuttal out of that concession. The "inferences and conclusions of the understanding" are effective. "They discover truths: but where the truths which they discover are indifferent, and beget no desire or aversion, they can have no influence on conduct and behaviour." As befits the position that morality precedes rational discourse by establishing its location, the rhetoric grows warmer and more direct. The answering aphorism yields immediately to a spirited evocation of the scene of moral activity, an extended narrative contrast between the "cool assent of the understanding" and the active vigor of the moral emotions at work in the world:

What is honourable, what is fair, what is becoming, what is noble, what is generous, takes possession of the heart, and animates us to embrace and maintain it. What is intelligible, what is evident, what is probable, what is true, procures only the cool assent of the understanding; and gratifying a speculative curiosity, puts an end to our researches.

Extinguish all the warm feelings and prepossessions in favour of virtue, and all disgust or aversion to vice: render men totally indifferent towards these distinctions; and morality is no longer a practical study, nor has any tendency to regulate our lives and actions. (P. 172)

In a simple sense, Hume's own position is a balance between these "plausible" arguments, or rather an exploration of the circumstances behind each of them. His part in the debate here is to restate both positions, purging them of their rhetorical grace notes and establishing a firmer and clearer narrative line in his exposition than either of them.

But in order to pave the way for such a sentiment, and give a proper discernment of its object, it is often necessary, we find, that much reasoning should precede, that nice distinctions be made, just conclusions drawn, distant comparisons formed, complicated relations examined, and general facts fixed and ascertained. Some species of beauty, especially the natural kinds, on their first appearance, command our affection and approbation; and where they fail of this effect, it is impossible for any reasoning to redress their influence, or adapt them better to our taste and sentiment. (P. 173)

As Hume explains in the conclusion of this introductory section, his *Enquiry* hopes "to discover the true origin of morals" by defining "Personal Merit." And that is to be accomplished by consulting his own feelings and examining the language of moral description, which "guides us almost infallibly in forming a judgement of this nature" (p. 174). The rhetoric behind the rational and sentimental positions is an essential part of Hume's material, part of the phenomena of moral self-definition and justification he is about to study. But the ideal reader of such a sequence must be able to discriminate among these rhetorical variations, separating and valuing Hume's improvements and refinements. The vexed question of where exactly Hume himself stands in the arguments of the *Dialogues Concerning Natural Religion* shows how good he could be at reproducing the persuasiveness of all positions. He is not always as generous to his opponents as he is here at the beginning of the *Enquiry*, but he is always ready to define all positions, including his own, as persuasive urging. What seems to mark the mature ethics and epistemology of the *Enquiries* is an extreme, almost precious or fastidious, bracketing of opinions within their rhetorical movements.

As these preliminary explorations may suggest, significant relationships exist between Locke, Berkeley, and Hume's writing and the elaboration of their thought. First, an important interplay takes place between thought and persuasive stylistic turns: local effects like diction, tone, rhythm, image, and other figures of speech, as well as larger and cumulative enforcements of meaning created by these local effects — dramatic setting, implicit narrativity, persona, and other supervising "scenic" tendencies. Secondly, these stylistic features sometimes constitute more than a persuasive superstructure; they become an implicit stabilization of the subversive implications and potential subjectivity of the philosophical project. They are a moral-literary defense against a wayward reader who might choose or overemphasize those negative implications. Style as "rhetoric" helps to promote ideological stability. But style is itself a source of instability, a personalizing force within a text that leads to a third level of connection between writing and thought. In a difficult sense, these writers sometimes try to pull away from the overtly rhetorical adjuncts of their thought by negating analogy, transcending persona, or canceling other self-sufficient or even playful properties in their writing. This repudiation is often attempted in the name of experience or unblinkered perception, a revived common sense or restored freshness and pertinence ironically threatened by the very enactment seeking to promote them. That recurring moment is the most profoundly rhetorical feature of these particular philosophical projects, and I think Hume understood this and made it central in his writing.

Perhaps, as Nietzsche asserted, truth is the solidification of old metaphors. At the least, philosophical exposition often finds to its discomfort that it cannot quite do without the persuasion summed up in terms like style and rhetoric. In describing the rhetorical enactments in their philosophical writing, I do not claim to alter radically the established or received versions of the thought of Locke, Berkeley, and Hume. Indeed, my analysis of their writing depends to some extent upon professional explanations of that thought. What I attempt is a gloss upon the literary surfaces and rhetorical movements of the texts as they promote philosophical issues, sometimes in the process creating ambiguity of a sort congenial to literary critics and hateful to philosophers. Philosophers may find such an inquiry irrelevant at best, at worst misleading for anyone in search of whatever clarity and truth are to be found in the British empiricists. I do not presume to resolve philosophical issues. For works that have clear literary force, I propose what Charles Altieri calls the literary critic's task: "to describe the elements of the actions which constitute the specific literary mode of the text."[77]

Chapter 2

Locke

In the detachment necessary to all thought is flaunted the privilege that permits immunity.

—Theodor Adorno, *Minima Moralia*

An Essay Concerning Human Understanding promises a modest exploration, although many readers have noted the delicate coexistence of modesty and such a grand subject. Locke's "Epistle to the Reader" reinforces modesty in many ways, presenting the author as an "Under-Labourer" working in the shadow of masters like Boyle, Sydenham, and Newton, "clearing Ground a little, and removing some of the Rubbish, that lies in the way to Knowledge" (p. 10). This elaborate self-depreciation is conventional enough, but Locke's modesty seems tinged with irony from the beginning.[1] His book, he says, was "not meant for those, that had already mastered this Subject, and made a thorough Acquaintance with their own Understandings; but for my own Information, and the Satisfaction of a few Friends" (p. 7). Anyone who thinks he has "mastered this Subject" is, of course, a fool, and one wonders who might be the object of such gratuitous intellectual contempt. No one, for the moment anyway, since the point of the "Epistle" is to flatter the reader and welcome him into what Rosalie Colie aptly calls an audience of colleagues "fit and few."[2]

Diffidence acquires in the course of the *Essay* a certain philosophical propriety and validity. But here in the "Epistle to the Reader" there is an implicit comedy in this reassuring persona, coming close to absurdity as

Locke tells us that when he began he thought all he had "to say on this Matter, would have been contained in one sheet of Paper; but the farther I went, the larger Prospect I had: New Discoveries led me still on, and so it grew insensibly to the bulk it now appears in" (pp. 7–8). Surprised discovery of complexity introduces the recurring comedy of philosophical activity, one of the sustaining themes of the *Essay*. Locke sounds at first like Pope's eager student in "An Essay on Criticism." As one reads on in the "Epistle," he begins to sound more like the voice of the prologue to "An Essay on Man." This emerging urbanity keeps Locke's comedy in line and focuses his modesty.

Pope urges Bolingbroke to the leisurely hunt of philosophical contemplation, to "catch the manners living as they rise"—like pheasants. Locke's "Epistle" contains a string of such cheerful analogies for his work; like Pope and Bolingbroke he is engaged in healthful and moral activity: the understanding's "searches after Truth, are a sort of Hawking and Hunting, wherein the very pursuit makes a great part of the Pleasure" (p. 6). And in the *Essay* itself Locke turns on occasion to similar illustrations and finds happy similitudes for the operations of the understanding drawn from the arts, both fine and mechanic.

"An Essay on Man" is a conversation between two old friends. Locke's *Essay* begins with five or six friends, who

meeting at my Chamber, and discoursing on a Subject very remote from this, found themselves quickly at a stand, by the Difficulties that rose on every side. After we had a while puzzled our selves, without coming any nearer a Resolution of those Doubts which perplexed us, it came into my Thoughts, that we took a wrong course; and that, before we set our selves upon Enquiries of that Nature, it was necessary to examine our own Abilities, and see, what Objects our Understandings were, or were not fitted to deal with. (P. 7)

Locke jots down some notes in preparation for the next meeting of these friends, and the *Essay* "thus begun by Chance, was continued by Intreaty; written by incoherent parcels; and, after long intervals of neglect, resum'd again, as my Humour or Occasions permitted" (p. 7).[3]

Philosophy exists alongside of a special kind of life, indeed grows spontaneously out of the conditions of leisure-class existence. There is no special urgency or professional intensity in the pursuit of truth, which emerges in the course of normal occupations and is in effect subordinate to the healthy irregularities of daily life. The modesty Locke is at pains to establish here, the aversion to terms of art, the tendency to anecdote and domestic and socialized analogy—these contribute to a self-consciously revised setting for philosophical activity. Locke's transparent modesty and mock confusion cooperate easily with the analogies unifying contemplative and social activities. The philosopher's ordinary good humor is part of his claim that philosophy is rooted in common life. Casual and spontaneous in origin, it occurs as naturally and easily as other leisure-class activities. Avoiding self-interest, obsession, or eccentricity, Locke's analogies defer to those activities in which philosophical generalizing and abstracting are subordinated to their particularity and practicality.

"Pride," Pope's "Essay on Criticism" finds, is the "never-failing vice of fools," and Locke's *Essay* begins by contrasting its own modesty with the traditional egotism of philosophy whereby hard words and esoteric notions are developed mainly to create a privileged class of professionals. The *Essay* is a consistent, sometimes heavy-handed attack on the Schoolmen, based on a moral-psychological analysis. Pride, Locke says often, explains it all:

> the Schoolmen since, aiming at Glory and Esteem, for their great and universal Knowledge, easier a great deal to be pretended to, than really acquired, found this a good Expedient to cover their Ignorance, with a curious and unexplicable Web of perplexed Words, and procure to themselves the admiration of others, by unintelligible Terms, the apter to produce wonder, because they could not be understood. (III.x.8)

The natural setting for thought Locke takes care to elaborate is obviously a guard against such self-serving professionalism. A sort of rival dramatization of the conditions of thought, Locke's scene excludes the solitary, potentially solipsistic philosopher as well as the conspiracy of thinkers or priests. The special leisurely circumstances of easy, unforced contemplation and study within which thought occurs are carefully developed as the "natural" and human way to think or as the only reliable origin for thought. This scene is in part an instinctive defense against the dangerously individualistic epistemology to be developed in the *Essay*, but it is also the beginning of what, following Roland Barthes, might be called a naturalization of the social and historical.[4]

The *Essay* depends upon the staging of this "natural" thought versus the unnatural way of thinking that has prevailed, Locke says, until now. His book is a dramatized version of the history of thought, the recovery of an original rational ability. It marks a journey out of the ludicrous complications of the history of philosophy to the sweet simplicity of thought as a natural activity. The circle of friends within which thought occurs is a reconstituted Eden. The polite deference and disinterested inquiry fostered there turn men away from the self-serving disputations of the

Schools in which the necessities of intellectual warfare have produced comically false resolutions. Locke invents a mocking myth of the psychosocial origins of scholastic axioms. To prevent the endless spinning out of disputations

between skilful Combatants, whilst one never fail'd of a *medius terminus* to prove any Proposition; and the other could as constantly, without, or with a Distinction, deny the *Major* or *Minor*; . . . certain general Propositions, most of them indeed self-evident, were introduced into the Schools . . . beyond which there was no going, and which must not be receded from by either side. (IV.vii.11)

The poor Schoolmen are inside the complicated moral-psychological inevitabilities of history rather than in the simple and fortuitously constituted circle of friends that is the backdrop for the *Essay*. Thought begins and must return, says Locke many times, to a prehistorical natural perception. Thus, Aristotle must have begun not with syllogisms but with "the original way of Knowledge, *i.e.* by the visible agreement of *Ideas*" (IV.xvii.4). In that beginning, the philosopher is like the child, who "when a part of his Apple is taken away, knows it better in that particular Instance, than by this General Proposition, *The Whole is equal to all its Parts*" (IV.vii.11). The experiment can continue. Aristotle, or the child, or any of the number of persons Locke pictures having experiences and coming to knowledge illustrates the point that the mind (or those operations and perceptions that are mind or that the mind examines and evaluates) has a native quickness and accuracy on which the cumbersome formulations of philosophy are based. Moreover, those formulations should always be tentative, subject to correction by experience, and the hero-narrator (as it seems proper to call him) of Locke's *Essay* belongs to no school or sect: "For no Definitions, that I know, no Suppositions of any Sect, are of force enough to destroy constant Experience; and, perhaps, 'tis the affectation of knowing beyond what we perceive, that makes so much useless dispute, and noise, in the World" (II.i.19).

This opposition easily extracted from the *Essay* is a conventional scenario. History, even current and present happenings, is riddled with the lies and distortions that follow from its record as a form of institutionalized self-seeking; truth has been suppressed by priests and politicians but preserved in the minds of the rational few in each generation who see through each epoch's particular distortions of it. Certainly, Locke knew firsthand the difficulties of surviving in the historical and political world. His writings often return to conspiratorial myths of political and religious origins. In the *Reasonableness of Christianity*, for example, he tells a familiar story of the degeneration of natural religion as men fell "into the hands of their priests, to fill their heads with false notions of the Deity, and their worship with foolish rites." Some men, the old story continues, the "rational and thinking part of mankind," worshipped God privately. "They kept this truth locked up only in their own breasts as a secret, nor ever durst venture it amongst the people; much less amongst the priests, those wary guardians of their own creeds and profitable inventions."[5] Such a myth disguises, or at least seeks to minimize, its class implications. The "rational few" owe their intellectual privilege to their leisure and freedom from drudgery but mainly, Locke makes clear, to the integrity and honesty separating them from history and its corruptions. Historical conditions make them free of history.

Locke seems to have been a gentle and deferential soul, but behind his mildness lies a clear contempt for those who lack the self-control he grants himself and his readers in the *Essay*. "The soberest man in the Kingdom," as he called himself once, turns on occasion in the *Essay* to drunkenness for images and speaks, for example, of those who have "imbibed" the doctrine of substantial forms and suffer from a sort of philosophical intoxication.[6] His political liberalism is matched by a nearly ferocious contempt for the lower orders and a stern program for their management that embarrasses some of his commentators.[7] The ideal amateur philosopher of the "Epistle" resembles in his industry a member of the deserving poor, "who has raised himself above the Alms-Basket, and not content to live lazily on scraps of begg'd Opinions, sets his own Thoughts on work, to find and follow Truth" (p. 6). That, however, is only an analogy, for thought is specifically a class privilege, and the sort of truth the *Essay* pursues is not available for "the greatest part of Mankind." Or so at least Locke says at vivid length in chapter xx of Book IV, "Of wrong Assent, or Errour":

These Men's Opportunity of Knowledge and Enquiry, are commonly as narrow as their Fortunes; and their Understandings are but little instructed, when all their whole Time and Pains is laid out, to still the Croaking of their own Bellies, or the Cries of their Children. 'Tis not to be expected, that a Man, who drudges on, all his Life, in a laborious Trade, should be more knowing in the variety of Things done in the World, than a Pack-horse, who is driven constantly forwards and backwards, in a narrow Lane, and dirty Road, only to Market, should be skilled in the Geography of the Country. (IV.xx.2)[8]

Locke retreats from such harshness. He suggests blandly that "No Man is so wholly taken up with the Attendance on the Means of Living, as to have no spare Time at all to think of his Soul" and that "there are none so enslaved to the Necessities of Life, who might not find many Vacancies, that might be husbanded to this Advantage of their Knowledge" (IV.xx.3). Even poor wretches have time to think about their immortal souls, but Locke has mentioned them and granted them this brief space for religious meditation only to castigate lazy leisured individuals, who are "as far, nay farther *from the Liberty and Opportunities of a fair Enquiry*, than those poor and wretched Labourers, we before spoke of " (IV.xx.4). He goes on in this chapter to make ignorance and error matters of human intractability, laziness, and pride, ethical rather than intellectual failings, which he presents satirically. Error is located in social and historical circumstances, since many men subscribe to notions enforced by accidents of birth and residence. Religious beliefs especially are perpetuated by such factors. Most men "are resolved to stick to a Party, that Education or Interest has engaged them in; and there, like the common Soldiers of an Army, shew their Courage and Warmth, as their Leaders direct, without ever examining, or so much as knowing the Cause they contend for" (IV.xx.18). Finally, most men realize this in some way and "there are fewer, that actually assent to them, and mistake them for truths, than is imagined" (IV.xx.18). Thought is indeed a class privilege neglected by most of the lazy inhabitants of the leisured classes, but all men, Locke insinuates in the course of this chapter, have an instinct for truth, an awareness at least of the relativity of opinion. From the "Epistle to the Reader" onward, the reader is invited to occupy a special place to which his class gives him ready access, but which is potentially natural, available to all men who will stir themselves. Locke steers us away from his own harsh analysis of knowledge as a class privilege to a redefined truth of which all men have some inkling.

As John Yolton has demonstrated, the *Essay* is a response to religious controversies of the time, despite Locke's repeated insistence that he was indifferent to such issues.[9] In fact, Locke's modesty and simplicity, those qualities he assigns to his work and to himself, are in the service of a comprehensive polemic directed at virtually the entire intellectual world of his time. The *Essay* is nothing if not contentious. Locke's exact location in that world of seventeenth-century polemics is a complex question and matter for intellectual historians. But his place in those disputes and his dramatization of his thought by means of style and setting as a matter beyond dispute create a situation full of ironies and ambiguities. Locke's strategy is to pretend to ignore controversy and to look down on disputation as something that simply cannot occur in his natural world of unobstructed perception. The style and tone appropriate to this strategy are implicitly ironic, since the "natural" scene in which that perception operates is a socially privileged world as well as a fiercely controversial scheme of things.

Locke manages those ironies by emphasizing another: a deference to truth whereby it is dramatized as a compelling and morally irresistible set of conditions. The speaker is not so much an expounder of a philosophical system as a patient observer and recorder of data, a functionally innocent outsider whose book is a compilation in a rhetorical sense of anecdote and observation punctuated by modest speculation and interrogation. The *Essay* presents itself as an antisystem; its founding anecdote, after all, is Locke's surprised discovery in leisurely and social discourse that first principles, the nature of the understanding, have never been really established or understood. The humility of such a sly questioner is transparent, yielding regularly to rigor with a disputatious tone at its edges. There is a polite challenge to an opponent, for example, after a discussion in the opening pages of Book I establishing that the idea of God is not innate: "But our minds being, at first, void of that *Idea*, which we are most concerned to have, it *is a strong presumption against all other innate Characters*. I must own, as far as I can observe, I can find none, and would be glad to be informed by any other" (I.iv.17). Self-effacement follows insistent rigor to create the recurrent stance of the essayist, who is an ingenuous "Lover of Truth" whose finest moments by his own standards are renunciations of certainty. He points proudly to his own revisions in Book II:

And now as a Lover of Truth, and not a Worshipper of my own Doctrines, I own some change of my Opinion, which I think I have discover'd ground for. In what I first writ, I with an unbiassed indifferency followed Truth, whither I thought she led me. But neither being so vain as to fancy Infallibility, nor so disingenuous as to dissemble my mistakes for fear of blemishing my reputation, I have with the same sincere design for truth only, not been asham'd to publish what a severer enquiry has suggested. (II.xxi.72)[10]

Locke distracts his reader from the social and intellectual location of his thought. He speaks of truth as a principle beyond any situation, a simple yet elusive entity that philosophical formulation can never get quite right or fix permanently. Locke and his circle of philosophical amateurs establish themselves in the natural scene of thought by holding themselves in readiness for those irregularities and readjustments which truth requires if it is to be followed. They are not infected by the competitive blindness of disputation because they are ready to acknowledge truth wherever and however it appears. *Amicus Plato sed magis amica veritas* is an old maxim. Locke's philosophical writing is founded on a pervasive and ironic deployment of it that gains force by dramatizing truth as available only to a radical openness hitherto unpracticed except by the innocent. Seeing the truth involves adherence to principles so clear and self-evident (and perhaps therefore difficult to admit) that Locke and his friends can only smile ironically at others' refusal to defer to truth as they do. What has been made difficult must be returned to its native simplicity, as Locke tried to explain to Stillingfleet. Accused by the bishop of being one of "the gentlemen of this new way of reasoning," Locke points out that the notion of substance is in fact destroyed by the comically elaborate word-spinning of the old logicians. To quote them is for Locke to point to their inadequacy:

He, that would shew me a more clear and distinct idea of substance, would do me a kindness I should thank him for. But this is the best I can hitherto find, either in my own thoughts, or in the books of logicians: for their account, or, idea, of it is, that it is, 'Ens, or res per se subsistens, et substans accidentibus;' which in effect is no more but that substance is a being, or thing; or in short, something they know not what, or of which they have no clearer idea, than that it is something, which supports accidents, or other simple ideas, or modes, and is not supported itself, as a mode, or an accident.[11]

Old definitions of substance represent a refusal to accept the deceptive simplicity of truth and a reluctance to live with its opacity or uncertainty. The old terminology in Locke's wide-eyed rendering of it is offensively technical as well as foolishly tautological, but its main weakness is actually moral. Such formulations claim to stabilize and contain truth. For Locke, these definitions must be exchanged for positions and perspectives that promote a dynamic truthfulness to experience, that create situations where truths reveal themselves. Thus, when Stillingfleet objected that "very little weight is to be laid on a bare grammatical etymology," Locke replied that such a derivation of substance "favours the idea we have of it." He reminded Stillingfleet of his point in the *Essay*, "that if we know the original of all the words we meet with, we should thereby be very much helped to know the ideas they were first applied to, and made to stand for."[12]

Etymology returns to an original historical moment when words were connected with an attempt to understand experience. Etymologizing defers to the experience contained in words, and its practice at crucial moments such as when we try to make sense of a term like "substance" is a self-effacing philosophical gesture. What really matters, in Locke's presentation, is the readiness to suspend systematizing and wordmongering and to let the truth or untruth recorded in words manifest itself. Locke's thought dramatizes itself as a set of instructions for watching the process of understanding rather than a formulation of just what it is we understand. Hence the ultimate irony in his writing. The *Essay* points to its own instrumentality, urging us to be ready for truth without promising to show it or deliver it in a stable or static form. Locke's urbane ironies continually affirm that self-denying philosophical project. The moral-intellectual solidarity of reader and writer thus projected helps protect against the chaotic possibilities of such a suspension of traditional certainties.

Locke himself provides quite moving testimony for such a view of his thought. Attacked by various prelates and apparently very ill with asthma, he wrote to Molyneux just two years before his death affirming his belief in the possibility of verification but expressing at the same time the necessary difficulty of that belief. Locke does not say that he has found truth but that he knows a certain kind of truth is available: he has experienced it and knows its effects if not its exact shape. The solution to uncertainty and opposition is the solidarity of a moral-intellectual class of men who occupy a position and take a perspective whereby truth can be seen.

If there be not an evidence of sense and truth, which is apt and fitted to prevail on every human understanding, as far as it is open and unprejudiced; there is at least a harmony of understandings in some men, to whom sense and nonsense, truth and falshood, appear equally in the respective discourses they meet with . . . If I could think that discourses and arguments to the understanding were like the several sorts of cates to different palates and stomachs, some nauseous and destructive to one, which are pleasant and restorative to another; I should no more think of books and study, and should think my time better employed at push-pin than in reading or writing. But I am convinced of the contrary: I know there is truth opposite to falshood, that it may be found if people will, and is worth the seeking, and is not only the most valuable, but the pleasantest thing in the world. And therefore I am no more troubled and disturb'd with all the dust that is raised against it, than I should be to see from the top of an high steeple, where I had clear air and sunshine, a company of great boys or little boys (for'tis all one) throw up dust in the air, which reach'd not me, but fell down in their own eyes.[13]

The urbanity and wit of this affirmation are striking. Locke reluctantly rejects the simplicity of a perfect empiricism in which truth would manifest itself to "every human understanding." But he also draws back from a trivializing physical relativism. Eating and playing at push-pin are activities the philosopher takes note of and perhaps pleasure in occasionally. However, the reading and writing of those men whose understandings distinguish truth from falsehood are not only superior activities but also "the pleasantest thing in the world." Seeking truth is an enjoyable worldly activity, a nobler but not an entirely distinct activity from eating and playing games. Locke affirms the truth many in fact accused him of negating, but avoids the potential solemnity or pomposity of such a moment by connecting the seeking of truth to a common world of innocent pleasure and ordinary variability that the philosopher never loses sight of (if he is a real philosopher and not a systematizing fool).

Perhaps the best moment in this passage is the closing image. Locke sees a clear, natural truth from a high steeple (ironically, of course, this is where his clerical opponents should be) and looks down on other thinkers, who try like dirty and mischievous urchins to obscure the view and healthy clarity by throwing dust in the air. Locke is not in his tower for contemplative isolation but to be in the clear air and sunshine that are the conditions for perceiving truth. Moreover, he retains an amused relationship to the lower world, where his philosophical opponents are busy with the childish games he has just rejected in favor of adult activities. A comic vignette rather than a hypostasized image of truth, this is a typical Lockean moment in its balancing of the natural scene of a reformed philosophical perception against the recurring historical comedy of self-interested disputation.

The cautious hesitation of the opening sentences of this passage echoes the modesty of the *Essay*, where Locke claims "not to teach, but to enquire" (II.xi.17). Like the letter, the *Essay* slides effortlessly from a circling modesty to a strength lent to it by the compelling force of a truth observed, and Locke continues by noting that he "cannot but confess here again, That external and internal Sensation are the only passages that I can find, of Knowledge, to the Understanding" (II.xi.17). Locke commits himself to interrogation and observation and thereby to steady alertness to the shocks and surprises of experience, those inescapable if puzzling or upsetting facts and conclusions in store for the inquiring intelligence. His persona has accordingly to be ready to testify to truth and affirm it strongly, to reach at times for an image or analogy that will shine forth with the same brilliance as truth. The passage from Locke's letter to Molyneux does quickly what the *Essay* accomplishes slowly and recurrently.

The world of Locke's philosophy demands such a literary manner, and that manner in turn enforces and supports the world. The primacy of an experienced reality or the language that articulates it is not something Locke seems to have worried about. In the *Essay*, reality—sensations, ideas, perceptions, and the world that provokes them—precedes language, and the problem is in fact to repress language and defer to truth.[14] The *Essay* bears almost innumerable traces of Locke's concern for the adequacy of his writing. It went through various early drafts, and Locke introduced thousands of textual changes into the editions that appeared in his lifetime, especially in the second and fourth editions. Most of these changes, as Gilbert Ryle noted, are "exegetically null corrections of misprints and misspellings, and his changes of semi-colons, parentheses, apostrophes, italics, etc."[15] But even that minor tinkering (as well as some substantive revision, the enlarged chapter "On Power" and new chapters on "Enthusiasm" and "Identity and Diversity" that followed the first edition) bespeaks an urge to revise and dramatizes the value of revision.

Locke is often criticized for his repetitiousness, and the *Essay* is careful and exhaustive to the point of prolixity. But his volubility, like the impulse to revise, serves to present language as an analytical instrument, a tool for extracting truth rather than a medium in which truth is expressed. Locke says as much in the "Epistle" when he remarks that rephrasing new and difficult matters makes them somehow clearer: "There are few, I believe, who have not observed in themselves or others, That what in one way of proposing was very obscure, another way of expressing it, has made very clear and intelligible: Though afterward the Mind found little difference in the Phrases, and wondered why one failed to be understood more than the other" (p. 8). The search is not exactly for the philosophical *mot juste* but for the phrasing that will somehow promote clarity in the mind of reader and writer, or perhaps for the necessary rephrasing of the same material that most readers require to come through to clarity in the difficult passages of thought. Locke told Molyneux that "some of the explications in my book" were "turned several ways, to make those abstract notions the easier sink into minds prejudiced in the ordinary way of education." He worried that such care for his readers had made the *Essay* too long, but Molyneux and some others found "the redundancy in it a pardonable fault."[16]

Rephrasing or rewriting will probably bring us nearer to the truth, not because we literally come closer to it in the new formulation but because the very act of reformulation often produces an operational clarity. But, paradoxically, Locke's prolixity is connected to his programmatic suspicion of language. Many words are necessary to avoid or warn against the distancing or distorting effect of language. Even when our knowledge terminates in "Things, yet it was for the most part so much by the intervention of Words, that they seem'd scarce separable from our general Knowledge." Words "interpose" themselves between us and truth and "like the *Medium* through which visible Objects pass, their Obscurity and Disorder does not seldom cast a mist before our Eyes, and impose upon our Understandings" (III.ix.21). Words are so unreliable that God chose, Locke says rather daringly, to put his most efficient and definite revelation in wordless terms, not in the Scriptures but in the "legible Characters of his Works and Providence" available even to those "to whom this written Word never came" (III.ix.23). Locke's lively literary manner and his persistent revision of his major work are, in a sense, a defense against the obscuring inertia of language, an attempt to sustain motion and activity in his text as well as in his thought. Language in such a view needs to be in constant process and to shun the final formulations of logic, the ossified terminology of the Schools, and the repeatable and formalized patterns of traditional rhetoric.

This last is like the logic of the Schools, an imposition of rule and form on what is best learned by example or perceived intuitively. Experience is best in education, as Locke's own experience has taught him: "I have seldom or never observed any one to get the skill of reasoning well, or speaking handsomely, by studying those rules which pretend to teach it . . . if you would have your son reason well, let him read Chillingworth, and if you would have him speak well, let him be conversant in Tully, to give him the true idea of eloquence." [17] Rhetorical theory, like the jargon of the Schools, is the enemy of truth and can also be explained in historical-psychological terms. The "Arts of Fallacy are endow'd and preferred," says Locke, because "Men love to deceive, and be deceived . . . And, I doubt not, but it will be thought great boldness, if not brutality in me, to have said thus much against it. *Eloquence*, like the fair Sex, has too prevailing Beauties in it, to suffer it self ever to be spoken against. And 'tis in vain to find fault with those Arts of Deceiving, wherein Men find pleasure to be Deceived" (III.x.34).

Locke never seems to lose his good humor, but the warnings against the deceptions of rhetoric occur with chorus-like regularity in the *Essay*. Just as he works to obscure the polemical point and social location of his thought, Locke seeks to neutralize his own rhetoric and to deny his own rhetorical self-consciousness. At its simplest, that means the refusal of "Wit and Fancy" and the moral, self-denying choice of "dry Truth and

real Knowledge" (III.x.34). "Truth" is revealed to the inquiring mind but
never fully articulated by the essayist, who maintains his diffidence
because he knows the inherent fallacy of final formulation, at least in normal language. So the problem he faces is to keep moving and to suspend
certainty. Locke defines freedom in Book II as the mind's "power to *suspend* the execution and satisfaction of any of its desires, and so all, one
after another," so that the mind "is at liberty to consider the objects of
them; examine them on all sides, and weigh them with others" (II.-
xxi.47). His style and identifying manner as a writer consist in a similar
suspension of normal assertion and arrangement; his deliberately loose
and informal rhythms, his sometimes prolix mixture of anecdote, data,
and reasoning are a refusal of balance and antithesis for the staged articulation of possibilities. Locke's prose might be called a negative force,
as it establishes what D. W. Harding calls a "functional" rhythm. Harding notes that Locke's writing is not overtly decorated in the manner of
Hooker or Browne, where the cadence of the prose is in effect aesthetic
and acts as a visible and dramatic accompaniment to meaning. Locke's
writing has qualities that are less apparent rhetorically but that "contribute to an evenness of tone consistent with low-pitched expectations,
with the insertion of provisos . . . and with reasonable rather than forceful
communication."[18]

Locke's thought finds the phenomenal world beyond our apprehension
and urges us to concentrate on ethics and religion. His style serves that
moral conclusion; it is full of qualification, reservation, and reflexive
turns, making the reader aware of the shortcomings and self-interest of
normal formulations. Here, for example, is Locke on the idea of infinity.
He notes that such an idea is the result of the mind's adding the idea of
space to space until it cannot see the end. But, he asks, can such an idea
actually exist at any moment in the mind?

This, I think, is the way, whereby the Mind gets the *Idea of infinite
Space*. 'Tis a quite different Consideration to examine, whether the
Mind has the *Idea* of such a *boundless Space actually existing*, since our
Ideas are not always Proofs of the Existence of Things; but yet, since this
comes here in our way, I suppose I may say, that we are apt to think,
that Space in it self is actually boundless, to which Imagination the *Idea*
of Space or Expansion of it self naturally leads us. (II.xvii.4)

This is Locke's deferential, truth-loving persona. His prose hesitates and
qualifies politely but it also inserts precise relations of cause and effect
and insists with a literalizing rigor upon exact distinction between an idea
(in that confusing seventeenth-century sense of a mental event something

like an impression or sensation) and an abstraction (a construction of the intellect). But even as he does that, his prose points to its temporality, and thought identifies itself as something happening right in front of us ("since this comes here in our way"). As that aside shows, the *Essay* is frequently like a narrative; the story of perception and how we at last arrive at correct understanding is inseparable from a narrative that goes back to specific anecdote and instance and, of course, back to the origins of each man's thought in some hypothetical primal moment of perception. Locke's sentences seek to record that perception and to achieve in their patterns an alternation that accompanies and to some extent matches the flow of narrative. The speaker puts experience before us and then tries to generalize; that is Locke's philosophical program in its simplest terms. Yet Locke's generalizations retain such dense and persistent qualification that in reading them we do not travel very far from the specific examples of experience.

The prose itself encourages this avoidance of the symmetries and patterns of generalization by a recurring habit of modifying clauses and concessive phrases. After describing what he calls the names of "mixed modes," that is, complex entities such as moral terms or qualities of things or actions, Locke begins to speak of the names of "substances." A transition paragraph moves from mixed modes to substances and illustrates the special quality of Locke's generalizing:

If the signification of the Names of mixed Modes are uncertain, because there be no real Standards existing in Nature, to which those *Ideas* are referred, and by which they may be adjusted, the *Names of Substances are of a doubtful signification*, for a contrary reason, *viz. because* the *Ideas*, they stand for, are supposed conformable to the reality of Things, and are *referred to Standards* made by Nature. In our *Ideas* of Substances we have not the liberty as in mixed Modes, to frame what Combinations we think fit, to be the characteristical Notes, to rank and denominate Things by. In these we must follow Nature, suit our complex *Ideas* to real Existences, and regulate the signification of their Names by the Things themselves, if we will have our Names to be the signs of them, and stand for them. Here, 'tis true, we have Patterns to follow; but Patterns, that will make the signification of their names very uncertain: For Names must be of a very unsteady and various meaning, if the *Ideas* they stand for, be referred to Standards without us, *that either cannot be known at all, or can be known but imperfectly and uncertainly.* (III.ix.11)

The paragraph begins with opposition between the names of mixed modes and substances, and the description of the former is a summary of the previous five sections, as the description of the latter forward to the next eight. It is an opposition only in the grammatical sense, however, since the names of both mixed modes and substances are uncertain and doubtful. An "if" clause promises, normally, a balancing certainty by means of a clear opposition; if we grant this, that will follow, or if this is true, that is clearly false. Here, we grant that mixed modes have uncertain names because they have no standard in nature and we are given by the successor to that conditional clause a positive contrary assertion about the names of substances, but one that makes them as unreliable as those of mixed modes. The opposition is to some extent an identity, and the symmetry of the sentence is in fact undercut by its logical content. The following sentences continue the description of the "opposition" and seem to establish a positive alternative to the hopelessly uncertain vagueness of the names of the mixed modes. In the third sentence in the paragraph, a reassuring parallel series of verbs ("we must follow Nature, suit our complex *Ideas* . . . and regulate the signification") seems to approve by its structure of the validity and efficiency of the process whereby we understand substances. The concluding "if" clause of this third sentence is an echo of the opening of the section and looks at first like an inverted variation of the conditional pattern with which we began. But the placement of the conditional clause in this sentence modifies the logical assurance such constructions provide, since here the "if" clause describes a condition that will turn out in the next sentence to be impossible. The built-in uncertainty of that project (to "have our Names to be the signs of" things and to stand for them) is underlined in the beginning of the last sentence by the concessive phrase "'tis true," a response to an implied and limited common sense. It is indeed true that "here" (and Locke's prose tends toward a virtual sort of location, the real space of perception as well as the logical place in the argument) we can refer to what Locke calls archetypes of simple substances, "Patterns" of things like *gold* or *apple*. But this last and most casually introduced of the sentences in this section, with its quasi-physical location and its polite concessive, is the most complex and the most rigorous in its examination of terms.

Two key terms, *patterns* and *names*, are repeated in succeeding clauses, each of which extracts further meaning from them, the first by modifying *patterns* and the second by explaining in a long independent construction the nature of *names* that are derived from such *patterns*. This last clause repeats the inverted conditional structure of the third sentence, only now the "if" clause that concludes matters in this section has an ironclad certainty and expresses an undeniable generalization rather than the tentative and observational hypothesis of the "if" clause that began the section. Locke is going to demonstrate in the next section that standards by which we refer to a substance such as gold and give it that name are, in fact, unknown or uncertain. But in this sentence he is establishing the axiom that an unknown or uncertain external standard for a word or name makes the idea associated with that name unclear and the name itself uncertain. The transition in this sentence is from observation and experimental comparison to an axiomatic utterance that takes for granted Locke's notions about the relationships among idea, word, and reality. This last construction is almost pseudoconditional and expresses rather a cause and effect relationship: unknown or uncertain external standards in simple utterances lead to unclear ideas and to the names deriving from them.

One purpose of this prose is to modify rhetorical symmetry, in this case to avoid mere anaphora. The "if" clauses are varied in position and, it turns out, in meaning, as we make our way from the observational and nearly conditional tone of the first sentence toward an increasing certainty that culminates in the near-axiom of the last independent clause of the concluding sentence. But there is an ironic narrative implicit in this section, as we follow a path from that initial observation of normal uncertainty about "mixed modes" to the emerging and more disturbing certainty that simple substances are themselves named without precision. The prose seeks to enact a reasonable investigation by its lack of ornament and by its substitution of varying experiential relationships for the exact repetitions of rhetorical pattern, and it also seeks by what Harding calls its "functional" rhythm to prepare us for paradox and even for denials of common sense and ordinary notions. The modest and deferential rationality of Locke's persona is a rhetorical necessity given the scope of his project and the radical implications of it that he draws out from time to time.

This section is carefully underwritten, as it were, and rhetorical and logical bluntness is avoided. Locke's tact as a writer is clearly visible in the *Essay*, especially in those moments when he turns to matters of faith and belief. For them he acquires momentarily another tone and rhythm, his style becomes formulaic, heavily allusive to religious texts, and given to the gnomic formulations of such discourse. The following paragraph stages very sharply the sort of modulation from the tactful analytical mode to this "religious" style:

Besides those we have hitherto mentioned, there is one sort of Propositions that challenge the highest Degree of our Assent, upon bare
Testimony, whether the thing proposed, agree or disagree with common

Experience, and the ordinary course of Things, or no. The Reason
whereof is, because the Testimony is of such an one, as cannot deceive,
nor be deceived, and that is of God himself. This carries with it
Assurance beyond Doubt, Evidence beyond Exception. This is called by
a peculiar Name, *Revelation*, and our Assent to it, *Faith*: which as absolutely determines our Minds, and as perfectly excludes all wavering as
our Knowledge it self; and we may as well doubt of our own Being, as
we can, whether any Revelation from GOD be true. (IV.xvi.14)

The first and last sentences in this paragraph are marked by the normal
inquiring tone of the *Essay*, a tone interrupted by those two short
sentences describing God's revelation. Locke goes out of his stylistic way
to separate them. Just as revelation is beyond analysis and commands immediate assent, the rhetoric appropriate to revelation features those compelling gnomic structures that call for acceptance (or rejection) but not for
the deliberately exhaustive Lockean manner. "Assurance beyond doubt,
evidence beyond exception" — those are precisely the conditions the *Essay*
in both form and content is out to question and often to undermine.
Form such as that of these pious sentences enforces assent, as Kenneth
Burke points out, by virtue of the reader's participation in the form.[19]
Locke's writing possesses its own subtle version of an enforcing form in its
continual deference and moderation, its steady modification of rhetorical
form, and its qualification of certainty.

Hobbes presents an instructive contrast and illustration of continuities
between form and philosophical content. *Leviathan* and Locke's *Two
Treatises of Government* invite us to imagine a primal political scene, the
state of nature. Hobbes's evocation is memorably stark; his primal man
lost and bewildered, surrounded by others in the same condition, fearful
and therefore dangerous. The scene in the early pages of *Leviathan* is
tragic-heroic; and Hobbes's style is roughly assertive, matching the assertions of power and the nearly desperate association of men that mark the
ways out of the anarchic state of nature. In a passage like the following
one, Hobbes displays a style powerful in ways Locke characteristically
avoids:

A fifth law of nature, is COMPLAISANCE; that is to say, *that every man
strive to accommodate himself to the rest*. For the understanding
whereof, we may consider, that there is in men's aptness to society, a
diversity of nature, rising from their diversity of affections; not unlike to
that we see in stones brought together for building of an edifice. For as
that stone which by the asperity, and irregularity of figure, takes more
room from others, then itself fills; and for the hardness, cannot be easily
made plain, and thereby hindereth the building, is by the builders cast

away as unprofitable, and troublesome: so also, a man that by asperity
of nature, will strive to retain those things which to himself are
superfluous, and to others necessary; and for the stubbornness of his
passions, cannot be corrected, is to be left, or cast out of society, as
cumbersome thereunto. For seeing every man, not only by right, but
also by necessity of nature, is supposed to endeavour all he can, to obtain that which is necessary for his conservation; he that shall oppose
himself against it, for things superfluous, is guilty of the war that
thereupon is to follow.[20]

Hobbes favors popular allusion, homely imagery, and common illustration; he achieves a loose and flowing discourse, homely yet eloquent with
a sort of quasi-biblical or near-proverbial simplicity. Like the edifice he
speaks of here, Hobbes's prose works by accumulation and addition;
clause gets piled upon clause in a hammering, driving manner far from
Locke's qualification and reservation. *Leviathan* is not divided and in-
secure but copious and confident, unviolated by Locke's constant insertion of modification and qualification.

There are moments in Locke's writing when he seems to aspire to a
purely nonassertive mode. As it moves along, the following passage from
the *Second Treatise* includes answers to objections as they arise.

For all the power the Government has, being only for the good of the
Society, as it ought not to be *Arbitrary* and at Pleasure, so it ought to
be exercised by *established and promulgated Laws*: that both the People
may know their Duty, and be safe and secure within the limits of the
Law, and the Rulers too kept within their due bounds, and not to be
tempted, by the Power they have in their hands, to imploy it to such
purposes, and by such measures, as they would not have known, and
own not willingly.[21]

The restraint and limitation urged here are matched by rhetorical
restraint; the legalistic balancing of power and obligation finds an
equivalent in the series of careful connectives, which are really modifiers
rather than links in a series. In effect, narrative possibility is negated. The
dramatic implications of a mythic political moment are left undeveloped
and unspecific. By contrast, the most well known passage in *Leviathan*
derives its strength from dramatic concreteness that has no parallel in
Locke's political or moral writings. The passage displays Hobbes's wealth
of allusion and biblical echo, his talent for common illustration and near-
proverbial formulation. But it also has a daring dramatic shape, beginning with an argument about the notion of time and the nature of war
and then leading to the biblical echoes in the anaphoric description of the
state of war and the memorable summary of the life of man. Hobbes's

prose is overtly rhetorical, designed to move its readers, unafraid to supplement theoretical surmise and philosophic argument with vigorously
imagined scenes:

> . . . and therefore the notion of *time*, is to be considered in the nature
> of war; as it is in the nature of weather. For as the nature of foul
> weather, lieth not in a shower or two of rain; but in an inclination
> thereto of many days together: so the nature of war, consisteth not in
> actual fighting; but in the known disposition thereto, during all the
> time there is no assurance to the contrary. All other time is PEACE.

> Whatsoever therefore is consequent to a time of war, where every man
> is enemy to every man; the same is consequent to the time, wherein
> men live without other security, than what their own strength, and their
> own invention shall furnish them withal. In such condition, there is no
> place for industry; because the fruit thereof is uncertain: and conse-
> quently no culture of the earth; no navigation, nor use of the com-
> modities that may be imported by sea; no commodious building; no in-
> struments of moving, and removing, such things as require much force;
> no knowledge of the face of the earth; no account of time; no arts; no
> letters; no society; and which is worst of all, continual fear, and danger
> of violent death; and the life of man, solitary, poor, nasty, brutish, and
> short.[22]

To be sure, I have matched an especially austere passage from Locke's
Treatise with perhaps the most vivid and memorable scene in *Leviathan*.
Locke in fact uses imagery and dramatic enactment a good deal in his
writings. But his images, frequent and even crucial as they sometimes are,
are always provisional and tentative. Hobbes seems to share that distrust
of metaphors and denounces them with characteristic vigor as "sensless
and ambiguous words . . . like *ignes fatui*; and reasoning upon them, is
wandering amongst innumerable absurdities; and their end, contention
and sedition, or contempt."[23] But his prose is heavily larded with extended analogies or often with marvelous, effectively surprising strings of
illustrations that take us out of the study and into a concrete world.
Describing the operations of memory, for example, Hobbes writes:
"Sometimes a man knows a place determinate, within the compass
whereof he is to seek; and then his thoughts run over all the parts thereof,
in the same manner as one would sweep a room, to find a jewel; or as a
spaniel ranges the field, till he find a scent; or as a man should run over
the alphabet, to start a rhyme."[24] Passages like this are reminders that
Hobbes enjoyed a liberty as a writer to range as freely as his frisky spaniel.
Subsequent philosophical prose developed a stricter decorum, obedient
to the demands of emerging scientific theory that did not admit easy connections and displayed more clearly separate and distinct orders of being.
Hobbes's easy analogizing is the most obvious sign of a robust stylistic

habit that looks back to a prescientific world full of analogy and similitude. The overwhelming concreteness of presentation found in *Leviathan* is perhaps the clearest difference between Hobbes's style (and the imaginative world evoked by it) and Locke's. Locke's storehouse of allusion, imagery, tonalities, and verbal possibilities is a much smaller building than Hobbes's, and when items are selected for use, they seem to be more carefully examined and justified as they are employed.

A network of historical circumstances helps to explain the visible alteration in philosophic style from Hobbes to Locke. Not the least important of these circumstances is the emerging scientific spirit. Locke qualifies as an amateur virtuoso and his travel journals are full of exact and minute data, from the pressing of olive oil and the fermentation of wine to the proportion of alloys in the coinages of Europe.[25] He also qualifies by successful practice as a physician, for as Peter Gay remarks he "was a physician before he was a philosopher, and a philosopher largely because he was a physician."[26] Locke collects symptoms as well as economic and agronomical data, just as in his philosophical program he observes and interrogates. On one level, his program is simply a continuation of the Baconian revolution, and the English seventeenth century is full of such curious and efficient virtuosos. His plainness is an expression of the flattening of the language of learning called for by Bacon and taken to literal lengths by Sprat in his *History of the Royal Society*. Moreover, Locke's severely unrhetorical manner and his commitment to the language of measurement, materiality, and relationship are part of the scientific depreciation of normal language that led to attempts to establish a universal character.[27]

But Locke's particular success in founding a new province of philosophical writing has distinct political implications. The ideals of scientific discourse that his writing serves are supported by and implicitly justify a political ideology. Locke's rhetoric—the calm, dispassionate manner, with its stylistic self-effacement and studied refusal of ornament and rhythm—defers elaborately to an objective, factual world. But the humble servant of reality is actually its powerful master, and Locke's style is a token of confident control. An *obiter dictum* in Marx's *Eighteenth Brumaire* sheds some light on this paradox. Just as the French revolution borrowed Roman forms and apparel, the seventeenth-century bourgeois revolution appropriated, says Marx, "the language, passions and illusions of the Old Testament. When the actual goal had been reached, when the bourgeois transformation of English society had been accomplished, Locke drove out Habakkuk."[28]

There is much more to Hobbes's style than biblical echo. But he possesses the prophetic voice and intensity Marx speaks of, even though he is the reactionary and secular antithesis of the Cromwellian revolutionaries. Locke's style is exactly appropriate to the liberal ideology with which he is now associated, and those habits of orderly deference and circumspection in his thought match carefully modulated and understated literary habits. From a philosophical point of view, Locke and Hobbes share certain assumptions about the nature of reality and the workings of the mind. But they live in separate imaginative worlds. Locke's style constitutes a coherently "bourgeois" philosophical manner rendered especially distinct when held against Hobbes's writing.

Although it has become almost strictly a term of abuse, "bourgeois" can serve as a neutral historical category that encompasses the political, moral, and psychological conditions created by what C. B. Macpherson has called a possessive market society, in which a class of men controls the land and labor, in which the products of that land and labor are treated as commodities to be bought and sold, and in which "men's relations to others are set largely by their ownership of these commodities and the success with which they utilize that ownership to their own profit." In such a society, power is visible and thought is naturally the privilege of a leisure class, as perhaps it has been in all societies. But that leisure class is now out to efface its power and to disguise domination; in the broadest historical terms, seventeenth-century bourgeois thought seeks to reconcile traditional Christian natural law morality with the power relations between classes that now constitute society.[29] For Marxist historians and political scientists like Macpherson, the bourgeoisie is necessarily involved in a dialectic between the freedom and self-possession of the individual and the various kinds of necessity created by the actions of the free individual, who is free by virtue of the bondage of many and whose freedom is itself compromised in the political and economic relationships that constitute the state and the market. Individuals are free because they give up a good deal of freedom to the state and because their free actions as economic individuals create a set of inexorable but beneficial conditions called the market.

Hobbes analyzed these paradoxes clearly, and his massively assertive style is an apt expression of his denial of natural law and his articulation of a self-conscious materialism and utilitarianism in politics and morality. Locke, says Macpherson, presented an easier, more ambiguous doctrine in which the power and domination of the propertied classes were located in nature and reconciled with the principle of individual freedom and moral responsibility. In the *Second Treatise* Locke managed to find that property rights are natural rights; each man is the sole proprietor of his own powers and naturally appropriates land and its products by exercising those powers. In time but still in the state of nature, there is no more land to be had, and some men can only sell their labor to those who have appropriated all the available land. Locke, as Macpherson interprets the *Second Treatise*, negates the imaginative darkness of the state of nature and makes it, in effect, a more complicated and extensive set of events, turning it away from the stark melodrama of Hobbes's formulation in *Leviathan* to another scenario in which it is hard to tell where nature ends and civil society begins. The power individuals exercise so visibly is attenuated and morally legitimized by being made part of a natural sequence of rational human development in which individuals yield to a collective, a civil society that guarantees the dominance of some individuals over others. The narrative mode, in effect, is altered, and the acquisition of land and of the power that goes with it is presented as the expression of a gradual process whereby natural morality and justice emerge. *Leviathan* alludes to a brutal historical record, and Hobbes's descriptions of the hypothetical origins of society read at times like the darkest moments in Malory. The *Second Treatise* imagines an inevitable and benign natural scene, and the difference in political doctrine between the two books is also a matter of their distinct means of literary enforcement and dramatization. Locke may be said to promote his political theory by reimagining the myth of political origins, and in part that restaging of origins is achieved by Locke's characteristic tone and manner as a writer.[30]

Two related aspects of that manner — the play of analogy and a recurring literalization — are brought into prominence by the subject matter. Both of these follow from the reimagining of nature that is central to Locke's political theory and crucial to his exposition of reality in the *Essay*. Locke's political theory begins with an attack on the false analogy between paternal and kingly power in Filmer's *Patriarcha*, and the ridicule he heaps on that book is a matter of literal analysis that resembles the analysis of terms in the *Essay*. Responding, for example, to Filmer's argument that paternity gives authority because it gives life, Locke points out that no one knows what "life" is:

How can he be thought to give Life to another, that knows not wherein his own Life consists? Philosophers are at a loss about it after their most diligent enquiries; And Anatomists, after their whole Lives and Studies spent in Dissections, and diligent examining the Bodies of Men, confess their Ignorance in the Structure and Use of many parts of Mans Body, and in that Operation wherein Life consists in the whole. And doth the Rude Plough-Man, or the more ignorant Voluptuary, frame or fashion such an admirable Engine as this is, and then put Life and Sense into it? Can any Man say, He formed the parts that are necessary to the Life of his Child? Or can he suppose himself to give the Life, and yet not know what Subject is fit to receive it, nor what Actions or Organs are necessary for its Reception or Preservation? (VI.52.pp.214–215)

Examination of common terms and untenable analogy is a matter of literal interrogation that leads to eloquent but temporary skepticism. The dramatization of human limitation is a recurring occasion for such eloquence in Locke's writings and often involves, as it does here, invoking social and even cosmic panoramas. From the ploughman to the voluptuary, from the grand speculations of philosophers to the minute and concrete investigations of the anatomist, Locke invites his readers to vary their perspectives and then to consider themselves in these shifting scenes. The ignorance we are invited to admit becomes a power to move with Locke through the social and intellectual world and to enjoy the special perspective that creates doubt around the idea of "life." Literalization is thus more than the refusal of analogy. Locke exchanges analogy for narrative. In his writings, to literalize is frequently to develop a complex narrative around a notion, to trace a term to its origin in the historical or mythic past or to elaborate its various present manifestations.

Filmer's analogy is untenable because it has no narrative complexity and is only a matter of simple movement from the family to civil society. Thus, Locke wonders what Filmer can mean by his claim that monarchy descends from Adam and proceeds to retell that simple story, literalizing and complicating it at once:

yet since Men cannot obey any thing, that cannot command, and Ideas of Government in the Fancy, though never so perfect, though never so right, cannot give Laws, nor prescribe Rules to the Actions of Men; it would be of no behoof for the setling of Order, and Establishment of Government in its Exercise and Use amongst Men, unless there were a way also taught how to know the Person, to whom it belonged to have this Power, and Exercise this Dominion over others. 'Tis in vain then to talk of Subjection and Obedience, without telling us whom we are to obey. For were I never so fully perswaded, that there ought to be Magistracy and Rule in the World, yet I am nevertheless at Liberty still, till it appears who is the Person that hath Right to my Obedience. (IX.81.pp.239–240)

Now, Locke employs a good deal of analogy himself throughout the *Two Treatises*, but he tends to imbed it in narrative and to validate it with literal and concrete instances. There is a central passage in chapter II of the *Second Treatise* that illustrates this procedure very well. Locke cites Hooker on the self-evident equality of men in nature and proceeds to extend Hooker's account of the ties that bind men to one another:

> But though this be a *State of Liberty*, yet it is *not a State of Licence*, though Man in that State have an uncontroleable Liberty, to dispose of his Person or Possessions, yet he has not Liberty to destroy himself, or so much as any Creature in his Possession, but where some nobler use, than its bare Preservation calls for it. The *State of Nature* has a Law of Nature to govern it, which obliges every one: And Reason, which is that Law, teaches all Mankind, who will but consult it, that being all equal and independent, no one ought to harm another in his Life, Health, Liberty, or Possessions. For Men being all the Workmanship of one Omnipotent, and infinitely wise Maker; All the Servants of one Sovereign Master, sent into the World by his order and about his business, they are his Property, whose Workmanship they are, made to last during his, not one anothers Pleasure. And being furnished with like Faculties, sharing all in one Community of Nature, there cannot be supposed any such *Subordination* among us, that may Authorize us to destroy one another, as if we were made for one anothers uses, as the inferior ranks of Creatures are for ours. Every one as he is *bound to preserve himself*, and not to quit his Station wilfully; so by the like reason when his own Preservation comes not in competition, ought he, as much as he can, *to preserve the rest of Mankind*, and may not unless it be to do Justice on an Offender, take away, or impair the life, or what tends to the Preservation of the Life, Liberty, Health, Limb or Goods of another. (II.6.p.311)

Locke's qualifying manner seems to be in control. Each assertion in the opening sentence is followed by distinction, refinement, and complication. The sentence expands the initial opposition between liberty and licence, and consists of an amplification of those terms that concludes with a qualification of the rule against destruction of the self or possessions. The legalistic exactness in the opening sentence is retained as the paragraph continues by the list of sacred personal rights, "Life, Health, Liberty, or Possessions." The last sentence in the paragraph serves as a summary and returns to the legalistic completeness of the first sentence. Obligations of self-defense and justice and prohibitions against violence in this last sentence define the situation with an obtrusive exactness that effectively blurs the whole issue by invoking a tangle of qualifications and precise exceptions to any rule the reader might try to extract immediately or in a careless reading.

But all this legalistic circling, both of the prose and the notions, surrounds a generalized ethical-political moment that is really of disarming simplicity. The center of this paragraph and the center of Locke's doctrine is a "Law of Nature" (identified as "Reason" only after it has been placed in the persuasive grammatical balance of the beginning of this second sentence—"The *State of Nature* has a Law of Nature"). That law is simply asserted, without origin or justification. Such "reason" is given in Locke's scheme, and the proof of its existence is quite simply that it is available to all but, Locke implies, neglected by most. Locke's voice establishes complexity and quasi-legal exactness as evidence of its *bona fides*, and then stages a tableau in which that careful qualifier and distinguisher listens to the voice of reason. The initial complexity serves that dramatic, radically simple moment, balancing it and locating it in a distinctly undramatic world. There is, moreover, an implied social and moral superiority given to the speaker and his audience. They do indeed "consult" reason; the verb has marvelous leisurely implications in which reason is an elegant volume or a wise and moderate friend. Grammatically, this second sentence resembles the opening one; it consists of a series of explanations with qualifications of an initial balanced assertion. But the sentence resolves itself into an enactment, as it were, of the mythical scene in which reason, nearly personified or objectified, speaks.

What reason finally teaches in this paragraph is a surprise, or at least the logical proof reason offers is unexpected. The peace of Locke's state of nature as enforced by the law of nature rests, it turns out, on an analogy whereby men realize they are the servants of God, artifacts of his fashioning, the property therefore of the divine master-artificer. Maker and Master are resonant, allusive terms, and reason has read the scriptures and echoes them effectively ("about his business" — see Luke 2:49). But reason modulates from that rather specific allusion to another kind of business, and the analogy that sees men as God's property works by literalization. The artificer's objects and the owner's property cannot destroy themselves or one another; they exist for the pleasure of their maker and master. So, too, men must be peaceful insofar as they realize that they are like objects or property. To preserve the stability of their own objects or property, the next sentence explains, men accept their own analogical status as objects or property. What these sentences do not say, of course, is that men are property or objects only analogically, whereas "the inferior ranks of Creatures" (animals, but in due course in Locke's theory, slaves and wage laborers) are actually property and objects. Analogy is used as proof in the third sentence and then attenuated by a literalization that returns the reader to the real world of objects and property. The paragraph skillfully recedes from the political and moral myth at its center, back to the exact and quasi-legalistic scene with which it began. The last sentence ends with a repetition of the catalogue of personal rights, but now they are varied slightly, the order changed and "Possessions" expanded to "Limb or Goods of another." The simple rhetorical point is variation, but the ideological point lies in surrounding the state of nature with the actual world of specific things and complex relationships.

Locke's implicit claim in much of the *Second Treatise* is that he is reviving literal and concrete truth. The political and moral myth he offers as ultimate proof of his theory of society is shored up by questions and observations that depend upon the unanswerable force of the literal. Property, for example, begins when man appropriates nature by his labor, and Locke at one point plays with the exact meaning of appropriate. Is it, he asks, a physiological, or a technological, or a physical term? It is, he concludes, a political term:

He that is nourished by the Acorns he pickt up under an Oak, or the Apples he gathered from the Trees in the Wood, has certainly appropriated them to himself. No Body can deny but the nourishment is his. I ask then, When did they begin to be his? When he digested? Or when he eat? Or when he boiled? Or when he brought them home? Or when he pickt them up? And 'tis plain, if the first gathering made them not his, nothing else could. That *labour* put a distinction between them and common. (V.28.pp.329–330)

There are, clearly, varieties of literalness, and Locke's definition of appropriate depends upon the establishment of a relationship rather than upon any substantial transformation. The acorns or apples become mine when they are no longer "common"; physical transformation by cooking or eating is literal but less important for establishing possession than labor.

What Locke is actually doing here, it seems to me, is blurring the distinction between the literal and the relational so that the latter acquires the solidity of the former, just as in the preceding example he blurs the distinction between the analogical and the literal for the same purpose. Locke's political theory depends upon a relationship between the state of nature and actual civil society that is inescapably analogical. His strategy as an imaginer of the state of nature is to move back and forth between that hypothetical state and the actuality of civil society so as to join them seamlessly, obscuring the point at which analogy occurs. The specificity, concreteness, and complication of his presentation distract us from the dramatic imagining of that state of nature, and the connection between the mythical and therefore schematic state of nature and the present, concrete civil society is seen as a temporal continuity. The literal truth of the present world therefore applies to that prehistorical world, and whatever analogy is available applies to both.[31]

Thus, Locke's reply to those who object that there is no historical record of a state of nature slips easily from a literal description of it to an analogical proof (decorated with historical examples):

That it is not at all to be wonder'd, that *History* gives us but a very little account of Men, *that lived together in the State of Nature*. The inconveniencies of that condition, and the love, and want of Society no sooner brought any number of them together, but they presently united and incorporated, if they designed to continue together. And if we may not suppose *Men* ever to have been *in the State of Nature*, because we hear not much of them in such a State, we may as well suppose the Armies of *Salmanasser*, or *Xerxes* were never Children, because we hear little of them, till they were Men, and imbodied in Armies. Government is every where antecedent to Records, and Letters seldome come in amongst a People, till a long continuation of Civil Society has, by other more necessary Arts provided for their Safety, Ease, and Plenty. And then they begin to look after the History of their *Founders*, and search into their *original*, when they have out-lived the memory of it. For 'tis with *Common-wealths* as with particular Persons, they are commonly *ignorant of their own Births* and *Infancies*: And if they know any thing of their *Original*, they are beholding, for it, to the accidental Records, that others have kept of it. (VIII.101.p.378)

There are two turns in these sentences, illustrations that flirt with a sort of analogical proof. We are taken from the connection between the childhood of mankind and that of certain famous armies of antiquity back to the generalized historical moment, which is then compared to the childhood of "particular Persons." Locke carefully grounds his first illustration in a sort of pseudohistorical record; we know that Xerxes and Salmanasser had armies and we can hardly deny that soldiers were once children. The historical and the natural are unobtrusively joined in this cunning illustration, and the state of nature is at once historicized and reinforced as a natural inevitability. We have all been children, although the experiences of childhood are now faded and indistinct. And most of us have heard of Xerxes and Salmanasser or even read about them or similar historical figures. We are less sure of their existence than of our own childhoods, but when Locke tells us that they and their armies were once children, then we are all gathered together in nature.

Locke's second generalization in these sentences ("Government is every where antecedent to Records") acquires strength from that implicit conjoining of nature and history. We are back in a generalized prehistorical scene, although we have to be very alert to draw a clear line between that scene and the superimposed childhood and antiquity of the previous sentences. When Locke returns to childhood to illustrate how civil society is necessarily ignorant of its formative years, he is appealing to our experience of our own childhoods and in context and by implication he is acquiring the truth of that which is only dimly remembered but incontestable. Common sense and the testimony of others tell us that we were once born and existed as infants; our own prehistory is an objective fact and a natural inevitability. The connection, by the way, between our ignorance of our own beginnings and the prehistorical phase of society is not very exact, since we can remember something even if we never learn to write or keep records. But Locke is not proving his point analogically; he is rather appropriating the qualities of his examples and edging his hypothetical construction of the state of nature over into the natural and historical worlds of experience.

One important result of this appropriation is an enforced and persuading continuity between the world of theory and the world of natural and historical experience. The political theory of the *Second Treatise* claims to return us to the origins of things, to the primal social moment that Locke insists can be accurately reconstructed. The reconstruction is a narrative that stretches back from our own experiences. Such narrative is enforced by analogy, but Locke skillfully surrounds his analogical links with precise facts and exact relationships, disguises his imaginative reconstructions with aggressively plain and literal speaking. Ironically in the light of Marx's epigram, Locke's talent as a writer involves just what the Lord commanded Habakkuk to do: "Write the vision, and make it plain upon tables, that he may run that readeth it" (Habakkuk 2:2).

The *Essay* displays a more problematical relationship to analogy and tends toward a recurring self-consciousness about its images and implicit dramatizations. Epistemology is necessarily more concerned than political theory with problems of metaphor and language and is largely defined as an activity by examining and questioning such terms. The *Essay* is a reenactment of thought itself rather than a reconstruction of the scene in which political thought originates. The events described or evoked in the *Essay* lack a location; the dramatic scene is internal, elusive. Locke approaches the moment when mental experience actually takes place and then finds that this moment escapes literal description and requires analogy. Analogy is proposed and indeed employed, but then it is frequently dissolved or, better, dismantled by the recurrent force of a literal view of things. Locke's tact and self-effacement fit perfectly within such a difficult dramatization, and those qualities are consistently supplemented in the *Essay* by a recurring thematics of loss, limitation, ignorance, and imperfection provoked by the difficulty of imagining the understanding and by the revelations about the understanding that emerge when it is imagined. If the state of nature as Locke reimagines it is a rational and historical location, then the scene where understanding operates is often dark, uncertain, confusing, strange to the point of absurdity. In the long run, as Locke announces at the outset, his investigation will assert the primacy of a "natural" perception that is individual and untutored. But at the same time he manages to expose the inadequacy of that same unaided natural understanding and to dramatize the need for an imposed moral and social order and for the intimations of order granted by divine revelation.

Locke's procedure is overtly reflexive, as the understanding seeks to understand its own operations, and seems to be founded from the opening pages on an optical metaphor. Wittgenstein once remarked, "Don't think, but look!" Locke begins by underlining the difficulty of looking at that which does the looking: "The Understanding, like the Eye, whilst it makes us see, and perceive all other Things, takes no notice of it self: And it requires Art and Pains to set it at a distance, and make it its own Object" (I.i.1). In *The Concept of Mind*, Gilbert Ryle points to the models philosophers have needed to describe or to imagine the intellect and finds Lockean epistemology dominated by a model whereby the mind can look at its own operations in the light produced by the metaphor of "reflection." For Ryle the consciousness Locke describes and depends upon in the *Essay* is a "piece of para-optics" and forms part of a metaphor of light made necessary by the Cartesian and Galilean representation of the world as a machine. Consciousness was given the role that light plays in the mechanical world and "the contents of the mental world were thought of as being self-luminous or refulgent."[32]

The point of that metaphor, as Ryle sees it, was to rescue mind from mechanism, to root mind in the material world but to provide a way out of the determinist implications of that world. Ryle considers such covert analogy a limiting assumption of post-Cartesian thought like Locke's. But Ryle is unfair to Locke when he implies that such a central metaphor is never critically examined. In fact, Locke is exceedingly self-conscious about his images and may be said to employ them mainly for dramatic purposes as part of the staged failure of the understanding to know itself adequately or of its discovery of the insufficiency of its knowledge of the world.

What is clear to any reader is the variety of images and analogies with which Locke decorates his discourse. Such variety suggests the arbitrary, almost playful nature of the imaging activity itself. There are pervasive optical images in the *Essay*, but they do not constitute a model for mind. Rather, they create narrative occasions within which various models can be temporarily employed self-consciously as clarifying images, discarded after serving their illustrative purpose. "Image" is perhaps a misleading term, then, for the *Essay* does not depend upon any one enforcing model for mind but upon a fictionalization of the activities of the understanding, a placing of mental operations in a narrative framework that employs images to evoke a process.

Locke uses his images in the casual and relaxed fashion that suits his manner as a gentleman-philosopher and amateur of common experience. His comparisons and illustrations come easily from leisurely circumstances he shares with his implied audience. Images to illustrate the workings of the mind lie at hand, but the very ease of employment and the variety of illustration available point to instability. These images are identified by Locke's manner of employing them as adjuncts to reasoning, since their availability contrasts with the heroically difficult task of picturing the operations of the understanding.

To take an obvious example, Locke is an observer and a traveler whose essay is a celebration of the intellectual and moral profit of thoughtful excursion. But at the same time he issues warnings that such travel is a dangerous and limited enterprise. He repudiates his own metaphors for ambitious inquiring even as he elaborates them. To observe, the *Essay* shows from its opening pages and images, is to travel through things, to mark a progression and a process, to make a trial run, to prepare for a journey, but also to discover navigational limits in order to plan future voyages no longer so grandly conceived:

6. When we know our own *Strength*, we shall the better know what to undertake with hopes of Success: And when we have well survey'd the *Powers* of our own Minds, and made some Estimate what we may expect from them, we shall not be inclined either to sit still, and not set our Thoughts on work at all, in Despair of knowing any thing; nor on the other side question every thing, and disclaim all Knowledge, because some Things are not to be understood. 'Tis of great use to the Sailor to know the length of his Line, though he cannot with it fathom all the depths of the Ocean. 'Tis well he knows, that it is long enough to reach the bottom, at such Places, as are necessary to direct his Voyage, and

caution him against running upon Shoals, that may ruin him. Our Business here is not to know all things, but those which concern our Conduct.

. . . . .

7. This was that which gave the first Rise to this *Essay* concerning the Understanding. For I thought that the first Step towards satisfying several Enquiries, the Mind of Man was very apt to run into, was, to take a Survey of our own Understandings, examine our own Powers, and see to what Things they were adapted. Till that was done I suspected we began at the wrong end, and in vain sought for Satisfaction in a quiet and secure Possession of Truths, that most concern'd us, whilst we let loose our Thoughts into the vast Ocean of *Being*, as if all that boundless Extent, were the natural, and undoubted Possession of our Understandings, wherein there was nothing exempt from its Decisions, or that escaped its Comprehension. Thus Men, extending their Enquiries beyond their Capacities, and letting their Thoughts wander into those depths, where they can find no sure Footing; 'tis no Wonder, that they raise Questions, and multiply Disputes, which never coming to any clear Resolution, are proper only to continue and increase their Doubts, and to confirm them at last in perfect Scepticism. Whereas were the Capacities of our Understandings well considered, the Extent of our Knowledge once discovered, and the Horizon found, which sets the Bounds between the enlightened and dark Parts of Things; between what is, and what is not comprehensible by us, Men would perhaps with less scruple acquiesce in the avow'd Ignorance of the one, and imploy their Thoughts and Discourse, with more Advantage and Satisfaction in the other. (I.i.6–7)

This marking of limits is a recurring theme in the *Essay*. The explicit moral purpose is to warn against the temptation to know the unknowable (and the ultimate effect and implicit promise from these opening pages is an enlargement of the unknowable). Hence the conventionally eloquent images in this passage enforce the idea that thought is like travel, the careful philosopher like an experienced sailor, and other rash thinkers like careless swimmers beyond their depth. But none of the images, vivid as they are, refers us to a model for mind. They are all quite openly ways of making the moral implications surrounding thought vivid rather than of visualizing thought itself. Thought is instead dramatized in a passage like this as movement and activity; it consists of surveying, examining, undertaking, running into, employing, and so on. Paradoxically, the movement of these images supports a literal movement and purposeful activity of the mind. The literal reality of mind is rendered concrete in large part by the difference between its activities and the patently metaphorical implications of those activities as they are imagined in conventional moral language. Locke describes his activity in these introductory paragraphs as beginning in a retreat from conventional moral metaphors and the founding of more modest, clearer, and in fact nearly literal terms for picturing thought and its moral implications. He began, he tells us, by simplifying metaphor and driving toward the literal, actually looking and examining rather than plunging into a "vast Ocean" or wandering into "depths" where there is no footing.

Locke's writings are full of images of travel, and he himself was a curious traveler who kept a lively journal and directed in his will that his executors purchase books of travel for the Bodleian. The image of the "way" is pervasive in his work and was perhaps an inescapable commonplace. The *Essay* asks its readers to follow along, to retrace the route of Locke's investigation, the ways of the understanding. The metaphor is hardly obtrusive. Way can be a manner, a method, or a path, and the word easily contains literal and metaphoric meanings. It suits Locke so well precisely because it is a nearly dead metaphor, yet alive enough to retain concreteness, practicality, and even a touch of moral idealism. The understanding requires such an elastic term. It is, after all, a faculty with no stable location, which reveals itself only in process and movement. "For what is not either actually in view, or in the memory, is in the mind no way at all, and is all one as if it never had been there" (I.iv.20). Innate ideas are an absurdity because we know ideas only by the process of having them, and the literal reality of things for us is the working through of our ideas. The travel from the world of experience to the registering of it constitutes the understanding. This is no metaphor; movement of this sort is literally what understanding is.

Locke's attack on innate ideas in Book I rests upon such an assumption of radical process. To evoke process without making it merely metaphoric he tends toward half-dead metaphors of common speech that are administrative and bureaucratic in their implications. Thus, like the idea of God the idea of substance would have been extremely useful for mankind:

If Nature took care to provide us any *Ideas*, we might well expect it
should be such, as by our own Faculties we cannot procure to our selves:
But we see on the contrary, that since by those ways, whereby other
Ideas are brought into our Minds, this is not, We have no such *clear
Idea* at all, and therefore signify nothing by the word *Substance*, but
only an uncertain supposition of we know not what; (*i.e.* of something
whereof we have no particular distinct positive) *Idea*, which we take to
be the *substratum*, or support, of those *Ideas* we do know. (I.iv.18)

The operation of the understanding is, let us say, nearly imagined and appears as a system of communication and supply, an abstract model that has its own peculiar concreteness, the way a map or a blueprint is both abstract and concrete. And, of course, these sentences conclude with a dismissal of substance as a mere etymology, or rather, a proof from etymology that "substance" is an idea rooted in common experience. Locke exposes that idea as a covert metaphor, half dead like his own but untenable because it doesn't really fit the dynamic and organizational model of the understanding that he is implicitly promoting. Perhaps a good deal of the scorn Locke heaps upon such hidden metaphors as substance is a sign of his own dependence upon the inevitable concretions of language.

That awareness is evident in the section that concludes Book I and prepares for the elaboration of ideas in Book II.

26. *To shew how the Understanding proceeds herein, is the design of the following Discourse*; which I shall proceed to, when I have first premised, that hitherto to clear my way to those foundations, which, I conceive are the only true ones, whereon to establish those Notions we can have of our own Knowledge, it hath been necessary for me to give an account of the Reasons I had to doubt of innate Principles: And since the Arguments which are against them, do, some of them, rise from common received Opinions, I have been forced to take several things for granted, which is hardly avoidable to any one, whose Task it is to shew the falshood, or improbability, of any Tenet; it happening in Controversial Discourses, as it does in assaulting of Towns; where, if the ground be but firm, whereon the Batteries are erected, there is no farther enquiry of whom it is borrowed, nor whom it belongs to, so it affords but a fit rise for the present purpose. But in the future part of this Discourse, designing to raise an Edifice uniform, and consistent with it self, as far as my own Experience and Observation will assist me, I hope, to erect it on such a Basis, that I shall not need to shore it up with props and buttresses, leaning on borrowed or begg'd foundations: Or at least, if mine prove a Castle in the Air, I will endeavour it shall be all of a piece, and hang together. Wherein I warn the Reader not to expect undeniable cogent demonstrations, unless I may be allow'd the Privilege, not seldom assumed by others, to take my Principles for granted; and then, I doubt not, but I can demonstrate too. All that I shall say for the Principles I proceed on, is, that I can only *appeal* to Men's own unprejudiced *Experience*, and Observation, whether they be true, or no; and this is enough for a Man who professes no more, than to lay down candidly and freely his own Conjectures, concerning a Subject lying somewhat in the dark, without any other design, than an unbias'd enquiry after Truth. (I.iv.25)

As befits the summarizing conclusion of an introduction, this paragraph gathers up the various commonplaces Locke began with in his "Epistle," although the diffidence of the "Under-labourer" clearing away rubbish in the world of learning has given way to the ironically qualified pride of the essayist turned philosopher as architect and general. This paragraph proposes images facetiously, playing with those which promise a disputatious and systematic discourse in their grandiose military and architectural analogies, that is to say, the very sort of discourse this first book claims not to be.

"Demonstration" must be for any reader who has come this far with Locke the special and therefore irrelevant activity of the corrupt philosophical tradition. There is a nice irony in the sentence where Locke asks that we allow him to take his principles for granted, for as alert readers of the *Essay* that is precisely what we cannot allow, even though and indeed because it has been "not seldom assumed by others." "I doubt not, but I can demonstrate too" is a wonderfully coy conclusion to this sentence and the sequence of images in the paragraph. The repetition of demonstrate, its placement in quoatation marks, labels it as a self-conscious moment and warns that the demonstration Locke has in mind is a revision or redefinition of that act. As it turns out, what he wants us to grant him is not a set of special and dubious philosophical postulates but our own experience and observations. What we had been led to expect would be a performance, a "demonstration," turns out to be something less and something more.

Locke pretends for a moment that he has been forced to take certain things for granted and thereby to edge over into systematic discourse, the borrowed ground of demonstration. Philosophical discourse is itself turned into a sort of metaphor, partly by contact with Locke's military and architectural images and partly by his redefinition in Book I of what it means to "demonstrate." Locke has encouraged his reader to deny the first principles of such discourse, but now he proposes to build his own "Castle in the Air." Should we expect "undeniable cogent demonstrations" in such an edifice? No, says Locke, unless you grant my principles. But who, at the end of Book I, can deny one's "own unprejudiced *Experience*, and Observation"? Locke's question is only superficially rhetorical. He will not be "philosophical" but he will claim the certitude provided by a new philosophical ground in which castles in the air descend to the bedrock of experience and observation. He slides away from metaphor and playful self-depreciation. His final sentence disclaims method and certainty, and in its studied lack of image and periodic structure depicts his activity in literal terms.

Locke ends with a return to the modest enquirer who uses no metaphor except the casual, colloquial phrase "in the dark" to set the scene. That common expression lies in some important sense at the heart of the *Essay*. It reminds us that the understanding, as Locke said at the outset, is like the eye, and it points to the natural concretions of the English language toward which Locke (and perhaps any thinker who makes his sort of claim) tends. To see is to comprehend or understand something irrefutable or inescapable; to observe is to watch and by natural extension to obey or accede to the reality of what is seen. Like the domesticated image of the way, those conventional expressions and half-dead metaphors surround the activity of seeing or observing, promote an enforcing concreteness, and point to a literal experience of things that claims to be nonmetaphorical.

Book II of the *Essay* is in part an attempt to find a means of talking about ideas and the operations of the understanding without allowing analogy to take over and within the enforcing concreteness and even literalness of common expressions. When he uses analogies, Locke is careful to identify them as such and to prepare us for an attempt to imagine a literal and unencumbered perception of the workings of the understanding. In the section on memory, for example, he explains our retention of ideas by rejecting one metaphor and substituting a more dynamic one:

> But our *Ideas* being nothing, but actual Perceptions in the Mind, which cease to be any thing, when there is no perception of them, this *laying up* of our *Ideas* in the Repository of the Memory, signifies no more but this, that the Mind has a Power, in many cases, to revive Perceptions, which it has once had, with this additional Perception annexed to them, that it has had them before. And in this Sense it is, that our *Ideas* are said to be in our Memories, when indeed, they are actually no where, but only there is an ability in the Mind, when it will, to revive them again; and as it were paint them anew on it self, though some with more, some with less difficulty; some more lively, and others more obscurely. (II.x.2)

Ideas are, literally, nothing; they are pure process or temporal occurrences. In like manner and by extension, the mind is not a place (although it seems to be a locus of activities), and ideas therefore cannot be stored anywhere in the mind (there is no "there" there). The mind exists in its own active sense by virtue of its varying artistic talents for representing experience, for imagining and presenting to itself an external world. But even the most vivid pictures the mind can draw *"are laid in fading Colours*; and if not sometimes refreshed, vanish and disappear" (II.x.5). The analogies Locke draws upon so readily in this section of Book II are meant to point to the weakness and instability of the understanding in its key function of remembering perceptions. "In all these cases, *Ideas* in the Mind quickly fade, and often vanish quite out of the Understanding, leaving no more footsteps or remaining Characters of themselves, than Shadows do flying over Fields of Corn; and the Mind is as void of them, as if they never had been there" (II.x.4).

The unexpected vividness or pathos of these images is really in the service of the literal, for the ideas vanish like shadows but the truth of process and passage remains. A succession of appearances and disappearances is what constitutes the materials of the understanding, and Locke later finds less poignant mechanistic analogies for its operations: "our *Ideas* do, whilst we are awake, succeed one another in our Minds at certain distances, not much unlike the *Images* in the inside of a Lanthorn, turned round by the Heat of a Candle" (II.xiv.9).

This resembles the earlier, more famous image of the understanding as a dark room or camera obscura: "For, methinks, the *Understanding* is not much unlike a Closet wholly shut from light, with only some little openings left, to let in external visible Resemblances, or *Ideas* of things without; would the Pictures coming into such a dark Room but stay there, and lie so orderly as to be found upon occasion, it would very much resemble the Understanding of a Man, in reference to all Objects of sight and the *Ideas* of them" (II.xi.17). What Paul Fussell calls the "elegiac action" of the earlier images for the memory has dropped out here, and the understanding is an efficient instrument, superior in some ways to that scientific curiosity, the camera obscura.[33] In the persuasive sequences of the *Essay*, there is a modulation from those elegiac moments to the neutral, serviceable analogies of the lantern and the dark room. That modulation helps to make the understanding a process, a set of regular phenomena whose locations and movements help us imagine the nowhere of the mind. The human images of loss and sensory impermanence dramatize the failures of memory, its instability as a cognitive guide. The human world of fading shadows and colors and dying children testifies, however, in Book II to the reality of a process in the material world in which the understanding is implicated, a process that sweeps away its constructions and images. Ultimately, that material world is essentially unknowable, for the world the understanding erects is at best adjacent to it, linked to it by the process Locke describes here in Book II.

Ernest Tuveson's point that Locke provided his age and succeeding generations with "the precious gift of a coherent and understandable way of visualizing the workings of the intellect" is thus misleading if one pays close attention to what happens in the imaginative world of the *Essay*.[34] The understanding, in Book II at least, is seen as a process, a confrontation with a succession of "ideas" that resists visualization. So Locke narrates the instability of memory, the obliquity of perception, and the inaccuracy of human formulations about the world. But his narrative depicts the regularity and dependability of the process of understanding itself. As the mechanical images of the lantern and the dark room suggest, understanding takes place in a location where certain relationships obtain, and perhaps the understanding itself is literally a space constituted by the occurrence of phenomena. The visual mode of conceiving or imagining the understanding is steadily eroded as Book II unfolds, exchanged in favor of spatiotemporal modes of dramatization that claim literalness as narrative sequences. Memory is fragile precisely because it depends upon the visual; it is limited by its aesthetic ambition for representation and the permanence that goes with it. Images fade and physical solidity crumbles; the memory may even depend upon the sequence of our own natural histories. We cannot be sure, says Locke, but "it may seem probable, that the Constitution of the Body does sometimes influence the Memory; since we oftentimes find a Disease quite strip the Mind of all its *Ideas*, and the flames of a Fever, in a few days, calcine all those Images to dust and confusion, which seem'd to be as lasting, as if graved in Marble" (II.x.5).

These images in chapter x of Book II point with special clarity, I think, to a crucial ambiguity in Locke's thought that is in some sense resolved by his skill as a philosophical narrator. John Yolton has argued that Locke was led by his opposition to innate ideas to suggest at times that the mind is essentially passive. Yolton adds that Locke did not really believe in that passivity and in due course presented the mind as improbably active and domineering.[35] Locke's defense against the implications of his own domination and control is to speak of the understanding as a process that is part of a shifting and uncertain phenomenal world. His good faith as observer and analyst of that world depends upon his renunciatory passivity in the face of truth, upon the cultivation of an open and receptive mind that never forgets its origins in a process that provides it with ideas, that shapes its contours with experiences. The narrator of the history of the understanding needs to establish a scrupulously stable self able to watch that process, to stand somehow apart from the world of fading memory and partial perception without taking on the logical and moral absurdity of philosophical independence or imaginative domination.[36]

Book II is a survey of the variety of ideas, proceeding from their simple origins to more and more complex notions. Locke identifies his analytical survey as a narrative grounded in the humble and literal beginnings of sensation and perception.

And thus I have given a short, and, I think, true *History of the first beginnings of Humane Knowledge*; whence the Mind has its first Objects, and by what steps it makes its Progress to the laying in, and storing up those *Ideas*, out of which is to be framed all the Knowledge it is capable of; wherein I must appeal to Experience and Observation, whether I am in the right: The best way to come to Truth, being to examine Things as really they are, and not to conclude they are, as we fancy of our selves, or have been taught by others to imagine. (II.xi.15)

Narrative depends clearly in these summarizing sentences upon those unobtrusive concretions and half-dead metaphors of travel, accumulation, and building. The mind can move purposefully, it can somehow store up its ideas like bricks and can construct with these materials. Locke's survey is an account of how mind comes to acquire those skills. As history, a search for origins and causes, the *Essay* balances these extraordinary metaphorically rendered accomplishments of the understanding against the limitations implicit in the particular perception of any entity and the literal situation in which perception begins. The mind is radically dependent, Locke stresses here, upon the initial reception of simple sensations by the mind-body organization. Its own subsequent busyness is a natural complicating and defensive response to the process whereby "ideas" are thrust upon it. Everyone can acknowledge such an originating process, and no images or analogies are necessary to render our sense of an external world of stimuli pressing upon us. But the reconstitution of that process by the understanding and its ascent from those simple sensations to complex representations are internal and mysterious matters. The great task of the *Essay* is to observe that ascent.

The difficulty lies in standing aside, in finding a formulation to do justice to an understanding that watches itself and traces its own rise from the literal. Where can such an observer stand? Locke says that his understanding has managed to free itself and stand apart from its own operations, recording events as the world moves into the understanding and as the understanding itself moves, traveling purposefully, acquiring materials, and building representations. The narrative movement in Locke's rendering is from the literal moment of an initial or original perception to the increasingly analogical and metaphorical constructions of the understanding. So, Locke stands on the simple and literal beginnings of experience. As the narrator of the ascent of mental complication, he presides over that division between the literal facts of perception and their figurative rearrangement by the understanding. His method as a dramatizer of mental activity is to appropriate the literal beginnings of experience, to imagine them with some insistence and a recurring moral irony as the physical fact that grounds all subsequent mental movement. The narrative mode of the *Essay* invites us to picture the understanding's activities as extensions of an initial literal moment in which ideas enter the mind or are impelled into it. There is a protective reservation in such narrative, for however high we may fly with Locke as we trace the flights of the understanding we can always return to the literal beginnings of experience as an unassailable, unfanciful, and unmetaphorical base—a moment of pure movement, temporal yet securely spatial, located here on the spot where Locke stands. Locke is not standing "apart" from his understanding, nor is he in any other metaphorical relationship to his material. As his rhetoric in the following passages makes clear, he claims to occupy in a special way the literal base from which reconstruction and rearrangement begin.

Thus, Locke opens the second book by speaking "Of *Ideas* in general, and their Original," and by grounding all ideas in sensation: "For since there appear not to be any *Ideas* in the Mind, before the Senses have conveyed any in, I conceive that *Ideas* in the Understanding, are coeval with *Sensation*; which is such an Impression or Motion, made in some part of the Body, as produces some Perception in the Understanding" (II.i.23). These simple transactions between the world and the senses are succeeded by more complex "*Ideas* of Reflection" when the mind considers its own contents and begins in Locke's inescapably metaphorical rendering to store itself with ideas, to construct itself, and to travel in pursuit of knowledge.

Thus the first Capacity of Humane Intellect, is, That the mind is fitted
to receive the Impressions made on it; either, through the *Senses*, by
outward Objects; or by its own Operations, when it *reflects* on them.
This is the first step a Man makes towards the Discovery of any thing,
and the Groundwork, whereon to build all those Notions, which ever he
shall have naturally in this World. All those sublime Thoughts, which
towre above the Clouds, and reach as high as Heaven it self, take their
Rise and Footing here: In all that great Extent wherein the mind
wanders, in those remote Speculations, it may seem to be elevated with,
it stirs not one jot beyond those *Ideas*, which *Sense* or *Reflection*, have
offered for its Contemplation. (II.i.24)

Locke occupies a base whereon "*Sense* or *Reflection*" provide ideas and on which all mental activity, no matter how exalted, is grounded, takes its "Rise and Footing." As a stable place, that location is a literal undermining of the metaphorical edifices or journeys of thought. The metaphor of location is effectively a literalization that denies the implications and the validity of other metaphors that follow from it. Sound and solid near-metaphors like "footing" drive out (or down) airy and elevated notions. "Reflection" seems to be a metaphorical retreat in some sense, but here it is almost a literal mirroring of what "sense" offers, even though introspection of this sort is elsewhere elaborated by Locke as a more powerful mental act. As Gilbert Ryle puts it, Lockean epistemology is founded on the optical metaphor whereby the mind "reflects" its own operations, sees them by means of a light it produces.[37] But here reflection is literalized, made a means of rendering a process that Locke insists is not a metaphor. Thinking and understanding, even of the highest sort, begin with a contemplation of what the senses offer (just what that means or how it invalidates "those remote Speculations" is not made clear here, although Locke will spend the rest of Book II working that out). Such looking as "reflection" involves can hardly be visual in a literal sense, and the contemplation Locke refers us to here is a sort of grounding in the material process of sensation. In other words, Locke imagines a situation in which metaphor is shifting and uncertain and in which a fiction of process and location operates against merely visual notions of how the mind works.

A common paradox among philosophical commentators is that Locke is not really what we normally understand by an empiricist. Book II in fact bears out Ryle's point that Locke is not the philosopher of an isolated consciousness who validates sensation and reflection. As Ryle puts it, "he is inquiring what it is to be in space, to be infinitely extensible, to be a substance, to be a person, etc., and not what it is to think of things as being one or other of these." Locke's definition of knowledge in Book IV, Ryle continues, adds up to "the assertion that knowing consists in seeing that a given character implies or excludes (i.e. implies the absence of) another character."[38] In other words, Locke is an imaginer of possibilities whose thought elaborates the strange eventualities neglected by philosophy and common sense alike. Book II involves a radical slowing of the normal tempo of experience, an altering of perception that extracts the misapprehensions of common formulations and imagines a strange, sometimes surprising world. Locke is a steady and still presence who asks us to compare our clumsy notions of sequence and duration, for example, with the actualities. The world is both faster and slower than we know:

. . . in the Impressions made upon any of our Senses, we can but to a certain degree perceive any Succession; which if exceeding quick, the Sense of Succession is lost, even in Cases where it is evident, that there is a real Succession. Let a Cannon-Bullet pass through a Room, and in its way take with it any Limb, or fleshy Parts of a man; 'tis as clear as any Demonstration can be, that it must strike successively the two sides of the Room: 'Tis also evident, that it must touch one part of the Flesh first, and another after; and so in Succession: And yet I believe, no Body, who ever felt the pain of such a shot, or heard the blow against the two distant Walls, could perceive any Succession, either in the pain, or sound of so swift a stroke. Such a part of Duration as this, where in we perceive no Succession, is that which we may call an *Instant*; and is *that which takes up the time of only one Idea* in our Minds, without the Succession of another, wherein therefore we perceive no Succession at all.

11. This also happens, *where the Motion is* so *slow*, as not to supply a constant train of fresh *Ideas* to the Senses, as fast as the Mind is capable of receiving new ones into it; and so other *Ideas* of our own Thoughts, having room to come into our Minds, between those offered to our Senses by the moving Body, *there the Sense of Motion is lost;*and the Body, though it really moves, yet not changing perceivable distance with some other Bodies, as fast as the *Ideas* of our own Minds do naturally follow one another in train, the thing seems to stand still, as is evident in the Hands of Clocks, and Shadows of Sun-dials, and other constant, but slow Motions, where though after certain Intervals, we perceive by the change of distance, that it hath moved, yet the Motion it self we perceive not. (II.xiv.10–11)

In this chapter, "Of Duration, and its Simple Modes," Locke imagines a phenomenal world that is fallacious insofar as it is visual. In the example of the bullet, the senses are at least sharply aware of pain and noise, and their accuracy in that regard is not in question. But when it comes to clocks and sundials, there is a gap between phenomena and our formulation, a blindness to motion and process that creates an empty space where there is in fact fullness.

Locke goes on in this chapter to present a world that imposes its motions on us, in which it is impossible, for example, to "keep one unvaried single *Idea*" in our minds for any significant stretch of time. Inevitably, other ideas or sensations drift in, and what lies in a man's power "is only to mind and observe what the *Ideas* are, that take their turns *in* his Understanding; or else, to direct the sort, and call in such as he hath a desire or use of" (II.xiv.13,15).

What cannot be questioned is the freedom of the philosophic observer to look at all of this activity and to imagine the literal reality that is the alternative to normal perception. This looking is not really an ocular activity but the imagining of a world more real than the merely visible or the merely verbal. The alternative world Locke imagines claims authenticity by negating both the ordinary visual world of common sense and the unexamined verbal world of philosophic formulation. But that alternative world is available only through the dramatization of human limitation, ignorance, and powerlessness. The triumphant literalizations of Book II are merely negations of the fictions of the understanding. The power of Locke's observing intelligence is, therefore, a kind of bureaucratic efficiency that defers to a natural and disorderly plenitude and can "direct the sort, and call in such as he hath a desire or use of."

Book II evokes a trying epistemological situation that promotes the courage and uncompromising honesty of the observer. Put simply, the mind necessarily alters phenomenal reality, and there is no real guarantee that the ideas and their arrangement in the understanding correspond to that reality in a significant way. Within the dramatizations of Book II at least, "reality" itself is an ultimate hypothesis, an extrapolation from the data experience provides. There is, as Locke goes on to say, a power in certain objects to produce sensations in us, but those sensations are not inherent or essential parts of those bodies. It is only what Locke calls the primary qualities of bodies that we can speak of with any certainty—"Solidity, Extension, Figure, Number, and Motion, or Rest"—and those qualities are presented in the *Essay* as problematical, liable to slip away from our crude perceptual organs and to lie outside a properly experiential world. They can form, in fact, a virtually inaccessible world of what Locke calls "Particles," which produce certain effects in us without necessarily revealing themselves thereby. God in Locke's reckoning is potentially a sort of ironic demiurge, who may have arranged matters to suit his own humor: "It being no more impossible, to conceive, that God should annex such *Ideas* to such Motions, with which they have no similitude; than that he should annex the *Idea* of Pain to the motion of a piece of Steel dividing our Flesh, with which that *Idea* hath no resemblance" (II.viii.13). Those possibilities form an effectively absurd backdrop to the organization provided by the secondary or properly human additions to the primal phenomenal world.

The particular *Bulk, Number, Figure, and Motion of the parts of Fire, or Snow, are really in them*, whether any ones Senses perceive them or no: and therefore they may be called *real Qualities*, because they really exist in those Bodies. But *Light, Heat, Whiteness*, or *Coldness, are no more really in them, than Sickness or Pain is in* Manna. Take away the Sensation of them; let not the Eyes see Light, or Colours, nor the Ears hear Sounds; let the Palate not Taste, nor the Nose Smell; and all Colours, Tastes, Odours, and Sounds, as they are such particular *Ideas*, vanish and cease, and are reduced to their Causes, *i.e.* Bulk, Figure, and Motion of Parts. (II.viii.17)

The "experiment" this passage performs issues instructions in a peculiar imperative tone that suggests the dismantling of the perceptual universe by a demonic parody of the creative word. The third sentence seems to echo I Corinthians' echo of Isaiah.[39] In its unusually dramatic repetitions, the sentence points to an epistemological antiworld that is the alternative to the prophet's and the apostle's ineffable heaven and whose existence supplies a good deal of the imaginative tension in Locke's thought. Such a world cannot be visualized or conjured up by analogy from human experience, but inferential knowledge of it is the result of Locke's deferential philosophic imagination, the logical residue after the centrifuge of philosophic possibility stops spinning.

At stake here is a central turn in what might be called the plot of the *Essay*. In a recurring moment in Locke's thought, the practical understanding is seen from the perspective of a contemplative intelligence. This intelligence transcends the play of ideas and objects in the understanding by slowing the tempo, separating ideas and objects, and thereby achieving an ontological stability that is at odds with the epistemological turbulence of the Lockean universe. For philosophical commentators, it is something of a scandal that Locke turned from an empirical epistemology to what appears to be a nonempirical ontology. Jonathan Bennett deplores Locke's recourse to the causal thesis whereby essences and substances exist as particles that cannot be perceived by the understanding but lie behind the veil of perception. As Bennett explains it, "in a perfected and completed science, all our secondary quality perceptions would be causally explained in terms of the primary qualities of the things we perceive. For example, our colour discriminations would be explained by a theory relating the colour aspects of visual sense-data to the sub-microscopic textures of seen surfaces."[40] As Bennett observes, Locke presents this situation as merely a question of human limitation. He is ready on more than one occasion to treat it as opportunity for satiric fantasy that rehearses his favorite moral themes of human limitation and appropriateness. If a man's senses were sharper, he "would come nearer the Discovery of the Texture and Motion of the minute Parts of corporeal things; and in many of them, probably get *Ideas* of their internal Constitutions" (II.xxiii.12). But he would then be an anomaly in the social world, unable to discourse with others who could not see the same things and unable to make his way "to the Market and Exchange." Or such vision might make him unfit for the properly human physical world: "perhaps, such a quickness and tenderness of Sight could not endure bright Sun-shine, or so much as open Day-light" (II.xxiii.12).

These are moral-rhetorical commonplaces such as Pope would later make memorable in "An Essay on Man." "Say what the use, were finer optics given, / To inspect a mite, not comprehend the heaven?" The question is how such commonplaces fit into the rhetorical structure of the *Essay*. Perhaps satiric equanimity is Locke's way of resisting the subversive implications of his approach. The epistemological investigations of the *Essay* uncover an unstable world of incomplete and unreliable perceptions consistently supplemented or even supplanted by an order that represents a human imposition, a cultural construct necessitated (or perhaps proved!) by our ignorance. Even the causal thesis can be regarded as a maneuver in the face of ignorance and a refusal (couched in terms of acceptance, or submission to a compelling scientific order of things) to give in to a disorderly phenomenal world. Locke, in John Yolton's formulation, refused to follow his thought through to its idealist or phenomenalist implications and instead had recourse to a "bold rationalism" whereby the idea of substance was seen as "an addition to the sensible qualities, as the locus of the real essence."[41]

Commentators like Yolton and Bennett direct us to a central problem in Locke's thought, which is resolved in a sense by his writing. His manner as a writer is an essential, perhaps inevitable adjunct to the delicate task of expressing both a deferential empiricism and a bold rationalism. His problem as a dramatist of the workings of the understanding is a situation wherein knowledge is a balance of ignorance and certainty, in which knowledge is acquired by moving through experience and charting the shifting boundaries between certainty and ignorance so that the latter reinforces the necessity of the former. To dramatize the severe limitations on our certainty and to establish ignorance and strangeness as the prevailing features of our perceptions and as the enabling context of certainty itself are the narrative problems Locke faces in much of the *Essay*. He literalizes the world of experience and thus allows the play of cultural activity and analogical understanding within that strange landscape; he admits that such activity and understanding are merely arbitrary human impositions, but that very admission is a form of control, a powerful deference as it were.

Inevitably, the complicated reciprocities and balances thus achieved bear an interesting resemblance to the political ideology and literary strategies of the *Treatises of Government*; the state is a human invention but rests on an ambiguously primal political base.[42] Society is historical and contractual, to some extent fortuitous and wonderfully artificial but also inevitable in the largest sense and therefore "natural." So, too, the understanding is historicized and temporalized; it comes to know its operations in Locke's narration by tracing out a process or sequence of events that takes it back to its temporal origins and follows its entrance into the cultural and social sphere. Locke's reconstruction of the history of each man's understanding reveals both its primal isolation and its need for ordering institutions such as society and language. In the process of evoking the disjunction between the reflexive queries of the understanding and the sensory confusions of the physical organism, Locke affirms a cultural and moral sphere of operational certainty and accuracy that measures the disjunction. That is to say, his confidently retreating language breaks away from philosophical certainty and system and affirms by ironic dramatization of its own limitations and self-enclosure.

In part, this is simply a matter in the first two books of making a virtue of necessity and rendering isolation, limitation, and pervasive uncertainty as epistemologically honest and morally resonant discoveries. But as Locke enters Book III and turns to language itself, his project grows nicely symmetrical. His literary manner exploits the paradoxical insufficiency and inevitability of language, and he thereby presents a strong case against language even as he dramatizes the necessity of its invention and employment. In other words, the third book presents the perfect opportunity for Locke's literary-philosophical project of balancing a number of opposing and sustaining themes: destruction of old notions and establishment of new ones, assertion of ignorance and limitation as a means of achieving relative certainty, evocation of a confused and disorderly perceptual world as a backdrop to a sustaining human and cultural order. Language serves beautifully for these presentations because it is both an index of disorder and inadequacy and, properly viewed and reformed, a means of establishing order. Or to put it dialectically, as I think Locke presents it in the course of Book III, to understand language is to grasp a process that establishes order because it simultaneously reveals disorder and maintains order as a constant possibility.

All of the *Essay* is a polemic against the untenable, merely verbal philosophy of the Schools, but Book III is, potentially, a radically disturbing investigation. More than philosophical terms of art are at stake. At first, however, the task of representing the origins of language seems much more manageable than the metaphorical contortions needed to understand the understanding. The strenuous literalizing effort of the first two books whereby the understanding is imagined as somehow seeking to know itself and to return to a time before it had thought about itself is exchanged for a less disorienting philosophical anthropology with a clearly rendered scene. Book III examines words in order to recover their origins and trace their history; Locke slides back to the primal moment when men crossed the civilizing threshold from isolated silence to socialized language. That moment is simple and rational. "The Comfort, and Advantage of Society, not being to be had without Communication of Thoughts, it was necessary, that Man should find out some external sensible Signs, whereby those invisible *Ideas*, which his thoughts are made up of, might be made known to others" (III.ii.1).

But Locke's rational anthropological scene is complicated by an epistemological qualification carried over from the previous books, for every man who speaks makes a continual adjustment between the meanings he gives his words and their social referents: "But though Words, as they are used by Men, can properly and immediately signify nothing but the *Ideas*, that are in the Mind of the Speaker; yet they in their Thoughts give them a secret reference to two other things" (III.ii.4). Locke explains that men must of necessity suppose there is agreement between their meanings and those of other men, and that they take a natural but false step from that position when "they *often suppose their Words to stand also for the reality of Things*" (III.ii.5). Throughout this preliminary elaboration of the origins of language and its primal workings, Locke insists with an interesting political implication on a radical separation between man and the language he invents, whereby man is still a prisoner of his own essentially incommunicable "ideas" and the possessor of an irrepressible linguistic individuality, much like that claimed by Carroll's Humpty Dumpty. Words, Locke says many times, "*signify* only Men's peculiar *Ideas*, and that *by a perfectly arbitrary Imposition*, is evident, in that they often fail to excite in others (even that use the same Language) the same *Ideas*, we take them to be the Signs of: And every Man has so inviolable a Liberty, to make Words stand for what *Ideas* he pleases, that no one hath the Power to make others have the same *Ideas* in their Minds, that he has, when they use the same Words, that he does" (III.ii.8).

Locke's rigorous particularization of experience in Book III follows from this radical individualizing of perception, and both recurring emphases are part of his self-conscious polemic against the older notion of an isomorphic relation between language and the world. Locke is clearly intent on asserting that language articulates the structure of the mind rather than that of the external world, and that language attempts to communicate each man's "ideas" to others. As Murray Cohen has defined it, Locke's innovation in describing this "Adamic moment" of linguistic creation lies in shifting the emphasis away from the lexical and taxonomic to the syntactical and logical.[43] In the dramatic context of the *Essay* as a whole, Locke's Adam is caught in the radical isolation and uncertainty evoked in the first two books as the conditions and results of understanding, and language is dramatized here as inseparable from a particularity of experience wherein its task is primarily and properly *political* (to clarify or to establish relationships among the different "ideas" men have) and improperly *metaphysical* (to establish an identity between words — and by extension the "ideas" words stand for — and the external world). The dramatic situation thus created has a potential for liberation as well as for a confining delusion, but as always in the *Essay* such a state of affairs is paradoxical and inherently ironic. Liberation means a recognition of human limits, an affirmation of the political and cultural constructs of the understanding and a sustained appreciation of them as such. The confining delusion from which these recognitions rescue us is the metaphysical arrogance implicit in older philosophical notions that enforce a stable and hierarchical world embodied in language, in this case the entire system of abstraction and classification, "this whole *mystery* of *Genera* and *Species*, which make such a noise in the Schools, and are, with Justice, so little regarded out of them" (III.iii.9).

To be sure, particularity and individuality are potentially overwhelming and in a pure state quite useless for communication and control. General terms are inevitable. What matters, Locke concludes, is to remember the historical dimension of language and to bear constantly in mind that generalization and abstraction are fashioned by the mind to enable men "to consider Things, and discourse of them, as it were in bundles, for the easier and readier improvement, and communication of their Knowledge, which would advance but slowly, were their Words and Thoughts confined only to Particulars" (III.iii.20). Validity and metaphysical certainty are replaced by usefulness in Locke's historical narration of language's emergence and employment, and the rigidities of system and classification give way in his presentation to a reiteration of particularity and the work of constructing order out of that particularity.

Locke, in a very clear sense throughout the *Essay*, shows us how he is at work in his book; he is a "busy" questioner and inquirer, dissolving certainty and moving through and around conventional formulations. The emphasis is always on the person speaking, on that Locke who examines his own thoughts and experiences and invites his reader to do the same.

Let any one examine his own Thoughts, and he will find, that as soon as he supposes or speaks of *Essential*, the consideration of some *Species*, or the complex *Idea*, signified by some general name, comes into his Mind: And 'tis in reference to that, that this or that Quality is said to be *essen-*

tial. So that if it be asked, whether it be *essential* to me, or any other
particular corporeal Being to have Reason? I say no; no more than it is
essential to this white thing I write on, to have words in it. (III.vi.4)

This insistent particularity extends to the present moment of Locke's composition of the *Essay* and asks us to imagine a moment when this book in
front of us did not exist, when its particularity as a document was inseparable from the particularity of white paper and ink and so on. Locke
is asking his reader to replace static philosophic entities such as "essence"
with a narrative reconstruction of our own creation of the general from a
constantly present particularity that extends to the book now in hand.

Book III is dominated by this staging and restaging of the history of
general terms, and the book is permeated by metaphors dramatizing
language as a fabrication of meaning whereby abstract and general notions are *"the Workmanship of the Understanding"* (III.iii.12,13,14).
Older philosophical notions are untenable precisely because they erase
the marks of the particular whereby human agency or intervention is
always visible. What Locke emphasizes throughout this book is not only
that "abstract ideas" (or general notions) are essentially boundaries set up
to mark species or kinds for our convenience and stability but that those
boundaries are difficult to fix, that the particular has an insistence and
plenitude that remind us as we invent language that human structuring is
absolutely necessary and absolutely arbitrary. This is even the case in that
species "most familiar to us, and with which we have the most intimate
acquaintance" (III.iii.14). Locke's example is man himself:

It having been more than once doubted, whether the *Foetus* born of a
Woman were a *Man*, even so far, as that it hath been debated, whether
it were, or were not to be nourished and baptized: which could not be,
if the abstract *Idea* or Essence, to which the Name Man belonged, were
of Nature's making; and were not the uncertain and various Collection
of simple *Ideas*, which the Understanding puts together, and then
abstracting it, affixed a name to it. (III.iii.14)

This example marks the beginning of what deserves to be called Book
III's recurring thematics of monstrosity, as Locke repeats at intervals the
difficulties not simply of definition but of human self-definition. Nature,
as presented here, is a place where a confusion of kinds is the rule, where
"Women have conceived by Drills" (III.vi.23), where the Abbot of St.
Martin was born in so hideous a shape that he was baptized conditionally,
where "monstrous productions" abound, and where "none of the Definitions of the word *Man*, which we yet have, nor Descriptions of that sort of
Animal, are so perfect and exact, as to satisfie a considerate inquisitive

Person" (III.vi.27). The external world is not fixed, its categories and species are infinitely fluid and drifting in a sea of boundless particularity. But Locke's enforcing dramatic example is appropriately personal and human. The *Essay* consistently returns to the personal and the local for its rhetorical if not its logical proof ("And I desire any one but to reflect on his own Thoughts, when he hears or speaks any of those or other Names of Substances, to know what sort of *Essences* they stand for"; III.vi.7). So, too, the recurring conclusive example that establishes this philosophical scene involves the reader in richly ironic self-doubt, in a querying of the "sacred Definition of *Animal Rationale*" (III.vi.26).

The monstrous and the violent Locke consistently evokes in Book III constitute a threatening and unpredictable world, closely linked to the unruffled analytic calm of the *Essay* itself. Such imaginative instability is partly a result of Locke's radical literalizing; new perspectives on familiar words and objects sometimes lead to the surprising and even the threatening. For example, Locke notes that light is a simple idea that cannot be defined and resists the attempts of both the Schools and the Cartesians. The tone is playful as Locke says that a scientific description of light that speaks of it as "a great number of little Globules, striking briskly on the bottom of the Eye" is no more revealing to someone who does not understand the word (who has not had the experience of light) "than if one should tell him, that *Light* was nothing but a Company of little Tennis-balls, which Fairies all day long struck with Rackets against some Men's Foreheads, whilst they passed by others" (III.iv.10). But then as Locke concludes from this that the true cause of light has nothing to do with our idea or experience of light, he turns without warning to a physical example that switches abruptly from the whimsical to the violent: "For granting this explication of the thing to be true; yet the *Idea* of the cause of *Light*, if we had it never so exact, would no more give us the *Idea* of *Light* it self, as it is such a particular perception in us, than the *Idea* of the Figure and Motion of a sharp piece of Steel, would give us the *Idea* of that Pain, which it is able to cause in us" (III.iv.10). A pressingly real world of knives and pain and necessary knowledge is placed next to a world of academic issues. Characteristically Lockean, these sentences dramatize the irrelevance of philosophical formulation and the primacy of experience. Experience in this case and in many others is not only painful but totally beyond verbal control or prediction. In the case of what Locke calls "simple ideas," the understanding can only proceed cautiously, remembering light and the pain a knife inflicts as irreducible and singular particularities.

The understanding can control monstrosity by defining terms, marking species and sorts, but that activity is only fully possible with what Locke calls "mixed modes," specifically human entities "made by a voluntary Collection of *Ideas* put together in the Mind, independent from any original Patterns in Nature" (III.v.5). This ordering is also partly accomplished by means of those human fictions Locke calls "nominal essences," with substances such as men, animals, plants, and elements. With the "simple ideas" such definition is impossible, since these "Ideas" (here clearly marked as experiences or impressions, the taste of a pineapple, the perception of light or color or motion or extension) cannot be understood by the understanding and cannot be presented in words. Language cannot represent the simple ideas by which it is initially constituted; and so it cannot know itself, has no control over its origins and is radically dependent on experiences to which it has only the misleading relationship natural to metaphors and other tropes. In effect, Locke's notions about language and simple ideas put us all in the position of that popular visitor to philosophical paradox, the man born blind who wonders about the world he cannot see but only hear about:

And no definition of *Light*, or *Redness*, is more fitted, or able to produce either of those *Ideas* in us, than the sound *Light*, or *Red*, by it self. For to hope to produce an *Idea* of Light, or Colour, by a Sound, however formed, is to expect that Sounds should be visible, or Colours audible; and to make the Ears do the Office of all the other Senses. Which is all one as to say, that we might Taste, Smell, and See by the Ears: a sort of Philosophy worthy only of *Sanco Panca*, who had the Faculty to see *Dulcinea* by Hearsay. And therefore he that has not before received into his Mind, by the proper Inlet, the simple *Idea* which any word stands for, can never come to know the signification of that Word, by any other Words, or Sounds, whatsoever put together, according to any Rules of Definition. The only way is, by applying to his Senses the proper Object; and so producing that *Idea* in him, for which he has learn'd the name already. A studious blind Man, who had mightily beat his Head about visible Objects, and made use of the explication of his Books and Friends, to understand those names of Light, and Colours, which often came in his way; bragg'd one day, That he now understood what *Scarlet* signified. Upon which his Friend demanding, what *Scarlet* was? the blind Man answered, It was like the Sound of a Trumpet. Just such an Understanding of the name of any other simple *Idea* will he have, who hopes to get it only from a Definition, or other Words made use of to explain it. (III.iv.11)

Paul de Man has argued that Locke's theory of language becomes in due course a theory of tropes by virtue of what de Man calls "the rhetorical motions of his own text."[44] This is obviously true at the level of the "simple ideas," which can only be approached by actual experience or in the synesthetic tropes of the ingenious blind man, but it is also true of the categorizing and fictionalizing process Locke presents as the essence of language. The particular is escaped by a generalizing and abstracting that is best understood by a metaphor of artifice, "the *Workmanship of the Understanding*" (III.iii.13,14). Those stable fictions the understanding composes out of the flux of particularity approach the status of figurative language. The "nominal essence" that allows language to speak of "men," for example, represents a comparison of particular entities (men or monsters) to a complex archetype labeled "man," which archetype is maintained as such only by constant commerce with particular "men" who enforce it by a linguistic act with distinct political overtones. The generality in the name or word is virtually in Locke's account of language a vehicle to allow temporary stability for the uncertain tenor contained in particular phenomena. Thanks to Locke's insistent separation of language and reality, the general and the particular effectively belong to different orders of being and are brought together only momentarily and in fact arbitrarily. Particular and general are like the tenor and vehicle that constitute metaphor, since in Locke's elaboration they are radically dependent on each other. A particular man is not a monster because he is like "man," and "man" is sustained in that relationship with particular men by a community of readers or speakers who understand and grant the similarity.

Indeed, the only time language escapes this comparative process with its figurative and political implications is at its hypothetical, presocial beginnings when the so-called mixed modes are invented. Locke tells a story in which Adam observes Lamech "more melancholy than usual" and wonders if he suspects his wife, Adah, of adultery. He therefore invents the two Hebrew words for jealousy and adultery in order to label his ideas about Lamech, and these words are perfectly adequate because they refer to no archetype but to Adam's own construction of the particular reality he sees around Lamech and Adah. With an irony that makes linguistic adequacy a very brief technicality, Adam finds he is wrong about Lamech, whose unease is the result of his guilt for committing a murder. But the adequacy of Adam's words remains, since he knows what jealousy and adultery are in the theater of his mind. However, as soon as Adam's sons come to use these words, they are forced into the comparative and social process language requires, and they must "conform the *Ideas*, in their Minds signified by these Names, to the *Ideas*, that they stood for in other Men's Minds, as to their Patterns and *Archetypes*" (III.vi.45).

In this same Adamic narrative, the father of mankind invents a name for "a glittering Substance" one of his sons brings home, *Zahab*. Here he bases his name on the obvious properties of the substance, on what he perceives as its natural archetype. But the properties of gold are multiplied by Adam's experimentation, and he adds ductility, fusibility, and fixedness to that archetype. Such experimentation and discovery are potentially endless, and there are by this time other men who "may have discovered several Qualities in Substances of the same Denomination, which others know nothing of" (III.vi.48). Language, as Locke always explains, is a political solution for both the variety of minds and the inexhaustible particularity of the world, and he finds that men have created a stable world of substances like gold by substituting "the name or sound, in the place and stead of the thing having that real Essence, without knowing what the real Essence is; and that is that which Men do, when they speak of Species of Things, as supposing them made by Nature, and distinguished by real Essences" (III.vi.49).

Both these social necessities are accomplished by an essentially figurative process, as the word "gold" is made to stand for the various properties a certain number of men have observed in their experiences of the substance. The word is a metonymic fiction, since it represents a part of what is in fact an endless particularity. "Gold" stands in an adjacent relationship to the inexhaustible manifold of qualities inherent in the material and it is thereby a linguistic convenience, a rhetorical-political device. Language is a political necessity in Locke's account of its origins because of the restless experimentation and continual revision of the external world natural to his individualistic and curious Adam. It is as much the inquisitive spirit and subversive privacy thus assumed to be natural to man as it is the inexhaustible particularity of the natural world that creates the complex linguistic situation Locke imagines. Although he does not bother with it, one can easily imagine another kind of human nature and social organization for which the world does not present these difficulties and for which language would be stable and easily limited.

Locke's theory of language is quasi-figurative, then, enforcing a constant self-examination of terms beautifully appropriate to the ironic balance of certainty and uncertainty that is his main literary strategy. Locke disparages language but exalts its linguistic and rhetorical powers. He reconstructs these primal linguistic moments to dramatize the intractability of the external world and to stage human cleverness, just as he himself makes his readers conscious of how deliberately oblique and rhetorical his own exposition must be in order to speak of things without falling into the traps set by ordinary unselfconscious language. Thus, the

Adamic narrative here in Book III is preceded by a passage about the difficulties of writing without forgetting that one is writing. Locke is telling his reader that the *Essay* differs from normal exposition or argument because he is aware of the misleading features of language and the difficulties of overcoming them:

> I must beg pardon of my Reader, for having dwelt so long upon this Subject, and perhaps, with some Obscurity. But I desire, it may be considered, how *difficult* it is, *to lead another by Words into the Thoughts of Things, stripp'd of those specifical differences* we give them: Which Things, if I name not, I say nothing; and if I do name them, I thereby rank them into some sort, or other, and suggest to the Mind the usual abstract *Idea* of that *Species*; and so cross my purpose. (III.vi.43)

A rethinking of the ordinary by means of narration is Locke's solution to this problem; such narration includes a naming that avoids mere labels, an active and continuously reflexive literary manner, a philosophical persona who by virtue of his individuality enjoys a clarifying relationship to this world of unstable language and the turbulent particularity it seeks to understand. Behind all this instability and arbitrariness there is the persistent reality of Locke's interrogating narrator. The polemic against the abuses of language that constitutes the last three chapters of Book III is launched by a narrator who has traveled back to the origins of language and thereby established his independence from the ordinary careless use of language. The only truly unexamined assumption is the reality of that individual, who is somehow spared the narrative instability of the particular. He, after all, is telling the story, and Locke makes sure from the very beginning of the *Essay* that his own story is included, that he is there as an anecdotal presence.

To some extent, the immunity the narrating self enjoys from the disturbing revelations of the *Essay* is a practical literary necessity, but Locke may be said to make it, as modern commentators complain, a means of philosophical enforcement. As Reginald Jackson puts it, "Locke throughout takes the view that there are persistent individual material substances, and that somehow we know this."[45] Jackson goes on to point out that this invariability Locke speaks of does not serve to distinguish one body from another and that therefore individuality turns out in the end to be a matter not of qualities but of relationships. Locke's writing is a means for accomplishing just such an accommodation, and the effect of the narrative-essay mode he develops is that the relational slides insensibly into the substantial. Locke's style is radically committed to self-observation, since as we have seen from the outset it is always examining itself for rhetorical excess and for terminological self-satisfaction and self-enclosure. The third book of the *Essay* provides a theory of language that intensifies Locke's distrust of language and makes linguistic reflexivity a philosophical as well as a moral imperative. The understanding's powers of self-observation are now extended, since it can observe itself in the process of using language. This observation can include a figurative but quasi-material situation, for example when Locke warns that in order to use prepositions and conjunctions properly a person must "enter into his own Thoughts, and observe nicely the several Postures of his Mind in discoursing" (III.vii.3). Or, such observation can be a simple and disarming return to the founding anecdote of the *Essay*, which illustrates "the Imperfection of Words" by describing "a meeting of very learned and ingenious Physicians, where by chance there arose a Question, whether any Liquor passed through the Filaments of the Nerves" (III.ix.16). Locke is there and tests his secret theory that "the greatest part of Disputes were more about the signification of Words, than a real difference in the Conception of Things." The character Locke reaffirms for himself in this vignette is Socratic, ironically deferential as he asks a simple question that undercuts argument and returns the "ingenious" company to unexamined assumptions and undefined terms. He asks them,

before they went any farther on in this Dispute, they would first examine, and establish amongst them, what the Word *Liquor* signified. They at first were a little surprised at the Proposal; and had they been Persons less ingenuous, they might perhaps have taken it for a very frivolous or extravagant one: Since there was no one there, that thought not himself to understand very perfectly, what the Word *Liquor* stood for . . . This made them perceive, that the Main of their Dispute was about the signification of that Term; and that they differed very little in their Opinions, concerning some fluid and subtile Matter, passing through the Conduits of the Nerves; though it was not so easy to agree whether it was to be called *Liquor*, or no, a thing which when each considered, he thought it not worth the contending about. (III.ix.16)

The merely verbal is banished by such self-examination, but Locke the sly Socratic questioner initiates the examination and his privacy and original apartness cannot themselves be examined. Who, after all, would examine them?

This apartness required for Locke's revisionist philosophical stance is also crucial in defining the origins of language and the epistemological-political situation behind those origins. The thinking self preserves throughout an apartness from its own processes of understanding, from the language it must use to organize the world it perceives, and of course from other men who are engaged in the same activities and practicing the same sort of isolation, if not with the philosophical narrator's clarity and self-consciousness. Locke's thought in one way or another constantly returns to this fundamental isolation. His position as a writer is equivalent to the placement of the self his thought describes, and both the style and substance of the *Essay* direct readers to a recurring relationship, which acquires by this repetition a virtual sort of substantiality. The isolated self by its deferential gestures occupies a stable space in which it is alone and from which it can observe and interrogate. Although Locke is hardly interested in putting his case so dramatically, Book III's investigations evoke a picture in which society and language are the structures devised by radically isolated individuals to resolve the chaos of particularity and to legislate a world by means of ingenious tropes. In the world available to the understanding and to the contemplative intelligence as Locke renders it here, the only dependable and recurring relationship is the space between the individual self and that which it observes, the phenomenal world and the language it finds available to deal with that world.

On the surface, Locke is trying to close that space, and a good half of Book III is spent attacking various forms of linguistic self-delusion and improper language that neglect or distort a "reality." Locke warns against the misuse of language and the "abuse of words" by returning again and again to a double theme: the confusion of words with things and an unsteady alignment between words and clear ideas. There is at times a sort of substantialism at work in this analysis, as when Locke says that words are useless when they stand for ideas that "agree not to the Reality of Things" (III.x.25). But essentially, Locke winds up promoting a human order founded on the substantiality of the perceiving individual, since the reality he dramatizes is never a stable world but one teeming with a particularity that borders on the absurd and sometimes on the violent and antihuman. However, Locke wishes to defer to another reality, a substantial world that is hidden and indeed quite "unknowable" within the boundaries the *Essay* describes. In part, that realm is a scientific and theological ideal that balances and perhaps diffuses the ideological subversion of Locke's conclusions. Locke's style turns self-consciously to those quasi-biblical rhythms and images that provide moral breathing space from the disturbing implications of the *Essay*.[46] But here at the very end of Book III such aphorisms give way to a triumphant declaration of human control over the world by means of language that must expand to meet the infinite needs of individual minds. In effect, "reality" is replaced by human needs.

Locke ends the third book by hoping that the linguistic-cognitive reforms he has been urging will take place and that thereby "many of the Books extant might be spared" and "many of the Philosophers (to mention no other,) as well as Poets Works, might be contained in a Nut-shell" (III.xi.26). That is a mild Lockean joke, since his implicit claim throughout is that the prolixity and indeed the repetitiousness of the *Essay* are caused by the persistence of error, and the ideal behind Locke's garrulity is always the short question of the cunning interrogator who knows that truth is cryptic and in some cases so private that it is unutterable or not susceptible to verbal demonstration (see III.ix.23). But the next and concluding section of this last chapter of Book III qualifies the joke and reintroduces the absolute necessity of language: "But after all, the provision of Words is so scanty in respect of that infinite variety of Thoughts, that Men, wanting Terms to suit their precise Notions, will, notwithstanding their utmost caution, be forced often to use the same Word, in somewhat different Senses" (III.xi.27). Locke may be said to try to balance the abuse of language and ignorance of "reality" involved in multiplying terms and preferring words to things and imagining that words are things against the necessity of modifying and enriching language so that terms are in effect multiplied almost to the virtual infinity of individuality. Those little pictures which he thinks might well be used alongside words that refer to things and substances cannot hope to do justice to the ideas in men's minds, and Locke admits it here.[47] The near-silence and the cryptic deferral to truth and experience that Locke recommends by precept and example are balanced and even put in question by the dynamic variety of individual minds, which demands an enormous expansion of language.

From one point of view, what Locke recommends is driving out the unsound linguistic currency of a bankrupt philosophical tradition of innate ideas and real essences and substituting a language backed by the solid bullion of experience. But experience as the *Essay* elaborates it turns out to be so varied and individualized that such a substitution has to be ironically qualified. Language is rescued from unconscious delusion and prideful certainty only to be delivered to an impossibly sensitive self-consciousness and an unacceptable epistemological relativism. The world Locke thus dramatizes is either richly varied or threateningly confused and arbitrary, rescued from its troubling implications only by Locke's recurring moral affirmations of the usefulness of uncertainty. Pope's line "Though man's a fool, yet God is wise" might serve as the epigraph for a good deal of the *Essay*.

In the context of these implications, then, the fourth book is both a conclusive summary of Locke's revision of the epistemological tradition and a restaging of the scene of thought and perception. Locke attempts to stabilize the turbulences and inconsistencies that appear with special clarity in the third book. He accomplishes this in part by the tone of finality and the sense of conclusion that dominate here, as Locke looks back to his previous work. But an opposition to the finality and rigidity of systematic thought is maintained by Locke's recurring dramatization of the limits of human knowledge that emphasizes our inability to have distinct ideas of things that are "*too remote*" and others that are "*too minute*" (IV.iii.24). To consider these limitations and to brood on our ignorance of our own world in the context of "the immense Universe" is to "discover an huge Abyss of Ignorance" (IV.iii.24). Moreover, if these limitations are placed within the uncertainty and actual ignorance the *Essay* has already uncovered, the situation is grave indeed. A few chapters later in the book Locke grows eloquent again and rehearses our ignorance of substances, since we are cut off from knowledge of that vast system of physical nature that creates and sustains them. Locke looks up to the sun, contemplates an unknowable network of particles and fluids, and finds "all these curious Machines" quite "beyond our notice and apprehension" (IV.vi.11).

It is clear, however, that what Locke here calls "this stupendious Structure of the Universe" does have an order and is a source of inspiration for human knowledge, serving as a balance for human imperfection and partiality. So, too, the imagination of an extraterrestrial perspective is possible if we reverse the normal human view. Somewhat in the manner of Johnson's malevolent experimental deities in his review of Soame Jenyns or of Voltaire's amused giant, Micromégas, Locke conjures up a race of exquisite perceivers, angelic intelligences "who see and know the Nature and inward Constitution of things" and with a "larger Comprehension, which enables them at one Glance to see the Connexion and Agreement of very many *Ideas*, and readily supplys to them the intermediate Proofs, which we by single and slow Steps, and long poring in the dark, hardly at last find out, and are often ready to forget one before we have hunted out another" (IV.iii.6). A version of angelic intelligence is constructed by speeding up human knowledge, by doing away with those painful and slow processes that constitute human perception and the reasoning that follows it. We come closest to angelic intelligence in those moments of intuitive knowledge when "the Mind perceives the Agreement or Disagreement of two *Ideas* immediately by themselves, without the intervention of any other" (IV.ii.1). And Locke's image for that moment is quasi-theological, a flash of light in the darkness so often established as the condition of our perception: "This part of Knowledge is irresistible, and like the bright Sun-shine, forces it self immediately to be perceived, as soon as ever the Mind turns its view that way; and leaves no room for Hesitation, Doubt, or Examination, but the Mind is presently filled with the clear Light of it" (IV.ii.1). Demonstrative knowledge, on the other hand, is mediated by language and reason, and it is "like a Face reflected by several Mirrors one to another . . . but 'tis still in every successive reflection with a lessening of that perfect Clearness and Distinctness, which is in the first, till at last, after many removes, it has a great mixture of Dimness, and is not at first Sight so knowable, especially to weak Eyes" (IV.ii.6).

This etiolation of light in demonstrative knowledge involves it in the flux of the phenomenal world and reinforces the psychological analysis of the operations of knowledge with which Locke began Book IV. Just as reflected light fades, so the memory of the proof behind knowledge fades. What even "Mr. *Newton*," for example, knows of the truth of any particular proposition in the *Principia* is based upon a memory of having gone through "that admirable Chain of intermediate *Ideas*, whereby he at first discovered it to be true" (IV.i.9). Locke then chooses an odd but I think revealing comparison to assert that Newton of course knows the proposition to be true: "remembring he once saw the connection of those *Ideas*, as certainly as he knows such a Man wounded another, remembring that he saw him run him through" (IV.i.9). Demonstrative knowledge of the most complex kind, even Newtonian physics, is effectively present to us at any particular time as if it were intuitive and immediate. The actual moment of knowledge of whatever sort is dramatized as incisive in a figurative and literal sense, a moment of violent penetration, as it were. Locke goes so far as to say that "every step in Reasoning, that produces Knowledge, has intuitive Certainty" (IV.ii.7). Our knowledge, therefore, is experienced as a set of isolated moments or intuitive insights within an unfolding process rather than as a continuity or a structure. The radical discontinuity between whatever we see or perceive or understand and our "understanding" is further underlined by the difference between the momentary and fragmentary quality of our knowledge and the totality it seems barely to touch: "the intellectual and sensible World, are in this perfectly alike; That that part, which we see of either of them, holds no proportion with what we see not; And whatsoever we can reach with our Eyes, or our Thoughts of either of them, is but a point, almost nothing, in comparison of the rest" (IV.iii.23).

The reader is left with an impression of little choice between human knowledge and ignorance, as the former is so carefully circumscribed that it is always founded on an awareness of the latter. Locke's elaboration of the differences between knowledge and ignorance here has the effect of bringing the two together, as ignorance appropriates knowledge and becomes a form of knowledge that is the prelude to a human self-sufficiency ironically grounded in the nearly absurd limitation of a geometrical "point" that is almost nothing, nearly "no where." On one level, the irony here is as old as Socrates, but in Locke's case an ignorance or at least an uncertainty about "natural philosophy" is a necessary prelude to a liberating empiricism that leads to practical material science and a rational theology and ethics.

> Experiments and Historical Observations we may have, from which we may draw Advantages of Ease and Health, and thereby increase our stock of Conveniences for this Life: but beyond this, I fear our Talents reach not, nor are our Faculties, as I guess, able to advance.

> 11. From whence it is obvious to conclude, that, since our Faculties are not fitted to penetrate into the internal Fabrick and real Essences of Bodies; but yet plainly discover to us the Being of a GOD, and the Knowledge of our selves, enough to lead us into a full and clear discovery of our Duty, and great Concernment, it will become us, as rational Creatures, to imploy those Faculties we have about what they are most adapted to, and follow the direction of Nature, where it seems to point us out the way. For 'tis rational to conclude, that our proper Imployment lies in those Enquiries, and in that sort of Knowledge, which is most suited to our natural Capacities, and carries in it our greatest interest, i.e. the Condition of our eternal Estate. Hence I think I may conclude, that *Morality is the proper Science, and Business of Mankind in general*. (IV.xii.10–11)

The problem is that Locke's investigations have been too thorough, his interrogations too searching. He has established an ignorance and subversive questioning of certainty reaching well past the demolition of old metaphysical or theoretical ambitions. Still, he is cautious and circumspect, adding as he continues that practical scientific discoveries such as iron, printing, the compass, and *quinquina* are what separate Europeans from benighted savages. But these summary reiterations of limitation here in Book IV reaffirm ignorance and subvert the very stability of selfhood and individuality on which Locke bases his limited humanism. There is at work throughout the *Essay* a gathering thematics of absurdity and monstrosity that emerges clearly in the final book. Locke's thought and the deferential manner of his writing are defined by their openness,

their readiness to entertain any possibility. In denying the availability of
an external order, Locke temporarily suggests that a zany solipsism is an
option, since an individual as such is cut off from other beings and
substances.

Paul de Man finds, with his customary dazzling subversion, that
Locke's argument has been haunted by the implicit conclusions drawn in
Book III. The monsters and changelings that complicate the old definition of man were, at first, says de Man, merely a "mock argument, a
hyperbolical example to unsettle the unquestioned assumption of defini-
tional thought." But here in Book IV mere argument becomes an "ethically charged issue," as Locke wonders where to draw the line between
monster and man, between infanticide and slaughter. Locke is trapped by
his theory of language, and "the substitutive text of tropes now has been
extended to reality." Locke's polemic against the "abuse of words" here in
chapter iv of Book IV is a recognition that all language is potentially a
disorienting catachresis.[48] Of course, Locke thinks that potentiality is
securely held in check by reason and the community of reasonable men
who enforce certain boundaries, by theological and political forces that
mean nothing to de Man. However, I think the text of the *Essay*, in what
de Man calls its "rhetorical motions," strives to repress particular instabilities it raises by its own logical vivacity.

Locke's incessant caution, his circling deference to possibility, allows
him to return again and again to the absurd antiscene or rival scenario to
the arrangements most men take for granted. The *"extent of our
Knowledge,"* for example, is "not only short of the reality of Things, but
even of the extent of our own *Ideas*" (IV.iii.6). Locke argues in this section that the failures of knowledge have been owing to "System, Interest,
or Party," and he affirms that human knowledge "may be carried much
farther, than it hitherto has been." But the limitation he then adds is
madly circular in its implications, since the world does not contain
anything equivalent to some of our key notions. This applies not only to
geometrical and mathematical constructions like a square, a circle, and
equality, but to self-descriptive notions like matter and thinking. It may
be, Locke concludes, that God has arranged matter and thought in ways
we cannot conceive, and in fact our world is illogical and mysterious for
us. The motion of physical bodies should produce nothing but other motion, but it seems "to produce pleasure or pain, or the *Idea* of a Colour, or
Sound," and we must "quit our Reason, go beyond our *Ideas*, and attribute it wholly to the good Pleasure of our Maker" (IV.iii.6). Not only
do we have to discard our conceptions of matter and thinking and confess

that we do not know the true relationship between our own elements, but we have no reason to exclude other possibilities and relationships God has established between matter and thought: "what reason have we to conclude, that he could not order them [the effects of motion] as well to be produced in a Subject we cannot conceive capable of them, as well as in a Subject we cannot conceive the motion of Matter can any way operate upon?" (IV.iii.6). A question like that, out of context, is a piece of rhetorical apologetics, but in the *Essay* it forms part of a larger pattern and is a contribution to Locke's implicit dramatization of the confusing alternative to his modest empiricism. There are, in a potential sense that Locke frequently insists on, other worlds and other arrangements, or, effectively for human perception, no particular or final arrangements (see II.viii.13).

What unfolds with a special clarity here in section 6 of chapter iii is the twisting, strangling nature of Locke's analysis. He refuses to give in to the diminished thing he makes of the understanding as he proceeds, drawing a tighter and tighter circle around the notion of the truth actually available to us. He draws back from unacceptable implications ("I say not this, that I would any way lessen the belief of the Soul's Immateriality: I am not here speaking Probability, but Knowledge"), but quickly passes on to license speculation ("it is of use to us, to discern how far our Knowledge does reach; for the state we are at present in, not being that of Vision, we must, in many Things, content our selves with Faith and Probability: and in the present Question, about the immateriality of the Soul, if our Faculties cannot arrive at demonstrative Certainty, we need not think it strange"). Locke negotiates between those who say that the soul is matter and those who say it is spirit. He spins in the center, from which other men go "running into the opposite Opinion" or "take refuge in the contrary."

Locke repeatedly invokes a knowledgeable ignorance, a temporary solipsism, whereby individual perception in all its limitations is used as a test of truth and then itself discredited as merely particular and thereby insufficient. This wavering between possibilities is something Locke controls very well here, as he proposes that we remember God's capacity to do just about anything and that we draw the conclusion that the question is imponderable.

He that considers how hardly Sensation is, in our Thoughts, reconcilable to extended Matter; or Existence to any thing that hath no Extension at all, will confess, that he is very far from certainly knowing what his Soul is. 'Tis a Point, which seems to me, to be put out of the reach of our

Knowledge: And he who will give himself leave to consider freely, and look into the dark and intricate part of each Hypothesis, will scarce find his Reason able to determine him fixedly for, or against the Soul's Materiality. Since on which side soever he views it, either as an unextended Substance, or as a thinking extended Matter; the difficulty to conceive either, will, whilst either alone is in his Thoughts, still drive him to the contrary side. (IV.iii.6).

This passage describes a built-in instability in thought, making a weakness of the mind's tendency for grasping and affirming by momentary intuitions rather than by sequential demonstration. But here the intuition is negative and to occupy one position is to be driven toward the other. The irresolution thus achieved disposes of the question without answering it, and in a sense that discarding of questions by involving them in psychological process and epistemological absurdity is what Locke substitutes for "answering" questions. Locke admitted as much when he confessed to Molyneux that he had trouble with the question of human freedom:

For I own freely to you the weakness of my understanding, that though it be unquestionable that there is omnipotence and omniscience in God our maker, and I cannot have a clearer perception of any thing than that I am free, yet I cannot make freedom in man consistent with omnipotence and omniscience in God, though I am as fully perswaded of both as of any truths I most firmly assent to. And therefore I have long since given off the consideration of that question, resolving all into this short conclusion, That if it be possible for God to make a free agent, then man is free, though I see not the way of it.[49]

Locke's conviction here flies in the face of logic and is a matter of necessary contradiction and of self-affirmation. In an important way, the questioner is always more important than the question, and Locke is understandably short and at times cruel with any ultimate skeptics who claim to doubt our knowledge of our own existence. Chapter ix, "Of our Knowledge of Existence," is the shortest one in Book IV, that brevity suggesting an impatience and anxiety perhaps something like Johnson's troubled retort to Boswell's nagging question: "We know our will is free, and there's an end on't."[50] Locke invokes experience as something that "convinces us, that *we have an intuitive Knowledge of our own Existence*, and an internal infallible Perception that we are" (IV.ix.3). Locke is quite content with the potential solipsism whereby the self guarantees its existence by observing its own activities and circumscribes itself in its own operations. Even our knowledge of the existence of God, he argues in the next chapter, is something available to the introspective self: "Thus from the Consideration of our selves, and what we infallibly find in our own Constitutions, our Reason leads us to the Knowledge of this certain and evident Truth, That *there is an eternal, most powerful, and most knowing Being*, which whether any one will please to call *God*, it matters not" (IV.x.6). Of course, as Locke notes several times, this knowledge is demonstrative rather than purely intuitive and "requires Thought and Attention; and the Mind must apply it self to a regular deduction of it from some part of our intuitive Knowledge" (IV.x.1).

Locke does just that in the tenth chapter and takes on various objections of the "men of matter" to the idea of an eternal and immaterial deity. The last objection he gives to his imaginary interlocutor is interesting, since it echoes Locke's own functional or dramatic skepticism. "But you will say, Is it not impossible to admit of the *making any thing out of nothing*, since we cannot possibly conceive it?" (IV.x.19). Locke's answer exploits the radical uncertainty of our conceptions, the extreme dislocation and alienation we sense even in our most basic notions and experiences. We are hardly in a position, he says, to restrict an infinite being to matters we can conceive, since we cannot really understand the operations of our own mind. On one level, then, our lack of knowledge of ourselves is evidence of God's existence, just as on another level our certainty of our own particular and finite existence is also thereby evidence for infinite diversity. We know that we are and yet our knowledge of what that being is and how it functions is an issue the *Essay* complicates tremendously. Locke's achievement as a writer is to exploit that complication so that his literary habits cooperate with an ideological control of unruly philosophical implications.

Modern commentators are often impatient with Locke for asserting the stability of personal identity in the face of the instability he himself uncovers at such length. Antony Flew, for example, finds Locke anxious to establish the notion of a continuous identity in spite of the clear implications in his thought that erode the supposition of the self as continuous. What Flew calls "the search for the real essence of personal identity" involved Locke's "abandonment of his greatest insight and a betrayal of the glorious revolution he was leading against the superstition of real essences and natural kinds."[51] It might be argued that Locke's insistence on something like a stable personal essence reflects the ideological necessity of individuality as the basic element of civil society. Whatever the reasons, Locke's literary practice in the *Essay* establishes a self that is stable precisely because it is at home with radical instability. In the fourth book Locke finds in such instability a rich opportunity for literary elaboration of his moral and philosophical themes.

The situation Locke evokes in the *Essay* accustoms the reader to a world of paradox, inconsistency, disruption, change, and even unexpected transformation. The narrator as sly questioner and ironic disposer of error and mere opinion makes us familiar and indeed comfortable with a reality always only partially revealed; or, he makes us satisfied with the ironic certainty of uncertainty, content with a diminished but nonetheless powerful selfhood, with an efficiently indirect assertiveness. Locke's philosophical posture encourages and is in turn reinforced by a literary manner based on textual disruption, on shifting our view from the book to the world and reminding readers of the process of writing. In terms of its literary enforcements, the *Essay* is essentially a comic, quasi-novelistic document in which process and a shifting reality are placed next to inelastic verbal formulations. The narrator's readiness for process and possibility exists next to the stiffness of a cast of characters who resist instability, at times to the point of comic madness. A recurring figure is the philosophical fool who demands certainty and refuses the normal. "He that will not eat, till he has Demonstration that it will nourish him; he that will not stir, till he infallibly knows the Business he goes about will succeed, will have little else to do, but sit still and perish" (IV.xiv.1). Locke's comic imagination delights at times in ridiculing those "Men whose Understandings are cast into a Mold, and fashioned just to the size of a *received Hypothesis*" (IV.xx.11). He loves antiphilosophical satiric moments in which radical doubt, to take an especially violent example, is punished. Let the skeptic who calls the evidence of the senses a dream "try, whether the glowing heat of a glass Furnace, be barely a wandring Imagination in a drowsy Man's Fancy, by putting his Hand into it, he may perhaps be wakened into a certainty greater than he could wish, that it is something more than bare Imagination" (IV.xi.8).

At the same time, the certainty of common experience is also vulnerable to satiric examination and the world of facts open to revision by new and ever changing perspectives. The King of Siam refused to believe the Dutch ambassador who told him that in his country water became so hard that men could walk on it. The probable is open to cultural limitations, and the king's skepticism is reminiscent of the incredulity of some of Gulliver's hosts. "*Hitherto I have believed the strange Things you have told me, because I look upon you as a sober fair man, but now I am sure you lye*" (IV.xv.5). Indeed, Locke's penultimate chapter, "Of wrong Assent, or Errour," contributes to the satiric safety valve he provides for his assertions. He describes with great energy and satiric vigor the diversity of men and their understandings, or rather the diversity enforced by political, social, and even moral-psychological individualities. If such diversity is placed next to the effort of the *Essay* as a whole to isolate the invariable and simple workings of *the* human understanding, the irony is a large and interesting one that saves Locke from the arrogance he attacks.

The satirical edges of Locke's discourse grow sharper in Book IV because he has to come rather close here to the finality he has warned against. This last book promises more generalized formulations, definitions of knowledge and error, or reason and faith. So Locke balances that potentially untenable final formulation and stable definition with controlled disruptions, sometimes by comic-satiric scenes, at other times by reiterating the limitations and potential absurd irrelevance of all human insight, and a significant number of times by turning to the literal process of reading and writing in which he and his audience are involved.

From the beginning of the *Essay*, he has been careful to present his thought in that active, present sense, and many times Locke lets us know that he has changed his mind about particular points or altered his emphasis. He claims that Book III grew out of a much smaller section, as he came to realize the importance of language. As he sets out in Book IV to define the varieties of knowledge, he describes that enormous, daunting project as a process whereby we perceive "the Agreement, or Disagreement of any two *Ideas*," and "its clearness or obscurity, consists in the clearness or obscurity of that Perception, and not in the clearness or obscurity of the *Ideas* themselves" (IV.ii.15). Knowledge is a power to observe a field of relationships, and it is obviously significant that Locke has already chosen an image from reading to illustrate the swiftness of such intuitive knowledge: there is in that moment of perception no doubt of agreement or disagreement, "no more than it can be a doubt to the Eye, (that can distinctly see White and Black,) Whether this Ink, and this Paper be all of a Colour. If there be Sight in the Eyes, it will at first glimpse, without Hesitation, perceive the Words printed on this Paper, different from the Colour of the Paper" (IV.ii.5). The illustration is part of Locke's visualization of the operations of the understanding. But there is an irony in the example that coincides with what I have called the literalizing and antimetaphoric drift of Locke's rhetoric. Knowledge here is not actually like reading, but simply and literally the perceptual act that precedes reading, distinguishing black letters on a white field. On several other occasions in Book IV when Locke turns to his text to illustrate various points, the same literalization is at work. For example, he makes the point that we receive knowledge of the existence of other things from sensation, even though we may not be aware of how this is happening:

v.g. whilst I write this, I have, by the Paper affecting my Eyes, that *Idea* produced in my Mind, which whatever Object causes, I call *White*; by which I know, that that Quality or Accident (*i.e.* whose appearance before my Eyes, always causes that *Idea*) doth really exist, and hath a Being without me . . . I can no more doubt, whilst I write this, that I see White and Black, and that something really exists, that causes that Sensation in me, than that I write or move my Hand; which is a Certainty as great as humane Nature is capable of, concerning the Existence of any thing but a Man's self alone, and of GOD. (IV.xi.2)

Reading and writing, at illustrative moments like this, are absorbed into a phenomenal world and are no longer privileged activities. Intuitive knowledge (and by extension all knowledge in an experiential sense) is a sudden seeing, a vision that in its momentary quality excludes the long sequences of writing and reading and for the moment insists on the phenomenal qualities of the text in front of us and thereby diminishes it as a text. Reading and writing are clearly associated with a discredited merely verbal philosophy in Locke's long attack here in Book IV on the syllogism. Ironically in a way, Locke retains traces of an oral and disputatious philosophical tradition in order to attack a philosophy that has become merely a series of written formulas and lost sight of the vitalizing pretextual origins of reasoning. A syllogism, as Locke explains, is a verbal repetition of simple truths that transposes and spins them out in "artificial Forms" rather "than in that short natural plain order, they are laid down in here, wherein everyone may see it; and wherein they must be seen, before they can be put into a Train of *Syllogisms*" (IV.xvii.4). Truth is edged back by implication to something preverbal or nonverbal, and Locke explains a bit further on in this chapter that rhetorical or metaphorical fallacies are much better detected by the way of ideas than by syllogisms. The violent aptness of rhetoric (for men are sometimes imposed on, "their phancies being struck with some lively metaphorical Representations") is countered by the equally violent restoration of simple order and visual immediacy.

Now to shew such Men the weakness of such an Argumentation, there needs no more but to strip it of the superfluous *Ideas*, which blended and confounded with those on which the Inference depends, seem to show a connexion, where there is none; or at least do hinder the discovery of the want of it; and then to lay the naked *Ideas* on which the force of the Argumentation depends, in their due order, in which Position the Mind taking a view of them, sees what connexion they have, and so is able to judge of the Inference, without any need of a Syllogism at all. (IV.xvii.4)

This is Locke's rhetoric at its most concrete. The various metaphors at work in such polemical passages are threaded through the entire *Essay*.

The overt image of undressing argument and revealing the bare body of the ideas is of course supplemented by a visualization of mental operations, but here as elsewhere Locke simultaneously turns away from the visual to a construction or arrangement by the understanding, which is made possible by sight but is also logical and nonvisual. Supervising these images is a tone of practicality and simple instruction; the mind is described in terms that fit a competent artisan rather than a subtle artist. Stripping off clothing to reveal the naked truth is a traditional satiric image, and it has the effect of turning the visualization into a moral imperative that distracts us from its metaphoric quality. This context makes visualization of the understanding's operations a moral-satiric gesture, which is directed against the nonvisual procedures of a merely verbal philosophical tradition that prefers reading and writing to experience.

Syllogisms, Locke concedes a few pages later, may be helpful; they are like "Spectacles," an aid in his time purely for reading. "Reason by its own Penetration where it is strong, and exercised, usually sees, quicker and clearer without Syllogism" (IV.xvii.4). Reason's "seeing" is not bound by the printed page. It is, rather, a muscular and instinctive activity, a power of perceiving relationships that in fact is diminished by reading, since Locke adds rather impishly that "use of those Spectacles" may so dim the sight "that it cannot without them see consequences or inconsequences in Argumentation" (IV.xvii.4).

Visualization, then, is Locke's rhetorical weapon for promoting a philosophy of what he calls "experience," and it is quickly absorbed by the larger rhetorical occasion of the *Essay*. I would define that occasion as a substitution of speech and virtual dialogue for the verbal forms of what Locke presents as the nonexperiential and merely textual concerns of an older philosophical tradition. The stylistic variety of the *Essay* and Locke's essayistic manner, with its modesty, concession, and uncertainty, are means of establishing a rhetoric of speech rather than writing; the textual surface is varied and sometimes undermined to bring the reader back to a personal voice that is using the text and never fully contained in it. There is an aptness in Locke's addition to the second edition of the chapter "Of Enthusiasm," since the self-deluding certainty of the enthusiast is a dangerous parody of the certainty provided by a superficial use of Lockean experience and by a literal acceptance of the visual metaphors for truth.

In section 8 of this chapter, Locke parodies the figurative language and the reasoning of an enthusiast, skirting dangerously close to his own metaphors for intuitive knowledge:

they see the Light infused into their Understandings, and cannot be mistaken; 'tis clear and visible there; like the Light of bright Sunshine, shews it self, and needs no other Proof, but its own Evidence: they feel the Hand of GOD moving them within, and the impulses of the Spirit, and cannot be mistaken in what they feel. Thus they support themselves, and are sure Reason hath nothing to do with what they see and feel in themselves: what they have a sensible Experience of admits no doubt, needs no probation. Would he not be ridiculous who should require to have it proved to him, that the Light shines, and that he sees it? It is its own Proof, and can have no other. When the Spirit brings Light into our Minds, it dispels Darkness. We see it, as we do that of the Sun at Noon, and need not the twilight of Reason to shew it us. This Light from Heaven is strong, clear, and pure, carries its own Demonstration with it, and we may as rationally take a Glow-worme to assist us to discover the Sun, as to examine the celestial Ray by our dim Candle, Reason. (IV.xix.8)

Locke quickly identifies this as a parody and notes its incoherence when the persuasive "Metaphor of seeing and feeling" is "strip'd" (IV.xix.9). And a few pages later he defines "Light, true Light in the Mind" as either self-evidence or the result of the "clearness and validity" of proof. "Light" may proceed from the devil, that deluding "Son of the Morning" (IV.xix.13). God makes a prophet but "does not unmake the Man." We must "bring this Guide of his *Light within* to the Tryal" (IV.xix.14). Locke is responding, I submit, to the persuasive instability of his own metaphors for knowledge. Coming here where it does in the *Essay* and in the sequence of Locke's revisions, "Of Enthusiasm" is his response to a plausible misreading of his writing that has missed its ironic literalizations and failed to grasp the powerful deferential method of understanding it recommends. So, Locke promulgates here a version of reason as old as Aquinas:

Reason is natural *Revelation*, whereby the eternal Father of Light, and Fountain of all Knowledge communicates to Mankind that portion of Truth, which he has laid within the reach of their natural Faculties: *Revelation* is natural *Reason* enlarged by a new set of Discoveries communicated by GOD immediately, which *Reason* vouches the Truth of, by the Testimony and Proofs it gives, that they come from GOD. (IV.xix.4)

There is another way in which the enthusiast represents a crucial misunderstanding of this revelation. The enthusiast is emphatically a speaker, and like the essayist his talk claims to come out of particular experience. The flaw in his speech is that he is essentially a monologuist. In the opening section of the chapter, Locke speaks of the enthusiast as someone who imposes upon himself and abuses his own mind, tricks himself and is liable to impose on others. Knowing, Locke explains and exemplifies throughout the *Essay*, is a situation in which a part of us talks to another part, in which there is a dialogue between the knowing part of the self and another and less obvious part that accepts or rejects what is proposed, according to the canons of reason. The only dialogue the enthusiast acknowledges is with God, but of course God never answers directly or has anything to gain from a human interlocutor. Locke's informing metaphor is social. Within the fiction of dialogue that depicts the workings of the understanding, there is a powerful political analogy whereby the enthusiast is a tyrannical absolutist and the man of judgment and reason a subscriber to the special sort of constitutional monarchy Locke favors. "Who does Violence to his Faculties, Tyrannizes over his own Mind, and usurps the Prerogative that belongs to Truth alone, which is to command Assent by only its own Authority, *i.e.* by and in proportion to that Evidence which it carries with it" (IV.xix.2).

Locke's *Essay* diminishes certainty, dismantles the world, disrupts ordinary tempo, sequence, and perspective. It tends to endanger the stability of treasured notions like identity and the immateriality of the soul. In a sense, Locke anticipates the Shandyean parody. His literary mode is implicitly comic and self-canceling. The *Essay* is an ambitious synthesis but leaves matters even more scattered than they were. The magnitude of the enterprise is undercut by the remarkable simplicity of its conclusions here at the end of Book IV, a simplicity that balances the rich confusion the *Essay* explores and extends.

Chapter 3

Berkeley

PHILONOUS. *Do I not know this to be a real stone that I stand on, and that which I see before my eyes to be a real tree?*
— *Three Dialogues Between Hylas and Philonous*

The smooth deference of the *Essay Concerning Human Understanding* manifests self-possession and power. Locke speaks as the representative of a truth that reveals itself as inevitable, inescapable, natural, and undeniable for any man of sense and candor. Locke's writing persuades by its modesty, its habitual concession to a fundamental moral and political stability that counterbalances the epistemological turbulence the *Essay* uncovers and pointedly fails to resolve. Such turbulence, for example, is ironically diminished by a series of knowing questions directed at "liberty" in the chapter "Of Power":

Without Liberty the Understanding would be to no purpose: And without Understanding, Liberty (if it could be) would signify nothing. If a Man sees, what would do him good or harm, what would make him happy or miserable, without being able to move himself one step towards or from it, what is he the better for seeing? And he that is at liberty to ramble in perfect darkness, what is his liberty better than if he were driven up and down, as a bubble by the force of the wind? The being acted by a blind impulse from without, or from within, is little odds. The first therefore and great use of Liberty, is to hinder blind Precipitancy; the principal Exercise of Freedom is to stand still, open the eyes, look about, and take a view of the consequence of what we are going to do, as much as the weight of the matter requires. How much sloth and negligence, heat and passion, the prevalency of fashion, or acquired indispositions, do severally contribute on occasion, to these *wrong Judgments*, I shall not here farther enquire. (II.xxi.67)

Locke's recurring scene of perception assumes self-control, counsels us to reserve judgment and postpone involvement. To some extent, images of cool apartness are necessary to counter the revelations of the *Essay* whereby the understanding discovers its implication in an uncertain external world, where it attempts to mark boundaries and works hard to define a properly human order. The problematic of representation lurks behind these activities, and Locke's unruffled manner often carries a protective irony. He begins here by characterizing freedom as the possibility of movement toward the good and by disparaging mere contemplative apprehension of the good. Understanding requires liberty, just as liberty without understanding is merely movement and loses the name of action. But in examining this paradox, Locke makes liberty the power to reserve movement in the light of the difficulty and uncertainty surrounding both the good and the idea of movement toward it. Action and involvement are promoted but not performed in Locke's scene, in which the moral agent is a modest, reasonable spectator somewhere off to the side rather than a reckless participant. Movement of any kind is ironically diminished by Locke's language; "impulse" is blind but freedom is essentially a matter of seeing while standing still, refusing movement without denying its necessity.

Vision in Locke enforces the objectivity of the viewer in a moral-epistemological situation where objectivity is severely compromised. Locke is openly skeptical about the possibility of any free action and, in effect, substitutes consideration for action. He will not speculate how moral, social, psychological, and even physiological factors can influence action. The rhetorical effect of such a refusal is clear enough, and the reader knows these factors are nothing less than the prevailing conditions of most actions. Locke's *Essay* at moments like this invites its readers to enjoy a knowing apartness and protective detachment; it assures them of their power by dramatizing their wise deferral of action. The *Essay* forms its readers into an audience sitting on the stage of perception, seeing so closely and accurately as to be amused rather than frightened by the play.

Berkeley never claims this sort of apartness and self-reservation. His entire philosophical and literary manner is founded on strenuous involvement in the world and characterized by persistent self-assertion which challenges philosophic deferral. In place of Lockean detachment and self-reservation, Berkeley speaks of a dangerous moral and intellectual struggle to come through to truth, to move fearlessly in those elements Locke evokes with such distaste in this passage. The moral activism and polemical urgency in Berkeley's writing are perfectly exemplified in compact form in the last paragraph of his last major work, *Siris*:

> The eye by long use comes to see even in the darkest cavern: and there is no subject so obscure but we may discern some glimpse of truth by long poring on it. Truth is the cry of all, but the game of a few. Certainly, where it is the chief passion, it doth not give way to vulgar cares and views; nor is it contented with a little ardour in the early time of life, active perhaps to pursue, but not so fit to weigh and revise. He that would make a real progress in knowledge must dedicate his age as well as youth, the later growths as well as first fruits, at the altar of Truth. (V,164)

Siris is a long series of aphorisms gathered in paragraphs like this, "a chain of philosophical reflexions and inquiries concerning the virtues of tar-water, and divers other subjects connected together and arising one from another" is how Berkeley summarized it on the title page in 1744. Although some modern commentators have found in the search for physical causes in *Siris* a modification, even a recantation, of Berkeley's defining system of "immaterialism," it is really a continuation and intensification of his philosophical style and characteristic scene, a rather more concrete and overt reprise of the themes and images promoting his thought from its precocious beginnings. From the youthful notebooks A. A. Luce has named the *Philosophical Commentaries* onward, Berkeley tended toward this aphoristic curtness, a sharp paradoxical manner from which he never essentially deviated. Where Locke is prolix, relaxed in his extended viewing of circumstances, detached and thereby ready to accept what leisurely investigation offers, Berkeley is crisp, taut in his formulations, armed with a hypothesis and placed steadily in a position, peering intently at a world which is in some difficult sense sustained by his alert gaze. The paragraph I have quoted, for example, exhorts us to action, both in the field and in the study. Truth is sought in a cavern but found by long "poring." The learned image of reading is supplemented by the physical and natural darkness which is its context and its challenge. The allusive strength of the language is Pauline, but the chase metaphor and the contemporary, polemical ring of "cry" and "game" save the passage from the solemnity of mere biblical paraphrase. The compact wit of that sentence is moderated by the stately rhythms of the next two, which are a miniature moral essay, balanced and considered after the sharp, arresting imagery of the opening two. The imagery subsides into moralized narrative but rises in the concluding sentence to a new scene of fertile consecration which replaces the dark cavern of the opening. The prose has a movement and an energy in its images and rhythms that are a formal accompaniment, in an almost musical sense, to the notions promoted in *Siris*. Youthful, athletic, witty, as well as eloquent in its pursuit of truth, Berkeley's literary manner in a passage like this stands in revealing contrast to Locke's middle-aged ironic mode and secular tolerance for diversity and incoherence.

In one way or another, philosophical style or statement is counterstatement. Berkeley is open and aggressive in his polemics. He names his enemies: skeptics, freethinkers, scientists, mathematicians, the men of matter and abstract ideas. In *Alciphron* he savagely parodies Shaftesbury and Mandeville, although his relationship to Locke's thought and manner is more complex. Berkeley is brash enough in his notebooks to declare that Locke is wrong (as is Newton), but "Mr. Locke" is never the object of scorn or ridicule. Of course, Berkeley set out to reassemble the Lockean dispersion of reality and to reestablish the authority of the central self Locke and other thinkers had scattered. His polemical stance is thus necessarily direct; irony and evasion would violate his program. Berkeley's assertive, lucid, straightforward literary manner is the appropriate enforcing vehicle for what he himself defined as a revolutionary simplicity. However respectful Berkeley was in public, his relationship to Locke had to involve repudiation and reversal of the Lockean doctrine and its attendant indirection of manner.

This is not to say that Berkeley's thought is merely a set of opposing variations on the Lockean system. Most commentators would allow that he passes beyond the response to Locke and into his own system. But Berkeley's self-imposed task is the invention of a new set of precise terms (or a radical revision of the old ones) for dramatizing the conditions of knowing. Sir William Hamilton complained of Locke that "of all philosophers" his language was "the most figurative, ambiguous, vacillating, various and even contradictory."[1] Berkeley proposes a new simplicity in his exploration of what he calls "first principles." In the *Principles of Human Knowledge*, he finds no "darkness and intricacy in the objects, or natural defect in the understanding" (II,25). The mind is, rather, "embarrassed" in its quest for truth by "false principles." In the context of Lockean complication, restoration of a natural clarity and simplicity is

Berkeley's repeated characterization of his program. To an important extent, Berkeley's task is a revision of the literary mode of Locke's *Essay*, which partakes of what Edward Said, following Lukács, calls the essential irony of the essay form, "patently insufficient in its intellectuality with regard to living experience."[2] Berkeley's literary mode is profoundly concrete and immediate, tending to aphorism and dialogue, dramatic forms rooted in social and moral experience and exactly suitable to an emerging clarity and certainty. The Berkeleian motto *"esse is percipi"* is a stage direction, a philosophical *coup de théâtre*, a radically clarifying imperative to resolve what Berkeley saw as Lockean muddle.

Locke's literary manner shuns dramatic simplicity, for the *Essay* in its circling meditations and ruminations erodes traditional assumptions about how and what we know. Locke's method as a philosophic essayist, with all the unsystematic looseness the title allows him, is to insinuate innovation, to cultivate what amounts at times to mock innocence in the face of the unorthodox conclusions he says we are drawn toward. The fairness and modesty Locke cultivates in his style are defenses against the polemical turbulence implicit in his findings. The *Essay* conjures up an epistemological world with disturbing implications, featuring the random, the arbitrary, and the essentially inscrutable. Locke's writing articulates a moral and political ideology as the human alternative to this irrelevant or unknowable or destructive world. His sweet reason is the only refuge in sight, and the point of his literary manner is to make it as much a natural inevitability as a philosophical position.

That is to say, Locke excludes opposition by presenting a philosophic scene where opposition cannot operate in any meaningful sense. His opponents quickly become irrelevant, invisible in the complicated flux Locke guides us through, simply part of the variety of representations offered to the detached and often amused inquiring essayist. In contrast, Berkeley's thought and literary manner are essentially oppositional. His editor, T. E. Jessop, remarks that "by instinct he thought polemically, in terms of objection and answer, projecting himself as his own opponent and bubbling with possible criticisms against his own case, yet all the time maintaining his singular serenity" (II,154). Berkeley needs his opponents as sustaining opposites for his radical simplicities. Without them, it can be argued, he risks lapsing into ordinary common sense or a potentially zany solipsism. Moreover, his intensely visual imagination and the special sort of seeing he urges require the abstract alternative worlds of mathematicians, materialists, and Deists. The sharp focus Berkeley wishes to achieve can appear only if his audience sees the fuzzy imaginings of these opponents or is encouraged to try to conceive their inconceivable entities. Leslie Stephen's paraphrase of Berkeley's purpose suggests that he achieved the desired literary effect: Stephen finds Berkeley out "to get rid of this gigantic corpse" called matter.[3]

Locke's tone implies a confident control of opposition; his philosophic project involves the dispersal or dismissal of any coherent alternative view. But Berkeley's assertiveness is to some extent a measure of his susceptibility to rival notions. The development and refinement of his thought take place within a series of sustained oppositions in which ideas emerge and are modified in the dynamic of debate. If Locke negates opposition, Berkeley's works present his opponents as both morally recurrent and historically threatening. They represent errors he is set against, but they also represent the various temptations philosophy as an activity is prone to, the moral dangers of philosophizing in general and at times the megalomania which is the risk of Berkeley's own thought. As we shall see, Berkeley eventually moves from exposition to philosophic dialogue as a means of self-protection, working out the misunderstandings his thought is liable to by placing many of them in the systems of his enemies. His philosophical program claims access to a moral, metaphysical, and theological totality, uncovers in effect a coherence in the universe otherwise unnoticed. Berkeley's opponents are a part of that totality; perennially skeptical and self-centered, they represent recurring possibilities given our fallen condition, and they are the human, all too human, inevitable opposition to the simple but strenuous features of the Berkeleian program for coming through to truth.

Locke's *Essay* is a complicating narrative full of blind alleys in which a negative sort of truth is forced on human inquiry, as uncertainty and arbitrariness are balanced by good-humored accommodation to our limitations. Berkeley's works are the heroic antithesis to that literary mode, claiming to restore a noble simplicity to the plot of philosophy, to depict truth and falsity engaged and struggling and to redefine human knowing as a sustaining operation. Perhaps pastoral is the most apt literary analogy for describing Berkeley's work, since he combines an idealized sense of human possibility with a satiric attack on the philosophers of matter and abstraction who deny the clarity of experience and block our direct and intimate participation in the natural world and, by extension, in the moral and political world. "America, or the Muse's Refuge," the poem he wrote before his disappointment there, is overtly pastoral, looking forward to those "happy Climes, the Seat of Innocence, / Where Nature guides and Virtue rules" (VII,373).

The alternative to his program is the reigning philosophical theory, what Berkeley calls a "forlorn scepticism" (II,25). If we adopt the position that we know only the "proportion or the relation" things bear to our senses, then the natural world is in danger of vanishing: "for aught we know, all we see, hear, and feel, may be only phantom and vain chimera, and not at all agree with the real things, existing in *rerum natura*" (II,78–79). Berkeley's mission is to rend the "veil of ideas," to drive out certain pernicious scientific and mathematical fictions which have been substituted for the discarded vital connection between men and the world. He defines his project as a cleansing of the entire field of human endeavor:

Matter being once expelled out of Nature, drags with it so many sceptical and impious notions, such an incredible number of disputes and
puzling questions, which have been thorns in the sides of divines as well
as philosophers, and made so much fruitless work for mankind; that if
the arguments we have produced against it, are not found equal to
demonstration (as to me they evidently seem) yet I am sure all friends to
knowledge, peace, and religion, have reason to wish they were. (II,82)

From these remarks in the *Principles of Human Knowledge* onward, Berkeley conceives his thought as the beginning of a program for unifying the worlds of learning, religion, and politics, and his career as a writer on various subjects is a sustained effort to accomplish that unification. Locke, we remember, makes a virtue out of modesty and failure. He defines his thought as mere clarification, a purging of old certainties that effectively allows matters to go on much as they were, severing speculative thought from practical life in such a way that management of self and society is in-dependent of the discoveries of the inquiring mind. Thus, his role in the *Essay* at least is hard to define; his modesty and qualified intellectual amateurism allow him to take a number of parts. Berkeley's work springs from motives that we regard as separate but that he tries to sustain at once in all his works, philosophical and nonphilosophical. The defender of common sense, the epistemologist-metaphysician, and the religious apologist are aspects of Berkeley's composite persona, even though one of these may dominate in a particular work.[4] His writing gains in force and persuasiveness, even if it loses logically, by using these roles and their rhe-torical resources to supplement one another. In the long run, Berkeley's project is to make these separate roles a single character, to treat them as inevitable, linked aspects of a unified view and style.

Berkeley's recastings of the characters and revisions of the plot of the philosophical story are often melodramatic, as the heroic scientists and mathematicians of a brave new intellectual order are transformed into villains. But his style, everyone agrees, is unfailingly lucid, no matter how lurid his polemics. Indeed, the conciseness of his utterance and the lean economy of his images are a counterbalance to his fervor, a distraction at times from the inconsistency and incompleteness of his arguments. In a sense, Berkeley's control as a writer, his management of image, theme, characterization, and philosophical scene, signals those contradictions and by its very smoothness invites a search for loose threads in the fabric of his thought. He is of great interest as a philosophical writer precisely because of his skill at interweaving his thought with persuasive literary form. His limpid and restrained style balances paradox and the outrages to commonsense notions in his system. As Hazlitt remarked, the "super-structure" of Berkeley's thought is "as light and elegant as possible," and "the most violent paradoxes and elaborate distinctions are rendered familiar by the simplicity of the style." Perceptively, Hazlitt speaks of an intensity in Berkeley's thought accompanied by a "careless freedom of manner as if he had never thought at all."[5] Whether we call it cool elegance or noble simplicity or plain speaking, Berkeley's literary manner stands in troubling and fascinating contrast to the difficulty or perhaps the contradictions of his philosophic position.

Berkeley faces most of those contradictions squarely in the notebooks or *Philosophical Commentaries*, where he seems to have worked out what he came to call "the Principle" or the "immaterial hypothesis" (I,10,#19). Some commentators tend to use the notebooks as a place to find contradiction; others, notably A. A. Luce, see them as a philosophic laboratory where Berkeley experimented with various notions and developed his mature doctrines. There, he sorted out intellectual influences, taking and refining ideas from Malebranche, coming to terms with Bayle and other skeptics, and settling himself in an adversary relationship with Locke and Descartes and especially with the mathematicians and scientists. Luce calls him a "perfect example of the 'inquisitive' man, all set to discover truth by consulting his own mind and looking into his own thoughts."[6] As intellectual autobiography, the notebooks are remarkable, although they do not seem as controlled as Luce says. J. O. Wisdom claims it is their "implied scepticism" that has made Berkeley an important thinker, and he offers another image of Berkeley as "a young philosophical dictator, confident, independent, scornful of mathematicians, sceptical of traditional philosophy, refreshing in the field of moral thought."[7]

Both these characterizations of the Berkeley of the *Commentaries* are true enough, since his jottings are as much a search for a style and a tone as for a philosophic position. To some extent, the search necessitates introspection and autobiography. For Berkeley is out to find a style that will do justice to his personality without compromising his thought: "Mem: to correct my Language & make it as Philosophically nice as possible to avoid giving handle" (I,27,#209). His fascinating autobiographical asides are often quoted: "Mem: that I was distrustful at 8 years old and Consequently by nature disposed for these new Doctrines" (I,33,#266). Another is a miniature self-portrait and scenario for future self-imagining:

I am young, I am an upstart, I am a pretender, I am vain, very well. I shall Endeavour patiently to bear up under the most lessening, vilifying appelations the pride & rage of man can devise. But one thing I know, I am not guilty of. I do not pin my faith on the sleeve of any great man. I act not out of prejudice & prepossession. I do not adhere to any opinion because it is an old one, a receiv'd one, a fashionable one, or one that I have spent much time in the study and cultivation of. (I,58,#465)

Such bravado is necessarily repressed in the published works, but the opposition sketched here between authority and unprejudiced experience is preserved. What Berkeley chiefly wants to modify for public presentation is his aggressive tone and contemptuous air. He was twenty-two or twenty-three when he made these notes, literally bursting with revolutionary notions and a self-confident scorn for his opponents. So, he resolves to be polite and not to call the mathematicians "Nihilarians." His next entry is a personal reminder: "N.B. to rein in y^r Satyrical nature" (I,77,#633–634). Some of his attempts at modesty, however, are still wonderfully haughty: "I wonder not at my sagacity in discovering the obvious tho' amazing truth, I rather wonder at my stupid inadvertency in not finding it out before" (I,34,#279).

In the second notebook Berkeley sketches the introduction to his written system, and among other plans he rehearses some traditional modesty tropes. He is a pigmy in relation to a giant like Locke, more successful because his task is narrower: "I am no more to be reckon'd stronger than a Gyant because he could throw of[f] the Molehill wch lay upon him, & the Gyant could only shake or shove the Mountain that oppresed him" (I,83,#678). A few entries later there is another "similitude" for the philosophers who have preceded him: "Adventurers who tho they them selves attained not the desir'd Port, they by their wrecks have made known the Rocks & sands whereby the Passage of aftercomers is made more secure & easy" (I,83,#682). He used neither of these bromides in his published work. Perhaps he found their self-satisfaction too obtrusive, perhaps such extended figures clashed with his plan, expressed earlier, to "abstain from all flourish & pomp of words & figures, using a great plainness & simplicity of stile" (I,37,#300).

Berkeley works in the *Commentaries* toward a manner that turns all that aggressive assertion into exploratory soliloquy and internal debate. His self-absorption and intellectual pride are sometimes used as materials for his epistemological project, and in the following entry he seems to address himself as much as an imagined opponent:

Consult, ransack y^r Understanding w^t find you there besides several perceptions or thoughts. W^t mean you by the word mind you must mean something that you perceive or y^t you do not perceive. a thing not perceived is a contradiction. to mean (also) a thing you do not perceive is a contradiction. We are in all this matter strangely abused by words. (I,72,#579)

"Ransack" violates the decorum of philosophical discourse, but the rest of the passage is echoed in Berkeley's published writings. He is working out a rigorously simple terminology based on a few key interrogations, stripped wherever possible of images or technical terms, and aimed to act as a sort of prod for thought rather than a depiction of thought or a representation of its operations. Here in the *Commentaries* he manages at times a cryptic intensity he did not care to try in his published works, but the ideal of a flashing, thought-provoking brevity is something Berkeley kept before himself when he wrote to be read. The pruning of self-serving aggressiveness and near-adolescent bravado is quite evident when we come to the published works. They represent, in the light of the exuberance of the *Commentaries*, a successful mature restraint in the service of a tactful literary strategy for presenting paradoxical doctrines.

As he wrote twenty years later, in 1729, to his American disciple Samuel Johnson, he "had no inclination to trouble the world with large volumes." His "small tracts," as he refers to them, were designed to give "hints to thinking men," to serve "the occasion of thinking." If such readers cooperate and go through the works "two or three times," then says Berkeley, all will be rendered "familiar and easy to the mind, and take off that shocking appearance which hath often been observed to attend speculative truths" (II,281–282). The reader Berkeley prepares to address must arm himself against "the Fallacy of Words" and "beware that I do not impose on him by plausible empty talk that common dangerous way of cheating men into absurditys." Berkeley never flatters his reader but challenges him, at times with a nearly contemptuous emphasis on the difficulties in store for him. The truth, he continues in this same entry, is not to be found in his book but in the reader's own mind : "w^{t}ever I see my self tis impossible I can paint it out in words" (I,85,#696).

In the published works a testy impatience with a slow reader is sometimes evident. In *A New Theory of Vision*, for example, Berkeley pauses after a demonstration of his notion that there are no ideas common to sight and touch: much more might be said, he offers, but "what has been said is, if I mistake not, sufficient to convince any one that shall yield a reasonable attention: And as for those that will not be at the pains of a little thought, no multiplication of words will ever suffice to make them understand the truth, or rightly conceive my meaning" (I,226).

Berkeley's ideal literary situation is thus an exceedingly lively one where the stability and integrity of the text are always in question, where both reader and author are openly critical of its finality and constantly vigilant against "Gibberish" and "Jargon" (I,85,#696). As he restates the case a bit later in a first draft of the *Principles of Human Knowledge*, the minute a notion is "cloathed with words" it may become "tedious and operose and hard to be conceiv'd, which yet being strip't of that garniture, the ideas shrink into a narrow compass, and are view'd almost by one glance of thought" (II,142). From these earliest sketches, Berkeley's theory of mind, in its upholding relationship with the world, is intimately related to his literary practice, for that involves suppressing language and its static formulations and promoting the questioning and reformulating activity of reader and writer. That active reader should be provoked by Berkeley's cryptic text; and this provocation begins the proving of Berkeley's system. The reading of an unsatisfactory text which is oblique, fragmented, and insufficient is part of a process leading to a unified vision, a "glance of thought."

Perhaps the best (or most extreme) example of that procedure in the *Commentaries* comes in a series of entries where the immaterialist doctrine is expounded in dialogue with an imagined interlocutor, who brings up problems like the existence of a chimera, the idea of infinity, and the question of continuity. The literary form of Berkeley's answers is aphoristic, logically unsound perhaps but linguistically complete in that the question provides its own answer. Do the books in the study exist now when we are not there? "Whenever they are mention'd or discours'd of they are imagin'd & thought on therefore you can at no time ask me whether they exist or not, but by reason of y^t very question they must necessarily exist" (I,59,#472). To the extent that you can frame a question

about a chimera, to that extent it "exists." Berkeley's wit in his developing strategy for presenting his thought lies in turning the inquiry toward
the reader's own mind, finding the answer in the interlocutor's objections
themselves: "In short be not angry you lose nothing. whether real or
chimerical w^{t}ever you can in any wise conceive or imagine be it ever so
wild or extravagant & absurd much good may it do you. you may enjoy it
for me. I'll not deprive you of it" (I,65,#518).

Such sarcasm drops out in the early published works, but the tactic of
turning the reader-interlocutor on his own thoughts is preserved. The
cryptic evocation of mental process provides its own answers, or proposes
that the reader examine the answers implicit in his own objections. "Ignorance," Berkeley remarks earlier in the *Commentaries*, is "in some sort
requisite in ye Person that should Discover the Principle" (I,35,#285).
That is to say, the objecting interlocutor represents a dramatic stage in
Berkeley's own development of his doctrine, and in a few entries he
records his own discoveries as he queries his own assertions and finds an
answer in the process: "To be sure or certain of w^t we do not actually
perceive (I say perceive not imagine) We must not be altogether Passive,
there must be a disposition to act, there must be assent, wch is active, nay
w^t do I talk There must be Actual Volition" (I,94,#777). As he makes
clear to himself in an earlier entry, Berkeley plans to be aggressive: "I
shall demonstrate all my Doctrines" (I,73,#586). For Locke, as Berkeley
notes here, "demonstration" could handle only abstract notions, and as
an enforcing philosophical term it belonged to the discredited lexicon of
traditional and Scholastic thought. Demonstration, for Locke, signifies an
impossible promise for philosophy to make or a self-enclosed achievement within the special boundaries of the old, merely verbal philosophical game. Berkeley declares that his "Introduction" will "set forth"
and insist on demonstration. What he has in mind is the self-examination
of writer and reader he hopes to set in motion. Demonstration begins in
cutting us loose from the text, shaping the work so that we pass directly
from it to our own thought or rebound off its hard surfaces into the vital,
airy medium of thought.

I think this view of Berkeley's literary-philosophic style explains in part
the ferocity of his attack on Shaftesbury. Of course, he objected
vehemently to Shaftesbury's moral and religious views and lumped him
with the infidels, freethinkers and Deists he called "minute philoso-
sophers." When he returned from America, Berkeley labeled Shaftesbury
"a loose and incoherent writer" (I,252).[8] And in the *Alciphron*, which he
brought back with him from Rhode Island, Berkeley went out of his way

to ridicule Shaftesbury's style, setting out as blank verse in the fifth
dialogue a passage from the first volume of the *Characteristics* (see
III,199). Alciphron, one of Berkeley's freethinkers, introduces it as a "noble specimen of fine writing." Jessop calls Shaftesbury's style "stiff, affected, tedious, and at times exasperating, successful in the effort to avoid
pedantry, but failing to reach the easy gentility aimed at" (III,11).
Euphranor, one of Berkeley's spokesmen in the dialogue, ridicules the
passage as "poetry," a "piece of tragedy" (III,200). Undaunted by
Euphranor's ironies, Alciphron defines Shaftesbury's aims by quoting the
Characteristics: "'by virtue of an intimate recess we may discover a certain
duplicity of soul, and divide our *self* into two parties,' or (as he varies the
phrase) 'practically form the dual number'" (III,200).

Shaftesbury's literary manner may have irritated Berkeley because it
suggested an affected and swollen version of his own procedure, a vulgar-
ization of Berkeley's rigorous self-examination and projection into
dialogue and debate. The Berkeleian program for rehabilitating the
authority of the perceiving self involves repression of an aggressive style
and a dramatized relocation of certitude in the reader and in the difficult
process leading from reading to thought. Shaftesbury imagines self-
knowledge as a smug Stoicism or serene Epicureanism:

Thus at last a mind, by knowing itself and its own proper powers and
virtues, becomes free and independent. It sees its hindrances and
obstructions, and finds they are wholly from itself, and from opinions
wrong conceived. The more it conquers in this respect (be it in the least
particular) the more it is its own master, feels its own natural liberty,
and congratulates with itself on its own advancement and prosperity.[9]

Mental life for Shaftesbury is self-observation transformed into self-
congratulation. His approach is ostentatiously leisurely, reveling in the
mind's freedom to range over the world from its privileged position. The
spectators in the *Characteristics* are aesthetes rather than Berkeley's
moralist-metaphysicians; their evocation of the mind's independence
leads away from body and toward a gushy neo-Platonism, a reversal of
Berkeleian muscular involvement in the actual and the physical. Berkeley's style marks his effort to preserve the continuous, nearly reciprocal
relationship between mind and things. Shaftesbury's style, in a passage
like the following one, dominates the physical world by treating it merely
as a source of images for the mind's self-inspection. Theocles seeks to persuade Philocles in *The Moralists* that beauty lies beyond its sensuous
forms:

For, taking rise from Nature's beauty, which transported me, I gladly ventured further in the chase, and have accompanied you in search of beauty, as it relates to us, and makes our highest good in its sincere and natural enjoyment. And if we have not idly spent our hours, nor ranged in vain through these deserted regions, it should appear from our strict search that there is nothing so divine as beauty, which belonging not to body, nor having any principle or existence except in mind and reason, is alone discovered and acquired by this diviner part, when it inspects itself, the only object worthy of itself. For whatever is void of mind, is void and darkness to the mind's eye. This languishes and grows dim whenever detained on foreign subjects, but thrives and attains its natural vigour when employed in contemplation of what is like itself. 'Tis thus the improving mind, slightly surveying other objects, and passing over bodies and the common forms (where only a shadow of beauty rests), ambitiously presses onward to its source, and views the original of form and order in that which is intelligent . . . he (he only) is the wise and able man, who with a slight regard to these things [the outward forms] applies himself to cultivate another soil, builds in a different matter from that of stone or marble; and having righter models in his eye, becomes in truth the architect of his own life and fortune, by laying within himself the lasting and sure foundations of order, peace, and concord.[10]

In his insistence on the conceit of vision rather than the facts of seeing, Shaftesbury is self-enclosed and self-indulgent. Prose like this is thought reduced to literary movement, variations of old philosophical-rhetorical commonplaces. Berkeley at his most vigorous wants to shake his reader out of the text; he strips it down (or tells us he is doing so) to a set of pointers at the particular, and his metaphors, as we shall see, are rooted in the literal realities of language and a vision that is related to the optical technicalities of actual "seeing." In this passage, Shaftesbury seeks to draw the reader away from the particular into a textual world where the problems surrounding self-definition become simply a matter of translation into an architectural metaphor (and an odd metaphor it is, passing from actual building materials to moral-psychological abstractions, asking us to imagine building without stone or marble). The normal procedure would ask us to picture "order, peace, and concord" as inner materials resembling stone and marble, but Shaftesbury's sequence reverses that. The physical world, in the prose as in the doctrines here, recedes in the face of a dominating literary manner, or rather, mannerisms. The problem for his "moralists," as Philocles puts it earlier, is "how to gain that point of sight whence probably we may best discern; and how to place ourselves in that unbiassed state in which we are fittest to pronounce."[11] Such an "unbiassed state" implies what Robert Uphaus calls "the impossible observer," who is the ideal reader for some neoclassical critics but is never, Uphaus argues, the actual reader in eighteenth-century writing.[12] Berkeley's thought is directly opposed to such an observer, for his revision of philosophical style depends upon an actively participating reader.

Berkeley's central philosophical statement, after all, is inseparable from his revision of the prevailing mode of imagining the perceptual world and his banishing of Uphaus' "impossible observer" from the epistemological scene: the knower sustains the known but without trivializing it as a mere representation. There is an enriching fullness and a sustaining dynamism in the epistemological transaction Berkeley describes rather than a thin and tenuous connection or an elegant or disdainful contemplation. In this regard, Shaftesbury is something of a philosophical vaporizer, more of a moral than a philosophical rival for Berkeley. Locke is always a more difficult implicit rival whose proposal for depicting the epistemological scene is persuasively complex. As Richard Rorty has put it, Locke tried to occupy a position somewhere between the Aristotelian notion that knowledge was an identity of the mind with the object known and newer conceptions of knowledge as a judgment about the accuracy of our representation of that object.[13] Such an ambiguity, as Rorty says, retained enough of Aristotelian identity to preserve an objective world but not enough to prevent skepticism. Locke's literary response to this uncertainty is a modesty that turns regularly into irony, questioning our representations in the name of an objective world that can never be accurately or fully represented but which is still out there in some sense. Berkeley enforces his position by canceling Locke's pervasive ironies about the relationship between us and the world. He insists our knowledge is more than a paltry representation or fading simulacrum; he seeks to transform the prevailing skeptical tone of philosophical discourse, the Cartesian method as translated into English philosophical style by Locke. Locke establishes irony as the condition of epistemological inquiry; Berkeley manages irony as a local affair, controlled and directed at his opponents to dramatize their inadequacies rather than ours.

To be sure, Berkeley's irony requires a certain forgetfulness of the reader. First, it is directed at abstraction in the name of an enlightened common experience of a psychological kind. Then Berkeley's system shifts and a similar corrective irony is turned on common experience itself, which is exposed as unaware of its own assumptions. That ultimate comic reversal is in the air as Berkeley begins his project indirectly in *A New Theory of Vision* by attacking geometrical falsifications of the actualities of sight. At first, all the irony is directed at theoretical optics from the vantage of an unencumbered and instinctive practice. But such practice is quickly revealed as bound by elaborate conventions and synthesizing artificialities.

Berkeley's position on the centrality of the perceiving self requires a confident, assertive voice, and that strong and clear speech enacts a personality who inevitably reinforces or supplements the argument. Berkeley's logic is surrounded and partly defined by this distinctive literary manner. In this passage from *A New Theory of Vision*, Berkeley's trust in the unimpeachable validity of our senses is enforced by a series of assertions in which a carefully recorded experience of the world is matched against the falsifying geometry of the scientists:

Nor do I see how I can easily be mistaken in this matter. I know evidently that distance is not perceived of it self. That by consequence it must be perceived by means of some other idea which is immediately perceived, and varies with the different degrees of distance. I know also that the sensation arising from the turn of the eyes is of it self immediately perceived, and various degrees thereof are connected with different distances, which never fail to accompany them into my mind, when I view an object distinctly with both eyes whose distance is so small that in respect of it the interval between the eyes has any conceivable magnitude. (I,174–175)

Following his thought, Locke's writing circles and eddies. Berkeley's drives forward, narrating a process, enumerating, evaluating, confident of its own strength, and drawing more strength from almost tautological self-affirmations: "And for me to make those judgments, and draw those conclusions from it, without knowing that I do so, seems altogether incomprehensible" (I,175). Like Berkeley's other works, *A New Theory of Vision* vehemently affirms the validity of actual human perception: "Every one is himself the best judge of what he perceives, and what not. In vain shall any man tell me that I perceive certain lines and angles which introduce into my mind the various ideas of distance, so long as I my self am conscious of no such thing" (I,173).

And yet, Berkeley's argument against the geometrical explanation of the operations of the eye depends upon a visual literalism by which, for example, the moon I see "is only a round luminous plain, about thirty visible points in diameter" (I,187). Were I to be carried toward the moon, I should in time see something entirely different. The eye is easily tricked, and proper seeing is eventually rendered by Berkeley as a rational, social act like reading. If visual language is upset by looking at objects in a concave mirror, the case resembles what would happen if a foreigner spoke English but used the words "in a direct contrary signification."

The Englishman would not fail to make a wrong judgment of the ideas annexed to those sounds in the mind of him that used them. Just so, in the present case the object speaks (if I may so say) with words that the eye is well acquainted with, that is, confusions of appearance; but whereas heretofore the greater confusions were always wont to signify nearer distances, they have in this case a direct, contrary signification, being connected with the greater distances. Whence it follows that the eye must unavoidably be mistaken, since it will take the confusions in the sense it has been used to, which is directly opposed to the true. (I,181–182)

Although the arguments about seeing in *A New Theory of Vision* are entirely derivative, passages like this one begin what might be called the consistent comedy of empirical perception peculiar to Berkeley.[14] His promotion of experience and of the vigorously argued certainties of ordinary sense perception leads to a rich confusion that can only be resolved in due course by something other than normal explanation. His clear-eyed persona eventually runs into a world of concave mirrors and altering perspectives and distorting angles, a multiplicity at variance with his strongly asserted unity. Visual language and its conventions for representing the world are as arbitrary as verbal language. Vision is, Berkeley proceeds to show, a construction of the mind whereby "tangible ideas" are conventionally connected with visual phenomena. Vision is an activity of mind, which operates rationally on materials provided by seeing and touching. Full human perception is a translation or recreation of the marks discerned by these partial senses: "in any act of vision the visible object absolutely, or in it self, is little taken notice of, the mind still carrying its view from that to some tangible ideas which have been observed to be connected with it, and by that means come to be suggested by it" (I,200).

A blind man suddenly given his sight would have to learn that his old tangible experience of two legs goes with his new visual experience of them:

So that in truth and strictness of speech I neither see distance itself, nor anything that I take to be at a distance. I say, neither distance nor things placed at a distance are themselves, or their ideas, truly perceived by sight. This I am persuaded of, as to what concerns my self: and I believe whoever will look narrowly into his own thoughts and examine what he means by saying he sees this or that thing at a distance, will agree with me that what he sees only suggests to his understanding that

after having passed a certain distance, to be measured by the motion of
his body, which is perceivable by touch, he shall come to perceive such
and such tangible ideas which have been usually connected with such
and such visible ideas. (I,188)

The forceful clarity of Berkeley's language undermines, for a time at least,
the very clarity and coherence of experience he promises to deliver. The
great source of Berkeley's paradoxes, Colin Turbayne points out, is his
habit of translating problems in vision (later in metaphysics) into "a problem of language." What is true in language, Turbayne says, "becomes,
when translated back into the language of nature, a shocking paradox."[15]

Now Berkeley chooses not to see the situation as a paradox but as a
parable, a highly traditional one echoing the argument from (or to)
design. "The proper objects of vision," he says near the end of *A New
Theory of Vision*, "constitute an universal language of the Author of
nature" whereby the world is revealed to us (I,231). A blind man, he continues, is amazed as he travels that his sighted guide can predict walls and
precipices. We should also find "cause of admiration" in the way the
visual world is organized: "The wonderful art and contrivance wherewith
it is adjusted to those ends and purposes for which it was apparently
designed . . . All these afford subject for much and pleasing speculation,
and may, if any thing, give us some glimmering, analogous praenotion of
things which are placed beyond the certain discovery and comprehension
of our present state" (I,231). This praise of the visual order has a problematic edge, since we are to the author of this language as the blind man
is to us. We are still merely slow readers of the visual language and not its
authors, and like all such readers we decipher those visual signs in an incomplete fashion, bowled over by the surface complexity of it all, marvel-
ing at the closely printed pages.

These were more than rhetorical tricks for Berkeley, and the visual
world was for him a source of delight and an opportunity for religious
apologetics. The single most salient feature of his sensibility as expressed
in all his writing, public and private, is an intense attraction to the spectacle of the physical world. The schoolboy who explored the cave of Dun-
more described it vividly seven years or so later: "tho' the intervall of time
may have rendered my ideas of severall particulars I there saw dim & imperfect, yet the dismall solitude, the fearfull darkness & vast silence of
that stupendous cavern have left lasting impressions in my memory"
(IV,260).[16] This same curiosity about the natural sublime led Berkeley to
fearless inspections of an eruption of Vesuvius when he was touring Italy
in 1717. He sent his friend, Dr. Arbuthnot, a letter describing his obser-

vations, the high point of which is the rendering of a river of lava. Upon hearing a terrible rumbling from the volcano, "a mixed sound made up of the raging of a tempest, the murmur of a troubled sea, and the roaring of thunder and artillery," Berkeley is moved by curiosity to approach the mountain.

I observed a mixture of colours in the cloud over the crater, green, yellow, red, and blue; there was likewise a ruddy dismal light in the air over that tract of land where the burning river flowed; ashes continually showered on us all the way from the sea-coast: all which circumstances, set off and augmented by the horror and silence of the night, made a scene the most uncommon and astonishing I ever saw; which grew still more extraordinary as we came nearer the stream. Imagine a vast torrent of liquid fire rolling from the top down the side of the mountain, and with irresistible fury bearing down and consuming vines, olives, fig-trees, houses, in a word, every thing that stood in its way. (IV,249)

These short reports of natural phenomena combine sharp, detailed observation with a care not to exceed the literal facts perceived. Berkeley does not repress his emotions in the face of this terrifying spectacle but he does defer to its power, trying to let the scene speak for itself and providing his reader with visual and aural materials. Of course, Berkeley's imagination plays a part in this evocation, and what he really does is to issue rather precise instructions for imagining the *son et lumière* of the eruption. His mind is visual but his instincts are rhetorical, drawn to pictorial arrangements that charm and compel and suggest meaning.

When during this same year he writes to Percival from Naples, his evocation of climate and landscape is a *locus amoenus*: "The air of this happy part of the world is soft and delightful beyond conception, being perfumed with myrtle shrubs and orange groves, that are everywhere scattered throughout the country; the sky almost constantly serene and blue; the heat tempered to a just warmth by refreshing breezes from the sea" (VIII,103).[17] Berkeley's Italian journal is full of similar touristic commonplaces, but the letter shows his talent for arrangement and persuasion. Italy is rendered as a coherent message whose physical features speak to our needs and entertain by their variety. Passing from nature to art in Italy, Berkeley displays a connoisseur's eye for the effects of paintings, statues, and architecture. He shows a special appreciation for visual rhetoric and an understanding of position and perspective as enriching visual complexities: "The eye is never weary with viewing the Pantheon. Both the rotunda itself and the vestibule discover new beauties ever time we survey them . . . The Church of S: Ignatius is richly painted. The ceiling is raised by the perspective of Padre Pozzo, and a cupola is so represented by the same hand in perspective that it wonderfully deceives the eye as one walks towards it from the door along the great Isle" (VII,252).

As *A New Theory of Vision* makes clear, Berkeley found a similar visual variety and rhetorical trickiness in the natural world, where the wonderful sublimity of extraordinary phenomena like the eruption of Vesuvius is matched in complexity by the normal sights the eye encounters, which are rendered by a synesthetic combination resembling Berkeley's evocation of the sights and sounds of the eruption. In fact, years later when he defended his theory of vision in *A Theory of Vision Vindicated* (1733), Berkeley made the artist an arbiter for perceptual paradoxes. In order to convince us that our judgments of size or distance "do not depend absolutely on the apparent magnitude," we "need only ask the first painter we meet, who, considering nature rather than geometry, well knows that several other circumstances contribute thereto" (I,273). Art, he continues, "can only deceive us as it imitates nature," and its "perspectives and landscapes" are a self-conscious version of normal, everyday procedure.

In his moral-theological meditations, Berkeley's language is characteristically drawn to evocations that emphasize both the grandeur of the visible world and its elusiveness for our limited if occasionally exalted faculties. When he writes to dissuade his friend Sir John James from Roman Catholicism, his images pass gracefully from Plato's cave to Paul's dark mirror: "We are like men in a cave in this present life seeing by a dim light through such chinks as the divine goodness hath open'd to us. We dare not talk in the high unerring positive style of the Romanists. We confess that we see through a glass darkly: and rejoice that we see enough to determine our practice and excite our hopes" (VII,147). The last clause is crucial. The traditional visual images of limitation serve a rhetoric of vision, whereby the visual expands with exercise and practice, by continued and informed looking. Berkeley's imagination, as it appears here and there in his miscellaneous writings and as it is elaborated in his thought, tries to enlarge the visual realm by focusing clearly on the available particulars as they are handled by the artful techniques of seeing, by looking closely and staring intently, making an advantage out of our myopia.

Berkeley thus brings a special pertinence to commonplace religious imagery, as in this passage from his sermon "On Eternal Life": "But the Christian religion enlargeth our view and extends our prospect. It raiseth our hopes from sensible things to things spiritual, from this life to that which is to come, from earth to heaven. That light which in its original was glimmering and obscure still shineth forth more and more unto perfect day" (VII,113). The carnal man, he says in another sermon, leads a "life of blindness and misrule," and for him "the image of God is blurred and defaced" (VII,88–89). In the epistemology and metaphysics, such resonant formulations of the ascent from seeing and understanding to "vision" arrive more gradually than in sermons. Berkeley has to deal in his philosophy with the opacity and potential abstraction of verbal language to describe the difficult synesthesia of visual language. He has, that is, to examine in precise detail the process of representation he can render so eloquently in his theological formulations. His various works on vision distinguish with great care between the phenomena available to the eye and what he calls the "images" projected on the retina, which are essentially imaginative reconstructions of the phenomena. Moreover, "throughout this whole affair the mind is wonderfully apt to be deluded by the suddain suggestions of fancy, which it confounds with the perceptions of sense, and is prone to mistake a close and habitual connexion between the most distinct and different things for an identity of nature" (I,269).

The verbal language Turbayne identifies as the stable vehicle of Berkeley's master metaphor has a turbulent uncertainty of its own, and Berkeley's literary facility collides with his own deep sense of the unreliability of language. After all, one can say anything, but experience seems to be limited. Berkeley frequently bases his arguments on the deluding adaptability of language and the difference between thought and speech. Thus, in 1735 he responded to James Jurin's attack on his attack on the freethinking implications of mathematics, the *Analyst*.[18] In *A Defense of Free-Thinking in Mathematics*, he replies to Jurin's accusation that he misunderstood Locke. In so doing, he sketches his suspicion of discourse and separates words from "ideas":

I entreat my reader to think. For if he doth not, he may be under some influence from your confident and positive way of talking. But any one who thinks may, if I mistake not, plainly perceive that you are deluded, as it often happens, by mistaking the terms for ideas. Nothing is easier than to define in terms or words that which is incomprehensible in idea; forasmuch as any words can be either separated or joined as you please, but ideas always cannot. It is as easy to say a round square as an oblong square, though the former be inconceivable. If the reader will but take a little care to distinguish between words or expressions and the conceptions of the mind, he will judge of the truth of what I now advance . . . Or, if the reader is minded to make a short work, he needs only at once to try whether, laying aside the words, he can frame in his mind the idea of an impossible triangle; upon which trial the issue of this dispute may be fairly put. This doctrine of abstract general ideas seemed to me a capital errour, productive of numberless difficulties and disputes, that runs not only throughout Mr. Locke's book, but through most parts of learning. (IV,135–136).

From his earliest writings, Berkeley issued similar challenges to his readers, entreating them to lay aside verbiage and attend, somehow, to their thoughts. Jurin's language, he warns us, is "confident and positive" — rather like his own, he fails to add. Berkeley's view of language, it needs to be said, includes a healthy respect for its power and for its dangerous adaptability. In a well-known passage in the *Principles of Human Knowledge*, he noted that language often enacts rather than represents, serving other ends than "the communicating of ideas marked by words." Language is thus for him capable of acting as an instrument for "the raising of some passion, the exciting to, or deterring from an action, the putting the mind in some particular disposition" (II,37). George Pitcher goes so far as to find Berkeley's position here an anticipation of what he calls the "instrumentalist view" of language, later developed and explored by Wittgenstein.[19] Luce notes that Berkeley moved in this position past the Lockean assumption that "all words stand for ideas" and that "all knowledge is about ideas" (IV,234). Words may represent ideas, of course, but they may also act rhetorically, enacting emotions or promoting motives that have no definite existence the way ideas or sensations do. Finally, words may indicate (they can hardly represent) notions like "spirit" or God.

  This rich and flexible theory is manifest in Berkeley's writing and in the crucial turns of his argument. Only someone as rhetorically skilled as Berkeley could extend the truisms of rhetoric into a theory of language. But his polemic against abstract ideas, like that against geometrical accounts of vision, is grounded in a severe psychological literalism, tightly restricting us to particular entities the mind can actually frame or conceive. Language can enact or express emotions, but the mind's operations and perceptions are restricted to representations of a limiting actuality. We can, he argues frequently, picture for ourselves only particular men or individual triangles. Those concrete entities will never resolve themselves into a universal but will retain a sharply defined particularity anchored in determinate characteristics.[20] At the same time, language is free to say anything, to claim otherwise, to utter nonsense and contradiction, and to move and persuade in spite of illogic. The recurring opposition between language and thought leads most of the time to a disparagement of the former, even to a denial of its power. "We know many things which we want words to express," Berkeley observes in his notebooks (I,29,#223). He evokes this concrete if unutterable particularity and satirizes the generalizing ambitions of philosophers, scientists, and mathematicians who substitute language for thought. Paradoxically, the brilliant fluency and facility of Berkeley's writing are enlisted in the service of this disparagement, and he defines his writing as a failure, an enactment of its own incompleteness. In the *Principles of Human Knowledge*, for example, he admits that common speech is inaccurate but necessary. Ordinary usage and philosophical truth, however, are incompatible. It is "impossible, even in the most rigid philosophical reasonings, so far to alter the bent and genius of the tongue we speak, as never to give a handle for cavillers to pretend difficulties and inconsistencies." The burden is on the "fair and ingenuous reader" who is able to operate rhetorically, in a negative sense, and "collect the sense, from the scope and tenor and connexion of a discourse, making allowances for those inaccurate modes of speech, which use has made inevitable" (II,63).

Berkeley's upholding of thought and of the intense particularity of mental experience not only is effected necessarily by verbal means but is, ultimately in his system, founded on a view of thought and perception that is fundamentally linguistic in its operations and that seems to disperse in time the very solidity of the world he begins with. As Turbayne explains it, the theory of reality initially presented in the *Principles of Human Knowledge* and repeated more vividly in *Siris* makes perception into a reading of phenomenal signs. Reality is a series of signs whose *esse* is *percipi*.[21] To consider my thoughts and to contemplate my short or tall individual men, equilateral or scalene triangles is to "read" them, that is, to grant them coherence and place them in a context provided by habit and convention. Or, when the mind looks out at the world of sense objects, it finds connection and meaning by a process Berkeley describes as a reading. The link between natural phenomena as I perceive it is not one of cause and effect "but only of a mark or *sign* with the thing *signified*. The fire which I see is not the cause of the pain I suffer upon approaching it, but the mark that forewarns me of it" (II,69).

Misperception and philosophical error are consistently dramatized by Berkeley as "misreading," in which the reader forgets the conventionality of the system and mistakes sign and signifier for the signified. Euphranor explains to Alciphron in the fourth dialogue that men are so immersed in the signs of visual language they think they see the signified rather than the visual signifiers, which strictly speaking are what they see. Just so, in reading

> we run over the characters with the slightest regard, and pass on to the meaning. Hence it is frequent for men to say, they see words, and notions, and things in reading of a book; whereas in strictness they see only the characters which suggest words, notions, and things. And, by parity of reason, may we not suppose that men, not resting in, but overlooking the immediate and proper objects of sight, as in their own nature of small moment, carry their attention onward to the very thing signifed, and talk as if they saw the secondary objects? which, in truth and strictness, are not seen, but only suggested and apprehended by means of the proper objects of sight, which alone are seen. (III,156)

Light, shade, color, and the rest of what Berkeley calls the proper objects of sight are a set of letters spelling out a language. Like so many of his assertions, Berkeley's insistence is both liberating and limiting, for in saving the appearances he risks a confused and dizzying phenomenal world where the objects of sight are a sort of alphabet soup of perceptual language. The mind is a magically constituted reader of these signs, for its reconstruction and recombination of them seems gratuitously external. Berkeley tends, however, to depict a less imperious self, whose very existence seems inseparable from the process of deciphering those signs.

God, of course, is behind that language, the author of the speaking script of natural process.[22] To pass from ideas and experiences to "notions" like God and spirit is to imagine and interpret, to admit new words into the lexicon and to "read" in another and higher sense, in fact to pass from reading to speaking or narrating. There is, therefore, a contradiction at the heart of Berkeley's thought that lends a special, specifically literary ambiguity to his writing. What contemporary literary critics call "difference" is pervasive in it. He makes his reader aware, philosophically self-conscious, that his text is merely and fragilely textual, incomplete and insufficient, potentially misleading in its solidification of process. The philosophic moment is defined by a moral-epistemological self-consciousness which is linguistic in focus. In *A New Theory of Vision*, for example, Berkeley describes the difficult interweaving of the primary objects of sight and the secondary objects suggested by them "most closely twisted, blended, and incorporated together" (I,190). An inattentive, naive use of the visual language makes the primary objects (light, color, shade) into the secondary objects or things of the world; it mistakes words and letters for things, omits the process whereby things are constructed out of perceptions. "And the prejudice is confirmed and riveted in our thoughts by a long tract of time, by the use of language and want of reflexion," Berkeley continues. Language is not only an analogy for seeing, it contributes further to the distortion of the world by repeating the forgetfulness of naive seeing. To use language is to be affected by its falsifications, to continue and reinforce the delusions of ordinary, unselfconscious seeing. Berkeley's emphasis falls not on the identity between seeing and reading but rather on the pressing need for staying alert dramatized by the weakness of language. Our suspicious attitude to language should be pulled back, Berkeley suggests here and elsewhere, to include our examination of everything else in the world. The value of the analogy from language seems primarily negative, a warning rather than an illumination.

In similar fashion, Berkeley's highly metaphorical discourse is built upon a disavowal of metaphor. As Colin Turbayne points out, Berkeley "was largely able to extricate his thinking from the physical connotations of 'in the mind'—his favorite metaphor."[23] One can note other, related difficulties. Berkeley's powerful handling of language and his suspicion of its falseness are parallel to the relationship between his strong sense of the physical and material world and his "immaterialism," whereby that world is sustained by thinking spirits in the "*esse is percipi*" formula. Just so, his denial of abstractions as signs unable to signify is placed within a dramatization of mental experience in which the objects of perception are made to signify by a percipient. Without that activity, those objects are as irrelevant and nonexistent as round squares or absolute space. Signifying only seems to be a matter of corresponding to an external world. That is a bankrupt representationalism Berkeley rejects, since it leads to Lockean turbulence and skepticism. As Harry Bracken summarizes the situation, Berkeley first affirms common sense by saying that things are simply as we perceive them; but then his "phenomenalism" forces him "to say that things are not *really* what they *appear* to common sense to be."[24] Now you see it, now you don't.

Berkeley's writing seeks to waver, like his thought, among affirmations and assertions and retreats, negations, self-canceling and complicating movements. The strong voice informing his writing reconstitutes a neglected phenomenal world but then defers to a process that dissolves it again. The process is then, in effect, repeated, as a new way of reading the phenomena is invented and a new, more powerful reader (the Berkeleian mind) is introduced, a mind that has to manage the difficult trick of sustaining the world and deferring to it at the same time.

Berkeley clearly recognized the need to trim his prose of its exuberance and to modify its tendency to the sensuous and potentially misleading particular. The first paragraph of the introduction to the *Principles of Human Knowledge*, for example, was originally much shorter, cryptic and intense in its rendering of error. The published paragraph is a comic narrative in which Berkeley compares the serenity of "the illiterate bulk of mankind that walk the high-road of plain, common sense" with the perplexity of philosophers, among whom Berkeley includes himself: "we are insensibly drawn into uncouth paradoxes, difficulties, and inconsistencies" (II,25). The manuscript of the first draft is an aphoristic rejection of philosophy as it has been practiced, and Berkeley speaks as its contemptuous opponent: "There is nothing these men can touch with their hands or behold with their eyes but has its dark sides. Something they imagine in every drop of water, every grain of sand which can puzzle & confound the most clear & elevated understanding" (II,121). Berkeley removed the drop of water and the grain of sand, and also the fine concentration of the image whereby philosophers are confronted by "dark sides" that recede from their light.

Through these contortions in his thought, Berkeley is a sort of philosophical lyric poet who is forced to restrain his powers, to curb his talent for rendering the world because he realizes (or rather his thought is out to make us realize) that such a world can easily be multiplied and extended illegitimately by cleverness or intensity like his. "Lengths abstract from breadths are the work of the mind, such do intersect in a point at all angles, after the same way colour is abstract from extension. every position alters the line" (I,15,#85). Observations like this are recurrent in the *Philosophical Commentaries*. "Why may we not conceive it possible for God to create things out of Nothing. certainly we our selves create in some wise whenever we imagine" (I,99,#830). Did Berkeley in his published works have to find a way to curb this imagination of the mind's incessant and potentially disruptive processing? Perhaps his visionary apologetics, in mid-career, is a way of reducing the buzz of perception by individuals to the stately and regular "imaginings" of God. First he had to find a way to represent the mind, itself the source of all representation, to write about the mind's operations without introducing a falsifying, self-certifying imagination.

Berkeley asserts in the *Commentaries* that "speech [is] metaphorical more than we imagine" and quickly goes on to see that neglect of this quality of speech has led to the "grand Mistake" whereby "we think we have Ideas of the Operations of our Minds" (I,24,#176,176a). Turbayne finds that Berkeley successfully emancipated himself from metaphors for mind, or always reminded himself that "in the mind" was a spatial metaphor.[25] Part I of the *Principles of Human Knowledge* opens by separating *"mind, spirit, soul,* or *my self"* from any of our ideas. It is "a thing entirely distinct from them, wherein they exist, or, which is the same thing, whereby they are perceived; for the existence of an idea consists in being perceived" (II,42). The mind for Berkeley, as I. C. Tipton puts it, "is something we know in and through its activities."[26] Turbayne suggests that Berkeley's view of mind is entirely phenomenalistic, the mind being actually a congeries of perceptions and volitions. Now, as Pitcher points out, that is a "secret" theory of mind, one that Berkeley publicly contradicts when he declares "mind is an unextended, active substance."[27]

On the one hand, Berkeley's writing is a series of insights, affirmations in which the specific particularity of perception is enacted and the sharply literalized facts of the process of understanding are rendered. But, on the other hand, mind itself for Berkeley is experienced as a continuity, something beyond or above or in some sense apart from the moments of perception it narrates. Berkeley wants it both ways, as Tipton remarks, and encourages us to think there is a *"rerum natura"* and that this objective order is dependent on our minds for its existence.[28]

Various commentators, notably A. A. Luce, have resolved this problem in Berkeley's thought by describing his method as dynamic and dramatic. For Luce, the *esse* Berkeley speaks of is not "essence" but rather an active principle *found* in the object by the mind rather than *made* by the mind. Luce says Berkeley took what Locke considered a "simple idea" and complicated it by denying that "to exist" and "to be" are equivalent. That is, Berkeley extends the narrative dimension of Locke's thought. Berkeley's "distinctive discovery," as Luce puts it, is that "the predicate *exist* by its very import and meaning brings all reality within the range and orbit of mind, perceiving or imaging or conceiving."[29] Locke's account of the mind performing those activities is, essentially, ironic. The various images and concretions that evoke or even attempt to represent mind are transparently inadequate but inevitable, given the nature of the understanding and its social, moral, and political needs. Locke wants us to "see," but his seeing is loose and inexactly analogical. Seeing, actual vision in the *Essay*, is radically insufficient and its use as a metaphor for knowledge is deeply compromised. Where Locke dramatizes the discovery of that irony and suggests moral adjustments, Berkeley begins with an elaboration of the mind's connections with the world in which visual and physical contiguity and adjacency are affirmed and then gradually transformed into deeper and more difficult relationships, first epistemological then metaphysical and theological.

In Berkeley's elaboration of its progress, mind changes its relationship to the world from extrinsic to intrinsic, learning in effect to imitate the divine mind, which maintains the forms of nature intimately and continuously. Berkeley's "mind" is a self-conscious narrator, potentially aware of the reflexive and self-supporting nature of narrative but also on the lookout for stabilizing anchors in an external world. Such an anchor is provided by God's original narrative, a story preceding all of ours. The theology behind Berkeley's epistemological sequence allows him to define our minds as entities that exist in order to experience a world that was made to be experienced and is unthinkable without being experienced.[30]

Given that theological underpinning, Berkeley may be said to replace Locke's supervising irony with a radical metonymic account of the world, turning our oblique relationship with it to a real contiguity. But then, to continue the analogy, metonymy turns to synecdoche as the mind discovers its implication in the process it describes.[31] Locke narrates the history of the mind, and his images for the understanding are concessions to our need for substance and static identity (although the images try to do justice to process and are suspended in the supervising irony of the *Essay*). Berkeley radicalizes the narrating process, literalizing in his thoroughgoing way the materials and surroundings of perception. Eventually, he claims to break through to mind itself as a substance whose identity *is* process. The insight that the *esse* of things is *percipi* leads by dint of repetition to the next step, that the *esse* of the mind is *percipere*. And there is a final step, from things and ideas to minds to "notions" about the configuration of these events. As Ian Ramsay puts it, Berkeley worked through "ideas" to "notions," since "an adequate empiricism" has to see that the situation of thought is not just ideas or ideas and minds but "personal activity terminating in ideas, activity about ideas."[32]

I think we have to pay attention to Berkeley's careful restriction of his terms. The expansion and validation of connection he seeks in his thought are paradoxically accompanied by a suppression of the false continuities and deceptive fullness of Locke's style and thought. Berkeley presents his writing as a reluctant verbalization of thought, a warning of its impoverishment by language. If we consider the history of the composition of his first major work, the *Principles of Human Knowledge*, and the format of later works like *Siris* and *The Querist*, there is justice in that characterization. The *Philosophical Commentaries* is a series of intense jottings, cryptic notes toward the *Principles*. And that work, as we know from an extant "first draft" reconstructed by modern editors, was written a paragraph or two a day. As a young man, anyway, Berkeley wrote in bursts, and this early writing approximates in its expression the form and experience he claimed for his thought, a series of insights, formulations that chart the literal, hesitating movements of mind. Locke's *Essay*, in contrast, is a sequence that grows and lengthens, developing and moving in quite another way. The *Essay* is a full and entirely adequate report of the circumstances of thought that, in effect, diminishes thought, places it in an enormous context. Berkeley's writing tries to give quite another impression; it is the bare recording of rational moments too pure and clear for mere language.

Locke multiplies terms and images, preferring terminological looseness ("I am not nice about Phrases," he says at one point; II.xxi.71) to pedantic exactness. Berkeley is as critical of outmoded and mystified philosophical jargon as Locke is, but he resists looseness and seeks to devise a set of terms exact enough to serve the rigorous literalism upon which his philosophical sequence depends. Luce notes that he deliberately dropped "person" as a philosophical term, partly, he tells us in the notebooks, out of prudence and to avoid giving offense. But "person" is not only a Trinitarian term, it is too superficially "unitary" and self-contained for Berkeley's mature thought. The term "mind," says Luce, maintains a distance whereby the object perceived "is in the mind, but not of the mind; it is for the mind, but not mental."[33] In Berkeley's evocations of the mind at work, the distance Luce speaks of is defined by being traversed. Locke's images lie, as it were, forever next to the inscrutable reality beyond our epistemological processes, hopelessly compromised but pedagogically useful. Overtly rhetorical in their extensions and elaborations, they prove the philosopher's comfortable relationship to common life and his disdain for technical language. Berkeley makes a point of rejecting vulgar images; even as easy illustrations from common life they are corrupting, obscuring representations. "For example, the will is termed the *motion* of the soul: this infuses a belief, that the mind of man is as a ball in motion, impelled and determined by the objects of sense, as necessarily as that is by the stroke of a racket" (II,107).

Berkeley seems to aspire to a kind of representation of the mind such as Michel Foucault attributes to the "Classical age," whereby "representations are not rooted in a world that gives them meaning; they open of themselves on to a space that is their own, whose internal network gives rise to meaning."[34] Berkeley says as much in the *Principles of Human Knowledge* when he complains that speaking of the nature and the operations of the mind "in terms borrowed from sensible ideas" has led to confusion (II,107). He advises retreat from such ideas and urges philoso-

phers "to retire into themselves, and attentively consider their own meaning" (II,107). What consistently matters for Berkeley, even if it is casually
expressed here, is movement through terminology, a contemplation in
which thought of a pure and intensely self-focused kind replaces reading,
with its analogies and clumsy equivalences; in which apprehension of a
perceptual whole replaces the slow constructing process of making out the
world.

There are really only two images in Berkeley's writing — language and
vision — and they quickly resolve themselves into one, since vision operates by analogy with language. Seeing and reading are activities, as Berkeley is obsessively concerned to show, that describe all action. They are
at once literalizing movements, as Berkeley renders them, but they aspire
to be creative, transcending activities which transform the signs we operate on. The governing metaphor of reading is literalized in the perceptual
process itself; the phenomena lie next to one another and seem to be
contiguous to the mind. But in reading those phenomena, the mind
enters into a relationship with them that is more than mere adjacency,
since the mind's location is an unresolved issue. Synecdoche must in some
sense take over from metonymy, since neither mind nor its objects can be
imagined separately. The original image whereby reality is a language we
read shifts, and reality becomes the language the mind speaks. Berkeley
not only narrows and refines the terms proper to epistemological description, he restricts the act of knowing to a particular process which
claims to be authentically literal but is in fact ambiguously metaphorical.
Grounded as reading is in the literal reality of signs and signifiers, it is also
always a matter of the construction or imagination of that same reality.

Texts are made to be read but would cease to exist as texts if literacy
were eradicated. Although Berkeley does not use our term, his world is a
text. His constant recourse to this basic and single image for epistemological process is the unifying balance to the intense particularity he
insists on, what rescues mind in effect if not in logic from the "intermit-
tency" problem and from the dilemma inherent in representing the mind
as a unified substance and narrating its constitutive and multiple operations. Berkeley's work redefines reading, restaging it so that it can overcome the gaps between text and reader and between language and
reality, so that the process ceases to be a reading and becomes a total
apprehension, an active speaking rather than a passive reading.

In his notebooks Berkeley states the case in extreme fashion: "Certainly
the mind always & constantly thinks & we know this too In Sleep & trances
the mind exists not there is no time no succession of Ideas" (I,79,#651). In

the published works he is more concerned to show that mental life is effectively continuous, that as we experience it time is nothing less than the succession of our ideas. Thus, in the *Principles of Human Knowledge* he says, "Time therefore being nothing, abstracted from the succession of ideas in our minds, it follows that the duration of any finite spirit must be estimated by the number of ideas or actions succeeding each other in that same spirit or mind. Hence it is a plain consequence that the soul always thinks" (II,83).[35] Berkeley explained to Johnson some years later that his conception of time led him to paradoxical (if not heterodox) opinions that he did not publish, "particularly the notion that the Resurrection follows the next moment to death" (II,293). These assertions come out of an imagination drawn by its vivacity to absurd implications and to arguments that operate by framing alternative narratives to illustrate impossibility. If time is not the succession of our ideas, then what is it? How can it be narrated? What other stories does that proposition entail?

Whenever I attempt to frame a simple idea of *time*, abstracted from the succession of ideas in my mind, which flows uniformly, and is participated by all beings, I am lost and embrangled in inextricable difficulties. I have no notion of it at all, only I hear others say, it is infinitely divisible, and speak of it in such a manner as leads me to entertain odd thoughts of my existence: since that doctrine lays one under an absolute necessity of thinking either that he passes away innumerable ages without a thought, or else that he is annihilated every moment of his life: both which seem equally absurd. (II,83)

This same inability to imagine or to narrate the implications of an opposing position or an alternative explanation for the undeniable facts of perception is what Berkeley offers in the *Principles* as a refutation of abstraction. Or better, he mimics the futile attempt of such an explanation to narrate or to conceive a clear idea:

Moreover, there being a great variety of other creatures that partake in some parts, but not all, of the complex idea of *man*, the mind leaving out those parts which are peculiar to men, and retaining those only which are common to all the living creatures, frameth the idea of *animal*, which abstracts not only from all particular men, but also all birds, beasts, fishes, and insects. The constituent parts of the abstract idea of animal are body, life, sense and spontaneous motion. By *body* is meant, body without any particular shape or figure, there being no one shape or figure common to all animals, without covering, either of hair or feathers, or scales, &c. nor yet naked: hair, feathers, scales, and nakedness being the distinguishing properties of particular animals, and for that reason left out of the *abstract idea*. Upon the same account the spontaneous motion must be neither walking, nor flying, nor creeping, it is nevertheless a motion, but what that motion is, it is not easy to conceive. (II,29)

Berkeley repeats that argument against abstract ideas many times in his work, taking delight as he does here in his mastery of the narrated particulars of the world and ironic satisfaction in the emptiness of abstraction. The insistence on time as nothing other than an experienced continuum is far less easy to justify, and he drops it after the *Principles*. Both these arguments appeal to narrative possibility as a logical proof; they challenge opponents to depict or narrate. The "reader" of the world in *A New Theory of Vision* makes way in the *Principles* for a narrator of experience who now appeals to common life and normal perception as coherent ways of representing the world. "Time, place, and motion, taken in particular or concrete, are what every body knows; but having passed through the hands of a metaphysician, they become too abstract and fine, to be apprehended by men of ordinary sense" (II,83).

Luce points out that *A New Theory of Vision* was a deliberately transitional work for Berkeley, a preparation for the radical doctrine of the *Principles* (I,56). As we have seen, his stress in the earlier work is on the defectiveness and limitation of the visual faculty. "Our sight is defective in that its view is not only narrow, but also for the most part confused: of those things that we take in at one prospect we can see but a few at once clearly and unconfusedly: and the more we fix our sight on any one object, by so much the darker and more indistinct shall the rest appear" (I,205). The other defect Berkeley speaks of here is our inability to see more than a limited number of visible points, so that whether I am in my study or outside it gazing at a prospect of "the circumjacent fields, mountains, sea, and open firmament," I see the same number of *minima visibilia* (I,205).

A recurring comic moment in Berkeley's exposition arrives when a theoretician is bewildered by an attentive observer of the actual and concrete; the magnificent panorama shrinks to the visual equivalent of the wall of my study. Donald Davie says very well that Berkeley's "idealism" is really a thoroughgoing empiricism, restricting reality to that which is perceived, in the most rigorous and exact sense possible.[36] The real comic twist in Berkeley's thought, however, is a matter of taking that empiricism and making it serve his immaterialism. Human knowing in the *Principles* comes to satisfy the "perfections" of sight he identified in *A New Theory of Vision* as corresponding to its defects: "1st, that of comprehending in one view a greater number of visible points [i.e. greater than those sight is restricted to]. 2ndly, of being able to view them all equally and at once with the utmost clearness and distinction" (I,205). Our view of the phenomena of the world is necessarily partial and depends upon position and perspective. Our understanding of the world is potentially, if rightly conceived, total and entirely coherent. We see oars bent in water, straight out of it; the moon and other objects grow and diminish as we approach or retreat; but we master that variety when we realize that our perception sustains it and that our seamlessly woven perceptions make such variety a coherent unity. Understanding seems at first to work by analogy with seeing and reading, but Berkeley's development of those analogies modifies and then negates them.

In a very simple sense, what Berkeley works toward in the *Principles* is the reassertion of a powerful self who acquires unity by traveling through and thereby negating the partiality and intense particularity of experience. The *Principles* draws to an end by proposing that the previous activity described in the treatise has proved the existence of an "I" who is not an idea nor like an idea "but that which perceives ideas, and wills, and reasons about them" (II,104). This entity mediates between static abstractions and unstable, radically shifting particulars. "Notion" is the term Berkeley puts forward for this rendering of our knowledge of self-knowledge.

Whatever there is to be said against this as a logical leap, it is a coherent moral gesture on Berkeley's part. The extraction of meaning and general purpose from the newly expanded phenomena of the sciences is the recurrent moral theme in his thought. The problem is to save the individual as agent without making him a moral-epistemological imperialist. Berkeley promotes the self, but only as a chastened perceiver who has experienced the humbling limits of ordinary perception. His strategy toward that end is a retreat, a temporary admission of human weakness whereby our "few, stinted, narrow inlets of perception" are depicted as quantitatively weak and scanty. "There may be, for aught that I know, innumerable sorts of ideas or sensations, as different from one another, and from all that I have perceived, as colours are from sounds" (II,75–76). But there is an indissoluble qualitative link between my mode of being and perceiving and any other conceivable entity, no matter how exalted: "yet for any one to pretend to a notion of entity or existence, *abstracted* from *spirit* and *idea*, from perceived and being perceived, is, I suspect, a downright repugnancy and trifling with words" (II,76).

Once again, perception is clarified by examining the paradoxes surrounding reading. Although it begins with submission to the rules of grammar and syntax and the substitution of language for experience, reading may well lead to the suspicion of a fullness beyond the text. Reading draws out a reader without whom there could be no text, and the reader finds his completeness in the gaps the text highlights by its very existence. Perception of sense data in Berkeley's rendering reveals the synthesizing wholeness of the mind or the understanding; the self is a unity realized by contrast with the fragments of its perception and in the operation of putting those fragments together. A book, in Stanley Fish's phrase, is a "self-consuming artifact," and for Berkeley the world of nature is a book that dissolves as we learn to read it, its fragments receding to reveal our sustaining wholeness and presence and then God's. Thus, at the end of the introductory sections of the *Principles* Berkeley summarizes the movement of his thought in a beautiful image that begins in ironic Lockean fashion and then rises to a special kind of affirmation featuring self-assertion and the negation of language: "In vain do we extend our view into the heavens, and pry into the entrails of the earth, in vain do we consult the writings of learned men, and trace the dark footsteps of antiquity; we need only draw the curtain of words, to behold the fairest tree of knowledge, whose fruit is excellent, and within the reach of our hand" (II,40). Philosophers like Locke speak of undressing nature and revealing truth naked, although what Locke leads us to is a darkness where some hypothetical angelic intelligences might be able to see. Berkeley's writings, overall, are full of tributes to a radiant physical world. He exploits the old rhetorical commonplace of the world as God's book, but only to modify it radically and to place his emphasis on reading in which the reader becomes an actor or narrator, a participant who draws back the curtain of words.

"The heavens declare the glory of God; and the firmament sheweth his handywork. Day unto day uttereth speech, and night unto night sheweth knowledge" (Psalms 19:1–2). As Curtius traces it, the book of nature received a new printing in the modern natural and mathematical sciences. For Renaissance writers and poets, that book had been instantly, immediately accessible, but for Galileo it was written in a special script, a "mathematical language."[37] Berkeley's approach to this commonplace makes the world more than an emblem in which the heart reads vaguely stirring messages from God and finds in order, complexity, or immensity signs of divine activity. And at the same time, Berkeley vehemently denies that the world is a divine cryptogram, a code cracked only by mathematical and scientific rearrangements. God, says Berkeley at the end of the *Principles*, is obviously revealed by nature, as both common sense and the scriptures testify abundantly. But there are certain apparent irregularities like "monsters, untimely births, fruits blasted in the blossom, rains falling in desert places, miseries incident to human life" (II,110). These argue that our senses grasp only the "motions and various phenomena" of "this mighty machine" and that "the hand which actuates the whole is it self unperceivable to men of flesh and blood" (II,110). It requires "an unbiassed and attentive mind" to read God's presence in the phenomena: "nothing can be more plainly legible, than the intimate presence of an all-wise Spirit, who fashions, regulates, and sustains the whole system of being" (II,111).

If we have come this far with Berkeley in the *Principles*, we know that an "unbiassed and attentive mind" is a reader of the "plainly legible" creation who is able to trace the divine hand because he knows that he is himself spirit. This reader realizes his spiritual identity by an intense concentration on the differences between the particularities of experience and *his* experience of the particular. In an outrageous but entirely consistent polemical maneuver, Berkeley finds that such a "reader" is more certain of God's existence than he is of other individuals. We know other selves not by the collection of sense data they represent to us but by an inference from those ideas of sense whereby we are directed "to think there is a distinct principle of thought and motion like to our selves, accompanying and represented by it" (II,109). Our skepticism about the normal proof for the existence of other selves leads to another, surer method of knowing them, which is the method for knowing God. Our certainty about God leads back to certainty about others.

Berkeley complicates the simplest, most emotionally direct evidence of God's existence, turning it away from a sensuously immediate intuition of divinity and making it a special kind of intellectual translation of the impressive sense data of the creation. Only after we learn to read our own perceptions do we read God's presence in the world they constitute; the creation first teaches us selfhood, not a humility in the face of an apparent creator. This bold stroke is of a piece with Berkeley's disciplined style, his repressed lyricism, his refusal to pass beyond the literal, his continual habit of suppressing and correcting metaphor. He redefines and sharpens the rhetorical commonplace of the world as God's book, in effect reversing it by saying that we read backwards from a primary knowledge of self to a knowledge of God and then of others. Those operations are parallel to his treatment of common experience, whereby perception is made, by paradoxical and literal insistence, to precede the objects it operates on. Berkeley works this way consistently, offering us a richly evoked particular world whose context is sharply altered by a reverse movement and abrupt shift back through things to a perceiver.

The opening section of Part I of the *Principles of Human Knowledge*, for example, surveys the "objects of human knowledge," rounds up the sense data that constitute things:

Thus, for example, a certain colour, taste, smell, figure and consistence having been observed to go together, are accounted one distinct thing, signified by the name *apple*. Other collections of ideas constitute a stone, a tree, a book, and the like sensible things; which, as they are pleasing or disagreeable, excite the passions of love, hatred, joy, grief, and so forth. (II,41)

The next section merely remarks that something is, of course, necessary to perceive this world, "what I call *mind, spirit, soul* or *my self*. By which words I do not denote any one of my ideas, but a thing entirely distinct from them, wherein they exist, or, which is the same thing, whereby they are perceived; for the existence of an idea consists in being perceived" (II,42). The enormity of this reversal is belied by Berkeley's matter-of-fact tone and his straight-faced equation of existence and being perceived. The sequence represents an epitome of Berkeley's dialectic, which is echoed in the movement of the prose. He vividly invokes a visible and tangible world and then seems to diminish or cancel it by analysis of the language (verbal or visual) available to render it; but that cancellation contains a promise of power or centrality for the perceiver. Berkeley's prose is also characterized by this appearance of cancellation, what I have called its reluctant verbalization and what many have praised as its spare economy.

In the following section from the *Principles,* for example, Berkeley seeks to explain the total separation of our knowledge of sense ideas from our knowledge of spirits.

After what hath been said, it is I suppose plain, that our souls are not to be known in the same manner as senseless inactive objects, or by way of *idea*. Spirits and *ideas* are things so wholly different, that when we say, *they exist, they are known*, or the like, these words must not be thought to signify any thing common to both natures. There is nothing alike or common in them: and to expect that by any multiplication or enlargement of our faculties, we may be enabled to know a spirit as we do a triangle, seems as absurd as if we should hope to *see a sound*. This is inculcated because I imagine it may be of moment towards clearing several important questions, and preventing some very dangerous errors concerning the nature of the soul. We may not I think strictly be said to have an idea of an active being, or of an action, although we may be said to have a notion of them. I have some knowledge or notion of my mind, and its acts about ideas, inasmuch as I know or understand what is meant by those words. What I know, that I have some notion of. I will not say, that the terms *idea* and *notion* may not be used convertibly, if the world will have it so. But yet it conduceth to clearness and propriety, that we distinguish things very different by different names. It is also to be remarked, that all relations including an act of the mind, we cannot so properly be said to have an idea, but rather a notion of the relations or habitudes between things. But if in the modern way the word *idea* is extended to spirits, and relations and acts; this is after all an affair of verbal concern. (II,106)

From the opening sentence, Berkeley is impugning the language he is forced to use, bracketing terms like "exist" and "know" and canceling them in regard to "spirits." The tone is that of an impatient school master who expects the worst from slow pupils or in this case from our inadequate and insensitive language. The distinction should by now be "plain" but at the same time such terms "must not be thought to signify any thing common to both natures." The warning in the second sentence reveals the uncertainty and pedagogic unease implicit in the first, and the third sentence extends the worried protest by insistent repetition that *spirit* and *idea* belong to distinct epistemological worlds. The etymological force of "inculcate" (to trample in, to impress) in the next sentence is apt. Berkeley has just resorted to his favorite rhetorical tactic, a literalizing absurdity, which is here actually an analogy from the world of the senses. We cannot see sounds, but sight and hearing belong to the same order of reality. Berkeley borrows the force of that synesthetic impossibility, applying it to another kind of distinction where it has no strict logical relevance. Berkeley's singular ambivalence toward the senses is often a matter of illustrating their impurity; we cannot see sounds but we manage our hearing and seeing by connecting habitual signs, using various senses at once. In this context, the "multiplication or enlargement of our faculties" Berkeley speaks of here refers us to that sensory confusion rather than to any possible meaningful exaltation. "Inculcation" in this paragraph and elsewhere in the *Principles* is a matter of rubbing our noses in sensory confusion. The "clearing" and "preventing" Berkeley speaks of thus acquire an overtly active sense, and the "moment" they serve implies both importance and movement. These sentences move through the available terms for sense knowledge of spirit, rejecting them by inviting us to watch as they whirl around the intellectual notion of spirit, which remains unmoved.

Berkeley then turns, as it were, from his audience and soliloquizes in austere philosophic style, saying (or claiming to say) the little that can be said about our "ideas" of spirit and extracting the stricter term "notion." These three sentences are the philosophic core of the section, preceded by persuasion and followed by a weary concession to the slack, merely verbal usage that is bound to set in. Philosophic statement is surrounded by warnings about the prevalence of error and misrepresentation in language, to the extent that the vigilance of the informed philosophical speaker is the rhetorical center of the writing. He utters a gnomic, "What I know, that I have some notion of," and then goes back to reprimanding language. This correction of language in the name of a primary experience of self is Berkeley's recurring literary gesture.

His philosophical project is the strenuous revision of the ordinary meaning of "existence," giving it an exhaustively continuous and paradoxical reversal in the name of a wordless experience. God in Berkeley's system makes this reversal possible. His sustaining presence in the natural world permits Berkeley to approach our direct experience of it with a lyrical appreciation he deliberately denies to our linguistic versions of that world. Here at the end of the *Principles* he allows himself a series of extended theological affirmations which seem to represent a release from the rigors of argument and the strain of paradoxical reversal. Berkeley has already paused in the course of the work to castigate atheists and to use arguments buttressed by theology, but the last eleven sections of the *Principles* are an intense polemical-lyrical conclusion, making it finally clear that a valid epistemology for Berkeley not only supports theology but begins in it.

This theological foundation of Berkeley's thinking has disturbed many modern commentators, especially because it seems to be logically incoherent. Denis Grey, for example, finds Berkeley in the *Principles* claiming that we know God directly through his works "in a context which denies the possibility of any direct knowledge of another mind."[38] George Pitcher points out, however, that Berkeley's definition of ideas as "visibly inactive" and totally devoid of "power and agency" makes the natural world and its effect on us nothing less than the direct operation of God's mind. As Pitcher says, "whatever plausibility there is in making God the cause of all our ideas of sense stems from the fact that the sensible world is so tremendously vast, complex, and orderly: only a single mind possessing infinite powers, so the reasoning must go, can be responsible for such a world."[39] God is an author, as tradition has it, and the world is caused by his mighty imaginings. If we "attentively consider," says Berkeley, the sweep of the natural panorama and "at the same time attend to the meaning and import of the attributes, one, eternal, infinitely wise, good, and perfect, we shall clearly perceive that they belong to the aforesaid spirit, *who works all in all*, and *by whom all things consist*" (II,108).

It would seem, then, that Grey is wrong, for Berkeley's claim is not that we know God directly but rather that we know God's imaginings by analogy with our own condition as creators.[40] Berkeley inserts a cross-reference here to an earlier section of the *Principles* where he defined the activity proper to mind as the power to make and unmake ideas: "I find I can excite ideas in my mind at pleasure, and vary and shift the scene as oft as I think fit. It is no more than willing, and straightway this or that idea arises in my fancy . . . when we talk of unthinking agents, or of exciting ideas exclusive of volition, we only amuse our selves with words" (II,53). Our ideas of sense rush upon us when we open our eyes from our fertile imaginings: those ideas of sense are steady and distinct, coherent in a way that separates them from "those which are the effects of human wills" (II,53). But just as we have produced worlds with our eyes closed, Berkeley argues that what we now see must have "some other will or spirit" which produces them. God's presence is the lesson Berkeley extracts from an intense concentration on both the powers and limits of human imagining.

Whatever their logical problems, such assertions license Berkeley to enter the physical world, allowing his imagination to elaborate it and to participate in its mystery and self-sufficiency, indeed to revel in its special aesthetic effects. Disruption of the normal assumptions about perception tears away the philosophers' alienating veil of ideas by tracing out an imaginative universe we share with the deity. Berkeley's argument tends to what many commentators call the specious and even contemptible position that conceiving something is equivalent to perceiving it, and his project as he expressed it in his notebooks is to expand the meaning of existence and give it "a larger sense than ordinary" (I,59,#473). Perception, as Tipton complains, can include for Berkeley anything the mind encompasses: dreams, hallucinations, or encounters with the world.[41] The burst of affirmation here at the end of the *Principles* releases the powerful self-assertion that is thus implicit in Berkeley's thought but repressed by the austerity of his style and literary manner and confused for a time by his complication of the conditions of perception. Berkeley's thought seeks to portray the world through the magnifying lens of what J. O. Wisdom calls "Theocentric Phenomenalism," which licenses what amounts to an intense solipsism.[42]

Clearly, there is a qualitative link between human and divine imagining. What we can conceive must exist. The world is like a human device, much of it as Berkeley renders it resembling the pictures and buildings he saw in Italy, employing similar aesthetic strategies, rhetorically conceived by some spirit to move and surprise us. Some of the world also seems gratuitous, contradictory, useless.

> We should further consider, that the very blemishes and defects of
> Nature are not without their use, in that they make an agreeable sort of
> variety, and augment the beauty of the rest of the creation, as shades in
> a picture serve to set off the brighter and more enlightened parts. We
> would likewise do well to examine, whether our taxing the waste of
> seeds and embryos, and accidental destruction of plants and animals,
> before they come to full maturity, as an imprudence in the Author of
> Nature, be not the effect of prejudice contracted by our familiarity with
> impotent and saving mortals. In *man* indeed a thrifty management of
> those things, which he cannot procure without much pains and industry,
> may be esteemed *wisdom*. But we must not imagine, that the inex-
> plicably fine machine of an animal or vegetable, costs the great Creator
> any more pains or trouble in its production than a pebble doth: nothing
> being more evident, than that an omnipotent spirit can indifferently
> produce every thing by a mere *fiat* or act of his will. Hence it is plain,
> that the splendid profusion of natural things should not be interpreted,
> weakness or prodigality in the agent who produces them, but rather be
> looked on as argument of the riches of his power. (II,111)

In effect, this is a meditation on human imagining, artistic and cunning or simply ordinary and capricious. God is understood as a painter or author, designing the spectacle of the universe for maximum effectiveness, and he is also thus conceived as an arbitrary human imaginer with his eyes shut who can as easily think of a clod or a pebble as of a solar system. The rich prodigality of the divine imagination is contrasted with human narrowness and necessity but also implicitly approached by analogy with a potentially unlimited human imagination. Properly understood, Berkeleian man as imagining "spirit" is the measure of all things, an adumbration of God at his most inexplicable but also most immediately available.

In this light, Berkeley's pressing literary-moral problem is to work forward to this divinely licensed solipsism and to distract his readers from the energy and authority of the imagining self by emphasizing process, location, and coherence in what can easily become a literary universe, something like Carroll's or Borges'. So, Berkeley's attack on rival theories of the world turns his opponents into irresponsible dreamers, liable to wake up like the Red King and blank out the material world. His writing in the largest sense—his analysis of language that literalizes metaphor and suppresses local stylistic effects, his recurring insistence on the difference between thought and language—is designed to present this centrality of the perceiving self as a sharply particularized moral sequence. Luce describes Berkeley's method in the *Principles* as a dramatization of uncertainty in which the reader has to entertain "for a time wrong and inadequate notions" and then "learn to interpret permanence, stability and reality in terms of mind and spirit."[43] When we get to the end of it all, dramatic surprise and literary force rest on a restored simplicity summed up in the "*esse* is *percipi*" formula, a renewed selfhood dependent upon our native innocence and the self-centered simplicity that treats the world as completely available. Berkeley offers us a choice between this newly powerfuly selfhood and the "forlorn scepticism" he says is its only alternative. The arrogance of such a self is necessarily diminished by its history of innocence and the humbling confusions Berkeley has led us through.

Berkeley tries to imagine a situation in which mind must be more than a mental projection room where representations of the world are viewed by an endlessly reflexive understanding. He advances from a discredited verbal representationalism to a clearly focused psychological representation that distinguishes carefully the varieties of material and intellectual experience without driving a wedge through them: "ffoolish in Men to despise the senses. if it were not . . . ye mind could have no knowledge no thought at all" (I,67,#539). He wants to lead his readers out of that elusive inner space where Descartes and Locke had seated the mind and into a richly elaborated phenomenal world, a scene of thought where world and perceiver actually and continuously intersect: "Mem: again & again to mention & illustrate the Doctrine of the Reality of Things Rerum Natura etc." (I,69,#550). The rest of his career after the youthful works in which he set forth his system is thus a literary elaboration and dramatic embodiment of this revised scene of thought. In dialogue and in lyric affirmation, Berkeley passes from the nowhere of the Lockean mind to moral, social, and physical locales where thought takes place.

Berkeley's major works after the *Principles* do not alter his thought in any major way. *Three Dialogues Between Hylas and Philonous* (1713) is, in one sense, a popularization of his doctrines, and *Alciphron* (1732) is an elaboration of the theological apologetics sketched out in earlier works. These dialogues offer release from the evenhandedness and stylistic restraint of the *Principles*. In them, the unity of the Berkeleian program can be fully staged; the characters who speak for Berkeley are free to embody and articulate a position as their particular way of being, and the same fullness extends to their opponents.[44] The urgent thematic implications of Berkeley's philosophical manner and the moral-religious origins and purposes of his thought become clear and apparent.

But these two works are impatient with their form and splendidly careless with the fiction of inquiry and exploration that philosophic dialogue proposes. They represent stages toward the perfect expression of Berkeley's literary sensibility in *Siris*. There he speaks at last without apparent constraint, a much older man who has weathered disappointment and held fast to his singular way of understanding the world. The relative tact and restraint, the narrative compromises and logical necessities of the earlier works drop out. The dialogues are punctuated with lyric affirmations and exalted exposition. *Siris* rises from the analytical to the lyrical, extravagant in its style and in its unrestrained exploration of the implications of the full Berkeleian program. It illustrates by its very openness and freedom the restrictions normal philosophical exposition imposed on Berkeley.

To be sure, those constraints are loosened in the polemical dialogues. In *Three Dialogues*, Philonous is the questioner who speaks from the security of a fully realized set of notions; he exposes the partiality and the unexamined assumptions in the answers Hylas provides. His questions reflect this confidence. Hylas complains that they presuppose answers, as is evident when Philonous asks if matter as substratum supports and therefore has extension, and Hylas answers, "You still take things in a strict literal sense: that is not fair, Philonous" (II,199). Hylas tries to reject Philonous' insistent, bantering literalism, but he is unable to describe any sense, "literal or not literal," in which he can articulate "matter's supporting accidents." The more he thinks about the question, the less he finds in it, and he concludes he knows "nothing of it" (II,199). Berkeley's philosophic comedy finds a butt in Hylas, who can occupy both the untenable opposing view of the materialists and the potentially disrupting skepticism and solipsism implicit in Berkeley's system, here dramatized and thereby rejected as Hylas' misunderstanding. By the opening of the third dialogue, Hylas is Berkeley's complete self-parody, his position what some readers imagined Berkeley's works contained.[45] Hylas has driven himself into that forlorn skepticism Berkeley speaks of in the *Principles*, only he transforms it by a ludicrous complacency into moral and intellectual self-congratulation: "Our faculties are too narrow and too few. Nature certainly never intended us for speculation" (II,227). Philosophers know nothing, and "that is the very top and perfection of human knowledge" (II,228).

Hylas clarifies the issue by his failure to manage the organizing principle of Berkeley's method as a thinker and writer: radical and corrective alterations are established by shifting distance and varying perspective; thought consists in maintaining such a balance, resisting intellectual vertigo by focusing on the stabilizing particulars of experience. The secret of that stability lies in arming the Berkeleian hero with "immaterialism," so Philonous can ride out these disorienting shifts he puts Hylas through. The polemical beauty of immaterialism is that all Philonous has to claim overtly is a simple and tenacious common sense: "I assure you, Hylas, I do not pretend to frame any hypothesis at all. I am of a vulgar cast, simple enough to believe my senses, and leave things as I find them. To be plain, it is my opinion, that the real things are those very things I see and feel, and perceive by my senses" (II,229). Such simplicity has shocking consequences, of course, and Philonous has already extended it far beyond the modest empiricism he claims here. In the second dialogue, for example, he insists that entities we cannot conceive do not exist, and he thinks this reply to Hylas concerning matter settles the issue: "When therefore you speak of the existence of matter, you have not any notion in your mind" (II,222).

Now, one rebuttal of Philonous' psychological literalism and limitation is to challenge its narrow pictorialism and argue that the mind's view may be partial and misleading. And at first Hylas brings up the veil of perception argument: even though we cannot be sure, there may indeed be qualities in matter such as those Philonous rejects. We cannot "conclude absolutely, that there is no heat in the fire, or sweetness in the sugar, but only that heat or sweetness, as perceived by us, are not in the fire or sugar. What say you to this?" (II,180). The answer is sharp and direct, single-minded and attuned to the rules of debate:

I say it is nothing to the purpose. Our discourse proceeded altogether concerning sensible things, which you defined to be the things we *immediately perceive by our senses*. Whatever other qualities therefore you speak of, as distinct from these, I know nothing of them, neither do they at all belong to the point in dispute. You may indeed pretend to have discovered certain qualities which you do not perceive, and assert those insensible qualities exist in fire and sugar. But what use can be made of this to your present purpose, I am at a loss to conceive. (II,180)

There are ground rules in philosophic dialogue that make it especially appropriate for Berkeley's contentious position. Silence is an admission of defeat within the challenges that constitute dialogue and keep it moving. From the first, Philonous challenges Hylas to keep talking about various notions that he knows are not susceptible to the kind of discourse he demands or that defy clear and simple description.

Now I am content to put our dispute on this issue. If you can frame in your thoughts a distinct abstract idea of motion or extension, divested of all those sensible modes, as swift and slow, great and small, round and square, and the like, which are acknowledged to exist only in the mind, I will then yield the point you contend for. But if you cannot, it will be unreasonable on your side to insist any longer upon what you have no notion of. (II,193)

What Philonous really means is that he will tolerate only those entities that can be spoken about; only notions that contribute to the expansive occasion of dialogue are allowed. Berkeley arranges the contest as a literary affair, for the dialogue makes coherent articulation the deciding factor. Philonous dominates because he is linguistically superior and able to operate within what he calls "strict propriety of speech." His theism in the third dialogue opposes Hylas' materialism by measuring a clear and present notion (spirit) against a vague "matter, or I know not what (I may add too, you know not what) third nature" (II,240). Philonous declares himself the winner in this exchange and others because he has a coherent story to tell, a series of clear and simple operations leading back in a strictly responsible way to the facts and relationships of perception.

From the effects I see produced, I conclude there are actions; and because actions, volitions; and because there are volitions, there must be a will. Again, the things I perceive must have an existence, they or their archetypes, out of my mind: but being ideas, neither they nor their archetypes can exist otherwise than in an understanding: there is therefore an understanding. But will and understanding constitute in the strictest sense a mind or spirit. The powerful cause therefore of my ideas, is in strict propriety of speech a *spirit*. (II,239)

Instead of insisting on the possibility of our ignorance or attempting to reject what Jessop calls the "analogy of experience" whereby mind is "the only owning, unifying, and productive kind of thing we *know*," Hylas plays Philonous' game and proposes terms like "instrument" and "occasion" to attempt to describe the secret operations of matter.[46] Philonous counterattacks that these are incomplete analogies, incapable of the metaphoric extension required to prove them. "An instrument, say you; pray what may be the figure, springs, wheels, and motions of that instrument?" (II,217). When Hylas fails to answer, Philonous introduces his own analogies to dismiss his opponent's: instruments are what we require for tasks impossible without their aid, and it follows that an "all-perfect spirit" would have no need of an "instrument" like matter for the operation of the universe, a task as direct for such an entity as the moving of a finger is for us (II,218–219).

Philonous' literalism is thus flexible, capable of resorting to metaphor to prove and disprove. But like Berkeley himself in the *Principles*, Philonous does not want to be understood as saying that objects actually exist in the mind or are imprinted on the senses. When Hylas attempts to literalize his theory or make him admit his reliance on metaphor, Philonous replies: "My meaning is only that the mind comprehends or perceives them; and that it is affected from without, or by some being distinct from itself" (II,250). As the intruding spatial relationship implicit in "without" indicates, keeping metaphor out of language is a constant struggle. Philonous claims that whatever metaphorical implications lie in his discourse come from the normal concretions of speech, the dead metaphors whereby mental operations are "signified by words borrowed from sensible things" (II,250).

These exchanges bring us back to Berkeley's ambivalence about language. Philonous manipulates metaphors to prove and disprove, but that is merely argument and rhetoric. He claims the epistemological transaction is entirely literal and yet describes his thought in moral and metaphorical terms as a strict "survey," which "the false lustre of error and disguise cannot endure" (II,208). Against what he can see only as the potential disorder and negative implications of this literalism, Hylas proposes a mechanistic model for cognition, "the modern way of explaining things," that is richly concrete and complete:

It is supposed the soul makes her residence in some part of the brain, from which the nerves take their rise, and are thence extended to all parts of the body: and that outward objects by the different impressions they make on the organs of sense, communicate certain vibrative motions to the nerves; and these being filled with spirits, propagate them to the brain or seat of the soul, which according to the various impressions or traces thereby made in the brain, is various [*sic*] affected with ideas. (II,208–209)

Hylas' model of the material organization of cognition is invalid, Philonous answers, because the brain which is its center can not be a "sensible" object and still be the cause of all other sensible objects. If we understand "brain," it is "in the mind" and therefore this model is a projection from and elaboration of the idea the mind has of it. Hylas is doomed to lose all these arguments because he lacks the position and perspective Philonous commands. What he initally neglects to tell Hylas is that what I must first perceive are not the objects of sense but the perceiver of those ideas, myself or mind. Mind is a viewer separate from the world, able to command the enormous prospect of experience not so much from a point outside it as from a moment inconceivable except as antecedent to it. Although mind can only situate itself in relation to the places it views, its temporal priority and epistemological dominance allow Philonous to baffle Hylas with arguments that are paradoxical and oxymoronic: outer is inner, the immediate is final, "appearances" are the things themselves, ideas are things solid and substantial:

PHILONOUS. You mistake me. I am not for changing things into ideas, but rather ideas into things; since those immediate objects of perception, which according to you, are only appearances of things, I take to be the real things themselves.

HYLAS. Things! you may pretend what you please; but it is certain, you leave us nothing but the empty forms of things, the outside only which sticks the senses.

PHILONOUS. What you call the empty forms and outside of things, seems to me the very things themselves. Nor are they empty or incomplete otherwise, than upon your supposition, that matter is an essential part of all corporeal things. We both therefore agree in this, that we perceive only sensible forms: but herein we differ, you will have them to be empty appearances, I real beings. In short you do not trust your senses, I do. (II,244–245)

Berkeley's immaterialism gives Philonous a literary identity; he is an enthusiastic reader of the perceptual world who turns into its narrator. In place of the merely ingenious constructions materialists and scientists devise to explain an opaque reality, Philonous substitutes this lyrical and creative relationship between the perceiver and the perceived world of sense. The concrete richness of this connection strengthens the claims of the perceiver in ways denied to the models and metaphors of Berkeley's opponents. There is an Empsonian pastoral turn to these dialogues, as there is in Berkeley's thought: the complicated perceptual world, here further bedeviled by Philonous' interrogations, is transformed by a reconstituted simplicity.

In philosophical dialogue, setting seems nothing but a decoration, a minimal or even ironic location if we remember the opening of Plato's *Phaedrus*. These dialogues begin in a vernal setting, Philonous making a special point of it. Their discussion he claims is inspired by "the solitude of a garden and tranquillity of the morning" (II,171). This seems merely a grace note at first, but the plot of the dialogues involves Philonous' preserving the sweetly coherent natural world against the dead abstractions, as Berkeley sees them, of the men of matter. "What treatment," asks Philonous in the second dialogue, "do those philosophers deserve, who would deprive these noble and delightful scenes of all reality? How should those principles be entertained, that lead us to think all the visible beauty of the creation a false imaginary glare?" (II,211). Philonous' argument allows him to appropriate the world of sense, that is, to turn away from argument to the reconstitution of a natural world which, for poor Hylas at least, has been alienated. In the third dialogue, Philonous offers our sensations as proof of the sensible world and by means of his lyrical insistence as proof of our priority as well: "I see this *cherry*, I feel it, I taste it: and I am sure *nothing* cannot be seen, or felt, or tasted: it is therefore *real*. Take away the sensations of softness, moistness, redness, tartness, and you take away the *cherry*" (II,249). The easy reciprocity of this moment carries enormous philosophical weight, disguising by its cheerful immediacy and literal psychological outline the difficulties of Berkeley's position.

Berkeley is thus a cunning philosophical dramatist, and *Three Dialogues* exemplifies his ability to exploit scene and setting and to make literary performance within them integral features of philosophical exposition. Perhaps the most coherent of these literary moments comes at the conclusion of the last dialogue, the well-known passage in which Philonous points to a fountain and sees in its operation two distinct things, one literal, the other metaphoric in a didactic and unexpected sense. The water in the fountain can rise only so high; "its ascent as well as descent" proceeds "from the same uniform law or principle of *gravitation*." Hylas' materialist principles lead "at first view" to skepticism, but "pursued to a certain point, bring men back to common sense" (II,263). The fountain is a human contrivance limited in its aspiration by the laws of nature, and Philonous plays in his image with its double movement. His particular accuracy and originality lie in seeing the water descend as well as ascend. The fountain is an image of the persuasive curve of Berkeley's thought in *Three Dialogues*. He stages the failure of a certain kind of aspiration, summed up in contrivances like the models and engines of the materialists, but such an exposé reveals the transparency of the world as perceived and discovers the perceiver in his centrality. In following the water in its double movement, Berkeley's thought presents what Donald Davie calls an "enlightened but still common sense."[47]

The serenity of these affirmations and the ease of the victory over a bewildered Hylas vanish in the harsh polemics of *Alciphron*, written during the bitter period in Rhode Island as Berkeley waited for the promised funds to establish his college in Bermuda. *Alciphron*'s intensity may have grown out of Berkeley's disappointment and his near-paranoid focus on "freethinking" as the root of all the evils of the day and the ruin of his college. He wrote to Percival from Rhode Island: "What they foolishly call free thinking seems to me the principal root or source not only of opposition to our College but of most other evils in this age . . . I am credibly informed that great numbers of all sorts of blasphemous books published in London are sent to Philadelphia, New York, and other places, where they produce a plentiful crop of atheists and infidels" (VIII,212).

The opponents Berkeley imagines here are much more formidable, fluent in exposition and confident of a power he sincerely feared they were acquiring. The eight long dialogues are an elaborate literary structure to contain these opponents and to embrace a much wider range of topics than the purely philosophical *Three Dialogues*. The "minute philosophers," Alciphron and Lysicles, have large roles to play, since the book sets out in the language of its "advertisement" "to consider the freethinker in the various lights of atheist, libertine, enthusiast, scorner, critic, metaphysician, fatalist, and sceptic" (III,23). To serve that variety, Berkeley balances the two freethinkers with two sensible and moderate opponents, Euphranor and Crito, who are recognizably Berkeleian in their positions but not obtrusively so like Philonous. Although each of these four main characters is reasonably distinct stylistically, the two groups they form represent clearly antagonistic and mutually exclusive ways of writing and thinking.

Alciphron is generally regarded as Berkeley's highest literary achievement; "the style is easy, the language plain, and the arguments are nervous" (that is, strong and sinewy), said a contemporary admirer.[48] Saintsbury, who ranked Berkeley above Addison and the equal of Dryden as a prose writer, said that *Alciphron* might be "read again and again with positive pleasure."[49] Jessop finds the style "astonishing in its sustained excellence," and yet defines that excellence as a simplicity based on "unforced confidence" (II,2).

Such praise is well earned, but Berkeley is no more lucid here than in his earlier works, and the unforced confidence Jessop speaks of is even more evident in *Three Dialogues*. *Alciphron* is distinct in Berkeley's career (it adds nothing to his thought, in fact it neglects some aspects of it) by virtue of its almost purely literary focus. The polemic against freethinking is a dramatization of its style, an elaborate mimicry and parody designed to reveal its moral, theological, and philosophical falsity by literary means. What makes this of great interest is the context provided by Berkeley's thought and his style in the earlier works. The minute philosophers in *Alciphron* assume in their shallow self-regard a dangerously similar version of the Berkeleian posture; like Berkeley, they propose a Ptolemaic reversal and renewal of thought, placing human knowing at the center of things. So, their self-satisfaction and stylistic self-enclosure need to be made distinct from the informed, powerful, but deferential self-understanding of Berkeley's thought. Their facility and fluency are rendered in the dialogues as moral errors, unmistakable signs of falsity or, rather, the essence of falsity. At the center of Berkeley's thought, as we have seen, lies the analogy of language: our constructions in visual perception resemble our constructions in reading, and by extension and intensification, this kind of reading reveals being and divinity. The freethinkers are guilty not simply of bad taste but of interfering with the complex processes whereby we perceive and reason. For if we use language badly or loosely (ignoring its fragility, its dependence on a communicating self), then the analogy for knowing the world, self, and God is much less useful or perhaps useless. The point of Berkeley's analogy from language is that language breaks down and reveals a mind or spirit. The freethinkers are perfectly contained by their language; they are their verbal constructions.

Berkeley's polemic is as much against improper language and its deluding satisfactions as it is against the generalizing doctrines of Deism and materialism. The minute philosophers are perfect antagonists for Berkeley because their position (as he defines it) is a revealing mirror opposite of his; their self-satisfied extravagance and utter confidence in language permit his spokesmen to define themselves by moderate counterpositions rather than self-assertions, and their style is effectively a quiet antistyle which defines itself by negating excess.

The opposition between the participants is thorough and begins in the moral and social stereotypes of the age. Euphranor is a rural contemplative, come from the university to settle in a "remote corner of the country," where "his mind is seldom idle while he prunes the trees, follows the plough, or looks after his flocks" (III,32). Alciphron, predictably, has gone from the Temple to an inheritance to a grand tour to a life of urban dissipation, "the amusements of the town, which being grown stale and tasteless to his palate, have flung him into a sort of splenetic indolence" (III,32). Lysicles, his companion, is a younger man whose "constitution and fortune" have been damaged by "an intimacy with men of pleasure and freethinkers" (III,32). Dion (Berkeley, the narrator) is introduced to these personages by Crito, a man of property and solid good sense whose character emerges in the dialogues as strongly ironic and skeptical of the claims of freethinking. He serves as the negative complement to Euphranor's positive expositions.

Crito and Euphranor rise slowly to eloquent heights, but the minute philosophers begin in full flight. Their speech is undermined from the first by its unhesitant, uncritical rhetorical fullness. For example, Alciphron responds in the first dialogue to Euphranor's question about freethinkers with an oration marked by exclamation, apostrophe, gesticulation — all governed by a keen sense of audience: "perceiving that Euphranor heard him with respect, he proceeded very fluently."

You must know, said he, that the mind of man may be fitly compared to a piece of land. What stubbing, ploughing, digging, and harrowing is to the one, that thinking, reflecting, examining is to the other. Each hath its proper culture; and as land that is suffered to lie waste and wild for a long tract of time will be overspread with brush-wood, brambles, thorns, and such vegetables which have neither use nor beauty; even so there will not fail to sprout up in a neglected uncultivated mind a great number of prejudices and absurd opinions, which owe their origin partly to the soil itself, the passions and imperfections of the mind of man, and partly to those seeds which chance to be scattered in it by every wind of doctrine, which the cunning of statesmen, the singularity of pedants, the superstition of fools, or the imposture of priests shall raise. Represent to yourself the mind of man, or human nature in general, that for so many ages had lain obnoxious to the frauds of designing, and the follies of weak men; how it must be overrun with prejudices and errors, what firm and deep roots they must have taken, and consequently how difficult a task it must be to extirpate them! And yet this work, no less difficult than glorious, is the employment of the modern free-thinkers. Alciphron having said this made a pause and looked round on the company. (III,34–35)

Alciphron extends his metaphor recklessly. He violates the decorum of philosophical utterance by dramatizing his cleverness, calling attention to his own artifice. Analogy is devalued by such overextension, and as matters proceed the minute philosophers' inventive variety grows loose and incoherent, as in this series of analogies offered by Lysicles:

We have cleared the land of all prejudices towards government or constitution, and made them fly like other phantasms before the light of reason and good sense. Men who think deeply cannot see any reason why power should not change hands as well as property; or why the fashion of a government should not be changed as easy as that of a gar-

ment . . . Those who are even slightly read in our philosophy know
that of all prejudices, the silliest is an attachment to forms. (III,77)

This particular self-exposing fullness is the freethinkers' stylistic
signature, reminiscent in its looseness of Swift's mad narrator in *A Tale of
a Tub*. As Lysicles makes clear, such a free and easy relationship to verbal
forms indicates an indifference to all other forms; the conceit illustrates
by its very fullness the emptiness of the world being rendered.

The zany inventiveness of the freethinkers is an index of their unsoundness, and Berkeley keeps coming back to it as a reliable philosophic
joke. Lysicles is still at it in the fifth dialogue when he mentions a
freethinker whose Pythagorean system divides men into former birds,
beasts, and fish, with "every individual retaining a tincture of his former
state, which constitutes what is called genius" (III,214). Lysicles sees
himself as a "flying fish: that is, a man of animal enjoyment with a mixture of whim." Thus, he concludes, freethinkers have their "creeds" and
"systems" but they can be "slipped off or on, as humour or occasion
serves" (III,214). Like Swift's "conscience" easily slipped down for the
sake of lewdness or nastiness, the truth Berkeley's freethinkers propose is
transparently unstable and unthinkable outside of their personalities.
And they themselves are mercurial, as indeed Alciphron boasts in the last
dialogue. "We have among us moles that dig deep under ground, and
eagles that soar out of sight. We can act all parts and become all opinions,
putting them on or off with great freedom of wit and humour" (III,320).

Euphranor's response to Alciphron's orations is, at first, brief and
pointed, an attack in form of the easy luxuriance of his metaphors of
cultivation and a questioning of their literal worth: "You make clear
work. The gentlemen of your profession are, it seems, admirable weeders.
You have rooted up a world of notions: I should be glad to see what fine
things you have planted in their stead" (III,45). In a way, this is merely
witty, a quick rather than profound response. In Berkeley's playfully contemptuous rendering, Alciphron's position is undercut by his own formulations, and the clichés of intellectual liberation are self-defeating.
The organic metaphor Alciphron rolls around here in the opening dialogue leads him to an implicitly satirical characterization of freethinkers,
"who have sprung up and multiplied of late years," rather like weeds or
flies (III,34). Eventually, Euphranor's rebuttal involves his shrewd and exact examination of Alciphron's carelessly applied metaphor of cultivation
and the restoration of the natural. He asks Alciphron a series of questions
about the natural, "what those things are which you esteem natural, or by
what mark I may know them" (III,55). Does the natural, an orange tree

for example, appear immediately, or does it depend for its nature on climate and soil and careful tending? Euphranor forces Alciphron to look at the facts his analogy implies, "that things may be natural to men" but require cultivation: "there being as great difference of culture, and every other advantage, with respect to human nature, as is to be found with respect to the vegetable nature of plants, to use your own similitude. Is it so or not?" (III,57).

Berkeley's skill as a philosophical dramatist is wonderfully evident in sequences like these, for Euphranor's advancing clarity and careful expansions of the initial metaphor drive Alciphron into short answers that represent a defeat for that voluble spirit: "It is"; "It seems so"; "Whatever is reasonable I admit to be natural" (III,57). Indeed, Euphranor's skill lies precisely in making silence the only valid response the freethinkers can offer; he reduces their inflated verbalizing to the simple motions of clarifying assent. Lysicles' peevish complaint in the second dialogue makes this explicit: to a question from Euphranor he replies: "If I say *yes*, you'll make an inference; and if I say *no*, you'll demand a reason. The best way is to say nothing at all. There is, I see, no end of answering" (III,75).

Euphranor's witty appropriation of Alciphron's governing analogy is complete, revealing in due course the latter's real preference for the cultivated and refined, even though his explicit endorsement appears to be of the natural.

And as those fruits which grow from the most generous and mature
stock, in the choicest soil, and with the best culture, are most esteemed;
even so ought we not to think those sublime truths, which are the fruits
of mature thought, and have been rationally deduced by men of the
best and most improved understandings, to be the choicest productions
of the rational nature of man? And, if so, being in fact reasonable,
natural, and true, they ought not to be esteemed unnatural whims, errors of education, and groundless prejudices [a lovely pun, in context],
because they are raised and forwarded by manuring and cultivating our
tender minds, because they take early root, and sprout forth betimes by
the care and diligence of our instructors? (III,57–58)

Euphranor is a gentleman farmer, a rural contemplative, for whom Alciphron's careless agricultural metaphor is really a vital synecdoche, and passages like this look forward to the mystical affirmations of *Siris*. Alciphron, in clear contrast, has no personal investment in his analogies and uses them merely rhetorically. The unsoundness of his thinking is partially revealed by his indiscriminate use of them. His bantering here in the first dialogue after Euphranor has clearly won the day expresses a moral relationship which places Alciphron outside his formulations, or better, makes it clear that he has no particular philosophical position but merely a set of attitudes or postures for self-assertion.

> Be of good courage, replied Alciphron [to Lysicles]: a skillful gamester has been known to ruin his adversary by yielding him some advantage at first. I am glad, said he, turning to Euphranor, that you are drawn in to argue, and make your appeals to reason. For my part, wherever reason leads I shall not be afraid to follow. Know then, Euphranor, that I freely give up what you now contend for. I do not value the success of a few crude notions thrown out in a loose discourse, any more than the Turks do the loss of that vile infantry which they place in the front of their armies, for no other end but to waste the powder, and blunt the swords of their enemies. (III,60)

There is in this language an odd combination of moral coarseness with a conventionally exalted dedication to the adventure of reason. Such uncertainty of tone marks Alciphron and Lysicles as caricatures of philosophic originality and vigor. Their pronouncements lack the tact, consistency, and quiet complexity Berkeley grants his spokesmen.

As the interrogators and commentators in the early dialogues, they have the advantage of corrective response; their encapsulating retorts are the antithesis of rhetorical self-indulgence. Euphranor summarizes the hedonism of his opponents memorably: "Why then it should seem that sensual pleasure is but a short deliverance from long pain. A long avenue of uneasiness leads to a point of pleasure, which ends in disgust or remorse" (III,89). The remarkable concision of this image is grounded in eighteenth-century landscape and optics. These two short sentences plant a moral pattern firmly in an observed world and suggest the disappointments of landed affluence. Of course, a "point of pleasure" is a profound Berkeleian irony in the context of his views on the falsity of geometrical representation. A "point" is a mere abstraction, for moral and psychological purposes an illusion.

Predictably, Lysicles misunderstands Euphranor and trivializes his protest, calling it merely "words and notions." The "wiser men of pleasure follow fact, nature, and sense" (III,89). Lysicles, Berkeley expects his reader to see, has it exactly backwards, for Euphranor and Crito command a connection between their language and the world it represents, while the freethinkers in their formulations effectively distort the world of experience. Crito here defends "notional pleasures" as lasting and, more sharply, finds that notions are implicated in "sensual pleasures" and embitter the most lively of them, "which at bottom will be found also to depend upon notion more than perhaps you imagine" (III,89). Berkeley stages the ethical debate in *Alciphron* around the issue of accuracy, identifying the freethinkers' language as self-serving cant because it ignores complexity of various kinds, turning the tables on their program for liberation, whose central claim is nothing less than a new realism in moral and philosophical analysis.

Berkeley proceeds against this persuasive claim by exposing its neglect of the actualities both of experience and of language. As emerges in the last dialogue, Alciphron is a sort of Lockean when it comes to the relationship between language and ideas. He calls for no words without correspondingly clear ideas. "Human learning and science" must proceed by "stripping" doctrines and tenets "of the words, and examining what ideas are underneath, or whether any ideas at all" (III,289). In a passage from this section cut from the third edition, Alciphron presents a theory of the psychology of abstraction whereby the mind constructs general representations in order to avoid the chaos that would follow if each particular thing or idea had a distinct name: "words must have been innumerable and language an endless impossible thing" (III,332). Euphranor questions the process whereby we form these "abstract general ideas" and finds Alciphron's account unfaithful to fact, unable to describe itself with any clarity or to explain the gap between specific experiences or ideas and abstractions.

It is a classic Berkeleian theme, then, this ironic scrutiny of falsifying abstraction which poses as liberating clarity. Euphranor suggests in place of Alciphron's mythical epistemological moment a history of notions whereby general ideas are constructed out of particular ideas by a process of signification, as "words become general by representing an indefinite number of particular ideas" (III,335). The word "man," Alciphron admits, does not always make him think of a particular individual, so he was led by lack of attention to think he had an abstract general idea called "man." Speaking for Berkeley, Euphranor promotes an epistemology founded on an awareness of the interplay between the conventionality of language and the particularities of experience. Such awareness resembles Augustan literary theory in its attention to the concrete in the universal and in its vigilance toward the solidification of universals in experience. Like so much of Augustan literature, Berkeley's thought sees language in a social and psychological dynamic:

the true end of speech, reason, science, faith, assent, in all its different degrees, is not merely, or principally, or always, the imparting or acquiring of ideas, but rather something of an active operative nature, tending to a conceived good: which may sometimes be obtained, not only although the ideas marked are not offered to the mind, but even although there should be no possibility of offering or exhibiting any such idea to the mind. (III,307)

Euphranor even beats his opponents at their own game, wittily using an image from the world of corrupt pleasure to evoke the special circumstances of language use: "Counters, for instance, at a card-table are used, not for their own sake, but only as signs substituted for money, as words are for ideas" (III,291).

In the sequence in dialogue VII where the canceled passage appears, Alciphron is rather more subtle and restrained than usual. He sounds like Locke, in fact. Berkeley finds in his position merely a rhetoric of clarity, intelligibility, and usefulness, which actually disguises a central incoherence. Like all mimicry, his rendering of Lockean rhetoric is not quite fair but for its own purposes maliciously accurate. What is grace? asks Alciphron, what "clear and distinct idea" does it mark? (III,290). He is for a clarity excluding "dust and disputes about tenets purely verbal," and he calls for evidence that "shines by its own light, and is admitted by all thinking men" (III,289). This is not the first time Alciphron appropriates these images of radiant, neglected common sense and experience. God, he says in dialogue VI, has given him reason and he "will judge by that unerring light, lighted from the universal lamp of nature" (III,251). In the first dialogue, he renders the minute philosophers' polemical strategy by a specific analogy from the nature of eyesight that seems to borrow a Berkeleian exactness about optical phenomena. Alciphron and his sort proceed gradually in demolishing "folly and supersitition," since "eyes long kept in the dark cannot bear a sudden view of noonday light, but must be brought to it by degrees" (III,40). But clarity like this is misleading, Berkeley's spokesmen show throughout these dialogues, because it is selectively literal and uses analogies and images cut off from the totality of experience.

Thus, to Alciphron's charge that scripture is obscure, Euphranor asks whether we should not compare revelation, literally, to the sun: should it not follow that "to expect in this world a constant, uniform light from God, without any mixture of shade or mystery, would be departing from the rule and analogy of the creation?" (III,236). From *A New Theory of Vision* onward, a naive analogy from visual experience for theological matters is unthinkable, but it makes little sense even in Locke's universe. Euphranor counters Alciphron's certainty here by reminding him of Locke's King of Siam, who refused to believe rivers could turn solid. It follows that I cannot "make my own observation or experience the rule and measure of things spiritual, supernatural, or relating to another world, because I think it a very bad one even for the visible and natural things of this" (III,240).

The light of truth, in a grand metaphor indifferent to experience, is unchanging, but "with respect to us," argues Crito, "it is variously weakened and obscured, by passing through a long distance or gross medium, where it is intercepted, distorted or tinctured, by the prejudices and passions of men" (III,281). Crito's eloquence is literalizing, his analogies specific, almost technically accurate. A man may "see enough for the purposes either of nature or of grace; though by a light, dimmer indeed or clearer, according to the place, or the distance, or the hour, or the medium" (III,281). Berkeley's language values accuracy and defers in its figures to natural sequence and process.

The rhetorical problem Berkeley faces in his polemical apologetics is to fashion an acceptable rise from this narrow, literalizing epistemology (or the rhetoric that accompanies it) to a lyrical rehearsal of the argument from (or to) design. The affirmative moments in these dialogues are marked by a combination of close analysis and large laudatory sweeps through the creation. "The soul of man," says Euphranor in dialogue IV, "actuates but a small body, an insignificant particle, in respect of the great masses of nature, the elements, and heavenly bodies, and system of the world" (III,146). That system is at once so immense as to be beyond total human understanding, but also able to be approached by analogy with sensible rules for understanding. Crito attacks Lysicles' questioning of the workings of divine revelation by means of a theatrical metaphor, which makes the unthinking skeptic like "a conceited spectator, who never looked behind the scenes, and yet would judge of the machinery; who, from a transient glimpse of a part only of some scene, would take upon him to censure the plot of a play" (III,249–250). Such analogies carry their own self-satisfaction, and this kind of commanding survey has its rhetorical dangers, exemplified in the high-flying self-characterizations of the minute philosphers like Alciphron, ready to soar at a moment's notice "on the wings of general maxims, while little minds creep and grovel amid mean particularities" (III,257). Easy sublimity and instant elevation are always rhetorically suspect, and Euphranor's irony grows thick here: "You, Alciphron, who soar sublime on strong and free pinions, vouchsafe to lend a helping hand to those whom you behold entangled in the birdlime of prejudice" (III,257).

Berkeley and his surrogates refuse to soar, because they claim to build their program on limitation, climbing up from an initially confused viewpoint to a clarifying height that stops quite short of an extraterrestrial vantage. Alciphron looks down on the earth and sees "the herd of mankind . . . divided and subdivided into numberless nations and tribes, differing in notions and tenets, as in language, manners, and dress" (III,220). Locke, we recall, tends to take this overview in a practical political and moral sense: the panorama is a check on useless pride and a spur to local action within "this little Canton" of ours (IV.iii.24). Berkeley's perspective, when he cares to invoke it, is angelic and leads to *contemptus mundi*. What is distinctive in Euphranor's rendering of this commonplace in the fourth dialogue is the specific ascent up to that perspective, as difficult a climb as the getting out of Avernus:

And, for aught we know, this spot, with the few sinners on it, bears no greater proportion to the universe of intelligences than a dungeon doth to a kingdom. It seems we are led not only by revelation, but by common sense, observing and inferring from the analogy of visible things, to conclude there are innumerable orders of intelligent beings more happy and more perfect than man, whose life is but a span, and whose place, this earthly globe, is but a point, in respect of the whole system of God's creation. We are dazzled, indeed, with the glory and grandeur of things here below, because we know no better. But I am apt to think, if we know what it was to be an angel for one hour, we should return to this world, though it were to sit on the highest throne in it, with vastly more loathing and reluctance than we would now descend into a loathsome dungeon or sepulchre. (III,172)

Note that Euphranor finds we are "dazzled" (one of Berkeley's favorite words) by a created world we never leave except by inference from the world of common sense. It is not the incomprehensible vistas of revelation or the ineffable third heaven glimpsed by St. Paul that Berkeley strives to imagine or invoke.[50] Instead, he has Euphranor move from an intense and sensuous appreciation of the world to an angelic height impossible to render without the "analogy of visible things."

Berkeley's spokesmen in these dialogues work toward a rhetoric that accommodates a richly rendered particular world and appreciates natural forms, ascending only gradually away from them. Euphranor defines the "natural" as cooperative involvement with such forms, not only in agriculture and education but in art. He points to "some prints after Raphael and Guido" on the wall and notes the contrast between the "unnatural" confinements of English garments and the simple, dignified "draperies that fall into such a variety of natural, easy, and ample folds" and "that cover the body without encumbering it, and adorn without altering the shape" (III,125). Implicitly, Berkeley's style and philosophical stance attempt to conform to classical values like these, cooperating with physical forms and processes and avoiding extremes of artifice, whether unnaturally covered or falsely naked. The thoughtful hero conjured up by Crito and Euphranor is very much like a judicious art critic or well-informed dramatic spectator. In the search for religious truth as Crito renders it at the end of the sixth dialogue, this spectator exemplifies the Berkeleian manner. The passage can stand for Berkeley's style at its active best.

> he that would, upon the foot of reason, erect himself into a judge, in order to make a wise judgment on a subject of that nature, will not only consider the doubtful and difficult parts of it, but take a comprehensive view of the whole, consider it in all its parts and relations, trace it to its original, examine its principles, effects, and tendencies, its proofs internal and external. He will distinguish between the clear points and the obscure, the certain and uncertain, the essential and the circumstantial, between what is genuine and what foreign. He will consider the different sorts of proof that belong to different things; where evidence is to be expected, where probability may suffice, and where it is reasonable to suppose there should be doubts and scruples. He will proportion his pains and exactness to the importance of the inquiry, and check that disposition of his mind to conclude all those notions groundless prejudices, with which it was imbued before it knew the reason of them. He will silence his passions, and listen to truth. He will endeavour to untie knots as well as to tie them, and dwell rather on the light parts of things than the obscure. He will balance the force of his understanding with the difficulty of the subject, and, to render his judgment impartial, hear evidence on all sides, and, so far as he is led by authority, choose to follow that of the honestest and wisest men. (III,283–284)

Crito and Euphranor divide the stylistic work between them, the latter given to sharp reasoning and irrefutable aphorism, the former to oratorical elaboration like this. Crito responds to the pointed flippancy of Lysicles, who says freethinkers approach religion with active minds "that tie knots and raise scruples" (III,283). By his hammering series of evaluating verbs, each governed by a thoroughness extending through an antithesis, Crito redefines activity. Like Crito's other speeches and like Berkeley himself in his own voice, this describes a series of operations, a chain of linked procedures which claims to narrate rather than to promote a position. It is an outline of method, but the Berkeleian method and its conclusions are inseparable. If you follow this procedure and use this particular vocabulary and adopt this sort of rhetorical posture, you come up with the Berkeleian perceiving self.

The rigorous deference Berkeley has Crito define points to the disruptive power of that self and its operations. The individual is involved in the world and judging demands a construction upward. To consider we must "erect" ourselves "upon the foot of reason," to an artificial height presumably, out of reach of our proper element. But "considering" still has an earthbound, strongly concrete sense; it is interchangeable with an actual seeing and as Crito concludes, it is joined by other ethically charged physical movements, silencing and listening. Actual thought, as this and other speeches describe it, is an active process, strenuously separated from and thereby strongly implicated in a world Berkeley tries to render as concretely as he can. As an enemy of abstraction, he devises a style that at times is as densely particular in its transaction with general terms and conditions as Johnson's.

Crito balances the grand ambition of this survey with a reiterated emphasis on volition. The seeker after truth exerts his will in the examination of all possibilities, and this willing is in the service of a deferral to truth that will reveal itself to an impartial observer and listener. Openness to truth is an ethical act requiring strength and purpose. Crito's repetitions are rhetorically simple, for thought is a series of purposeful observations in which the self maintains its judicial stance and resists the temptations to rearrange and appropriate the world in writing, opportunities eagerly embraced by the freethinkers. In Crito's rendering, thought is depicted in the rhythm of his prose as a massive holding back of energy. In *Alciphron* as a whole, Berkeley's writing for his side is defined by restraint, in part a defensive maneuver against the enemy's confident assertions but also a self-defense against his own stylistic fluency and systematic completeness.

Berkeley sounds in his enthusiasm in one of his *Guardian* essays very much like a minute philosopher. Philosophy, he says, enlarges the mind by "general views" and "by the contemplation of more numerous and distant objects than fall within the sphere of mankind in the ordinary pursuits of life" (VII,207). *Alciphron* parodies a self-serving version of that enthusiasm. The intensity of the attack and the careful fashioning of an antithetical manner in Crito and Euphranor make the polemic a therapeutic exercise in which Berkeley disciplines himself, holding back a fullness and enthusiastic exposition of his own views in favor of a cleansing operation on the moral-intellectual world.

The minute philosophers have given knowledge a bad name. Euphranor sets out in the seventh dialogue to show that their objections to faith are not the effect of knowledge but "proceed rather from an ignorance of what knowledge is" (III,303). He goes on to rehearse a comprehensive theory of signs which finds it "natural to assist the intellect by imagination, imagination by sense, and other senses by sight" (III,306). Knowledge is a vital, incessant work of substitution:

We illustrate spiritual things by corporeal; we substitute sounds for thoughts, and written letters for sounds; emblems, symbols, and hieroglyphics, for things too obscure to strike, and too various or too fleeting to be retained. We substitute things imaginable for things intelligible, sensible things for imaginable, smaller things for those that are too great to comprehend easily, and greater things for such as are too small to be discerned distinctly, present things for absent, permanent for perishing, and visible for invisible. (III,306)

All this is properly accomplished within Berkeley's rhetorically sophisticated qualification of how language operates, and Euphranor is careful to add that signs also work to raise emotions, to produce dispositions, and to direct our actions "in pursuit of that happiness" which "sets rational agents at work" (III,307). Hylas had complained that Philonous left us "nothing but the empty forms of things, the outside only which strikes the senses" (II,244). But Berkeley is protesting that outer is "inner," that an invidious opposition of outer and inner is nonsense. His program from his earliest writings promotes that subversion of normal location by describing philosophical experience as an intense participation inseparable from a judicious and distanced evaluation of the world. This shift comes easily to Berkeley. He employs a version of it in the Tory homily he wrote called *Passive Obedience* (1712). There he argues for the inviolable loyalty owed to the king by urging his audience to shift their perspective, from "the too near view of the little present interests of ourselves, our friends, or our country" to an imagining of "ourselves to be distant spectators of all that is transacted and contained" in the world. Distance is necessary to judgment, and "he who stands close to a palace can hardly make a right judgment of the architecture and symmetry of its several parts" (VI,32–33).

Berkeley's achievement in *Siris* is philosophical narrative in an unrestrained, lyrical style that brings those activities and perspectives together. *Siris* turns away from the polemical tactics of the earlier works, with their comic dramatizations of philosophical error and moral-theological absurdity. In a sense predicted by some of the more assertive entries in the *Philosophical Commentaries,* Berkeley was always slightly uncomfortable with the implictly ironic mode of philosophical discourse in the tradition of Descartes and Locke. His arguments and elucidations are often marked by impatience with their slowness, and they are invariably accompanied by a certain shortness with opponents. *Siris* is apart from this world of polemics and is not a work of argument at all, as that term is normally used. It represents a release of Berkeley's implicit lyricism, a sometimes breathtaking elaboration of the process of signifying that Euphranor describes in *Alciphron*, and an extension of the images and representations of thinking and perceiving threaded through the earlier works.

It is appropriate in a number of ways that *Siris* should begin as a carefully detailed recipe for making tar-water. Berkeley's interest in tar-water's medicinal properties grows out of his Christian activism, his response to what Jessop reminds us was the "appalling sickness and mortality" in Ireland after the famine of 1739 (V,vi). His extraordinarily keen attention to the particular and his essentially empirical sensibility are behind his strange faith in tar-water. As he explained to Thomas Prior, he had made "experiments in many various and unlike cases" and "on those trials is founded my opinion of the salutary virtues of tar-water; which virtues are recommended from, and depend on, experiments and matters of fact, and neither stand nor fall with any theories or speculative principles whatever" (V,178). He adds, however, that theories "enlarged" his views of the medicine and led him to a "greater variety of trials, and thereby engendered and nourished my suspicion that it is a panacea" (V,178).

Berkeley falls easily into organic metaphors, and the connection between theory and such metaphors is what *Siris* is about. *Siris* passes from the recipe for tar-water and an explanation of its properties to an exalted account of the created universe in which the processes by which tar is made and by which it repairs the body are intricately related. The progress, as Donald Davie puts it, is from physic to metaphysics, but the link is a "chain" whereby connections are neither plain metaphor nor literal repetition.[51]

This balsam, weeping or sweating through the bark, hardens into resin; and this most copiously in the several species of pines and firs, whose oil being in greater quantity, and more tenacious of the acid spirit or vegetable soul (as perhaps it may not improperly be called), abides the action of the sun, and, attracting the sunbeams, is thereby exalted and enriched, so as to become a most noble medicine: such is the last product of a tree, perfectly maturated by time and sun. (V,44)

Observation and imagination (a sort of metaphorical reimagining of what is observed) are the features of Berkeley's prose here, and that process suggests an analogy with his epistemology. The resin, properly viewed, is in a relationship to the sun that exalts and enriches it. What begins as an ex-

ternal operation in nature is completed and perfected by a subtle appropriation of solar energy, just as ordinary perception, properly understood
in Berkeley's epistemological scheme, borrows its form from divine creation and is a kind of radiation of an inner light or energy. The Hebrew
words for "fire" and "light," Berkeley notes a bit later, are identical except
for the pointing (V,92). The pure fire animating the physical universe is
not the flickering flame and smoke but "that which is collected in the
focus of a mirror or burning glass." Without it, "the whole would be one
great stupid inanimate mass" (V,96). This subtle force is grossly visible in
solar fire but known through its operations. Its *esse* is in its creative and
upholding effects, and Berkeley's strange rendering of it makes it like the
"light" that is an image of perception correctly understood.

The universe Berkeley evokes in *Siris* is alive with connections. His
paraphrase of physics and biology is an animating version of them, fired
by his visionary rhetoric:

These native spirits or vegetable souls are all breathed or exhaled into
the air, which seems the receptacle as well as source of all sublunary
forms, the great mass or chaos which imparts and receives them . . .
Whatever perspires, corrupts, or exhales, impregnates the air, which, being acted upon by the solar fire, produceth within itself all sorts of
chemical operations, dispensing again those salts and spirits in new
generations, which it had received from putrefactions. (V,77)

This panorama is not Berkeley's retreat from immaterialism. These spec-
tacular phenomena show "there is a Mind that governs and actuates this
mundane system." The "pure aether, fire, or the substance of light" is ad-
ministered in the macrocosm "by an Infinite Mind," just as it is "in the
microcosm with limited power and skill by the human mind" (V,83).

What is stylistically remarkable about *Siris* is its modulation from technical biological or pharmacological details to these broad celebrations of
the universe, from exactly rendered physiology to an eloquent, densely
metaphorical, quasi-archaic prophetic utterance that achieves its power in
managing these striking shifts. Scientific exactness combines with a prophetic brevity and simplicity, a lyrical intensity shares the stage with phys-
ico-theological aphorism, The Berkeleian prophetic style is nearly imperative; its gnomic observations suggest the animating power of mind, both
human and divine: "The whole atmosphere seems alive. There is
everywhere acid to corrode, and seed to engender. Iron will rust, and
mould will grow in all places. Virgin earth becomes fertile, crops of new
plants ever and anon shew themselves; all which demonstrates the air to be
a common seminary and receptacle of all vivifying principles" (V,78).

Berkeley also moves in his survey from the tiny particles of creation to the moral and social world they constitute. If we think back to *Alciphron*, there is a resemblance between this kind of literary virtuosity and the rapid fluency Berkeley satirized in his freethinkers.

As the body is said to clothe the soul, so the nerves may be said to constitute her inner garment. And as the soul animates the whole, what nearly touches the soul relates to all. Therefore the asperity of tartarous salts, and the fiery acrimony of alkaline salts, irritating and wounding the nerves, produce nascent passions and anxieties in the soul; which both aggravate distempers and render men's lives restless and wretched, even when they are afflicted with no apparent distemper. This is the latent spring of much woe, spleen, and *taedium vitae*. Small imperceptible irritations of the minutest fibres or filaments, caused by the pungent salts of wines and sauces, do so shake and disturb the microcosms of high livers as often to raise tempests in courts and senates; whereas the gentle vibrations that are raised in the nerves by a fine subtle acid sheathed in a smooth volatile oil, softly stimulating and bracing the nervous vessels and fibres, promotes a due circulation and secretion of the animal juices, and creates a calm satisfied sense of health. (V,60)

The descent from the grand spiritual analogy whereby the body clothes the soul to the exact workings of the nervous system is rapid and satiric in its force, stretching from the salts in wines and sauces which upset their consumers to the disturbances they cause in courts and senates. The soul is involved in these material relationships, and if its relationship is inharmonious it suffers accordingly. Berkeley's version of hylozoism is aggresively exact, not merely mystified or mysterious but morally, socially, and physically complete. He returns again and again in these pages to a miraculously interconnected world whose lesson is antimechanistic by virtue of its analogical richness. The internal arrangements of the individual bodies have external results, personal and social: "life holds together the bodies of animals, the cause whereof is the soul, and as a city is held together by concord, the cause whereof is law, even so the world is held together by harmony, the cause whereof is God. And in this sense the world or universe may be considered either as one animal or one city" (V,131). Consistent with Berkeley's earlier notions, this vast system of interconnected phenomena is "a sort of rational discourse" that needs to be read, "not only [as] a magnificent spectacle, but also a most coherent, entertaining, and instructive Discourse; and to effect this, they are conducted, adjusted, and ranged by the greatest wisdom" (V,120,121).

Berkeley's prose avoids the scattering energy and gratuitous domination he satirized in Shaftesbury by trying to serve as a faithful rendering of that discourse. His style in *Siris* seeks to enact the connections it talks about, the deep-seated harmonies of the universe rendered by recurring images of fire and light and by lyrical cadences that mimic the grand cosmic movements:

Nevertheless, as the mind gathers strength by repeated acts, we should not despond, but continue to exert the prime and flower of our faculties, still recovering, and reaching on, and struggling into the upper region, whereby our natural weakness and blindness may be in some degree remedied, and a taste attained of truth and intellectual life. (V,155)

In the administration of all things, there is authority to establish, law to direct, and justice to execute. There is first the source of all perfection, or *Fons Deitatis*; secondly the supreme reason, or [*Logos*]; and lastly, the spirit, which quickens and inspires. We are sprung from the Father, irradiated or enlightened by the Son, and moved by the Spirit. Certainly, that there is Father, Son, and Spirit; that these bear analogy to the sun, light, and heat; and are otherwise expressed by the terms Principle, Mind, and Soul, by One or [*Tò hen*], Intellect, and Life, by Good, Word, and Love . . . (V,162)

The latter paragraph translates the systems of the ancients, "Platonists, Pythagoreans, Egyptians, and Chaldeans," into Berkeleian idiom. The summarizing smoothness and regularity of construction in the prose parallel the philosophical point. The universe is sustained in motion by God "according to various rules or laws of motion" (V,112), and Berkeley's prose moves rhythmically with it, tracing and enforcing resemblances and connections between celestial vistas and the minute organization of plants and animals. In these sentences, for example, the stately rhythm cooperates with intensely concrete, poeticized scientific terminology to produce the living world Berkeley wants us to imagine:

The heaven is supposed pregnant with virtues and forms, which constitute and discriminate the various species of things. And we have more than once observed that, as the light, fire, or celestial aether, being parted by refracting or reflecting bodies, produceth variety of colours; even so, that same apparently uniform substance, being parted and secreted by the attracting and repelling powers of the divers secretory ducts of plants and animals, that is, by natural chemistry, produceth or imparteth the various specific properties of natural bodies. Whence the tastes, and odours, and medicinal virtues so various in vegetables. (V,92)

As Donald Davie has put it, Berkeley's "diction" revivifies the dead metaphors in our normal understanding of the material world but leaves them neither metaphoric nor literal. The chain *Siris* describes, Davie continues, "does not lead from one territory into another. Rather it is coiled and piled, physical or metaphysical according as we look on this coil or on that."[52]

In his elegant refutation of the "idealism" built on Berkeley's formula "*esse is percipi*," G. E. Moore found it made nonsense of part and whole as meaningful categories: "*esse* is held to be *percipi*, solely because *what is experienced* is held to be identical with the *experience of it*." For Moore, it is necessary to conceive that something exists apart from our sensation of it; the notion of experience, he seems to say, includes its own partial relationship to a whole. In *Siris* at least, Berkeley's answer to the necessary incompleteness of perception is the fullness of his rhetoric, which blurs the distinction between sensation and thought. He evokes a plenitude in which *esse* and *percipi* are not merely tautologically connected, as in Moore's rendering an awareness of something is simply our awareness of our awareness.[53] Rather, Berkeley's rhythmic prose and reiterated, vivified imagery promote "*esse is percipi*" as a series of grand narrative moments in which the reader discovers that *esse* is also *percipere*, participation with Berkeley in the perception of the universe in a rich and oddly particularized way. Berkeley's vivid imagination of the cosmos seeks to transform the potentially absurd world of the immaterialist hypothesis into a regular, beautiful physicotheological spectacle, to prevent the solipsism and narrow skepticism that misunderstanding is liable to make of the hypothesis.

And yet for all its eccentric splendor, *Siris* has an ironic plot and a didactic, rhetorical purpose. Berkeley's radiant images of the world are governed by a Platonic irony, and "we in this mortal state are like men educated in Plato's cave, looking on shadows with our backs turned to the light" (V,124). *Siris* leads the reader through acid, salt, sulphur, air, aether, and visible corporeal fire in order to "ascend through all those mediums to a glimpse of the First Mover, invisible, incorporeal, unextended, intellectual sources of life and being" (V,137). Berkeley's images have an almost Blakean forcefulness and density as he depicts the soul's efforts to "snatch a glimpse of pure light." It is "soon drawn backward and depressed by the heaviness of the animal nature to which she is chained." Berkeley wants his reader to feel the intensity of these contraries, and this passage as he draws near the end of *Siris* leads the soul once more, in a sort of frenzy, "amidst the agitation of wild fancies and strong affections, to spring upwards." But, "a second relapse speedily succeeds into this region of darkness and dreams" (V,154–155).

The transcendence Berkeley renders in *Siris* is slow and gradual, and he deliberately returns from the visionary to the textual. Whatever progress upward is possible he describes in specifically rhetorical terms, "by insensible transitions, [to] draw the reader into remote inquiries and speculations, that were not thought of either by him or by the author at first setting out" (V,138). Berkeley is wary of transcending his bookishness. He balances lyric enthusiasm with caution about the difficulties of true understanding and formulates those difficulties in a metaphor which brings us back to the literal fact of our reading and his writing.

But, if there are many links in the chain which connects the two extremes of what is grossly sensible and purely intelligible, and it seem a tedious work, by the slow helps of memory, imagination, and reason— oppressed and overwhelmed, as we are, by the senses, through erroneous principles, and long ambages of words and notions—to struggle upwards into the light of truth, yet, as this gradually dawns, further discoveries still correct the style and clear up the notions. (V,137)

We seem to be soaring out of sight, shaking off words and notions in the ascent to "the light of truth," but our discoveries correct our style and clarify our notions. *Siris* is what Berkeley calls at its end an "essay," a series of "hints to awaken and exercise the inquisitive reader" (V,157). Berkeley seeks even in this most visionary and uninhibited of his works to be rhetorical in a crafty and instructive sense; he wishes to subordinate the grand rhetorical movements of *Siris* to the essential clarity and simplicity of his style and his philosophical position. His procedure makes sense of one of Derrida's sibylline utterances about writing and meaning: "Meaning must await being said or written in order to inhabit itself, and in order to become, by differing from itself, what it is: meaning."[54] Even at his most lyrical, Berkeley is a philosophical rhetorician who arranges this dramatization of the dance of meaning.

Chapter 4

Hume

*I know not anything more pleasant or more instructive than to compare
experience with expectation or to register from time to time the
difference between idea and reality. It is by this kind of observation that
we grow daily less liable to be disappointed.*

—Johnson to Bennet Langton, *Boswell's Life of Johnson*

Shortly before he died in 1776, Hume looked back in a short
autobiography whose calm introspection and ironic modesty strike comically against the fervor of youthful ambition by which he was "seized
very early with a passion for literature, which has been the ruling passion
of my life, and the great source of my enjoyments." For Hume and his
age, "literature" embraced all of letters, writing available to the generality of educated men, and excluded (with certain exceptions from antiquity) books addressed to the specific needs of the professions. Hume's
passion turned to "the pursuits of philosophy and general learning"
(Cicero and Virgil are his examples) and away from the legal tomes of
Voet and Vinnius his family thought he was studying. A few years later,
when he set out in his mid-twenties to revolutionize western thought in
deliberate solitude at La Flèche, Hume was following a "plan of life"
which regarded "every object as contemptible, except the improvement
of my talents in literature."[1] Like Berkeley, Hume was utterly convinced
of his originality, but he imagined his work in even broader, more heroic
fashion as reconstituting "the republic of letters." This, in the coy third-
person preface to the "Abstract," is the implicit claim of *A Treatise of
Human Nature*:

The book seem'd to me to have such an air of singularity, and novelty as claim'd the attention of the public; especially if it be found, as the Author seems to insinuate, that were his philosophy receiv'd, we must alter from the foundation the greatest part of the sciences. Such bold attempts are always advantageous in the republic of letters, because they shake off the yoke of authority, accustom men to think for themselves, give new hints, which men of genius may carry further, and by the very opposition, illustrate points, wherein no one before suspected any difficulty. (Pp. 643–644)

Like Locke and Berkeley, Hume sought to avoid the specialization that undermines the freshness and pertinence of philosophical writing; he wished to act not so much as a reviser of systems and perennial problems as a repudiator of them and a founder by radical reformulation of a new tradition, which would turn from books to experience and speak to a broad if discerning audience. In part, this ambition is a rhetorical gesture, a set of stylistic habits supporting a moral and political program to liberate and secularize knowledge. So, too, the republic of letters Hume wished to address was a narrow commonwealth at best, an ideal group of readers whose presence served to sharpen discourse and preserve it from professional dullness. But this idea of an audience served Hume well, for his thought is deeply embedded from its beginnings in persuasiveness. The self-advertisement of his abstract appeals to readers alert enough to sense an "air" and catch insinuations. But the "men of genius" who will continue his philosophic program are also readers in this regard, able to seize those "hints" the *Treatise* contains and thereby follow Hume into the higher reaches of his thought.

To some extent, Berkeley treated writing as an obstacle to clarity, or he tended at least to dramatize thought and apprehension as first and foremost wordless activities compromised by language. Locke's garrulity is a sign of his concession to the limits of thought and reason; the digressive easiness of his manner marks a refusal to attempt to persuade in matters not provable. Locke and Berkeley are writers who often claim to put writing aside, to subordinate it to thought and sometimes to disparage it. Hume always conceived of his philosophy in literary terms and saw his problems as essentially rhetorical. Locke knew he was right and projected an often careless confidence. Berkeley wished that men would see how right he was and how wrong they were; his manner is full of passionate intensity, despising mere persuasiveness. Hume wished to persuade a broadly conceived audience that he was right and that they might easily share his confidence. If we are to believe the letter he wrote but never posted to Dr. Arbuthnot describing his first efforts, that desire was intense and led to intellectual despair: "I had no Hopes of delivering my Opinions with such Elegance & Neatness, as to draw to me the Attention of the World, & I wou'd rather live & dye in Obscurity than produce them maim'd & imperfect."[2]

A Treatise of Human Nature is densely argued and difficult. Hume often fails to achieve "Elegance & Neatness," but the book nevertheless is "written" in a manner that distinguishes it from the work of Locke and Berkeley. In part, Hume's distinctiveness is a matter of essayistic fluency, a careful tonal control and delicate sense of audience his predecessors to some extent neglected. Although he did not wholly integrate it with his thought until the *Enquiries*, Hume's style in the *Treatise* has the Addisonian "smoothness" Irvin Ehrenpreis says is meant to startle and delight by its contrast with the doctrines expounded.[3] For example, as he moves in Book I of the *Treatise* toward a redefinition of belief as "a more vivid and intense conception of an idea, proceeding from its relation to a present impression," Hume summarizes his extraordinary conclusion as if it were a harmless notion, indeed as if philosophy were thereby as elegant as the poetry and music he places it next to:

Thus all probable reasoning is nothing but a species of sensation. 'Tis not solely in poetry and music, we must follow our taste and sentiment, but likewise in philosophy. When I am convinc'd of any principle, 'tis only an idea, which strikes more strongly upon me. When I give the preference to one set of arguments above another, I do nothing but decide from my feeling concerning the superiority of their influence. Objects have no discoverable connexion together; nor is it from any other principle but custom operating upon the imagination, that we can draw any inference from the appearance of one to the existence of another. (P.103)

"Nothing but" and "only" are harshly reductive conjunctions, but Hume's reassuring manner takes readers into his confidence and serves to distract us from these implications. By virtue of clarity and simplicity, the writing refuses its implications and treats an arbitrary universe as a natural one, where our choice of arguments is associated with the pleasure we give ourselves by discriminating in music and poetry. An attitude emerges from summarizing passages like these that accepts a dispersed reality with equanimity, without surprise or anxiety. The passage is thereby both a summary of the close reasoning preceding it and a rhetorical seal for that argument, its embodiment in an attractive persona. A reluctant reductionist, Hume is a modest observer careful to affirm a world of custom and habit even as he politely demolishes philosophical expectations.

Modesty becomes a simple rhetorical signal, a clear, ironic counter-point to actual arrogance. Thus, Hume is at his most deferential when he arrives at the most compactly outrageous revisions in the *Treatise*. He presents a subversive ethical insight as if it were a mere textual refinement, a polite if firm enforcement of a strictness of speaking. Hume chooses to dramatize his activity as the correction of prevailing loose ways of talking, irresponsible and inattentive discourse, which he has discovered, in all modesty, by careful reading and neat marginal notation:

I cannot forbear adding to these reasonings an observation, which may, perhaps, be found of some importance. In every system of morality, which I have hitherto met with, I have always remark'd, that the author proceeds for some time in the ordinary way of reasoning, and establishes the being of a God, or makes observations concerning human affairs; when of a sudden I am surpriz'd to find, that instead of the usual copulations of propositions, *is*, and *is not*, I meet with no proposition that is not connected with an *ought*, or an *ought not*. This change is imperceptible; but is, however, of the last consequence. For as this *ought*, or *ought not*, expresses some new relation or affirmation, 'tis necessary that it shou'd be observ'd and explain'd; and at the same time that a reason should be given, for what seems altogether inconceivable, how this relation can be a deduction from others, which are entirely different from it. But as authors do not commonly use this precaution, I shall presume to recommend it to the readers; and am persuaded, that this small attention wou'd subvert all the vulgar systems of morality, and let us see, that the distinction of vice and virtue is not founded merely on the relations of objects, nor is perceiv'd by reason. (Pp.469–470)

"Hume's law," as it is now often called, is the last paragraph of the opening chapter of Book III, "Of Morals," a straightforward exposition of the logic behind his denial of rational ethics. The transparent pseudodeference of this paragraph concludes a series of sharp assertions, and its fiction of amateurism is preceded by the synthesizing claim in the previous paragraph that vice and virtue are like the secondary qualities such as sounds, colors, heat, and cold, which "according to modern philosophy, are not qualities in objects, but perceptions in the mind" (p.469). Hume's rhetoric involves the disparagement of philosophical discourse itself, an undermining of its pretense to systematize reality and, worse, to regulate our conduct. So, this momentary professionalism, which notes that "this discovery in morals, like that other in physics, is to be regarded as a considerable advancement of the speculative sciences" (p.469), is canceled in the next clause. Like the demotion of secondary qualities to epiphenomena, the relegation of ethical discrimination to feeling "has little or no influence on practice" (p.469).

The casual "addition" of the concluding paragraph tips the balance against philosophical systems, defeats them in the name of an unprejudiced observer, a witty amateur very much like the persona behind the eighteenth-century familiar essay who wanders into these professional precincts with a modest and thereby satirical perspective. For the moment, spontaneity compels Hume; he cannot "forbear adding" and he recalls his own surprise at discovering illogic. Hume is a reader who sides with other readers, now armed with a "small attention" or "precaution" commonly neglected by "authors." It will require a good deal more than small attention to follow Hume's argument, and this distinction is itself a matter of some rigor. The guiding irony in moments like these consists of Hume's essentially rhetorical transformation of the difficult or abstruse into the neglected obvious. What he shares with his readers is not only the distinctly literary satisfaction of an assumed naiveté but also the knowledge that clear and simple expression, a rigorous literalism in language and a rejection of terms of art are the ultimate principles of a reformed philosophy. Hume at his best offers readers clarity and firm assurance, earned in victorious debate with muddled reasoners. Into their large and clumsy assertions, we are enabled to insert small corrections which overturn whole systems. Hume's law is an aphoristic translation of tangled controversy, a witty condensation and refutation of volumes in a simple rephrasing.

At such moments, Hume's writing has an oratorical polish, a rhythm and measured pace he tries to sustain even in the many difficult sections of the *Treatise*. Sensitivity to style is something Hume takes so much for granted he can use it to make a philosophical point. When viewing moral qualities not directly or closely related to us, he argues near the end of the *Treatise*, we can feel a limited sort of involvement. Imagination allows men to establish justice and property by giving them some notion of what others deserve. One of Hume's analogies for this sympathy is stylistic in a sense almost too exquisite to be credible:

When I run over a book with my eye, I imagine I hear it all; and also, by the force of imagination, enter into the uneasiness, which the delivery of it wou'd give the speaker. The uneasiness is not real; but as such a composition of words has a natural tendency to produce it, this is sufficient to affect the mind with a painful sentiment, and render the style harsh and disagreeable. (Pp.585–586)

Many modern commentators find it hard to forgive Hume his stylish persuasiveness. Most are too concerned with narrowly defined problems in his thought to worry about the larger, cumulative effects of Hume's writing, but to those who stop to consider them he seems acute rather than profound. His style, as Stuart Hampshire puts it, "was designed to persuade rather than to prove."[4] Acuteness, elegance, persuasiveness—these are qualities which actually undercut Hume's philosophical achievement, concealing what C. H. Sisson calls "the fundamental sleight-of-hand" at work in his thought.[5] Hume's arguments, says A. P. Cavendish, are "persuasive rather than conclusive," and he often fails to prove his case strictly but presents "his opinion in a persuasive manner."[6] These complaints are not mere boorishness or the jealous hostility of logical technicians. Persuasion and proof, as Hampshire notes, may be considered quite distinct, and Hume's stylishness seems a sign of bad faith or evasive shallowness.[7]

One answer to such critics is to treat Hume's writing as a distinct rhetorical enactment and a crucial supplement to his thought. Michael Morrisroe attempts such a defense when he finds that summaries of the arguments "do not reflect the mind of Hume. Only his writing does."[8] Morrisroe suggests that Hume's mind is a richly varied, supremely interesting aesthetic phenomenon, which supplements the "conceptual content" of his thought. Hume's element was language. He was as sensitive to style and its variations as a fish to excessive oxygenation. Given a choice between "being esteem'd a Friend to Virtue" and "a Writer of Taste," he wrote to Francis Hutcheson in 1739, he would choose the latter, "otherwise I must despair of ever being servicable to Virtue." The moralism Hutcheson apparently found lacking in the *Treatise* would have violated the decorum of literary taste, introducing an "Air of Declamation amidst abstract Reasonings."[9] Hume aspired to correctness and simple elegance in his writing; he scorned rhetorical excess and obtrusive verbal ornament. Like so many of his contemporaries, including Adam Smith, Hume preferred Demosthenes to Cicero, who as he said in his essay "Of Eloquence," was sometimes "too florid and rhetorical." Demosthenes was "more chaste and austere," his manner "rapid harmony, exactly adjusted to the sense: it is vehement reasoning, without any appearance of art: it is disdain, anger, boldness, freedom, involved in a continued stream of argument." Demosthenes is a nearly perfect orator because he conceals artifice, sustains an argument by emotional effects whose rhetorical causes are not easily apparent. Vehemence is part of the "stream" of argument rather than a visible supplement. Cicero's figures, on the other hand, "are too striking and palpable," and his wit sometimes stoops to the "artifice even of a pun, rhyme, or jingle of words."[10]

Hume concluded "Of Eloquence" conventionally enough, finding real eloquence lacking in modern times, which possess a lesser kind of "Attic eloquence, that is calm, elegant, and subtile, which instructed the reason more than affected the passions, and never raised its tone above argument or common discourse."[11] In "Of Simplicity and Refinement in Writing" however, Hume wondered whether a sort of "Asiatic" decadence was setting in as an "excess of refinement" after the recent progress in learning. "The endeavour to please by novelty leads men wide of simplicity and nature, and fills their writings with affectation and conceit." Given the self-consciously subversive implications of his thought, Hume is interested in cultivating a special tact in his writing to avoid adding to the scandal and to cut himself off from the series of polemics which is the literary history of philosophy. He begins "Of Simplicity and Refinement in Writing" citing Addison to the effect that fine writing "consists of sentiments which are natural, without being obvious. There cannot be a juster and more concise definition of fine writing."[12] Hume's thought has, of course, a paradoxical relationship with the "natural." He presents a recovery of the natural in the face of accumulated obtuseness and nearly universal blindness to its truth. What he elaborates is not "obvious," but it is natural only by virtue of his moderating manner as a writer: paradox and subversive difficulty are suspended within a tightly controlled style dominated by terse understatement, irony, mock concession, and the austerity of ornament he so admired in Demosthenes.

To some extent, Hume's opinions in the *Essays* are glossy commonplaces, but they do reflect his practice. All his life, Hume shunned stylistic extravagance of whatever kind or persuasion. Writing to William Strahan, his publisher, in 1771, he thanked him for sending Samuel Johnson's pamphlet on the Falkland Islands, a work Hume found "very diverting from the Peculiarity and Enormity of the Style."[13] Johnson's massively deliberate style was merely amusing. Rousseau's extravagant eloquence met with a sterner response. As he told the Comtesse de Boufflers in 1763, Rousseau's "domineering force of genius" is "always intermingled [with] some degree of extravagance." Although he denies it, Rousseau seemed to choose "his topics less from persuasion, than from the pleasure of showing his invention, and surprizing the reader by his paradoxes."[14]

Stylistic extravagance for Hume erodes persuasiveness, calls attention to language as self-serving performance, and separates the writer's activity from a community of discourse with deeply held standards of useful clarity and intelligibility. Hume's writing takes place, it seems to me, within the following paradox: on the one hand, he sought to write for the discerning public who formed the ideal republic of letters and he aspired to establish an easy clarity around the traditional philosophic problems; on the other hand, he uncovered and relentlessly articulated in the *Treatise* an epistemological and moral world of turbulent uncertainty where the common sense and humanist continuities supporting the republic of letters are canceled or at best rendered arbitrary and imperiled. Hume was often accused of the same intellectual sensationalism he found in Rousseau, and Johnson said he and "other sceptical innovators" had gone off to milk the bull of mere paradox. Hume's thought thus presents him with an occasion for intellectual melodrama and moral extremity. Even as a young man, he was uneasy with this temptation.

Part of his well-known apology to Hutcheson reflects this uneasiness vividly but suggests a solution that fits perfectly within what he eventually made the social, moral, and aesthetic program of his thought. His letter echoes closely the last paragraph of the *Treatise*, and Hume repeated the sentiments almost exactly in the first section of *An Enquiry concerning Human Understanding*. One may consider both mind and body, he wrote to Hutcheson, "either as an Anatomist or as a Painter." The latter describes "the Grace & Beauty of its Actions," the former seeks "to discover its most secret Springs & Principles." But one must choose, since to "pull off the Skin, & display all the minute Parts" reveals the trivial "even in the noblest Attitudes & most vigorous Actions." [15] The words of the *Treatise* are slightly harsher: the anatomist presents "something hideous, or at least minute" (p.621). Justification of the anatomist's grisly art (still in Hume's day associated with mutilation and the punishment of criminals) is in each of Hume's rehearsals of this dramatized apology for his inquiring philosophy a matter of a resolving aphorism, which links artistic and intellectual work in their contribution to human ease. The "Anatomist," Hume wrote to Hutcheson, "can give very good Advice to a Painter or Statuary: And in like manner, I am perswaded, that a Metaphysician may be very useful to a Moralist." [16] The *Treatise* concludes by putting this more positively. A painter can hardly hope to excel without exact advice from an anatomist: "We must have an exact knowledge of the parts, their situation and connexion, before we can design with any elegance or correctness" (p.621). And the *Enquiry*, less assertive and more smoothly generalizing, generates a maxim: "Accuracy is, in every case, advantageous to beauty, and just reasoning to delicate sentiment. In vain would we exalt the one by depreciating the other" (p.10).

The *Treatise* is a pure exercise in anatomizing; its harshly literalized renderings of the perceptual world and its reiterated skeptical toughness insist on close attention to the shocking implications of a minute examination of knowledge and morals. But an ignorant painter, like a superficial moralist, can produce only offensively inaccurate representations. Hume's even-handed, restrained rhetoric in the *Treatise* is the verbal equivalent of strict accuracy. His refusal of overseeing and organizing analogies or of master metaphors, his modulations away from declamation or clamorous insistence, the studied moderation of his style, and the ironic modesty of his claims—these gestures try to balance the extreme implications of his findings, framing radical propositions with a conservative literary manner. Behind this style lies Hume's claim to promote utility, beauty, and ease; his observations are contributions to a revised representation of man, bound in its accuracy, as the *Enquiry* puts it, to make life better.

In some of his moral and religious writings, Hume's delicacy is merely discretion in the face of powerful intolerance. As he remarked of Rousseau's *Confessions of the Savoyard Vicar*, "the liberty of the press is not so secured in any country, scarce even in this, as not to render such an open attack on popular prejudices somewhat dangerous." [17] But Hume's circumspection extends to issues that held no threat of prosecution, although they excited the wrath of philosophical contemporaries like Thomas Reid.

After he read the *Treatise*, Reid was moved to vigorous challenge of Hume's ideas, and in a series of papers read before the Aberdeen Philosophical Society (which he later published in 1764 as *An Inquiry into the Human Mind on the Principles of Common Sense*), he attacked what modern philosophy had wrought and promoted what he called "Common Sense." According to Reid, modern thought had removed the intellectual rubbish of the past but in so doing had erected new barriers between men and philosophy. Berkeley had completed the work of Descartes, Malebranche, and Locke and undone "the whole material world." Hume had dismantled what remained, "the world of spirits," leaving "nothing in nature but ideas and impressions without any subject on which they may be impressed." Reid complained, with some justice I think, that the theory of "ideas" on which modern thought stood and with which it atomized and in effect dispersed the world of experience was an unjustified fiction, a nonempirical formulation. He called the "ideal philosophy" a hypothesis with no solid proof of the existence of these ideas, these representations of the material of existence, which are always conceived as something past and which turn the operations of the mind into memory and imagination exclusively. "Upon the strictest attention, memory appears to me to have things that are past, and not present ideas, for its object."[18]

Hume complained to Hugh Blair when he was asked to comment on Reid's work: "I wish that the Parsons would confine themselves to their old occupation of worrying one another, and leave Philosophers to argue with temper, moderation, and good manners."[19] But after reading some sections of Reid's manuscript he was somewhat mollified and wrote a complaisant if, as Mossner notes, a faintly ironic letter in which he praised Reid's style at the distinct expense of his thought: "It is certainly very rare, that a piece so deeply philosophical is wrote with so much spirit, and affords so much entertainment to the reader . . . when I enter into your ideas, no man appears to express himself with greater perspicuity than you do; a talent which, above all others, is requisite in that species of literature which you have cultivated." Hume corrected one of Reid's Scotticisms and with clearly ironic deference said he was pleased his "errors" had by their force led Reid "to perceive their futility."[20]

Hume's irony is clarified by looking briefly at Reid's writing and his rival dramatization of the epistemological scene. Reid's notions are considered but his rhetoric tends toward the declamation Hume so carefully avoided. Even when he responded to Hume's cagy letter, Reid laid out the scene in garish colors and melodramatic tones: if Hume's principles are solid, his "system must stand; and whether they are or not, can better be judged after you have brought to Light the whole system that grows out of them, than when the greater part of it was wrapped up in clouds and darkness."[21] The *Inquiry* itself is often self-dramatizing in similar fashion. For example, this introductory section on the present state of philosophy combines a clumsy ironic attack on modern thought with a heavy-handed apostrophizing of Philosophy and Common Sense:

Des Cartes, Malebranche, and Locke, have all employed their genius and skill to prove the existence of a material world; and with very bad success. Poor untaught mortals believe undoubtedly that there is a sun, moon, and stars; an earth, which we inhabit; country, friends, and relations, which we enjoy; land, houses, and moveables, which we possess. But philosophers, pitying the credulity of the vulgar, resolve to have no faith but what is founded upon reason. They apply to philosophy to furnish them with reasons for the belief of those things which all mankind have believed, without being able to give any reason for it. And surely one would expect, that, in matters of such importance, the proof would not be difficult; but it is the most difficult thing in the world. For these three great men, with the best good will, have not been able, from all the treasures of philosophy, to draw one argument that is fit to convince a man that can reason, of the existence of any one thing without him.

Admired Philosophy! daughter of light! parent of wisdom and knowledge! if thou art she, surely thou hast not yet arisen upon the human
mind, nor blessed us with more of thy rays than are sufficient to shed a
darkness visible upon the human faculties, and to disturb that repose
and security which happier mortals enjoy, who never approached thine
altar, nor felt thine influence! But if, indeed, thou hast not power to
dispel these clouds and phantoms which thou hast discovered or created,
withdraw this penurious and malignant ray; I despise Philosophy, and
renounce its guidance — let my soul dwell with Common Sense.[22]

Facile sarcasm informs Reid's attack on modern thought and on Hume's
skepticism in particular: an assertive catalogue of the ordinary dares
Hume to reject what he never in any event denied. Placed next to Hume's
careful ironies, Reid's writing is spirited but essentially hasty, coarse, and
vulgar. To be sure, this is a polemical passage, an introduction to Reid's
defense of "common sense" against the "ideal philosophy." But his opposition between common life and philosophy is a simpleminded antithesis. The entertainment Hume found in Reid's work may have come
from seeing the complex and delicate negotiations between philosophy
and common life he stages in the *Treatise* reduced to these easy exhortations. Reid's tone is uncertain, almost out of control. The praise of "Philosophy" is a literary joke to some extent, mock reverence to a discredited
personification which sets up the choice of Common Sense in a climax at
first comic and then deadly serious. A few paragraphs later, Reid arranges
a reconciliation between these abstractions, a restoration he calls it of
their natural friendship, in which philosophy realizes its dependence on
common sense: "Philosophy (if I may be permitted to change the metaphor) has no other root but the principles of Common Sense; it grows out
of them, and draws its nourishment from them. Severed from this root,
its honours wither, its sap is dried up, it dies and rots."[23]

Reid is competent and earnest but his rhetorical self-consciousness at
moments like these reveals an uncertainty with language and with the
essentially simple metaphoric enforcements of his thought. Slightly embarrassed by his metaphors here (this is about the fifth clear shift in this
section), he plunges ahead and his polemic against philosophy serves to
justify metaphoric excess. For Reid common sense is over and over again a
nearly embodied entity, an unquestionable and unexaminable set of
powers granted by "Nature." "Such original and natural judgments are,
therefore, a part of that furniture which Nature hath given to the human
understanding. They are the inspirations of the Almighty no less than our
notions or simple apprehensions."[24]

Reid's understanding of modern thought is far from naive, and his elaboration of perception is often shrewd. But his rhetorical enforcements are less than subtle, returning regularly to a philosophic scene where apostrophe and personification do much of the work of persuasion, where analogy and simple metaphor obtrude as Reid attempts to clarify his own position and condemn others. The transaction with reality that Hume complicates and bedevils with uncertainty, Reid turns into a visit from divinity manifest in human uniformity and natural regularity. Cause and effect become signified and sign in the language Nature speaks.[25]

Reid's program has a refreshing simplicity and directness; indeed it might be called a substitution of naive and childlike perception for the adult complications and ironic reciprocities Hume establishes. The essential philosophic moment, says Reid, is best rendered by considering children looking at every thing curiously, directed by Nature "to handle every thing over and over, to look at it while they handle it, and to put it in various positions, and at various distances from the eye."[26] For Hume, such pastoral moments are postlapsarian fictions; sweetly innocent common sense cannot be restored because its categories and the representation of its defining moments such as Reid sketches are lower-order versions of philosophical formulations, essentially simplified and rhetorical reconstructions of a complex sequence which is social and historical rather than mythic or recurrent. The common sense Reid enshrines is untenable for Hume because its existence rests on an incomplete narration, a less than wholly attentive or accurate rendering of the actualities of experience or perception. As Reid himself notes with tiresome frequency, thinkers like Hume have to live in the common world. What such predictable objections miss totally is the operation and sequence of Hume's writing. That records among other things a strenuous, consistent effort to retain common experience and everyday understanding by accounting for their rearrangement of actual perception. The effort is required precisely because of the newly founded complexity and even the elusiveness of ordinary happenings. Reid wishes to live in a world where the operations of the mind, the mind itself, and the objects of experience are distinct. He complained in a later work that for Hume these clarities and distinctions are lost: "When he speaks of the ideas of memory, the ideas of imagination, and the ideas of sense, it is often impossible, from the tenor of his discourse, to know whether, by those ideas, he means the operations of the mind, or the objects about which they are employed."[27]

Quite simply, Hume's radical notions contain no compromise with these mixed and shifting mental configurations. In the face of their disorder, he cultivated stylistic austerity and rhetorical coolness. He had to resist the temptation to dramatize this scene of thought and establish narrative clarity where he did not actually find it. Hume's literary fastidiousness is part of his ambition to persuade by communicating abstruse matters with a new kind of clarity, but the special sort of concinnity that is his literary signature is related to the difficult nature of his central insights. The *Treatise* is an attempt to retain clarity in rendering an epistemological scene where, as Reid complained, clarity has no place, where sequence and order seem to be imposed rather than discovered. Irony, as many have noted, must be the prevailing tone in such an effort, since clarity seems a gratuitous invention under these circumstances.

As any reader can see, Hume's irony is pervasive, stretching in the *Treatise* from contempt for philosophical rivals to a recurring amusement with philosophizing itself. Irony is what Stuart Hampshire calls a "fitting style" for the secular mind, "which can accept and submit itself to the natural order, the facts of human nature, without anxiety, and therefore without a demand for ultimate solutions." Hume's irony, as Hampshire describes it, "exhibits as persuasively as possible both the demand for a complete solution of the problems and the frustration of this demand, and then finally leaves the matter there, with no further conclusion, no happy ending."[28] The sequence in such irony seems clumsy when applied to Hume's writing, where the reader's anticipation of actual solutions is never really an issue, where a supervising tone prepares us for what are actually mock surprises, and where the artificial disappointments of philosophical inquiry, as Hume stages it, are nothing less than moral-rhetorical consolations.

As he thought about the kind of philosophical irony embodied in Socrates, Kierkegaard found that its "first potency" lay in "formulating a theory of knowledge which annihilates itself." Irony in such a view is the writer's predisposition, a trope that overwhelms philosophy, a negation of the phenomenal: "It flees back into itself instead of going out of itself, it is not in the phenomenon but seeks to deceive by means of the phenomenon, the phenomenon is not in order to manifest essence but to conceal essence." Hume's writing avoids the daemonic whirling in Kierkegaard's rendering of irony. Hume approaches the phenomenal world and, to use Kierkegaard's terms, discovers a vast gap between himself and that world; his thought elaborates something that seems to be neither self nor world and finds, even more alarmingly, that these "phenomena" do not simply conceal their own essence but call the investigator himself into question. What is left for Hume is not quite rendered by Kierkegaard's formulation of the distinct movements of dialectic and irony: "dialectic infinitely expands itself and flows out in extremities, irony leads the movement back into personality, induces it to round itself off in personality."[29] Kierkegaard's ironist is flirting with nothingness, thumbing his nose at emerging Hegelian "objectivity," and preparing this hollowed out selfhood for God. Hume the ironist, in the *Treatise* at least, is staging a philosophical process in which he is less a personality in the melodramatic sense imagined by Kierkegaard than a representative character, a revised version of that literary invention, the philosopher. What is generally overlooked about the *Treatise* is its deliberate scenic self-consciousness, the narrative frame Hume sets it in and pauses quite often to remind the reader of. Hume's local ironies and their implications are part of a larger moral-literary occasion, a narrative meant to give readers pleasure as well as instruction.

This is not to say Hume was in complete literary control of the *Treatise* and always managed to place his philosophical project within a moral fable. Rather, his elaborate literary framing is the key to his attempt to stabilize his thought, to avoid the static conventionality of secular skepticism and the unacceptable (perhaps to him inconceivable) intellectual and moral melodrama his thought could provoke, that "metaphysical agony" some commentators find in the *Treatise*.[30] "Nothing is more usual and more natural for those, who pretend to discover any thing new to the world in philosophy and the sciences, than to insinuate the praises of their own systems, by decrying all those, which have been advanced before them" (p.xiii). This opening sentence of the "Introduction" to the *Treatise* offers a generalization that turns gracefully into a compressed narrative, in which the neutrality of "pretend" is undercut by the force of "insinuate." The old joke is the inevitability of thinly disguised self-seeking in philosophers, and indeed this self-promotion is a "natural" activity Hume himself will engage in before this opening paragraph is over. From the outset, Hume's irony is self-implicating, since he implicitly claims here to avoid the verbal clumsiness that goes with this self-seeking. Philosophers transparently promote themselves by attacking their predecessors; they should merely confess ignorance, their own as well as their rivals'. Hume's "ignorance" in this paragraph is a formidable affair, a sweeping dismissal of philosophy itself: "Principles taken upon trust, consequences lamely deduced from them, want of coherence in the parts, and of evidence in the whole, these are every where to be met with in the systems of the most eminent philosophers, and seem to have drawn disgrace upon philosophy itself" (p.xiii). The control of scene in this sentence rebukes the verbal clumsiness "usual" in philosophers; the inclusive panorama of ignorance seems to satisfy Hume's call for a repression of self-interest.

In the following paragraph, the joke becomes broader, the scene livelier, and the comic emphasis more sharply verbal. Philosophy as it appears even to the "rabble without doors" is a mere babble, a "noise and clamour." Again, Hume's analysis is both moral and rhetorical; careless language and irresponsible declamation violate elementary rules of coherence: "Disputes are multiplied, as if every thing was uncertain; and these disputes are managed with the greatest warmth, as if everything was certain. Amidst all this bustle 'tis not reason, which carries the prize, but eloquence; and no man needs ever despair of gaining proselytes to the most extravagant hypothesis, who has art enough to represent it in any favourable colours" (p.xiv). Hume assumes an audience who shares his delight in disorder thus viewed and controlled. The *Treatise* returns regularly to these comic evocations of philosophy as noisy wrangling, a favorite and recurring moment in eighteenth-century philosophy and writing about philosophy. What Hume adds to this commonplace is a witty rendering of symmetrical absurdity, an exact inversion of order: instead of canceling each other, uncertainty and certainty coexist and feed on each other. Such verbal wit depends upon abhorrence of extremes and simple formulations; it satirizes an ignorance of the psychological inevitability of linguistic deception. This wit takes pleasure in generalized representations of human nature and draws its tendentious strength from observing the ignorance or forgetfulness of human inevitability displayed in human affairs. The *Treatise* often sounds in its literary moments like one of Johnson's *Ramblers*, predicting by its symmetrical wit the inevitability of its disclosures. In short, Hume's literary manner at the very opening of his book is founded on the broad ironies of a moral-rhetorical tradition, which he has no desire to undermine and which in his own way he eventually seeks to reaffirm as even more necessary in the light of his epistemology. Unlike Kierkegaard's subversive ironist, Hume's persona in the *Treatise* is ready to protect himself and his audience with a literary manner that invokes as a consoling constant the intrinsic and absolute limitations of human understanding. Hume thus affirms an irony implicit in the moral-literary culture in which he lived.[31]

Having set the scene and struck the stylistic keynote, Hume goes on to sketch his Baconian ambitions for his science of man, indulging himself in a rather grandiose image which echoes the earlier, mocking rendering of the philosophical scene. There, a false eloquence wins the day and "the victory is not gained by the men at arms, who manage the pike and the sword; but by the trumpeters, drummers, and musicians of the army" (p.xiv). Now Hume proposes philosophical audacity:

. . . instead of taking now and then a castle or village on the frontier, to march up directly to the capital or center of these sciences, to human nature itself; which being once masters of, we may every where else hope for an easy victory. From this station we may extend our conquests over all those sciences, which more intimately concern human life, and may afterwards proceed at leisure to discover more fully those, which are the objects of pure curiosity. (P.xvi)

But the "science of man," as Hume proceeds to explain, is limited by "experience and observation" and the mastery promised in the conceit excludes in practice "the ultimate original qualities of human nature" (p.xvii). The introduction is itself a moral essay on the inevitability of ignorance and indeed on the satisfaction implicit in acknowledging ignorance of ultimates. Hume seems to turn the joke on himself and on the book that follows, since human nature adjusts to despair as it does to enjoyment: "we are no sooner acquainted with the impossibility of satisfying any desire, than the desire itself vanishes" (p.xviii). That there is no going beyond experience is "the reason of the mere vulgar," but the writer may lapse into self-congratulation in his skillful confession of ignorance. Hume's irony is directed for the moment at the easy irony which is the honest thinker's temptation:

And as this impossibility of making any farther progress is enough to satisfy the reader, so the writer may derive a more delicate satisfaction from the free confession of his ignorance, and from his prudence in avoiding that error, into which so many have fallen, of imposing their conjectures and hypotheses on the world for the most certain principles. When this mutual contentment and satisfaction can be obtained betwixt the master and scholar, I know not what more we can require of our philosophy. (P.xviii)

This last sentence undercuts the special self-satisfaction setting in, one "more delicate" than the easy ignorance of the vulgar. Hume's assertion acquires an ironic edge and turns into a rhetorical question, for the context of the introduction excludes "contentment and satisfaction" between master and scholar, indeed denies the cozy subordination in the world of learning implicit in such titles. Writing like Hume's in the *Treatise* involves a challenge to the reader to follow intricate reasoning, of course, but also, as this introduction exemplifies and initiates it, to understand ironic twists and tonal modulations. The philosophical text and the project it records are full of moral as well as intellectual pitfalls for writer and reader; conjectures and hypotheses may turn into "certain principles," and the mere confession of philosophical ignorance may transform inquiry into the delicate satisfaction in which master and scholar are content. The final paragraph of the introduction makes it quite clear such contentment is untenable.

Hume's final point makes "this impossibility of explaining ultimate principles" (p.xviii) the condition of all knowledge. None of the sciences and arts "can go beyond experience," although moral philosophy has a special disadvantage not found in natural philosophy. Introspection or self-examination is always problematical; if I place "myself in the same case with that which I consider, 'tis evident this reflection and premeditation would so disturb the operation of my natural principles, as must render it impossible to form any just conclusion from this phaenomenon" (p.xix). One must look out at the "common course of the world" and by "cautious observation" of men "in company, in affairs, and in their pleasures" hope to form a collective and comparative view, "which will not be inferior in certainty, and will be much superior in utility to any other of human comprehension" (p.xix). The satisfied master and scholar of the previous paragraph, content with an elegant negative formulation, are hardly capable of such observation, which as Hume evokes it is a process of constant adjustment and correction for bias and self-interest. Self-regulation is built into Hume's moral-literary manner, in which generality qualifies self-assertion or subsumes individuality into familiar patterns and categories. Each term in Hume's "science of man" is subject to ironic scrutiny: man is a category existing only within the history of men as comically predictable creatures, and "science" is built on an examination of terms always distorted by individual men and always therefore to be supplemented by social observation. Philosophical inquiry takes place within these conditions; it must guard against the ambiguity of the philosopher's motives as well as take into account the unreliability and partiality of introspection. Understanding perception and charting the movements of the understanding, as Hume will show in Book I of the *Treatise*, involve an almost impossible reflexiveness, a determined turning back to the corrections and arrangements of the perceiver. Hume's literary manner prevents that reflexive process from stopping, placing that self in a pattern of observed human behavior, which logically follows these investigations but in practice accompanies them, negating a solipsism or self-satisfaction that would terminate inquiry. Hume's philosophizing is inseparable, then, from the moral-rhetorical chorus which places it (and re-places it) in a human context.

The introduction to the *Treatise* is brief and impersonal, with Hume in control of his various ironies. The concluding Part IV of Book I is by contrast an extended, complicated, even confused personal narrative, which claims to interrupt the *Treatise*, as Hume wonders aloud where his thought has led him and whether he should continue. The artifice of this development, the literary shape implicit in these bursts of spontaneity, surprise, and bewilderment, seems obvious enough. And yet this chapter has often been read with little regard for its literary context and even less appreciation of its function as a comic transition toward Books II and III. I take it as given that Hume manages all his rhetorical effects in the *Treatise*, that these obtrusively self-conscious autobiographical moments are an enjoyable aspect of its persuasiveness. Perhaps these broadly rendered retractions and hesitations were in some way part of the actual sequence of Hume's thinking as he drafted the *Treatise*. This particular arrangement is certainly his rhetorical exploitation of whatever difficulties he had.

A cardinal rule of Hume's stylistic decorum is the avoidance of self-satisfied paradox, just as a guiding principle of his thought is the denial of static substance or the undermining of any fixed position in our relationship to the world. That commitment to movement extends, I think, to his rhetorical fashionings. The epistemological arena evoked in Book I is a place of constant motion, and Hume's rendering of his thought responds to that. He stages an instructive dialogue with a lay audience, an ironic bantering with philosophic rivals, and a mock-serious soliloquizing in which he places his own expectations and ambitions for pattern and coherence against the inevitably scattered or confusingly dynamic realities he uncovers. Book I proposes an extended passage *through* uncertainty, through a rigorously literalized account of mental processes. Book I is appropriately a text through which Hume himself as vigorous persona travels, by means of irony of course but also by various other disturbances of his own systematic process of inquiry. Just as the traditional stability surrounding notions like cause and effect, probability, and belief is disrupted by his investigation, so Hume disturbs his own literary personality to establish his good faith. Only deluded systematic reasoners pretend to escape disruption. Hume questions traditional philosophic practice and thereby alters the character of the philosopher, philosophizing and then writing ironically and humanly about it. All this disruption, needless to say, is qualified by the rhetorical occasion, and the confused or embarrassed persona who makes his appearance in "Of the Sceptical and Other Systems of Philosophy" (Part IV of Book I) is in short order exposed as part of the philosophical point.

The first three parts of Book I have relentlessly enforced skepticism, the last section of Part III taking evident pleasure in equating the instincts of animals and human reason. "To consider the matter aright, reason is nothing but a wonderful and unintelligible instinct in our souls, which carries us along a certain train of ideas, and endows them with particular qualities, according to their particular situations and relations" (p.179). But this triumphant reductionism is followed as Part IV opens by a generalizing passage that strikingly repairs (or at least qualifies) by moral sentiment and aphorism what systematic analysis has crumbled. Writing like this is a rich supplement to analytic bleakness. Hume's moral generality creates a monitory resonance, turning the paragraph into much more than a methodological warning:

In all demonstrative sciences the rules are certain and infallible; but when we apply them, our fallible and uncertain faculties are very apt to depart from them, and fall into error. We must, therefore, in every reasoning form a new judgment, as a check or controul on our first judg- ment or belief; and must enlarge our view to comprehend a kind of history of all the instances, wherein our understanding has deceiv'd us, compar'd with those, wherein its testimony was just and true. Our reason must be consider'd as a kind of cause, of which truth is the natural effect; but such-a-one as by the irruption of other causes, and by the inconstancy of our mental powers, may frequently be prevented. By this means all knowledge degenerates into probability; and this prob- ability is greater or less, according to our experience of the veracity or deceitfulness of our understanding, and according to the simplicity or intricacy of the question. (P.180)

A humanized, almost allegorical scene of perception, this is a moral- ized fable in which the inevitable weakness of human nature is supported scrupulously by a reformed reasoning. However, Hume places reason in the infinitely troubled context of causes and effects, reminding us that the effort for certainty is always in fact doomed to failure. The connection between our reason and truth, the *Treatise* has already shown at length, is an impossible one, as indeed the next sentence declares when it labels all knowledge "probability." The fable, then, is ironic, especially since this probability is subject to such varied circumstances. But the irony cannot touch the moralizing perspective enforcing this formulation; indeed, the perspective supplies the situation wherein irony can operate effectively. The comic commonplace tracing human aspiration, the discovery of weakness and fallibility, and the verbal resolution of the discovery precede Hume's epistemology and must to some extent influence it. Hume constructs aphorisms that contain human variability and uncertainty; he presides over this spectacle and manages a steady assertion of inevitability, both moral and intellectual. His writing in this sense is more than his command of expository language and mastery of a clarifying and simple eloquence. Those stylish features arrange his philosophic materials so that the findings of neutral, analytic inquiry struggle meaningfully with common predispositions to order and coherence. Eventually, Hume's thought ratifies common life by traveling through the chaotic alternative life just to the side of it or underneath it. Hume arrives at common life rather than beginning with it. He stages the literary rediscovery of the ordinary contained by strong implication from the beginning of the *Treatise* in his moral-literary manner.

Part IV concludes Book I by explicitly recognizing this affinity, by "discovering" what has been rhetorically evident from the start. If all knowledge "resolves itself into probability, and becomes at last of the same nature with that evidence, which we employ in common life" (p.181), then the task remaining is to examine how we actually operate in the world. What follows is a destructive analysis of the validity of the evidence used in common life but also inevitably a dramatization of the necessity of such evidence. The "Nature" Hume conjures up to resolve the paradoxes of total skepticism is a literary personification of inevitability who has hovered benignly over the *Treatise* from the beginning.

Reason as Hume imagines it here in "Of scepticism with regard to reason" is represented by a scrupulous, introspective gentleman, a "man of the best sense and longest experience" who must be conscious by virtue of that disposition and his own history "of many errors in the past" and a "dread [of] the like for the future" (p.182). The discourse Hume makes "natural" is deeply self-critical, simultaneously aware in the very act of thought of the difficulty of knowing objects and of the weakness of this faculty of knowing.

When I reflect on the natural fallibility of my judgment, I have less confidence in my opinions, than when I only consider the objects concerning which I reason; and when I proceed still farther, to turn the scrutiny against every successive estimation I make of my faculties, all the rules of logic require a continual diminution, and at last a total extinction of belief and evidence. (P.183)

Equally "natural," however, is the transitory quality of total skepticism. The skeptical questions, says Hume in the next paragraph, ignore the human realities whereby such a statement describes a psychological event or intellectual moment rather than a position that can be occupied.

Thought, even at its most skeptical, is part of a process of representation whereby "Nature" is imagined as imagining us:

> Shou'd it here be ask'd me, whether I sincerely assent to this argument, which I seem to take such pains to inculcate, and whether I be really one of those sceptics, who hold that all is uncertain, and that our judgment is not in *any* thing possest of *any* measures of truth and falshood; I shou'd reply, that this question is entirely superfluous, and that neither I, nor any other person was ever sincerely and constantly of that opinion. Nature, by an absolute and uncontroulable necessity has determin'd us to judge as well as to breathe and feel; nor can we any more forbear viewing certain objects in a stronger and fuller light, upon account of their customary connexion with a present impression, than we can hinder ourselves from thinking as long as we are awake, or seeing the surrounding bodies, when we turn our eyes towards them in bright sunshine. Whoever has taken the pains to refute the cavils of this *total* scepticism, has really disputed without an antagonist, and endeavour'd by arguments to establish a faculty, which nature has antecedently implanted in the mind, and render'd unavoidable. (P.183)

Hume only seems to be arguing, and those who attempt to answer him find themselves caught in foolish soliloquy, arguing in spite of themselves with a disappearing anatagonist. Hume actually illustrates the necessity of a process of judgment, enacting in the skeptical movements of his thought a truth in human activity, reconstituting truth in the course of negating truth in its older, now discredited substantial form. The dim light of the philosopher's study is every bit as compelling as "broad sunshine"; the abstractions and deliberate formulations of even the most intellectual judgment are linked to the involuntary swings of visual perception. The eyes "turn," just as a few pages later the mind has a "posture" and "the attention is on the stretch" (p.185). For Hume, mind is not so much an entity realized by images as a nearly literal extension of the physical individual in his surroundings and social circumstances. Hume's skepticism operates by returning to the incontrovertible physicality of experience. He affirms what many of his critics thought he denied, in order of course to dismantle the fictions implicit in the old dualistic formulations concerning the untroubled traffic between mind and the world.

The elaboration of skepticism is part of a larger purpose, "to make the reader sensible of the truth" of the hypothesis "*that all our reasonings concerning causes and effects are deriv'd from nothing but custom; and that belief is more properly an act of the sensitive, than the cogitative part of our natures*" (p.183). Hume's text is a means to an end, profoundly rhetorical in its effort to move the reader and make him "sensible" of the truth of a position. This section is a series of expositions designed to fail and prove their point by the indirection of literary enactment. The overseeing irony in this skeptical twisting cancels the logic of skepticism by the immediacy of narration. We seem to be following an argument about the total fallibility of the judgment but discover we are participating with Hume in a process establishing the circumstances of its inevitability. Judgment is a concrete reality quite apart from questions of truth or falsity. Skepticism cannot be answered, Hume concludes, because it is a series of natural dispositions, fading away by virtue of its own "subtility," lacking the "natural and easy" connection with our imagination requisite for belief (p.186). Skepticism fails to convince us because it speaks to a discredited reason and depends upon a judgment caught up in custom and habit; reason is not a faculty but part of a world of narrative inevitability rather than logical possibility.

These connections imposed by the imagination, as Hume calls it to separate it from the "senses" and "reason," are the subject of the much longer next section, "Of scepticism with regard to the senses." Hume conducts a long reprise of his system with great show of fairness and an obtrusive rigor.[32] This section is a sort of parodic philosophic essay in which various attempts to clarify the conditions of perception are examined with a slow, detailed thoroughness. Hume surveys both philosophical and vulgar accounts of our transaction with the external world, partly to continue his bantering of philosophy but mainly to remind his reader of the unsettled nature of the issues surrounding common perception. Tempo is crucial here. Hume conducts a rehearsal of his fundamentals, a shaping of the problem by comic slow motion in which the frustration of easy or traditional resolutions is always inevitable but delayed by an exaggerated deliberation.

And indeed, whatever convincing arguments philosophers may fancy they can produce to establish the belief of objects independent of the mind, 'tis obvious these arguments are known but to very few, and that 'tis not by them, that children, peasants, and the greatest part of mankind are induc'd to attribute objects to some impressions, and deny them to others. Accordingly we find, that all the conclusions, which the vulgar form on this head, are directly contrary to those, which are confirm'd by philosophy. For philosophy informs us, that every thing, which appears to the mind, is nothing but a perception, and is interrupted, and dependent on the mind; whereas the vulgar confound perceptions and objects, and attribute a distinct continu'd existence to the very things they feel or see. (P.193)

Hume seems to be out to correct vulgar notions as he moves in this section to more and more tangled versions of ordinary experience. Philosophical reductionism insists on the isolation of our perceptions and Hume illustrates this by personal anecdote. With a deliberateness predicting the comic absurdity to come, he turns to his paper, his desk and pen, the fire in his chamber for examples of stability. Further consideration of commonplace events, the opening of the study door by a porter, the arrival of a letter from a friend "who says he is two hundred leagues distant" (p.196), reveals their strangeness and the necessity for common living of imagining a world of connections of which we have no direct perception. "Here then I am naturally led to regard the world, as something real and durable, and as preserving its existence, even when it is no longer present to my imagination" (p.197). Slow and self-conscious thinking like this is implicitly comic, a violation in its dull literalism of the vivacity and sharp brevity Hume admires as a writer and always comes as a thinker to identify as the defining and conclusive features of our experience.

The incisive Hume rescues the plodding philosopher from his bewilderment, or replaces him, switching voices and resuming his command of paradoxical refinement. Regularity in our perceptions is insufficient "for us to infer a greater degree of regularity in some objects, which are not perceiv'd; since this supposes a contradiction, *viz.* a habit acquir'd by what was never present to the mind" (p.197). In due course in this section, Hume will find that the "imagination" is our natural inclination in the face of our scattered experience to give ourselves perceptual ease by inventing essential notions like unity and identity. The imagination is "seduced" by the resemblance of certain perceptions and "produces the fiction of a continu'd existence" (p.209). Hume marshalls philosophical insights to describe the situation which provokes these necessary fictions, but he ends by undermining the ability of philosophy to account for them. Where, he asks, did the fancy ever find this notion of another existence resembling its perceptions "but yet continu'd, and uninterrupted, and identical" (p.213)? The notions of the ordering imagination, as Hume evokes it, are constantly checked by a little philosophical reflection, but these notions are so necessary that philosophy itself comes to cooperate in their fashioning. To "set ourselves at ease," philosophy contrives the "double existence" of perceptions and objects. This "pleases our reason, in allowing, that our dependent perceptions are interrupted and different; and at the same time is agreeable to the imagination, in attributing a continu'd existence to something else, which we call *objects*" (p.215).

All these elaborate inventions, and common perception is as clever as philosophy in devising them, are gathered under the sign of nature. Philosophical description, with the dominance it seems to involve, turns inevitably into a recognition of natural patterns, and the epistemological arena is the battleground for a broadly rendered psychomachia. Even though "reflection tells us" that our perceptions are interrupted and essentially different, we invent new fictions: "Nature is obstinate, and will not quit the field, however strongly attack'd by reason; and at the same time reason is so clear in this point, that there is no possibility of disguising her" (p.215). Caught between these conflicting human needs, "we endeavour to set ourselves at ease as much as possible , by successively granting to each whatever it demands, and by feigning a double existence, where each may find something, that has all the conditions it desires" (p.215).

The primal scene of perception, whether conceived by the vulgar or by philosophers, is an elusive place, constituted in Hume's tricky meditation by the mind thinking about itself in different contexts in order to satisfy various, shifting needs. In theory, Hume seeks to describe that time when we perceive without the filters of custom and habit, but his practice makes that moment unimaginable, able to be spoken of only by contrast with actual perception, which is inconceivable without custom and habit and which is normally nothing but custom and habit. The unalterable, incessant reciprocity thus dramatized as the central quality in perception serves to dissolve mind into its operations, and to render mental life as the pure process in which mind repairs its fragmentary glimpses of its own impressions of what it takes to be the external world. Hume resists the hypostatization of mind that Locke and Berkeley in their separate ways encourage. His account of epistemological complexity is an implicit diminishing of mind, which becomes not only an easily bewildered set of human powers but a transparently self-seeking entity, out for its own ease and ready to prefer its own fictions of wholeness, unity, and continuity to the isolated data it perceives.

Epistemology in these chapters is really a form of moralized psychology in which independence and substance are canceled by an introspective narrator who is alive to the context and process rendered by his own writing and thereby ready to endorse the necessity of the fictions he dismantles. To write, Hume's persona makes clear, is to construct a world where formulations challenge one another, where rhetoric involves the ability to defend contradictory positions with equal skill and conviction. Rhetoric like Hume's balances instability against the formulas and patterns of recurrence and inevitability; the epistemology he traces has a similar shape, as the instability inherent in perception is redefined as a paradoxical inevitability. To rehearse those systems, "both popular and philosophical," which attempt to account for the external world we seem to perceive is to discover their inadequacy and in due course to affirm the inevitability of the needs they represent. The spontaneity Hume claims to record at the conclusion of his examination of sense perception is a prelude to an ironclad summary of the total unreliability of the senses. That such logic should commence in an inclination, a momentary conviction which claims to take place in front of us as we read, predicts the irrelevance of logical systems which attempt to overrule common life. Hume's logical summary takes place in a situation in which logical summarizing itself may easily become impossible:

> I begun this subject with premising, that we ought to have an implicit faith in our senses, and that this wou'd be the conclusion, I shou'd draw from the whole of my reasoning. But to be ingenuous, I feel myself *at present* of a quite contrary sentiment, and am more inclin'd to repose no faith at all in my senses, or rather imagination, than to place in it such an implicit confidence. (P.217)

A summary of the reasons that have led Hume to this reversal ends with rhetorical questions: "What then can we look for from this confusion of groundless and extraordinary opinions but error and falshood? And how can we justify to ourselves any belief we repose in them?" (p.218).

Another speaker seems to arise in the next paragraph, or the ingenuous persona seems to adopt another pose, sliding into an authoritative analysis of the implications of the preceding reasoning, switching from the metaphysical melodrama of these sweeping rhetorical questions to a cool essayistic mode. "This sceptical doubt," the paragraph begins, is a "malady, which can never be radically cur'd, but must return upon us every moment, however we may chace it away, and sometimes may seem entirely free from it" (p.218). The force of this demonstrative opening is to label the preceding paragraph a rhetorical exercise, a species of philosophizing from which the narrator now distances himself. Hume does not repudiate his conclusions. The senses and understanding cannot be defended "upon any system" and "we but expose them farther when we endeavour to justify them in that manner" (p.218). But he does insert his reasoning into a sequence that exemplifies the ironic pattern he is committed to as a moral essayist. Skeptical doubt, the Hume of this final paragraph says, "arises naturally from a profound and intense reflection."

Doubt "always" increases as we pursue such a topic, "whether in opposition or conformity to it" (p.218). The resolving axiom is wonderfully trivial, a witty debasement of the opening medical diagnosis, which treats the "malady" as nothing more than part of a normal imbalance: "Carelessness and inattention alone can afford us any remedy." From the impassioned reviewer of his own ironclad reasoning, Hume changes into the ironic commentator on the psychological dynamics of intense study, diminishing only the inhuman commitment to systematic discourse rather than its conclusions, placing carelessness next to rigor not to prefer the former but to acknowledge its inevitability. Skepticism is contained within the same theory of human nature which accounts for day-to-day belief and affirmative philosophical systems. Like them, skepticism is situated within the possibilities of persuasive statement, at those junctures where human nature at particular moments and according to individual dispositions makes us ready to be convinced. As Barry Stroud puts it, Hume does not say that nature refutes skepticism but rather that natural instincts "submerge" our doubts.[33] "Balance" might be a more accurate and appropriately rhetorical term, for whatever the reader may think "at this present moment" (and Hume himself is "*at present*" convinced by his skeptical analysis), "an hour hence he will be persuaded there is both an external and internal world" (p.218). Hume includes himself and his own certainty by virtue of what he pointedly marks as his spontaneous conviction at this moment. This is nothing less than a rhetorical qualifying of the offensively systematic completeness of skepticism without repudiating its defining insights.

Inevitably, Hume's concern is the nature of conviction rather than the nature of truth. Norman Kemp Smith found the origins of the *Treatise* and the opening up of what Hume called "a new Scene of Thought, which transported [him] beyond Measure" in the insight, derived from Hutcheson, that all "judgments of *value* of whatever type, are based not on rational insight or on evidence, but solely on feeling." This notion, said Kemp Smith, led to Hume's conviction that all judgments are thus matters not of knowledge but of belief, which "rests always on feeling, and never in ultimate analysis on insight or evidence."[34] And belief, as Hume elaborates it in the *Treatise*, is something we are led to by our comparative examination of the sequences of our "impressions," in which lively and distinct perceptions convince us of the truth of certain things within that sequence. "Convince" may misrepresent Hume, since the impressions persuade or irresistibly enforce belief by their vividness. Hume's terms are strikingly aesthetic, for the perceptions operate rather like the motions of art in their persuasive effect. As Hume renders it in the first book of the *Treatise*, the process whereby we understand is a difficult reciprocity between entities, which we designate for convenience as the mind and the world; but it is the quasi-aesthetic psychological force in our experience that determines belief and settles (for a time) the reality question. We resolve the issue by deciding to believe, albeit falsely as Barry Stroud notes, in certain relations between objects and events in the world.[35]

Robert Paul Wolff finds a key turn in Hume's thought: he began the *Treatise* assuming empirical knowledge could be explained by reference to the contents of the mind, but he discovered in the process of writing the book "that it was the activity of mind rather than the nature of its contents, which accounted for all the puzzling features of empirical knowledge."[36] It seems to me that in Hume's writing the mind has a double activity as audience and speaker. The epistemological process takes place within a naturalistic psychology that resembles a rhetorical situation: our ideas are "representations" of impressions, copies that are more or less vivid; we are persuaded to belief not by argument but by image and forceful sequence. The impressions that dominate us are effective because they are vivid, easier than others for us to grasp and remember.

Commentators like John Passmore find Hume's position odd and inconsistent, for Hume cannot really decide "whether or not a cogitative act takes place or whether there is simply a more vivid idea driving out a less vivid one." Belief for Hume, says Passmore, should be purely sensitive but shades over into the cogitative.[37] This shading over that Passmore speaks of resembles the moment in which an audience is pleased by the force and shape of performance; the mixed sensitive/cogitative act is like an aesthetic response and the situation is very much like the theory of audience engagement Hume later described in his essay, "Of Tragedy," where he concluded that an audience's pleasure in tragic representation proceeds from delight in observing mastery of the difficult techniques of such representation. His first example is from oratory: Cicero's description of Verres' slaughter of the Sicilian captains allows us the pleasure of watching a master of eloquence at work and of noting the disparity between our pleasure and the horrible events described. Tragic drama obeys the same laws, only there the pleasure of watching an imitation of action is added; the art of painting also illustrates the process clearly. "Objects of the greatest terror and distress please in painting, and please more than the most beautiful objects that appear calm and indifferent. The affection, rousing the mind, excites a large stock of spirit and vehemence;

which is all transformed into pleasure by the force of the prevailing moment."[38]

Obviously, these comments describe something other than normal psychology. The aesthetic reaction Hume evokes in "Of Tragedy" presupposes an informed moral and literary sensibility. As Ralph Cohen puts it with great exactness, Hume's spectator at a tragedy attends first to the artistry of language, then to the management of the semantic content.[39] The semantic content itself is simply a rhetorical factor, an intensifer of eloquence. Hume's spectator, however, is moved and thereby in an aesthetic sense convinced by eloquence he has learned to recognize and value. His emotion and belief presuppose a history of cogitative acts of education and then, more immediately, an act of recognition. But the aesthetic moment is still for Hume primarily a sensitive one wherein the judgment is, to some extent, out of control and thus "objects of the greatest terror and distress" can please.

Common perception is, naturally, less powerful than Cicero or Shakespeare, but the "belief" it entails is as compelling if less explicable an experience than aesthetic pleasure. Hume's account of belief in the *Treatise* is complicated, even confusing and ambiguous as Passmore decides. But his theory of belief, as he elaborates it in Section VII of Book I ("Of the nature of the idea of belief") is clear and insistent on one point: belief is "a particular manner of forming an idea," and the only way to vary an idea is by adjusting "its degrees of force and vivacity" (p.97). Hume's concluding illustration is a literary experiment: observe two readers of the same book, one thinking it a "romance," the other "a true history." Both receive the same semantic content, but the force of genre stimulates the imagination and produces conviction in the latter, "while the former, who gives no credit to the testimony of the author, has a more faint and languid conception of all these particulars" (p.98). Current understanding of literary genre might argue for almost the reverse of that, and Hume wondered in the "Appendix" just what this "manner" is that separates our notions of truth and fiction. He admitted the awkwardness of his terms, conceding that "an idea assented to *feels* different from a fictitious idea . . . And this different feeling I endeavour to explain by calling it a superior *force*, or vivacity, or solidity, or *firmness*, or *steadiness*" (p.629). But as Barry Stroud notes, Hume never retreated from the notion that belief derives from the qualities of some ideas in relation to us, not from the addition of the idea of belief to our experience.[40] Again, Hume's illustration of this process is aesthetic, another experiment, this time with colors. Vary a color by "a new degree of liveliness or brightness" and it remains the same, only more effective; but any other variation changes the shade or color (p.96). Thus with an idea: if we attempt to interfere intellectually, to judge or understand, then the idea "represents a different object or impression" and belief concerning the original idea is no longer possible. Whatever else it may be, belief is a relationship between us and experience in which we are persuaded, ultimately, by a force we cannot resist.

I would stress, therefore, the importance of Hume's examples in the body of the *Treatise*. The connoisseur of shade and color and especially the discriminating reader of history and fiction are characters who live within the confusing perceptual world Hume evokes; they manage quite well to keep their bearings, even though their judgments are temporarily usurped by the force of belief and the instability of light. Stroud is only half right to complain that Hume's account of the difference between reading fact and fiction is untenable, for Hume's reader is someone who has a firm sense of literary hierarchies and who has positioned himself so that fact and fiction produce appropriate effects in him. What Hume presents as natural and inevitable is, in part, a response promoted if not arranged by a cultural and moral predisposition. That, I think, is a recurring moment in his thought, part of its logical weakness from a modern standpoint but also a sign of its literary enforcement.

Our reconstruction of the world from our impressions of it is designed to give us ease, comfort, and even pleasure, to make life as agreeable as possible. We persuade ourselves that this is the real world, but mean in fact it is the best world for us. Our conventionalized representations are fictional equipment for living, rhetorical inventions in a very important sense. Hume's irony it should be added never seeks to destroy those fictions, only to keep them balanced as such between chaos and untenable absolutes.

Hume's tact and restraint as a writer, his scorn for what he called "declamation," his almost exaggerated value for the exact phrase, and the careful aphoristic shape of his prose (which may be what Johnson meant when he complained to Boswell that the structure of Hume's sentences was "French")[41] — all these traits are modifying responses to the compulsive mechanism he uncovers. In the middle of the obtrusive shapings of normal perception, Hume's philosophic observer cultivates a special neutrality that resembles aesthetic contemplation; he appreciates effects, awards marks, and makes distinctions between the truth of sequence and the illusion of substance. Indeed, the moment in Book I Hume marks as climactic both reiterates his central principle of sequence and finds that

his entire argument has required a sequentiality which appears "prepos-
terous" in a literal sense. "Experience," Hume explains, "never gives us
any insight into the internal structure or operating principle of objects,
but only accustoms the mind to pass from one to another" (p.169). Only
after establishing this principle by examining our inferences from the
relation of cause and effect can we define the latter terms.

> . . . the nature of the relation depends so much on that of the in-
> ference, we have been oblig'd to advance in this seemingly preposterous
> manner, and make use of terms before we were able exactly to define
> them, or fix their meaning.
>
> . . . . .
>
> There may two definitions be given of this relation, which are only dif-
> ferent, by their presenting a different view of the same object, and making
> us consider it either as a *philosophical* or as a *natural* relation; either as a
> comparison of two ideas, or as an association betwixt them. (Pp.169–170)

The two "definitions" Hume offers are aggressively literal descriptions of a
pure sequentiality, which can be affirmed only now that the reader has
come this far. A cause can be "'an object precedent and contiguous to
another, and where all the objects resembling the former are plac'd in like
relations of precedency and contiguity to those objects, that resemble the
latter.'" Or if this definition seems either to impoverish the perceiver or
claim a false originality for him, Hume offers a "natural" description:
"' A CAUSE is an object precedent and contiguous to another, and so
united with it, that the idea of the one determines the mind to form the
idea of the other, and the impression of the one to form a more lively idea
of the other'" (p.170). Hume follows this contentious pair of definitions
(the latter a rejection by refinement of the former) with a further defiance
which describes his own movements. Those who are dissatisfied with his
formulation "should substitute a juster definition," but he can offer no
other because he has deliberately locked himself into the sequences he
describes with such accuracy. His narrative repeats the argument, enacts
in a personal and specific manner the sequence he claims is the ultimate
extent of knowledge:

> When I examine with the most utmost accuracy those objects, which are
> commonly denominated causes and effects, I find, in considering a
> single instance, that the one object is precedent and contiguous to the
> other; and in inlarging my view to consider several instances, I find
> only, that like objects are constantly plac'd in like relations of succession
> and contiguity. Again, when I consider the influence of this constant
> conjunction, I perceive, that such a relation can never be an object of
> reasoning, and can never operate upon the mind, but by means of cus-

tom, which determines the imagination to make a transition from the idea of one object to that of its usual attendant, and from the impression of one to a more lively idea of the other. However extraordinary these sentiments may appear, I think it fruitless to trouble myself with any further enquiry or reasoning upon the subject, but shall repose myself on them as on establish'd maxims. (P.170)

Jonathan Bennett is troubled by the limitations of such a program, which makes Hume's thought merely "a theory about what must occur before there can be understanding, rather than about what understanding is, or about what it is for an expression to have a meaning." Bennett seems to find fault with Hume because he is not an Oxford don who has read Wittgenstein and Austin, but his complaint is useful testimony to the negative purity of Hume's discourse and to his success in dramatizing his neutrality as philosophic observer. Bennett criticizes Hume for stopping short of explaining the irrational or the customary basis of belief, but Hume's self-appointed (and specifically literary) task here in Book I is to drive out explanation and to reside in the literal facts of the case, that is, to diagram process and locate origins without seeming to impose explanation. The difficulty of establishing a stationary position amid the buzzing movements of perception is underlined by Bennett's irritation with Hume for writing "as though someone might be aware of a stream of impressions while making no predictions about what lies ahead; and it is against this background that he can represent us as having to make predictions, as though refraining from them were an intelligible alternative which we are psychologically powerless to adopt."[42] Hume grants a temporary possibility to what he in fact dramatizes as psychologically impossible. We can speak as if a suspension of prediction were possible, partly to render more sharply its practical impossibility and partly to provide moral-intellectual comedy to the scene of perception and thought. In the passage after he defines "cause," the narrator "finds," "examines," "considers," "inlarges" his view, and "perceives"; neutral operations that confirm his objectivity and whose efficiency is ironically contrasted with his declared "incapacity" in the sentence preceding this passage for substituting "a juster definition" of cause. These activities are defined, in one of Hume's characteristic turns, as a rueful submission to the facts in the case. The narrator's elegantly weary disclaimer at the end is what he calls a choice to "repose," to lie still in the middle of "extraordinary" sentiments. That, I submit, is a wonderfully skilled transformation by stylistic modulations of Hume's subversive philosophical alertness into a mock indolence and submission.

In part, as James Noxon notes, Hume's attack on causality is a rejection of "metaphysical constructions," a preparation for the "psychological explanations of the errors and illusions which generate pseudo-problems."[43] Purely philosophical commentators like Bennett fail to appreciate Hume's context: a defiant narrative of his own mental operations, a rhetorical refusal to employ explanations which have been debased by the opposing rhetoric of metaphysical speculation. Hume's analysis consistently includes a virtuous refusal to deal in ultimates and absolutes; what might be called the plot of Book I pits Humean awareness of limits against speculative foolishness. "Nothing is more requisite for a true philosopher, than to restrain the intemperate desire of searching into causes, and, having establish'd any doctrine upon a sufficient number of experiments, rest contented with that, when he sees a further examination would lead him into obscure and uncertain speculations" (p.13).

Here and throughout the *Treatise*, Hume is also refusing another temptation by avoiding the sanctimonious self-congratulation Locke liked to indulge in at such moments. Locke almost celebrates human ignorance; he establishes it as a ground for moral and political submission. His analysis of the operations of mind tends to defer to a scientific physiology of mental phenomena that might conceivably be developed. Hume refuses to call limitation ignorance and tends to work within the boundaries of our experience, as he understands them, tends to find within those boundaries a rich field for assertive philosophical activity.

As part of its self-definition, empirical inquiry of the kind both men practice claims a diffidence in the face of things as they are experienced. Hume offers in place of speculation and ultimate explanation "experimental" observation and a detailed and precise rendering of the proximate, that which is nearest to us in psychological time and space. "To explain the ultimate causes of our mental actions is impossible. 'Tis sufficient, if we can give any satisfactory account of them from experience and analogy" (p.22). That might serve as a motto for the whole *Treatise*. An "account" is a narrative quite opposed to explanation, which is a resolving commentary on it. Book I may be said to arrange a confrontation between systematic explanation and this rhetoric of limitation, nonintervention, and disinterested observation.

Eventually, Hume will summarize matters by calling experience a pure passage, a series of entirely discrete events, a principle of superficiality: "Now the nature and effects of experience have been already sufficiently examin'd and explain'd. It never gives us any insight into the internal structure or operating principle of objects, but only accustoms the mind to pass from one to another" (p.169). Like so much of Hume, this modest sentence carries a huge subversive burden. For much eighteenth-century discourse, movement through the world and immersion in its details were the defining human activity. As J. Paul Hunter puts it, for the Augustans the universe was additive and progressively discoverable; "experience and education were equated with the conquest of space."[44] Hume's conquest of space is a restoration of its strangeness, its emptiness perhaps. He seems to take pleasure in cancelling the additions whereby the discrete parts of experience are formed into wholes. The following passage describes the process whereby we pass by inference from one object to another:

'Tis therefore by EXPERIENCE only, that we can infer the existence of one object from that of another. The nature of experience is this. We remember to have had frequent instances of the existence of one species of objects; and also remember, that the individuals of another species of objects have always attended them, and have existed in a regular order of contiguity and succession with regard to them. Thus we remember to have seen that species of object we call *flame*, and to have felt that species of sensation we call *heat*. We likewise call to mind their constant conjunction in all past instances. Without any farther ceremony, we call the one *cause* and the other *effect*, and infer the existence of the one from that of the other. (P.87)

Hume is good at rendering what he tells us are the mere notions of the understanding. His style is suddenly simple and direct, a diagram rather than a description. "The nature of experience is this" is a sort of arrow in the margin. The following sentences match in their directness the sharp simplicity of the movements of the mind, which omits "ceremony" and quickly devises the useful connection called cause and effect.

But this mimicry of the mind's narration of reality leads Hume to a further step in his own narrative. He notices that in our reasoning about cause and effect only one is "perceiv'd or remember'd, and the other is supply'd in conformity to our past experience" (p.87). Hume claims we have thus "insensibly" been led to discover a new relation between cause and effect, "when we least expected it, and were entirely employ'd upon another subject" (p.87). "Constant conjunction" is added to contiguity and succession, although it quickly turns into a blind alley for finding the "*necessary connexion*" Hume claims to be tracking. A sentence begins in hope and concludes with its negation: "There are hopes, that by this means we may at last arrive at our propos'd end; tho' to tell the truth, this new-discover'd relation of a constant conjunction seems to advance us but very little in our way" (pp.87–88). Within the narration of the sequentiality of mental experience is the mock narrative of philosophical discovery, a staged and consequently ironic progress in which movement leads in Hume's rendering to the discovery of even more movement: "From the mere repetition of any past impression, even to infinity, there never will arise any new original idea, such as that of a necessary connexion; and the number of impressions has in this case no more effect than if we confin'd ourselves to one only" (p.88). Hume goes on to complicate matters, but his procedure remains the same: apparent meaningful movement is analyzed into its discrete particulars and the ambitious formulations he proposes are dispersed by the force of those particulars. Hume's rendering of epistemological sequence is so literal that it prevents any narrative progress in his explanation of that sequence. A rhetoric of limitation and nonintervention overcomes in mock struggle Hume's attempt to find an organizing principle for his narrative. His account of how we know is made to break down into a description of what we know. Book I of the *Treatise* may be said to stage a confrontation between systematic explanation and this discovery of limitation and analytic frustration. Such modesty is, however, enforced by what Hume later regretted as a "positive Air which prevails in that Book, & which may be imputed to the Ardor of Youth."[45]

I think Hume was too harsh on himself, although his ironic self-depreciation is a habitual mode that has misled later readers. As he remarked to Henry Home, the expurgated *Treatise* he showed to Bishop Butler represented a blameless "cowardice," since he "was resolved not to be an enthusiast in philosophy, while [he] was blaming other enthusiasms." Hume's youthful bravado in the *Treatise* needs to be reconsidered in the light of the literary sensibility he displayed as a young man and, especially, in the context of those regular modifications of systematic order that recur within the unfolding of the *Treatise*. Hume did indeed set out to establish the "science of man" and he boasted in this same letter to Home that his principles were capable of producing "almost a total alteration in philosophy."[46] As John Passmore puts it, the attempt to establish this new science is "one of the most important of Hume's intentions, affecting the structures of his argument at point after point."[47] But Hume's moral posture within those intentions includes a habitual intolerance of unqualified ambition, an awareness of a recurrent, comic psychological limitation undercutting grandiose intentions. Thus, he adds this note in the letter to Home: "You'll excuse the frailty of an author in writing so long a letter about nothing but his own performances.

Authors have this privilege in common with lovers, and founded on the same reason, that they are both besotted with a blind fondness of their object."[48]

James Noxon has recently wondered why so many commentators, literal as well as rigorous, have expected Hume in the *Treatise* to act like a Newton of the human sciences. Noxon says, aptly enough for my purposes, that the *Treatise* is about as mathematical as Ovid's *Metamorphoses* and is experimental and observational only in the loosest possible sense. Hume, Noxon concludes, did not have a scientific sensibility and was uninterested in experimental science.[49] But Noxon does regard the *Treatise* as a failed system, especially Book I in which the destructive analysis of ideas is never really harmonized with the psychological theories based on associationism. Noxon sees Hume's career as a retreat from an "early, reclusive, system-building period" to the elaboration of moral and historical topics, guided as Hume matured by a developed literary sense. Compared to a book like Descartes' *Meditations*, which moves "inexorably toward a well-planned denouement," the *Treatise* "drags" the reader through "tortuous thought, and when in the end [Hume] admits that his doubts cannot be excised by local means, it is far from sure that he had foreseen that conclusion."[50] My argument is that Noxon and others have read the first book of the *Treatise* too literally, finding in its hesitations and "expressions of metaphysical agony" a purely expressive rather than a largely rhetorical means of staging uncertainty, demolishing metaphysics, and preparing the ground for the psychological and moral reimagining of man in Books II and III.

Even as a young man caught up in the ardor of philosophic innovation, Hume was not simply a frustrated systematizer or a malicious skeptic. He was a man of genuine moral sympathy, and his empiricism, as T. E. Jessop says very well, marks a "deep sense of the precariousness of all theorizing, which Locke had in a much lesser degree, and which Berkeley scarcely had at all (he was a metaphysician)."[51] Resolved not to be an "enthusiast" in anything, Hume seeks a language that matches the complex neutrality of his philosophic stance and avoids the implicit self-satisfaction of rigid positions or even of fixed attitudes. He is sometimes accused of lacking a true position or of occupying so fluid and shifting a set of positions that it is nearly impossible to pin him down.

From the beginning of his career, Hume sought to respond to this essentially stylistic problem. The *Treatise* explores ways of expressing detachment from thought and its commitments, or of enacting a moral and intellectual resistance to the finality of systematic utterance. In his early twenties, Hume sought what Raymond Williams calls "a proper relationship between reasoning and experience at much more than a formal level."[52] The precocious systematizer, who wondered if his dry despair after "profound Reflections" was similar to the effects of enthusiasm on religious "Fanatics," needed to drive a wedge between reasoning and experience, to retain a rigorously examined experience as a valid category and a check on the autonomous drift of abstract thought.[53] In parts of the *Treatise*, the result is a situation that modern commentators find philosophically irresponsible but which Hume attempts to make morally and rhetorically satisfying.

Such balancing of rhetorical satisfaction and philosophical irresolution is perfectly exemplified in section VI of Book I of the *Treatise*, "Of personal identity." An influential essay typical of modern commentary finds Hume's logic wanting and his tonalities irrelevant ("however tolerant of our linguistic behavior Hume may be, there is nothing for him to be tolerant about"). Terence Penelhum bases his refutation of Hume on the efficiency, accuracy, and stability of ordinary language and the orderly world it ensures and establishes. He claims we make no real "mistake in saying that a succession of related objects may form a unit of a certain kind, or that the same thing may undergo radical changes." Hume's error, says Penelhum, lies in "supposing that invariance is the standard of identity in all cases, when it is only the standard in a very few (those in which invariance is part of the concept of the thing)."[54]

Penelhum's revisions of the problem seem convincing. And yet he relies on and stoutly defends precisely the ordinary language that Hume's chapter (and the whole of the *Treatise*) throws into question, not so much by direct challenge as by a consistent undermining of the ways available to represent the process of understanding. Moreover, Hume's discussion of personal identity does not take place in the special intellectual arena of a philosophical problem (Penelhum's essay is a detailed analytic response to one text, a small part of that text, addressed to a group of academic philosophers), but is set with some flourish and some irony as well on the largest stage possible. The issue is nothing less than the nature of man and, more important, the founding acts of meaning and utterance that make "man" possible. "Invariance" in Hume's exposition of the situation has a long moral and philosophical history; it is a notion with a threatened ontological status to which Penelhum and other unsentimental moderns are necessarily indifferent. Hume's self-appointed task is thus exceedingly delicate: his investigation of selfhood is conducted in a literary manner that both defers to and corrects "ordinary language," just as his reexamination of "invariance" and "substance" and other notions behind personal identity describes and refines them, not so much deriding them (as Penulhum puts it) as satirizing their misuse and misunderstanding by philosophers.[55]

Penelhum's incisive point is simply that there is no identity problem and that Hume's elaboration of an intricate complex of epistemological adjustments is irrelevant, completely unnecessary given the stability of language in ordinary use. For an example, he finds Hume inconsistent in speaking of "'an *object* that remains invariable' and 'several *objects* existing in succession,' because he is here using the same norm in each case, viz., 'object'; and although this is the vaguest norm in the language, the mere fact that he uses the same one in each case suggests very easily that in the two phrases he is thinking of objects of the same kind, e.g., a single and uninterrupted note and a succession of distinct notes."[56] Hume, it seems to me, is worried by just this predisposition of language to solve problems. He concludes "that all the nice and subtle questions concerning personal identity can never possibly be decided, and are to be regarded rather as grammatical than as philosophical difficulties . . . All the disputes concerning the identity of connected objects are merely verbal, except so far as the relation of parts gives rise to some fiction or imaginary principle of union" (p.262). What Penelhum considers a definitive principle of order, Hume declares an end to speculation, or rather a redefinition of order in this case as merely verbal.

"Of personal identity" is a relatively self-contained essay, one of the "several topics" Hume says he has been "led" into by his "miscellaneous way of reasoning" (p.263). Of course, this essay rests on notions developed in the preceding parts of Book I; the theory of impressions and the trinity of resemblance, contiguity, and causation control the direction of the argument. Given the inevitable analytic dead end this background imposes, Hume's exposition is striking in its leisurely expansiveness. Hume arranges this discussion, I believe, to provide his readers with an amusing and instructive sequence, rehearsing or staging the rediscovery of notions central to the *Treatise* and carefully working into his discourse rhetorical equivalents of the false or untenable positions leading to those notions.

He begins with a favorite trick and recurring stylistic opposition: mimicry of fatuously self-satisfied soliloquy is followed by ironically deferential dialogue, which offers in its rejoinders an incisive reasoning based on what the *Treatise* has already established.

There are some philosophers, who imagine we are every moment intimately conscious of what we call our SELF; that we feel its existence and
its continuance in existence; and are certain, beyond the evidence of a
demonstration, both of its perfect identity and simplicity. The strongest
sensation, the most violent passion, say they, instead of dis-
tracting us from this view, only fix it the more intensely and make us
consider their influence on *self* either by their pain or pleasure. To attempt a farther proof of this were to weaken its evidence; since no proof
can be deriv'd from any fact, of which we are so intimately conscious;
nor is there any thing, of which we can be certain, if we doubt of this.

   Unluckily all these positive assertions are contrary to that very experience, which is pleaded for them, nor have we any idea of *self*, after
the manner it is here explain'd. For from what impression cou'd this
idea be deriv'd? This question 'tis impossible to answer without a
manifest contradiction and absurdity; and yet 'tis a question, which
must necessarily be answer'd, if we wou'd have the idea of self pass for
clear and intelligible. It must be some one impression, that gives rise to
every real idea. But self or person is not any one impression, but that to
which our several impressions and ideas are suppos'd to have a reference.
If any impression gives rise to the idea of self, that impression must continue invariably the same, thro' the whole course of our lives; since self
is suppos'd to exist after that manner. But there is no impression constant and invariable. Pain and pleasure, grief and joy, passions and sensations succeed each other, and never all exist at the same time. It cannot, therefore, be from any of these impressions, or from any other, that
the idea of self is deriv'd; and consequently there is no such idea.
(Pp.251–252)

The turn in "unluckily" controls the comic tempo, since it abruptly halts
the paraphrase of the philosophers of self, whose energetic "proof" spins
in a logical and rhetorical circle, positing sensation and even "the most
violent passion" as the demonstration of a fact beyond demonstration and
on whose truth is founded all demonstration. This position in Hume's
paraphrase is a series of untroubled paradoxes; each sentence repeats
another aspect of the paradox whereby selfhood is asserted as preceding
any conceivable rational analysis. Hume is often accused of loving
paradoxes, but in this case he argues against easy acceptance of paradox
and premature surrender of reason. "Unluckily," then, not only halts the
self-satisfied paradoxical whirl but expresses Hume's characteristic contempt for specious or superficial reasoning.

   The second paragraph poses a question in place of reckless assertions:
merely verbal paradoxes are exchanged for dilemmas from experience.
The narrator plunges back, as it were, into the strict speaking of ideas and
impressions established by the *Treatise*: "from what impression" is the
idea of self derived? "This question 'tis impossible to answer without a

manifest contradiction and absurdity; and yet 'tis a question, which must necessarily be answer'd, if we wou'd have the idea of self pass for clear and intelligible." This sentence follows, with one key variation, the paradoxical pattern set in the first paragraph. The contradiction holding these clauses together is a challenge leading to further activity rather than a repetition that doubles the paradox of selfhood back on intuition. What follows imitates dialogue, not only forming an analytic sequence but turning to the sensations the philosophers of self claim establish it—"Pain and pleasure, grief and joy, passions and sensations"—and making them into a fast-moving sequence rather than single and conclusive entities.

The rebuttal ends with a Q.E.D. "Consequently" seems a return to a sort of certainty, a dangerously positive assertion. Moving away from static assertion, Hume launches out into "particular perceptions," indeed his own perceptual adventures. In the context of the opening paragraph, his choice of verbs in this narrative is deliberate: "For my part, when I enter most intimately into what I call *myself*, I always stumble on some particular perception or other, of heat or cold, light or shade, love or hatred, pain or pleasure. I never can catch *myself* at any time without a perception, and never can observe any thing but the perception" (p.252). Hume freely admits he lives in the same linguistic world as the philosopher; he has something he *calls* himself. But he depicts himself in the process of refining common usage, stumbling and unable to catch the static abstraction called self. Most readers have seen this passage as merely ironic. I think it is comic, human in the Humean sense that the right to live with contradiction is earned by active inquiry. This scene reaffirms the special features of Hume's narrator in the *Treatise*, an elaborate mock-humility mixed with defiance by which he gives up the idea of a unitary self: "And were all my perceptions remov'd by death, and cou'd I neither think, nor feel, nor see, nor love, nor hate after the dissolution of my body, I shou'd be entirely annihilated, nor do I conceive what is farther requisite to make me a perfect nonentity" (p.252).

The defiance in this sentence is brash enough, as Hume slides into the "positive air" he later regretted, thumbing his nose at any metaphysician who "may, perhaps, perceive something simple and continu'd which he calls *himself*" (p.252). Contemptuous dismissal is followed, however, by a generous image of the mind as a "kind of theatre," generous in the sense that it modifies Hume's tendency to a mechanical naturalism. He begins by reducing mankind to "nothing but a bundle or collection of different perceptions." We are at the mercy of our bodies: "Our eyes cannot turn in their sockets without varying our perceptions." But when Hume turns to his theatrical image, a cultural richness and aesthetic intensity briefly moderate natural harshness. "The mind is a kind of theatre, where several perceptions successively make their appearance; pass, re-pass, glide away, and mingle in an infinite variety of postures and situations" (p.253).

The analogy contains a hint of human steadiness, a spectator somehow apart from all that flux, moved and delighted in a precise manner by its various patterns. And of course the image signals the logical contradiction in Hume's attempt to reduce the self. There is at work throughout this section of the *Treatise* what John Passmore calls a myth of prior and pure understanding, whereby the series of perceptions supposed to generate the fiction of identity can operate only "if there is something which is at first misled by, and then, after reconsideration, can discover that it was misled by, a series of similar perceptions."[57] Hume seems aware of this paradox and moves quickly to stop the reverberations of his comparison, which "must not mislead us," for it is intended to signify only the motion of the perceptions. We have not even "the most distant notion of the place, where these scenes are represented, or of the materials, of which it is compos'd" (p.253). But such a retraction admits the possibility of imagining a scene and understanding the dramatic materials used in this theater. The image is a glimpse of a certain organization of experience that negates, at least in part, the severe naturalism of Hume's theory.

Presiding over the reduction of self and the language used to contain it, then, is a narrator whose control and ironic challenges to his opponent are modified by a manner that encourages self-implication and expresses a steady reluctance to take satisfaction in mere paradox. Hume's problem, especially clear in this section, is to avoid the tone of triumph in his reductionism and to neutralize the smug acceptance of disorder implicit in his dismantling of common notions. A reluctant skeptic, what Richard Popkin calls a "schizophrenic Pyrrhonist," Hume was thus a writer who wished to avoid the finalities of systematic exposition.[58] Summarizing Hume's complicated exposition of personal identity, Norman Kemp Smith says that the self is "like everything else in experience, to be understood (so far as 'understanding' is humanly possible at all) solely in terms of relation."[59] In Hume as he asks to be read, writing is the ultimate and sure relation, providing almost in spite of his intentions as a thinker a perspective tending to stabilize or at least to ground in dependable rhetorical relationships the unruly perceptual relationships his thought so intensely explores. His diffidence in the face of his clarifying image of the mind as a theater grants the power of such representation. His tactful retreat from its facility gives him and his reader an identity as discriminating users of language, implicitly earns coherence for his writing by a self-conscious awareness of its limits. But Hume recognizes in his reluctant rejection of analogy our recurring need to mislead ourselves.

Hume carefully notes the compensating movements of imagination as it fabricates notions and transforms diversity into identity:

> Our propensity to this mistake is so great from the resemblance above-mention'd, that we fall into it before we are aware; and tho' we incessantly correct ourselves by reflexion, and return to a more accurate method of thinking, yet we cannot long sustain our philosophy, or take off this biass from the imagination. Our last resource is to yield to it, and boldly assert that these different related objects are in effect the same, however interrupted and variable. In order to justify to ourselves this absurdity, we often feign some new and unintelligible principle, that connects the objects together, and prevents their interruption or variation. Thus we feign the continu'd existence of the perceptions of our senses, to remove the interruption; and run into the notion of a *soul*, and *self*, and *substance*, to disguise the variation. (P.254)

Hume's logic in passages like this is supported by moralized narrative. In the context of the *Treatise*, our inability to sustain a philosophical view of diversity is a sign of inescapable humanity. The situation Hume dramatizes in the first sentence rests upon a natural pattern which it is foolish, in a sense, to resist, and the reader is invited to take momentary pleasure in the inevitability of our common weakness. But the next three sentences describe an assertion rather than a process, an attempt to escape the human comedy of process by legislating and "imposing" absurdity. The tone shifts in these sentences from comedy to satire, a blame emerges steadily from the mock-heroic of "boldly" asserting identity to the foolish "feigning" of false principles of identity, and finally to the deliberate and thereby blameworthy "running" into untenable notions (the verb hints at cowardice, retreat from the painful facts). Groups of sentences like this recur in Hume's discussion; they have an insistent moral-literary shape inseparable from the psychological exposition that reduces identity to a fiction. Hume's account of introspection transforms it into revealing soliloquy wherein the categories of selfhood are generated by clumsy rationalization.

As perhaps every single modern commentator observes of the *Treatise*, its psychologism is thus not experimental or even properly observational. Antony Flew puts the case for responding to these complaints. Hume's concern, he says is not strictly with logical analysis "but with issues of psycho-social fact" that contribute to the construction of "some sort of mental geography" of man.⁶⁰ By its narrative arrangements, these sequences with their rather delicate control of tone and moral attitude, Hume's writing makes those psychosocial facts consistently relevant to a reimagining of man that seeks to demystify human nature and to make the truth about us readily accessible (within the density and complexity of the *Treatise*, there is a promise of liberating simplicity in its conclusions). Hume's account of mental happenings is geographical in the broadest sense, a description of human economy and ecology, not just a record of topography and a positioning of land masses but a marking of the tidal movements and trade routes of the mind as it negotiates for ease and stability.

As the section progresses, Hume's tolerance for what he calls the artifices of the imagination increases. His examples are from the stable world of common life as he turns to the identity we ascribe to vegetable and animal bodies as well as to useful structures like buildings and ships. When he comes at last to attempt a new explanation of personal identity, he begins with a joke whose irony serves an ultimate simplicity Hume always claims. Personal identity has become, he notes, "so great a question in philosophy, especially of late years in *England*, where all the abstruser sciences are study'd with a peculiar ardour and application" (p.259). The larger context of the *Treatise* and the immediate surrounding argument yield a comic tableau: the question as transformed by Hume is no longer "abstruse," for his rigorous but simple and exact narrative has dispelled the quirkiness and eccentricity in that "peculiar ardour and application" of English philosophers. For the clumsy intellectual exertions of philosophers Hume substitutes radical simplicity, his insistence that perception is restricted to particulars and that the understanding "never observes any real connexion among objects" (p.259).

Although the identity of the mind must be "fictitious," like that "we ascribe to vegetables and animal bodies" (p.259), Hume invites his readers to consider (actually to reconsider) the issue in the light of the basic assumptions of the *Treatise*. They amount to an insistence on the literal facts of perception, a heightened emphasis on the separate strands of perception as forever separate. Identity can only be what Hume labels "a quality, which we attribute" to our perceptions "because of the union of their ideas in the imagination, when we reflect upon them" (p.260). Hume talks about this potentially disturbing conclusion as something evident and transparent and to that extent reassuring; his literal and in one sense fantastic epistemological world is treated as if it were normal

and natural. The merely logical necessity of separate and distinct perceptions becomes an empirical fact, an easily experienced set of conditions.
The fiction of personal identity issues from connections provided by
resemblance and causation. A visualized rendition of memory illustrates
the image-collecting activity of that faculty:

> . . . suppose we cou'd see clearly into the breast of another, and observe
> that succession of perceptions, which constitutes his mind or thinking
> principle, and suppose that he always preserves the memory of a con-
> siderable part of past perceptions; 'tis evident that nothing cou'd more
> contribute to the bestowing a relation on this succession amidst all its
> variations. For what is the memory but a faculty, by which we raise up
> the images of past perceptions? And as an image necessarily resembles
> its object, must not the frequent placing of these resembling perceptions
> in the chain of thought, convey the imagination more easily from one
> link to another, and make the whole seem like the continuance of one
> object? In this particular, then, the memory not only discovers the iden-
> tity, but also contributes to its production, by producing the relation of
> resemblance among the perceptions. (Pp.260–261)

This linking leads, Hume continues, to the more complex operation of
causation whereby certain perceptions (impressions) "give rise to their
correspondent ideas; and these ideas in their turn produce other impressions" (p.261). What commentators call the "copy principle" in Hume's
thought is strongly at work in this exposition, which depends upon granting the mind a dominating vivacity and clarity in its imaginings. Identity
is quite simply the most audacious of the imagination's fictions, since as
Hume concludes we sustain it in the face of an inevitable forgetfulness of
its constituents. Once we establish the self by grasping "that chain of
causes and effects" which constitutes it, "we can extend the same chain of
causes, and consequently the identity of our persons beyond our memory,
and can comprehend times, and circumstances, and actions, which we
have entirely forgot, but suppose in general to have existed" (p.262).
Memory, Hume insists, "does not so much *produce* as *discover* personal
identity" (p.262).

Hume finds nothing that can justify personal identity, but his writing
as he proceeds establishes it as an eminently clear entity. A. P. Cavendish
remarks that in Hume's theory we can never conceive of something as
necessarily existing, "because for him an idea is a kind of picture, and it is
perfectly obvious that nothing in a picture makes it necessary that what it
is a picture of should exist."[61] Identity appears as just the sort of on-
tologically uncertain picture Cavendish finds recurrent in Hume, a picture the mind sustains by powers of composition implicitly analogous to

literary or artistic fashioning. As an image, Hume's evocation of the links forged by memory is unobtrusive, and his "chain" of causes and effects is a nearly dead metaphor. But the memory is an active power, a faculty, Hume calls it, for raising up images of past perceptions; it is a force that manages this spectacle and arranges a convincing clarity which more than distracts us from ontological uncertainty. Hume's own analogy is boldly clear and suggests his own ultimate preference for experience that neutralizes such uncertainty. The soul is "properly" compared to "a republic or commonwealth," which "may not only change its members, but also its laws and constitutions; in like manner the same person may vary his character and dispostion, as well as his impressions and ideas, without losing his identity" (p.261).

A complex analogy like this differs only in its self-consciousness from the image making of the memory. The clarity of Hume's writing in the face of irreducible ontological confusion is parallel to the psychological clarity with which he surrounds the dark notion of identity. By facing the paradox calmly and indeed making it the climax of Book I, Hume redefines reason into a power inseparable from the imagination and treats the self's relationship with the world as essentially rhetorical. Reason becomes for Hume, as T. E. Jessop formulates it, "a process of associatively determined causal inference."[62] Hume's writing controls its associations but is nonetheless limited to them, bound by conventional analogies like "chains" or "bundles" of perceptions to evoke the mind's activity, occasionally reaching for more complex and suggestive images like the soul as commonwealth but always making the reader aware of the tangential and merely rhetorical relationship of such discourse to any conceivable reality. Hume's writing regularly displays its persuasive efficiency even as it admits its philosophical limitations. Indeed, Book I is largely a matter of such admissions:

When I reflect on the natural fallibility of my judgment, I have less confidence in my opinions, than when I only consider the objects concerning which I reason; and when I proceed still farther, to turn the scrutiny against every successive estimation I make of my faculties, all the rules of logic require a continual diminution, and at last a total extinction of belief and evidence. (P.183)

This sentence cheerfully predicts the steady movement in this last part of Book I toward a radically diminished knowing. In its firm control of sequence and its clear analysis of its own powers of representation, Hume's writing records as well its own compensating strength. The enormous implications of his system become relatively harmless in the context of the literary control Hume exercises over them. The notorious "Conclusion" of Book I is only an externalization of what has been implicit in a commanding literary manner.

That conclusion is the broadest philosophical comedy, featuring a persona who begins in clowning mock terror and isolation and passes gradually to a paralyzing crisis. The crisis itself, with superb comic symmetry, has been caused by Hume's conclusion, as he reviews the extreme implications of his system, "that reflections very refin'd and metaphysical have little or no influence upon us." No sooner has he committed himself to that rashly absolute generalization than the emotional effects of a denial of the validity of all belief and reasoning set in and cancel even that tiny certainty. He fancies himself "inviron'd with the deepest darkness, and utterly depriv'd of the use of every member and faculty" (p.269). But this paralysis is resolved abruptly by the "natural" cycle that returns him to social distraction from these "chimeras": "I dine, I play a game of back-gammon, I converse, and am merry with my friends; and when after three or four hour's amusement, I wou'd return to these speculations, they appear so cold, and strain'd, and ridiculous, that I cannot find in my heart to enter into them any farther" (p.269). This narration is in the experimental present tense; the persona is a suddenly vivid version of the writer of the *Treatise* who has allowed himself to forget the commanding literary distance he has been putting between actual experience and the literal dissections of it by his system. Hume observes this character and imagines his reactions within the exaggerated immediacy that now intrudes in a patently rhetorical sequence and span:

Can I be sure, that in leaving all establish'd opinions I am following truth; and by what criterion shall I distinguish her, even if fortune shou'd at last guide me on her foot-steps? After the most accurate and exact of my reasonings, I can give no reason why I shou'd assent to it; and feel nothing but a *strong* propensity to consider objects *strongly* in that view, under which they appear to me. Experience is a principle, which instructs me in the several conjunctions of objects for the past. Habit is another principle, which determines me to expect the same for the future; and both of them conspiring to operate upon the imagination, make me form certain ideas in a more intense and lively manner, than others, which are not attended with the same advantages. (P.265)

The crisis Hume stages around his persona is a vindication of this view, a marking out once again of the dynamic redefinition of "truth" in a personal sequence. His melancholy turbulence, subsidence into normality through social pleasures, and eventual return to contemplative pursuits are illustrations of the truth of human process, which emerges within the exposition of metaphysical limitations, defining and also restraining his system. The Hume of this conclusion enacts those confusions bound to beset the understanding which the *Treatise* has already explored. Even the Baconian ambition to reorganize the "learned world, which lies under such a deplorable ignorance in all these particulars" (p.271) is placed by Hume's comic narrative within the framework of his moralized psychology, in which natural inclinations bring him back to the invigorating pleasures of philosophy. For all its dangers, philosophy is an appropriately human exercise which at its best cooperates with our natural rhythms. It is "almost impossible for the mind of man to rest, like those of beasts, in that narrow circle of objects, which are the subject of daily conversation and action" (p.271); so philosophy as Hume now defines it is the establishment of "a system or set of opinions, which if not true (for that, perhaps, is too much to be hop'd for) might at least be satisfactory to the human mind, and might stand the test of the most critical examination" (p.272). In part, this diminished ambition marks the passage of the *Treatise* to the passions and morals, the true subject of philosophy for Hume, but it also underlines once again his commitment to persuasiveness and indeed to the pleasures of philosophical discourse as such.[63] The "Conclusion" rehearses in its modulation from melodrama to comedy the plot of Hume's thought: the displacement of philosophy by philosophical writing, which is not truly skeptical as such but is a literary deployment of skepticism to place thought in psychological and moral reality.

By itself, this literary adjunct is not surprising. Even the most complex philosophical exposition may turn on occasion to a guiding rhetorical opposition or polemical thrust which serves to highlight logical rigor and perhaps to sustain nonphilosophical readers. Locke and Berkeley, like Hume, have an active distaste for purely professional discourse and place their writing in an overseeing, clarifying dramatic scene. In Locke's *Essay*, modest rationality and moral-political compromise hold steadily against epistemological confusion. Locke's tactful retreats from certainty to pragmatic, operational clarity take place against a potentially threatening backdrop of absurdity and violence. Berkeley enforces a purer clarity by a paradoxical simplicity, epistemological and theological at once. Richly metaphoric, his thought dramatizes itself as points of light in obscurity, a vital, corrective seeing in a darkening, corrupt moral-philosophical world. Hume avoids Berkeleian melodrama as well as the politicized Lockean scene. The sustaining thematic adjunct to his thought is nothing less than the problem of philosophical writing itself. As the most cunningly rhetorical of the three, Hume bases the persuasiveness of his work on his resistance as a writer to the systematic and thereby untenable implications he uncovers at the bottom of all philosophical discourse, including his own in a sense. As I read the *Treatise*, it contains the gradual permeation of Hume's thought by that resistance; it records a growing sense of the near incompatibility between stylish clarity and abstract difficulty, between reassuring, shapely aphorism and the disturbing rigor of his philosophical revolution. As Raymond Williams puts it with unique incisiveness, Hume "must forbear insisting, renounce any pretension to be graceful and engaging, even while he engages and insists. In this tension, a whole movement of thought—in effect the transformation of empiricism—is being slowly and unevenly brought to light."[64] Hume retreats in due course from obtrusive rigor and abstruse difficulty (without renouncing them) to the aphoristic persuasiveness of the *Enquiries*, but the drastic recasting he gives his thought is implicit in the difficulties, both stylistic and thematic, he encounters in Books II and III of the *Treatise*.

As he opens Book III, Hume speaks of the silencing effect of some abstruse reasoning, irrefutable but unpersuasive as he later said of Berkeley's skepticism.[65] A "long chain of reasoning" like the *Treatise* may cause the reader to forget initial principles and to "lose sight of all the most receiv'd maxims, either of philosophy or common life" (p.455). Hume hopes to make the *Treatise* "acquire new force as it advances" and sees a sustaining natural progression in its topics: as *"morals* will corroborate whatever has been said concerning the *understanding* and the *passions"* (p.455). Moreover, "morality is a subject that interests us above all others" (p.455), and no one can consider it with indifference. The *Treatise* is a succession of related and progressively involving subjects. Hume is not only encouraging readers; he is making the persuasive movement of his thought part of its substance and reaffirming its relevance for an active, interested reader.

Hume's persuasiveness has all along displayed itself against various implicit forms of unpersuasive discourse. The repudiation of metaphysics in Book I is enforced by a supple literary manner that runs rings around the stiffness of previous systems, as Hume evokes them of course. Epistemological process is the mind's imaginative construction of order, and Hume's writing returns consistently to the tentative fragility of the conversion. His irony is ready to remind readers of the certainty of human uncertainty and thereby to prevent the dominance of rigid schemes or inflexible categories. But this moral turn in his thought is seriously imperiled by the mechanistic associationist psychology to which Hume was committed. In Book I the polemic against metaphysical rigidity makes that psychology a liberating force, a natural process to set against the creaking machinery of the philosophers; it provides ingratiating anecdote and personal narrative as well as conclusive empirical testimony against false objectifying schemes. In Books II and III, however, Hume necessarily defers to his own machinery, which begins the task of objectifying passions and morals. His problem is to retain his literary presence, with all the humor and engaging good sense it has accumulated thus far, and to sustain the ordinary reader's attention and interest as Hume now actually sets out to elaborate his "science" of man and to pursue what his title pages dauntingly call "the experimental Method of Reasoning." Where Book I revises metaphysics in generous human terms, these books offer to explain passions and morals in a rigorous and potentially abstract manner. The paradoxes in Book I are troubling mainly to the thoughtful, first to those who adhere to a misconceived philosophy and then to Hume himself, who offers his own merely temporary disorientation as evidence of the ultimate prevalence of common experience over the paradoxes of even a corrected philosophy like his own. But Hume's project now focuses on certain calculated outrages to common emotional and moral notions. These books transform and complicate daily experience, making the ordinary strange as well as difficult. Hume the moral essayist is crossed with the anatomist of the passions and moral sentiments. The resulting hybrid produces a divided, sometimes uncertain literary manner within which Hume struggles to retain persuasive poise and clarity.

The passions of pride and humility Hume sets himself to trace as he opens Book II are an intermediate psychological entity, not derived purely from "natural and physical causes" (p.272) or from particularized external causes, but from the mind's perceptions, what he calls "secondary and reflective" impressions which arise "either from the original impressions, or from their ideas" (p.276). Even as he sketches this difficult mental entity and distinguishes between calm and violent impressions, Hume's "experimental" mode attempts to stabilize a richly concrete world of human occurrences, to speak in general terms about matters that threaten to become either abstractly schematic or diversely particular. The associationism basic to Hume's thought, as John Passmore points out, is inconsistent, negating the determinism it seems to claim by speaking so insistently of propensities of the mind. Unlike ideas, impressions are connected only by resemblance, but Hume's rendition of the movements of our passions lends them an involving moral shape, turns what should be mere sequence into narrative with a plot featuring pathos and what

Passmore calls "the mind's own interests and inclinations rather than the conjunctions and repetitions of its perceptions."[66]

> All resembling impressions are connected together, and no sooner one arises than the rest immediately follow. Grief and disappointment give rise to anger, anger to envy, envy to malice, and malice to grief again, till the whole circle be compleated. In like manner our temper, when elevated with joy, naturally throws itself into love, generosity, pity, courage, pride, and the other resembling affections. 'Tis difficult for the mind, when actuated by any passion, to confine itself to that passion alone, without any change or variation. Human nature is too inconstant to admit of any such regularity. Changeableness is essential to it. And to what can it so naturally change as to affections or emotions, which are suitable to the temper, and agree with that set of passions, which then prevail? (P.283)

The animating force in this generalized language works against systematizing. "Mind" acquires an identity and a dominance in this account of its instinct for ease and appropriateness. Humean "ideas" are linked by the controlling triad of resemblance, contiguity, and causation, and these ideas can easily cooperate with the more volatile "impressions" rendered in this paragraph. The result is "a double impulse" on the mind and a powerful emotional effect. Hume conjures up a brief example, a sketch for the pathological potential in ordinary human relationships: "Thus a man, who, by any injury from another, is very much discompos'd and ruffled in his temper, is apt to find a hundred subjects of discontent, impatience, fear, and other uneasy passions; especially if he can discover these subjects in or near the person, who was the cause of his first passion" (p.284). Hume's language drifts toward individual volition and design; this aggrieved individual finds new reasons for enmity and is to a large extent the author of his enlarged passion. Hume concludes this section with a curious analogy for this process from "an elegant writer"—Addison.[67] The visual beauty of an object is intensified when it is supplemented by effects upon another sense. Addison's spectator finds a power in simultaneous sensory experiences greater than their sum if taken separately. Addison's psychological aesthetics is like Hume's mechanism of the passions, for both involve a deliberate and to some extent a delighted assent to the mind's multiple and original operations. Hume seems to want to sketch a determinism, but the introduction of Addison's spectator in the presence of landscapes and paintings marks his uneasiness with that direction of his thought. The flowering of passion Hume evokes is dangerous and destructive of self, and the perspective of the Addisonian aesthete may serve as an instinctive correction.

Balanced against the drive toward systematic and even mechanistic ex-

planation is Hume's repeated invocation of the moral commonplaces surrounding the idea of human nature: "Can we imagine it possible, that
while human nature remains the same, men will ever become entirely indifferent to their power, riches, beauty or personal merit, and that their
pride and vanity will not be affected by these advantages?" (p.281).
Hume enlists these commonplaces to serve systematic explanation, using
them as a sanction for scientific simplicity and regularity. Since human
nature is everywhere and always the same, it follows that certain "few and
simple" principles must account for the multiplicity of effects to be
observed in mankind (p.282).

The balance between the moral essayist and the analyst of the passions
is disturbed in short order, as Hume tracks the causes of pride and
humility and conducts one of his "experiments," actually no more than
an introspective rendering of his examination of mental circumstances to
determine "whether these causes be regarded, as the qualities, that
operate, or as the subjects, on which the qualities are plac'd" (p.285). The
conclusion of the experiment is partly a schematic, quasi-mathematical
diagram in which mental occurrences are transformed into forces and
"movements," and then a biologizing analogy turned literal as Hume
speaks of the "organs of the human mind" (p.287). But he seems uneasy
with such terms. This "discovery" is prefaced by attempts at anecdotal
directness, which maintain a present-tense enactment of thinking this
problem through, which adopt for a moment a mannered spontaneity in
the middle of rigorous exposition: "the true system breaks in upon me
with an irresistible evidence" (p.286). Hume's experimental present tense
stages the discovery of the "causes" of the passions; he writes as if the
systematic truth about them has emerged gradually in actual empirical
inquiry that negates (or at least distracts from) the mechanistic implications of a system of the passions.

The difficulty, then, is only to discover this cause, and find what it is
that gives the first motion to pride, and sets those organs in action,
which are naturally fitted to produce that emotion. Upon my consulting
experience, in order to resolve this difficulty, I immediately find a hundred different causes, that produce pride; and upon examining these
causes, I suppose, what at first I perceive to be probable, that all of
them concur in two circumstances; which are, that of themselves they
produce an impression, ally'd to the passion, and are plac'd on a subject, ally'd to the object of the passion. When I consider after this the
nature of *relation*, and its effects both on the passions and ideas, I can
no longer doubt, upon these suppositions, that 'tis the very principle,
which gives rise to pride, and bestows motion on those organs, which

being naturally dispos'd to produce that affection, require only a first
impulse or beginning to their action. Any thing, that gives a pleasant
sensation, and is related to self, excites the passion of pride, which is
also agreeable, and has self for its object. (P.288)

Two voices divide the work: the neutral experimentalist who thinks in
terms of a human machine and the tentative essayist who "consults" experience. The latter briefly introduces diversity, a "hundred different
causes" in place of the single one the experimenter speaks of so confidently in the opening sentence. Diversity resolves itself quickly into "two
circumstances" and the essayist yields as he "examines" and "considers,"
his doubt turning to certainty as the multifarious moral-psychological
world summed up in pride gives way to a simplifying physics of the passions whereby motion is bestowed on "organs" by means of a "first impulse."

Hume's unhappiness with this transformation is manifest. Before proceeding, he inserts a separate section, "Limitations of this system," which
complicates the axiom that pride and humility are produced in a sort of
magnetic field of impressions and ideas, "by which one of them, upon its
appearance, naturally introduces its correlative" (p.289). Although he
promises to resolve these complications later on, Hume concedes in these
limitations a ruling contradiction in human affairs, a historical density
produced by time and circumstances. Moral-psychological generalities
and paradoxes begin to crowd out the rhetoric of associationism, and
Hume concludes "with a reflection deriv'd from these five limitations"
which undermines the theoretical validity of his project, which warns
readers not to suppose these theories cancel human irregularity, "as may
at first sight be imagin'd from this system."

An evil may be real, tho' its cause has no relation to us: It may be real,
without being peculiar: It may be real, without shewing itself to others:
It may be real, without being constant: And it may be real, without
falling under the general rules. Such evils as these will not fail to render
us miserable, tho' they have little tendency to diminish pride: And
perhaps the most real and the most solid evils of life will be found of
this nature. (P.294)

Pride and humility are accounted for within Hume's mechanisms, but a
subject exists somewhat to the side of systematic regularity, converting by
the peculiarities of imagination and temperament what is philosophically
invalid or incomplete into psychological reality. Moral "reflection" uncovers a separate realm of predictable perversity, as regular in its way as
the associative mechanisms Hume is elaborating but dependent upon

particular circumstances and to that extent undetermined and contingent. Moreover, as a "reflection" Hume's concluding paragraph is a carefully labeled literary epitome of the "limitations" of this system, a reminder not only of its supervision by common experience but of the writing that defines experience by opposing moral qualification to systematizing. The oratorical repetitions refer readers to each of the five enumerated limitations; each sentence is an aphoristic rendition of the numbered preceding paragraphs, now part of a sequence whose climax forms no part of the section itself and which is not directly connected to Hume's philosophical aims. We are inevitably miserable because of a world of experience quite impervious to philosophical analysis, and the last two sentences of this conclusion are a moral-literary moment only incidental to Hume's tracing of causes. His analysis turns by a kind of cultural habit to generalized moral narrative which takes pleasure in paradox and which doubles such pleasures by stylistic arrangements that both enhance and contain contradiction.

Even Hume's most ostentatiously objectified moments are compromised by the concrete richness of his examples. His "experiments" take place in such a sharply rendered moral-psychological scene that he is hard pressed to maintain the abstract simplicity of his diagrams. For example, he proceeds from pride and humility to love and hatred and devises in Section II of Part II a long summarizing experimental chapter "to confirm this system" (p.332). The chapter's eight numbered experiments are a series of vignettes in which Hume imagines himself first "in company with a person, whom I formerly regarded without any sentiments either of friendship or enmity" (p.333) and then with a son or brother or someone united to him "by a long and familiar acquaintance" (p.337). The guiding analogy for these relations is geometrical, with "four affections, plac'd, as it were, in a square or regular connexion with, and distance from each other" (p.333). By the end of the chapter, Hume claims to have established a sort of emotional Pythagorean theorem in which pride and humility or love and hatred arise from the "double relation of impressions and ideas" with an absolute regularity: "An object without a relation, or with but one, never produces either of these passions; and 'tis found that the passion always varies in conformity to the relation" (p.347).

But geometrical relations and emotional vectors are inescapably complicated in the telling by those social and psychological circumstances to which Hume attends with such exactness. In the longest of the experiments, the seventh, "we find, that when we either love or hate any person, the passions seldom continue within their first bounds; but extend themselves towards all the contiguous objects, and comprehend the friends and relations of him we love or hate" (p.341). That describes a disorderly, quasi-organic motion rather than the mechanical or mathematical transfer of force Hume is outlining. But he restores this wayward analogy, since observation proves that "our passions, like other objects, descend with greater facility than they ascend" and we tend to hate a whole family when our quarrel is with the father rather than with the son, or to love "the subject for the prince, rather than the prince for the subject" (p.342). The passions differ in this regard from the imagination, which passes with more facility from the lesser to the greater than vice versa. The thought of the servant leads to the master, Jupiter's satellites to the planet itself, and "the mention of the provinces of any empire conveys our thought to the seat of the empire; but the fancy returns not with the same facility to the consideration of the provinces" (p.342).

A modern reader may feel rather like Uncle Toby listening to his brother Walter's explanations. The social and political assumptions behind this contradiction are remarkable; hierarchy and subordination support the associative mechanisms of Hume's "imagination," but the passions in obeying those very principles seem to violate physical laws by resisting the passage from inferior to superior. Moreover, the passions are stronger than the imagination; they are "impressions," connected in Hume's scheme only by their resemblance, difficult to predict or manage. Degrees of passion, he notes, may easily produce differences in kind and introduce a diversity difficult to classify. "A man, when calm or only moderately agitated, is so different, in every respect, from himself, when disturbed by a violent passion, that no two persons can be more unlike; nor is it easy to pass from the one extreme to the other, without a considerable interval betwixt them" (p.344).

It is left to an entity called "mind" (a wholeness and unity never really far from Hume's atomistic analysis of mental operations and implicit in his command of so complicated a sequence) to reconcile contradiction. The passion "prevails" over the imagination but it does so by tactfully "complying with it, and by seeking another quality which may counterballance" the opposition (p.345). When we are surrounded in Hume's concluding vignette by the children or servants of a father or master of a family we love, their "nearness and contiguity in this case encreases their magnitude, or at least removes that opposition, which the fancy makes to the transition of the affections" (pp.345–346). The passions facilitate the transition for the fancy by arranging a social scene "which brings the matter to an equality, and leaves the way open from the one passion to the other" (p.346). The passions are accommodated to the imagination, at least in the tender scene Hume evokes here; they have a guidance system he introduces without explanation or origin. He speaks consistently of the separate parts of the mind and insists rigorously on the central distinction between impressions and ideas, but he inevitably conjures up a balancing and unifying sensibility which encompasses this mental machine and directs it to serve human needs of which the machine can have no notion.

Theodor Adorno remarks that even though he dismisses the self as a prejudice, Hume "bears witness in every sentence to his real humanism."[68] What Adorno sensed is evident in even the most ostensibly technical moments in the *Treatise*, where the vivacity of Hume's writing and the breadth of moral imagining it supports produce the philosophical exercise Johnson recommended to Langton. "Of the Passions" is inevitably true to the generality and speculative openness promised by its title: a series of essays in which Hume not only balances experimental terminology and systematic expectations against emotional experience but in due course transforms his analysis of the passions into a redefinition of them which is a defense of their autonomy.

Hume's distinctiveness as a moral writer lies in his provocative refusal to assign blame. When he speaks of "those who take a pleasure in declaiming against human nature" (p.352), the wholly negative significance in Hume's lexicon of declamation as incomplete, unobservant, merely verbal moralism is quickly made clear. Such satirists find man "altogether insufficient to support himself" and look disapprovingly at his "continual search after amusement in gaming, in hunting, in business; by which we endeavour to forget ourselves, and excite our spirits from the languid state, into which they fall, when not sustain'd by some brisk and lively emotion" (p.352). Hume celebrates the social necessity sour moralists deplore and finds in the formation of social groups and activities not only an attractive scene but the specifically human emotional moment his system aspires to comprehend, in every sense of the word.

Sympathy is at the center of this human nature, and Hume speaks of man's "ardent desire of society" with something less than anthropological distance when he observes that "a perfect solitude is, perhaps, the greatest punishment we can suffer" (p.353). And a bit earlier in Book II, he finds the mind "insufficient, of itself, to its own entertainment"; it "naturally seeks after foreign objects" (pp.352–353). In these recurring moments, Hume evokes a social scene as the center of his thought, which stands in startling contrast to the solitary analytic pursuits of the *Treatise* as it casts a cold eye on the passions. "Of the love of relations" quickly cancels the locational neutrality of "relation," seeing it with suddenly heightened rhythm as a vital connection.

On the appearance of such an object [the mind] awakes, as it were,
from a dream: The blood flows with a new tide: The heart is elevated:
And the whole man acquires a vigour, which he cannot command in his
solitary and calm moments. Hence company is naturally so rejoicing, as
presenting the liveliest of all objects, *viz.* a rational and thinking Being
like ourselves, who communicates to us all the actions of his mind;
makes us privy to his inmost sentiments and affections; and lets us see,
in the very instant of their production, all the emotions, which are
caus'd by any object. Every lively idea is agreeable, but especially that of
a passion, because such an idea becomes a kind of passion, and gives a
more sensible agitation to the mind, than any other image or conception. (P.353)

The analysis of the passions, then, depends upon transcending the self-enclosure of the solitary philosopher by imagining or recreating those instants when emotions are produced and communicated. "Company" ratifies the rationality the *Treatise* renders so tentatively, and communication allows us to see, perhaps for the first time in Hume's imagining of man, a real connection between objects and a particular subject. Ideas, those weak copies of powerful "impressions," become at this moment uniquely moving and convincing imitations of them. The idea of a passion becomes in company itself "a kind of passion." That telling phrase looks back to Hume's nervously technical rendering of the emotions. The enthusiasm of this sequence is implicit even in his most difficult and abstract explications, since his writing seeks to render a version of the invigoration unique to company, endeavors that is to dramatize his own reality as "a rational and thinking Being" and to give the talking philosopher the immediacy and vitality of a human subject enlivened by "foreign objects."

Within the unfolding of the system of the passions in Book II are certain problems, exceptions, and contradictions, which Hume treats as a succession of essay topics and occasions for moral-literary rumination. The passions are not only diagrammed; they are redefined and reviewed as elusively powerful but essentially benign, directed if properly understood to our ease and satisfaction. Hume redramatizes emotional life, turning it away quite self-consciously from the destructive turbulence of the moralizing tradition, as he evokes it. His acceptance of the properly understood passions recognizes their power and grants them some unpredictability. Hume matches analytic objectivity with moral neutrality, supports the rationality and consistency of his system by conceding the necessary inconsistency of the passions. Thus, the regularity Hume is at pains to establish contains instances that violate rational expectation, as here in "Of the love of relations," where it is "remarkable" that "whoever is united to us by any connexion is always sure of a share of our love, proportion'd to the connexion, without enquiring into his other qualities" (p.352). Even friends in whom we cannot "discover any very valuable quality" are preferred "to strangers, of whose superior merit we are fully convinc'd" (p.352). Psychological accuracy is also a persuasive honesty on Hume's part, and the exceptions to system are his refusals to hide irrationality and promises of moral complexity.[69]

A persona emerges in the final part of Book II who takes full advantage of these ingratiating failures of system; the physicist of the passions defers to the dramatist of the emotional life as Hume turns to what he calls the *"direct* passions" such as desire, aversion, grief and joy, hope and fear (p.399). Partly because the relevance of his whole epistemological scheme may be at stake on this point, Hume's defense of a kind of necessity in the operations of these passions against what he calls "this fantastical system of liberty" (p.404) has a distinct polemical edge and a set of elaborate oratorical enforcements.[70] By means of what he labels strict philosophical speaking (which means following his account of the mind's operations), Hume claims merely to observe common life, to rescue normal emotions from the distorting representations of moralists. The will, he says, obeys the principles we see at work in matter; both respond to circumstances, and our knowledge of them is a matter of observing the constancy of that response and inferring a regularity therefrom. "Now I assert, that whoever reasons after this manner [that is, whoever expects the actions of men to follow from "their motives, temper and situation"] does *ipso facto* believe the actions of the will to arise from necessity, and that he knows not what he means when he denies it" (p.405). Necessity of this implicit kind is not, Hume stresses, "a conclusion of the understanding, but is merely a perception of the mind" (p.406). We may not care for the terms ("perhaps we may avoid those expressions"; p.406) but we live in the world they define.

The literalizing of common experience is a familiar Humean tactic, which leads at times to a bemused, anthropological distance whereby Hume treats psychological commonplaces as if they were strange and newly discovered phenomena. "I have frequently observ'd, that those, who boast of the antiquity of their families, are glad when they can join this circumstance, that their ancestors for many generations have been uninterrupted proprietors of the same portion of land, and that their family has never chang'd its possessions, or been transplanted into any other country or province" (pp.307–308). Detachment enforces mechanistic regularity; empirical modesty is a transparent cover for full and thereby slightly contemptuous control. But here Hume's relationship to his material has shifted, and his effort to see common life as proof of his doctrines operates from within that life. He claims now to reside within the experiences he analyzes. His persona has established its integrity and reliability by the inclusiveness of his moral analysis and the sympathetic range of his social observations. Emotional experience, as Hume comes to render it, is increasingly coherent, but unified and paradoxical rather than atomized and mechanical. For example, a few pages earlier in this section Hume offers a social panorama as evidence of the diversity which maintains "such a uniformity in human life." This rendition of a large scene begins with physical minutiae: "The skin, pores, muscles, and nerves of a day-labourer are different from those of a man of quality: So are his sentiments, actions and manners. The different stations of life influence the whole fabric, external and internal; and these different stations arise necessarily, because uniformly, from the necessary and uniform principles of human nature" (p.402). Within the social machine, there is a seamless continuity between what Hume goes on to call "*natural* and *moral* evidence" (p.406), that is, between the world structured by our perceptions and that enforced by our passions. The fateful bodies of the day-laborer and the man of quality evoke for a moment a world of drastically narrowed rationality and an organic, encompassing compulsion from which the philosopher cannot hope to exempt himself.

Perhaps this self-implication is owing partly to the fullness and paradoxical insistence of Hume's rhetoric as he argues for a revised "necessity." This section marks the victory of a new representation of the passions to replace the schematic diagram with which he began. A condemned prisoner is Hume's concluding example of the continuity and unity of experience (the example suggests a metaphor Hume will take pains to correct). This prisoner sees both the solidity of his jail and the "obstinacy" of his jailer; he wisely chooses in all attempts for freedom to work at the stone and iron of his jail rather than "upon the inflexible nature" of his jailer. Conducted to the scaffold, he "foresees his death as certainly from the constancy and fidelity of his guards as from the operation of the ax or wheel" (p.406). The recurrent inevitability of the passions is absolute, iron clad and rock hard, indeed harder.

At the end of Book III, Hume refuses to separate natural abilities from virtues or moral qualities, finding the traditional distinction between dispositions like good sense and virtues like benevolence merely verbal and the province of grammarians. "There is a sentiment of esteem and approbation, which may be excited, in some degree, by any faculty of the mind, in its perfect state and condition; and to account for this sentiment is the business of *Philosophers*" (p.610). Recognition and approval by others constitute the moral world, not the exertions of solitary ethical individuals.

As Hume made even clearer in the *Enquiry concerning Human Understanding*, the philosopher overrides conventional distinctions in order to narrate experienced continuities.[71] Just so, Hume's cancellation of the traditional "combat of passion and of reason" (p.415) takes place in this world of continuities, and his self-consciously witty reversal of the relation between those merely literary abstractions depends upon a denial of the distinction between them. "Reason is, and ought only to be the slave of the passions, and can never pretend to any other office than to serve and obey" (p.415). Even that formulation turns out to be too generous and falsely symmetrical, for the passions in Hume's rendering are part of the indivisible world of experience. Reason, as Hume more and more narrowly defines it, can only observe their operation and attempt to arrange conditions for their beneficial or efficient operation. Passions are in fact opposed by other passions, although some of them like benevolence, resentment, love of life, kindness to children, or aversion to evil are calm or mild enough to appear reasonable to unphilosophic observers. Hume uncovers the virtual autonomy of the passions, and he takes pleasure in imagining their arbitrary irrationality: "'Tis not contrary to reason to prefer the destruction of the whole world to the scratching of my finger. 'Tis not contrary to reason for me to chuse my total ruin, to prevent the least uneasiness of an *Indian* or person wholly unknown to me" (p.416).

The mind Hume evokes in these concluding pages of Book II is an easily disrupted entity rather than the well-oiled machine with which he began. The "calm passions" easily become violent ones "by a change of temper, or of the circumstances and situation of the object, as by the borrowing of force from any attendant passion, by custom, or by exciting the imagination" (p.438). Philosophy, Hume adds, cannot hope to understand the "smaller and more delicate revolutions" of what he admits appears to be a "war." The struggle not only "diversifies human life" and makes men different from one another, but also "from themselves in different times" (p.438). Qualified instantly ("this struggle of passion and reason, as it is call'd"), the temporary lapse into the rejected psychomachia is crucial, I think, for it is one of the markers here at the end of Book II of a reassertive literary control provoked by the failure of Hume's systematic physics of the passions (or the inadequacy of his experimental terminology and its mechanical model of mind). Hume's drift has been toward concrete psychosocial instances which enforce an emerging thematics of diminished rationality and endangered identity. Men are different "from themselves" at various times, partly because of their intense relationship as imagining selves to the circumstances of experience. The force of a passion, Hume observes earlier, "depends as much on the temper of the person, as the nature or situation of the object" (p.427). But both those factors are tremendously variable. As Hume considers them in the "influence of the imagination on the passions" (Section VI) and the role "Of contiguity, and distance in space and time" (Section VII, VIII), his account is complicated to the point of contradiction. Contiguity to self, whether in space or time, would seem to be crucial: "Ourself is intimately present to us, and whatever is related to self must partake of that quality" (p.427). Distance in space and in future and past time seems to weaken passion progressively, but Hume wonders why an exact reversal of that process is also true: "Why a very great distance encreases our esteem and admiration for an object: Why such a distance in time encreases it more than that in space: And a distance in past time more than that in future" (p.432).

The emotional moments in question are essentially cultural: our admiration (in the stronger sense current then, exciting "wonder") for ancient civilizations, our excitement in front of large vistas, "a wide plain, the ocean, eternity, a succession of several ages" (p. 432). High and low, descent and ascent, are merely gravitational accidents, but they are universally charged with human meaning, precisely because of our physical difficulty in ascending and ease in descending. A physical accident is a source of moral and psychological necessity. Language and perception obey that necessity. The effects of distance upon the imagination extend the mechanistic diagram of the mind's movements, but these movements as Hume considers them have an inevitable cultural and ethical force which counters (or at least accompanies and modifies) his scientism.

The mind, elevated by the vastness of its object, is still farther elevated by the difficulty of the conception; and being oblig'd every moment to renew its efforts in the transition from one part of time to another, feels a more vigorous and sublime disposition, than in a transition thro' the parts of space, where the ideas flow along with easiness and facility. In this disposition, the imagination, passing, as is usual, from the consideration of the distance to the view of the distant objects, gives us a proportionable veneration for it; and this is the reason why all the relicts of antiquity are so precious in our eyes, and appear more valuable than what is brought even from the remotest parts of the world. (P.436)

In spite of our hopelessly compromised sense of personal identity, and in the face of his own mechanistic reductions, Hume's language inclines to a secularized physicotheology. In the special cultural moment of historical retrospection that Hume makes a special point of including in his psychology, "elevation" (and the difficult movement it argues for) replaces mere "transition" through time and space. "Imagination" transforms mere separation and vast distance, changing difficulty into value, prizing the mind's own exertions.

Mind for Hume, as J. V. Price puts it, is a process rather than a fixed entity. The various metaphors for mind in the *Treatise* help us distinguish its function from its structure, and the point of Hume's metaphoric variety, according to Price, is that structure cannot be known except by function.[72] In fact, Hume is wary of such metaphors; they are clustered here at the end of Book II and constitute part of his response to certain recalcitrant or even anomalous features of the mind that arise in considering the "direct passions." Chief among these is the uncertainty surrounding hope and fear, as "probability" prevents the understanding from determining the reality of an object of desire or aversion. "So that as the understanding, in all probable questions, is divided betwixt the contrary points of view, the affections must in the same manner be divided betwixt opposite emotions" (p.440). In the complex musical analogy that follows, Price's distinction makes good sense, for the nature or structure of the instruments themselves emerges by comparision with each other within the orchestral ensemble. The passions resemble string instruments, "where after each stroke the vibrations still retain some sound, which gradually and insensibly decays" (pp.440–441). They do not, Hume begins by saying, resemble a wind instrument, "which in running over all notes immediately loses the sound after the breath ceases" (p.440). That agility and celerity belong to the fancy. The passions move slowly and retain resonances, so that as probability points to good or evil, "the passion of joy or sorrow predominates in the composition" (p.441). Emotional confusion is thus like a musical alternation whereby one theme slowly succeeds another, each one coloring the other, one perhaps emerging dominant, or perhaps neither: "it sometimes happens, that both the passions exist successively, and by short intervals; some times, that they destroy each other, and neither of them takes place; and sometimes that both of them remain united in the mind" (p.441). Flexible and physical, this elegant analogy serves as a bridge between the difficult psychological relations and locations Hume seeks to diagram and to spatialize. When the imagination views an object or situation, that is like a particular stroke of the bow or finger plucking the strings of the passions: "Each view of the imagination produces its peculiar passions, which decays away by degrees, and is follow'd by a sensible vibration after the stroke" (p.442).

What is especially striking about this analogy is its extension well past the point of local clarification. Stretching a metaphor past its immediate illustrative purpose in an argument has hitherto in the *Treatise* been reserved for comic characterization: to depict the grandiose and futile ambitions of philosophy or to evoke the playfully self-depreciating persona Hume assumes at times.[73] Neutralizing discourse about mental phenomena, featuring abstract entities like relations, sensations, and impressions, seems to yield without reservation here in a richly metaphoric evocation in which Hume is first a musician, then a chemist, and finally in this sequence a student of optics. Contrary passions may attach themselves to objects intimately connected; then "the passions are like an *alcali* and an *acid*, which, being mingled, destroy each other" (p.443). The experiment can continue: when fear and hope are balanced as the possibility of grief or joy in events is equal:

Throw in a superior degree of probability to the side of grief, you immediately see that passion diffuse itself over the composition, and tincture it into fear. Encrease the probability, and by that means the grief, the fear prevails still more and more, till at last it runs insensibly, as the joy continually diminishes, into pure grief. After you have brought it to this situation, diminish the grief, after the same manner that you encreas'd it; by diminishing the probability on that side, and you'll see the passion clear every moment, 'till it changes insensibly into hope; which again runs, after the same manner, by slow degrees, into joy, as you encrease that part of the composition by the encrease of the probability. Are not these as plain proofs, that the passions of fear and hope are mixtures of grief and joy, as in optics 'tis a proof, that a colour'd ray of the sun passing thro' a prism, is a composition of two others, when, as you diminish or encrease the quantity of either, you find it prevail proportionably more or less in the composition? I am sure neither natural nor moral philosophy admits of stronger proofs. (Pp.443–444)

The control in these stylish conceits (hardly "plain proofs") is actually an admission of defeat, a surrender to the fullness of analogy and the merely literary clarity Hume has pointedly rejected in outlawing the psychomachia of passion and reason and in his continual insistent literalization of mental processes. The experimental virtuosity of the image rules out actual experimentation; the calibrated precision of all these analogical realms corrects the uncertainty that surrounds the passions as Hume finds them, in practice and experience more and more entangled and complicated. The elaborate rhetorical question surrounding optics simply underlines the persuasive function of the analogizing, just as the assertion of unassailable proof in the last two sentences indicates a certain uneasiness with the analogies. In effect, Hume offers his own cleverness and a rhetorical appropriation of scientific terms rather than the "experimental method" promised by his title page. These passages predict Hume's rejection of Book II of the *Treatise* as he recast his thought into the *Enquiries*.

Hume's late-nineteenth-century editor, L. A. Selby-Bigge, was fairly scandalized by Hume's desire for literary fame, his readiness to take "the line of least resistance" in the *Enquiries* and to exchange the difficulty of the *Treatise* for "elegance, lucidity and proportion."[74] Charles Hendel defends Hume, finding him true in the *Enquiries* to his old arguments, accommodating public taste only in the "manner of presentation."[75] My view is that Hume's revision toward elegant simplification is part of the natural drift of his thought as he advances into Book III of the *Treatise*, where abstract difficulties and knotty elaborations necessarily defer to the concreteness of those "moral subjects" announced on the title page of this volume. The first two books not only complicate the understanding and the passions themselves but totally redefine the relationship between reason and emotion by denying their stability as descriptive terms. Moral reality no longer consists, says Hume, of struggle between opposing faculties, since those "faculties" are merely literary inventions, part of the representation of man he discredits. As Richard Kuhns puts it, Hume's skepticism assualts the imperfections of reason "so that we become open to the coordinate view that experience is possible because of our rich endowment of sentiment and feeling."[76] But sentiment and feeling are themselves compromised by Book II, complicated immensely by Hume's wavering dramatization of them as he slides from his own confident rationality about their locations and relationships to an essentially rhetorical presentation of them whereby they are stabilized by clever and extended analogizing.

Hume's discovery in the *Treatise*, to turn again to Robert Paul Wolff's formulation, is that reality as we possess it is not in the contents of the mind but is the result of mental activity. As Wolff notes, that theory has to free itself from associationism and the "copy theory of ideas" in which it is "embedded."[77] Hume thus moves toward an appreciation or ratification of human activity (he calls it "artifice" at one point) in the face of the disorderly "natural" plenitude his thought uncovers. That is to say, as Hume proceeds he recognizes (in part by virtue of his literary control) that something other than the play of associations or the passive copying of an external world is at work in human self-understanding and definition. In its self-conscious rhetorical virtuosity, Hume's writing moves him toward the centrality of human artifice. Implicit in the "elegance, lucidity and proportion" Selby-Bigge complained of in the *Enquiries* is a recognition of the necessity of rhetorical effect for rendering the discovery philosophy makes about itself: knowledge is a reflexive alertness in the face of experience, an awareness by definition of the terms and methods needed to represent experience. Philosophy, as Hume eventually delivers it in the *Enquiries*, attempts to balance our lingering sense of knowledge as discovery of matters of fact with the pressing realization that knowledge is largely the experience of human self-enactment.

But this situation is already apparent in the *Treatise*, especially in Book III where Hume's sentimental ethics involves, as Barry Stroud summarizes it, attributing certain characteristics—virtue or goodness—to certain actions or characters. In fact, says Stroud, for Hume there are no such characteristics in them but our feelings lead us inevitably to these attributions. Moreover, "we express the feeling by way of making an assertion but not an assertion about the contents of our minds. Our moral judgments, like our causal judgments, are 'projections.'"[78] Our assertions in this case are self-conscious pronouncements rather than spontaneous expressions of feeling like a cry or a cheer. For Stroud, Hume thus avoids "the pitfalls of psychologism and emotivism," but that negative movement is also an affirmation of morality as a constructive process rather like writing itself, a decision to participate in a useful, necessary, and often delightful fiction.

The transforming process of attribution and projection in moral judgment matches the local stylistic movements of Hume's writing, which operates a good deal of the time in the *Treatise* by visibly persuasive sequences with clarifying images and subtle tonal modulations, by generalized moral rumination and soliloquizing introspection, and by vivid interrogation of opponents or implicit dialogue or forensic combat with them. These movements do not so much reveal the process of actual thought as project its results by rhetorical means. The subversive effect of philosophical writing lies in its open employment of these rhetorical formulations, which tend to subordinate logic to persuasiveness. Commentators sometimes complain that Hume thus conceals (or never realizes) a thinking entity whose wholeness and self-possession contradict the fragmented and compelling natural process he claims operates in psychology and ethics. My argument is that Hume suspends the question by treating philosophical discourse as a set of rhetorical gestures; he dramatizes thought and restores it to its status as largely another sort of speaking. Language has speakers; reality has perceivers and philosophers claim a privileged and final perception. Hume cancels that finality. He invites readers to watch as he adds the pleasures of rhetorical form and stylistic ease to difficult philosophic notions or, sometimes, as he cancels traditional philosophical controversy by witty redefinition of terms and redramatization of the issues. In the process, he makes his persuasive discourse an activity that not only describes but in a sense parallels human knowing and valuing.

Hume begins Book III with a denial of rational ethics based on the strict recalling of his epistemology, which insists that the only relations we ever manage to perceive are "resemblance, contrariety, degrees in quality, and proportions in quantity and number" (p.464). To those who object that morality involves the discovery of another relation, Hume answers with two closely reasoned challenges. If the moral relation exists, it can only obtain between our internal actions and external objects and never within the actions and objects themselves, for then "we might be guilty of crimes in ourselves, and independent of our situation, with respect to the universe" and "even inanimate beings wou'd be susceptible of moral beauty and deformity" (p.465). Secondly, if there is a moral relation discoverable by reason it must be "eternal and immutable" and must have the same effect on every rational creature, having "no less, or rather a greater, influence in directing the will of the deity, than in governing the rational and virtuous of our own species" (p.465). But there is no necessary connection between knowledge of virtue and the will to perform it. As Hume reminds us, his epistemology proves that such regularity and inevitability are untenable. He concludes his reasoning with a retrospective image of this Humean universe, a simplified rendering earned by the preceding rigor: "All beings in the universe, consider'd in themselves, appear entirely loose and independent of each other. 'Tis only by experience we learn their influence and connexion; and this influence we ought never to extend beyond experience" (p.466).

That formulation edges away from rigor, promotes an easy visualizing

of spatial relationships as a way of understanding the difficult negation of
moral relationships Hume has just explained. This summary also invokes
the cautious Humean observer, who keeps beings apart by a scrupulous
adherence to first principles and who reserves judgment as he defers to experience in a special literal sense. By contrast, "philosophers" want to establish moral relations where they do not exist. Hume confronts them
with an extended analogy between occurrences in the moral and natural
world, which grants, in the name of experience and unprejudiced observation, every sort of connection and relationship except the one that matters.

To put the affair, therefore, to this trial, let us chuse any inanimate object, such as an oak or elm; and let us suppose, that by the dropping of
its seed, it produces a sapling below it, which springing up by degrees,
at last overtops and destroys the parent tree: I ask, if in this instance
there be wanting any relation, which is discoverable in parricide or in-
gratitude? Is not the one tree the cause of the other's existence; and the
latter the cause of the destruction of the former, in the same manner as
when a child murders his parent? 'Tis not sufficient to reply, that a
choice or will is wanting. For in the case of parricide, a will does not
give rise to any *different* relations, but is only the cause from which the
action is deriv'd; and consequently produces the *same* relations, that in
the oak or elm arise from some other principles. 'Tis a will or choice,
that determines a man to kill his parent; and they are the laws of matter
and motion, that determine a sapling to destroy an oak, from which it
sprung. Here then the same relations have different causes; but still the
relations are the same: And as their discovery is not in both cases attended with a notion of immorality, it follows, that that notion does not
arise from such a discovery. (P.467)

The fullness in this observation of natural process is tendentious, since
the purpose of the elaborate parallel between murderous saplings and un-
grateful children is to illustrate utter discontinuity. Hume speaks here
with self-conscious forensic verve, constructing an embarrassing analogy
designed to collapse the more it is elaborated. The succession of acorns
and mighty oaks is a benign inevitability and an image of order; parricide
a rare and monstrous option that strikes at the heart of human order.
Hume's rhetorical questions force his imagined interlocutor to reject the
connection, but the speaker insists on these exact but untenable relations.
Indeed, he continues them with another, briefer example, as he asks
"why incest in the human species is criminal, and why the very same action, and the same relations in animals have not the smallest moral turpi-
tude and deformity?" (p.467). These examples evoke a natural order
whose fullness is a moral emptiness. Hume elaborates this naturalism for

a transparent purpose; he issues a forensic challenge to rational ethics, which is invited to locate moral principles in a sharply rendered, comprehensive natural sphere. As Hume arranges the argument, all reason can do is affirm human difference by pronouncements about vice and virtue.

Take any action allow'd to be vicious: Wilful murder, for instance. Examine it in all lights, and see if you can find that matter of fact, or real existence, which you call *vice*. In which-ever way you take it, you find only certain passions, motives, volitions and thoughts. There is no other matter of fact in the case. The vice entirely escapes you, as long as you consider the object. You never can find it, till you turn your reflexion into your own breast, and find a sentiment of disapprobation, which arises in you, towards this action. Here is a matter of fact; but 'tis the object of feeling, not of reason. It lies in yourself, not in the object. So that when you pronounce any action or character to be vicious, you mean nothing, but that from the constitution of your nature you have a feeling or sentiment of blame from the contemplation of it. (Pp.468–469)

Moral theory, in Hume's context, is only talk, a defensive self-assertion provoked by the naturalistic universe of "certain passions, motives, volitions and thoughts." Hume's argument stages a debate between an exaggerated naturalism that makes room for parricide and incest and an offended rational morality that collapses in mid-speech, able only to deny the specious analogy between man and natural process. These early pages of Book III turn moral philosophy into a rhetorical contest over which Hume merely presides, claiming in effect to judge the insufficiency of rational ethics and the untenability of scientific naturalism. Both become merely rhetorical positions, unaware of their status as pronouncements.

Hume pretends elaborately to look for that quality which makes action moral, and he discovers a tautology: "we have naturally no real or universal motive for observing the laws of equity, but the very equity and merit of that observance" (p.483). Since moral action requires a motive separate from itself, it follows "that the sense of justice and injustice is not deriv'd from nature, but arises artificially, tho' necessarily from education, and human conventions" (p.483). Book III becomes an examination of moral terminology which substitutes an elegant descriptive anthropology of moral behavior for an awkward science of morals. Hume transforms moral categories into moral narratives. He examines the context and causes of moral language and instructs his readers to value morality as a means of human expression and self-definition, a self-justifying activity in part but also implicitly a refusal of a merely naturalistic world that Hume elaborates with distaste and contempt. Nature, he observes at the beginning of

Book III, is of all philosophical terms the most "ambiguous and equivocal," for it includes everything except the miraculous and is thereby a worthless comprehensive notion (p.474). Hume redefines what is traditionally labeled natural for man as mere spontaneous behavior, occurring "without the intervention of thought or reflexion"; but in the same breath he finds that "mankind is an inventive species" drawn by its circumstances toward certain "artificial" but not "arbitrary" arrangements like justice (p.484). These can properly be called "*Laws of Nature*; if by natural we understand what is common to any species, or even if we confine it to mean what is inseparable from the species" (p.484). Nature is thereby most available or most clearly described not by narrow philosophical terms but by flexible, broadly conceived evocations of man that are historical and anthropological in focus.

When he examines the "origin of justice and property" in Part II of Book III, Hume finds that moral philosophers have constructed the "suppos'd *state of nature*" (p.493) by borrowing the experimental technique (if not the candor) of natural philosophers, who operate by treating "any motion as compounded and consisting of two parts separate from each other, tho' at the same time they acknowledge it to be in it self uncompounded and inseparable" (p.493) The state of nature is just such an analytic fiction, created by separating the "affections" from the "understanding" so that "the blind motions of the former, without the direction of the latter, incapacitate men for society" (p.493). "Full of war, violence and injustice," this fiction is the inversion of the poets' golden age of milk and honey, where "Even the distinction of *mine* and *thine* was banish'd from that happy race of mortals, and carry'd with them the very notions of property and obligation, justice and injustice" (p.494). But the poets' "idle fiction" is in fact intensely coherent, drawn from human instinct and desire, whereas the philosophers' construct is an abstract simplification. Poets have realized by their myth that justice depends upon scarcity: "They easily perceiv'd, if every man had a tender regard for another, or if nature supplied abundantly all our wants and desires, that the jealousy of interest, which justice supposes, could no longer have place; nor would there be any occasion for those distinctions and limits of property and possession, which at present are in use among mankind" (p.494). Philosophers have failed to see what poets and even "common experience and observation" teach, that love and abundance obviate society but that animosity and scarcity produce it, nay require it. "Here then is a proposition, which, I think, may be regarded as certain, *that 'tis only from the selfishness and confin'd generosity of men, along with the scanty provision nature has made for his wants, that justice derives its origin."* (p.495).

The "experimental method of reasoning" Hume continued to advertise on the title page of this final volume of the *Treatise* has effectively vanished, replaced in this sequence by the pointed rejection of a pseudo-scientific philosophical fiction. Moreover, the refutation of moral philosophy's misguided attempt to ape the abstractions of natural philosophy is contained within an elaborate rhetorical feint. Hume seems at first to lump mistaken philosophers with deluded poets, but then turns a leisurely paraphrase of their golden age into a proof of common experience. Poetry, he explains, is a model for true philosophy by virtue of its "taste or common instinct, which in most kinds of reasoning goes farther than any of that art and philosophy, with which we have been yet acquainted" (p.494). The verifying modulations of experience Hume proposes now occur within a supervising anthropology for which the poets are excellent guides: "Encrease to a sufficient degree the benevolence of men, or the bounty of nature, and you render justice useless, by supplying its place with much nobler virtues, and more valuable blessings" (pp.494–495).

Like the poets, Hume is an imaginer of the human scene whose quarrel with the abstractions of moral and political philosophy is implicit in the fullness and sharpness of his renditions. Hume reintroduces as generalized literary anthropology the "nature" he has banished as a philosophical term. Other animals have their needs balanced by their abilities; the lion's voracity is matched by his power as a hunter, the docility of the sheep and ox compensated by their moderate and tolerant appetites. Man alone is paradoxically situated, for by himself "he is provided neither with arms, nor force, nor other natural abilities, which are in any degree answerable to so many necessities" (p.485). In fact, Hume argues, man is immediately social, virtually unimaginable as the creature he is without some form of society: " 'tis utterly impossible for men to remain any considerable time in that savage condition, which precedes society; but that his very first state and situation may justly be esteem'd social" (p.493). "Of the origin of justice and property" is a series of such tableaux, seeking to persuade by a symmetry that matches the easeful symmetry of self-expression in human institutions like society.

For example, Hume observes that the "love of gain" can only be channeled and not restrained by other passions.

There is no passion, therefore, capable of controlling the interested affection, but the very affection itself, by an alteration of its direction.

Now this alteration must necessarily take place upon the least reflection; since 'tis evident, that the passion is much better satisfy'd by its restraint, than by its liberty, and that by preserving society, we make much greater advances in the acquiring possessions, than by running into the solitary and forlorn condition, which must follow upon violence and an universal licence. The question, therefore, concerning the wickedness or goodness of human nature, enters not in the least into that other question concerning the origin of society; nor is there any thing to be consider'd but the degrees of men's sagacity or folly. For whether the passion of self-interest be esteem'd vicious or virtuous, 'tis all a case; since itself alone restrains it: So that if it be virtuous, men become social by their virtue; if vicious, their vice has the same effect. (P.492)

The mythic-historic moment dissolves as Hume considers it, turning in the description to a psychological instant rather than a true sequence. And he quickly adds "that nothing can be more simple and obvious than this rule," established by every parent to preserve peace among his children (p.493). Society is the expression of the passion for acquisition; human nature is defined by that passion, as every individual instinctively serves his own ease. No matter what moral terms we choose to designate those instincts, society is the invariable result of human inevitability. Hume at moments like this does not propose to explain human nature or to judge it; he rejects the partial fictions of moral and political philosophy by delighting in what he presents as the self-evident and self-contained wholeness of human nature. The concluding aphorism turns moral distinctions into a rhetorical surface, counters that can be moved around to create symmetry and to disparage ironically the urge for explanation. Society is a fact deriving from the expression natural to the human organism; vice and virtue are merely names for the expression.

Distinctly Humean, this passage defers to fact and action, staging their inaccessibility to reason. As he puts it in the opening pages of Book III, our passions, volitions, and actions are "original facts and realities, compleat in themselves, and implying no reference to other passions, volitions, and actions. 'Tis impossible, therefore, they can be pronounced either true or false, and be either contrary or conformable to reason" (p.458). Philosophy, as Hume comes to practice it, is thereby a deference to "original facts and realities," a rehearsal of anthropology and psychology that seems to lead to explanation and then deliberately stops short of it, turning into compressed summarizing of circumstances, consoling us with aphorism and its tonality of control and satisfaction.

Confronting over and over again the inaccessibility for reason of "original facts and realities," Book III converts the elaborate rhetorical postures of the *Treatise* into a major philosophical point, turning a set of destructive tactics into a positive position. Given the shift in Hume's emphasis from reality as the content of the mind to reality as the activity of minds, the disingenuous persona of the first two books, with his transparent modesty and massively delayed and deflated revelations, now fairly represents a position and a program for knowing. Specific narrative is substituted for general explanation, artifice and contrivance are found in the place of truth and nature, and Hume makes knowing itself into a convention and true knowing an awareness of the genre of knowledge. Here, for example, is his answer to those who argue that our approbation of moral qualities is a constant that precedes the variations of experience. Whether he finds them close to home or in China, moral qualities "appear equally virtuous, and recommend themselves equally to the esteem of a judicious spectator" (p.581). The sympathy varies but the esteem is a constant, affirmed by moral reason. Against this view, Hume argues that our esteem is the result of "certain sentiments of pleasure or disgust, which arise upon the contemplation and view of particular qualities or characters" (p.581). Those sentiments vary according to our situation. What holds them together is an agreement to ignore the variations. As Hume sketches the scene near the end of Book III, morals like aesthetic perception involve the representation of a stabilizing fiction:

Our situation, with regard both to persons and things, is in continual fluctuation; and a man, that lies at a distance from us, may, in a little time, become a familiar acquaintance. Besides, every particular man has a peculiar position with regard to others; and 'tis impossible we cou'd ever converse together on any reasonable terms, were each of us to consider characters and persons, only as they appear from his peculiar point of view. In order, therefore, to prevent those continual *contradictions*, and arrive at a more *stable* judgment of things, we fix on some *steady* and *general* points of view; and always, in our thoughts, place ourselves in them, whatever may be our present situation. In like manner, external beauty is determin'd merely by pleasure; and 'tis evident, a beautiful countenance cannot give so much pleasure, when seen at a distance of twenty paces, as when it is brought nearer us. We say not, however, that it appears to us less beautiful: Because we know what effect it will have in such a position, and by that reflexion we correct its momentary appearance. (Pp.581–582)

The shifting, partial perspectives of human knowing provoke Lockean regret and Berkeleian moral intensity but lead Hume to appreciation of human cleverness as it arranges perception to suit convenience and maintain beauty. In place of earlier polemics and forensic intensity, Hume as he nears the end of the *Treatise* offers calm, dispassionate renderings of the psychological process behind moral notions, excluding intellectual melodrama by treating this convention for knowledge as if it were a sensible and self-conscious arrangement rather than an instinctive reflex for coherence.

Moral process is part of a larger epistemological process, and both moral and sense knowledge involve the correction of "the momentary appearance of things" and the overlooking of "our present situation" (p.582). Our general moral notions require us to forget that situation, but Hume's anthropological view makes such forgetfulness, in practice, impossible: " 'Tis seldom men heartily love what lies at a distance from them, and what no way redounds to their particular benefit; as 'tis no less rare to meet with persons, who can pardon another any opposition he makes to their interest, however justifiable that opposition may be by the general rules of morality" (p.583). We seem, however, to manage to think rationally about moral action: "We blame equally a bad action, which we read of in history, with one perform'd in our neighbourhood t'other day" (p.584). Such thought is the result of our "reflexion" as we imagine the distant action closer to us: "the former action wou'd excite as strong sentiments of disapprobation as the latter, were it plac'd in the same position" (p.584). "Reflexion" is not reasoning, then, but rather a certain representation of the world whereby we imagine ourselves in other situations or locations and let this version of the actual move us to a conviction that is real if "inferior to belief," as Hume puts it. (p.585).

In fact, every sort of thinking Hume describes in the *Treatise* requires a similar exercise of and qualified surrender to imagination and its reconstructive representations of the world. Truth as it is available always involves a self-persuasive mechanism, and Hume's examination of moral process defines moral truth as nothing less than the mechanism itself. He seeks to assure readers this is a normal, untroubling state of affairs, instinctive and automatic yet easily comprehended and controlled by analogy with other human arrangements. The opposition between a compelling naturalism and a controlling (or at least a compensating) intelligence is, quite simply, the paradoxical, unresolved center of Hume's thought and the problem his subsequent writing wrestles with. We convince ourselves about moral regularity, just as we adjust our perceptions in order to have identity, causality, and other features of a world we need in order to live properly and comfortably. Inescapably, these adjustments are instinctive; philosophical reflection cannot make process itself self-conscious or totally available to reasoning. What philosophical writing can do is formulate the process and oppose it to the compensatory fictions of rationality, giving us a literary relationship to our own in-evitabilities and providing a textual *tertium quid* where intelligence and control can actually operate. By the time he concludes the *Treatise*, Hume's literary problem is to perfect a mediating manner that acknow-ledges the revisions of actuality deeply implicit in all experience without surrendering all our claims to self-determination.

In the *Dialogues Concerning Natural Religion*, Demea is scandalized when Philo suggests that matter may acquire motion without a first mover. Philo's response begins with a maxim, balancing the constructions implicit in "experience" and the intractability of the material presented to that same experience: "Every event, before experience, is equally difficult and incomprehensible; and every event, after experience, is equally easy and intelligible." Both a witty verbal balance and a shrewd observation with moral and psychological applications, Philo's sentence is the prelude to a skeptical "cosmogony." [79] But considered as a rhetorical opening for an argument, it places Philo somewhere outside of its an-tithesis, makes him a managing literary presence rehearsing possibilities and postponing commitment. By their insistent shapeliness, the *En-quiries* make stylish formulation a way out of mere naturalism or untenable rationalism. Whatever their shortcomings as philosophical ex-position, the *Enquiries* represent a literary attempt to stabilize a philosophical problem.

Hume described the *Enquiries* as an abridgement. "By shortening & simplifying the Questions," he wrote to Gilbert Eliot in 1751, "I really render them much more complete. *Addo dum minuo*." [80] Their radical compression is partly popularization of the *Treatise*'s complication of epistemological process, partly a removal of unresolved issues like per-sonal identity and abstruse ones like the nature of space and time, the idea of substance, and the immateriality of the soul, and partly a modula-tion of tone as brashness and paradoxical bravado are exchanged for a uniformly polite, silken, insinuating manner. This manner is well described by Hume's evocation in the *Enquiry concerning the Principles of Morals* of the behavior proper to "facilitate the intercourse of minds": "A mutual deference is affected; contempt of others disguised; authority concealed; attention given to each in his turn; and an easy stream of con-versation maintained, without vehemence, without interruption, without eagerness for victory, and without any airs of superiority" (p.261). [81]

Hume's abridgement is actually an addition of these tonalities of power and control. His brevity and suavity call attention to themselves as artful avoidance of prolixity, futile complications, and endless polemics. [82] His elegantly compressed simplicity signals partial retreat from philosophical argument. Hume is now essentially a mimic of various positions, an ironic ventriloquist who paraphrases with controlled incredulity, affected deference, thinly disguised contempt, and above all thereby with power-fully implicit authority the various traditional claims or ambitions of philosophy. In the *Treatise*, he offers a rich, sometimes confusing mixture of the essayistic and analytic styles. In the *Enquiries*, he presents an almost purely essayistic version of the analytic; he subordinates philosophy as a project for finding truth to philosophy as a persuasive manner of talking about the issue of truth. From the assertive, overtly commanding, and superior position with which he began the *Treatise*, Hume arrives in the *Enquiries* at a disinterested, "enquiring" approach which never quite leaves the self-interrogating mode, never ceases to con-sider philosophical speculation as severely limited and potentially deluding, and never forgets the justifying and guiding purpose of thought in moral-social utility. And, most important, the *Enquiries* con-sistently return to a rhetorical self-consciousness by which Hume freely surrenders the finality of thought and displays his reliance upon analogy and other illustrative, persuasive turns.

In part, this stylistic shift is a thematic reorientation of Hume's thought, a clearer emphasis upon the moral and social relevance of philosophy. With its chapters on miracles and providence and a future state, *An Enquiry concerning Human Understanding* looks closely at metaphysics and religion as disturbers of the peace, both personal and public. Where the *Treatise* pits Humean revisionism against the entire philosophical tradition, often rendered as an absurd monolith, this *En-quiry* begins with an essay distinguishing "the different species of philos-ophy," actually only two, one "easy and obvious," the other "accurate and abstruse" (p.6). At first, the choice itself seems obvious, between elegant moralists like Cicero and Addison and difficult thinkers like Aristotle and Locke. Cicero's fame "flourishes at present" while Aristotle's "is utterly decayed," and "when Locke shall be entirely forgotten," Addison will perhaps "be read with pleasure" (p.8). Hume seems to endorse useful moralizing, but his supervising, almost officiously objective manner sug-gests he is paraphrasing standard arguments for social usefulness and in-tellectual moderation. Nature, fully personified, is the last and most overtly rhetorical of these defenders as she warns against philosophical ex-cess: "Indulge your passion for science, says she, but let your science be human, and such as may have a direct reference to action and society." This would seem to be Hume's own position, and Nature's concluding maxim, "Be a philosopher; but, amidst all your philosophy, be still a man" (p.9), is often taken as his last word on the subject.[83]

But such a maxim rests on the very opposition between philosophy and common life that Hume's thought denies. Nature's advice can sustain both the smug professionalism and the shallow anti-intellectualism Hume derides. In fact, Nature's edict is followed by a severe historical qualification of her limited wisdom. The "generality of mankind" tend to reject "all profound reasonings" out of hand and turn the moderation Nature advises into facile anti-intellectualism. The rest of Section I is a consideration of the uses of the "accurate and abstruse philosophy," but it is an even-handed defense, which finds the ultimate value of such thought precisely within the moral world the "easy philosophy" claims the exclusive right to serve.

Metaphysics, as Hume calls this activity, is a human inevitability, and the search for ultimate understanding is founded in and perpetuated by vanity and ambition, rendered by broadly ironic strokes: "Each adventurous genius will still leap at the arduous prize, and find himself stimulated, rather than discouraged, by the failure of his predecessors; while he hopes that the glory of achieving so hard an adventure is reserved for him alone" (p.12). Hume defines the function of a reformed philosophy as the final reversal of this recurring historical comedy. The *Enquiry* is to be a passage through human understanding which will disabuse it of illusions about itself. Hume's summary reveals the priority of a moral-literary balance, elaborates a nearly allegorical plot in which various philosophical positions and psychological tendencies struggle for dominance.

The only method of freeing learning, at once, from these abstruse questions, is to enquire seriously into the nature of human understanding, and show, from an exact analysis of its powers and capacity, that it is by no means fitted for such remote and abstruse subjects. We must submit to this fatigue, in order to live at ease ever after: And must cultivate true metaphysics with some care, in order to destroy the false and adulterate. Indolence, which, to some persons, affords a safeguard against this deceitful philosophy, is, with others, overbalanced by curiosity; and despair, which, at some moments, prevails, may give place afterwards to sanguine hopes and expectations. Accurate and just reasoning is the only catholic remedy, fitted for all persons and all dispositions; and is alone able to subvert that abstruse philosophy and metaphysical jargon, which, being mixed up with popular superstition, renders it in a manner impenetrable to careless reasoners, and gives it the air of science and wisdom. (Pp.12–13)

Intellectual narrative leads to resolving actions (first ironically conceived as fatigued submission, then rising to heroic husbandry) which redefine philosophy as psychological necessity and social responsibility. Philosophy is not a progress through error to truth but a subversion of error and an establishment of a civilized, knowing balance in place of extremes of indolence and extravagant, doomed curiosity. The reasoning Hume promises will appeal to "all persons and all dispositions," thereby negating the initial division of the thoughtful part of mankind into partisans of either the easy or the abstruse philosophy. Moreover, that division of philosophy misrepresents the actual state of affairs in which a union of false abstruseness and popular superstition undermines the authority of all thought.

As Hume admits, this is a negative recommendation, and he suggests the possibility of positive discoveries "at least in some degree" of the "secret springs and principles, by which the human mind is actuated in its operations" (p.14). We cannot simply rule out ultimate knowledge, nor can we reject abstract philosophy as false because it is difficult. In any event, such attempts are made "every day," even "by those who philosophize most negligently" (p.15). It is therefore imperative, as he remarks at the end of this introduction (p.16), to reconcile "profound enquiry with clearness, and truth with novelty!" With suspicious modesty, Hume defines his function as mere adjudication between the differing satisfactions of philosophical investigation. As it appears in due course, however, clearness negates profound enquiry and novelty is canceled by truth, so Hume leaves us with his adjudication itself as the only untouched satisfaction.

Consider, as a representative example, the "sceptical solution" of the "sceptical doubts" Hume raises "concerning the Operations of the Understanding" in *An Enquiry concerning Human Understanding*. Part I of this solution is a drastic simplification of the tangled problem of belief, labeled and affirmed as such: "What, then, is the conclusion of the whole matter? A simple one; though, it must be confessed, pretty remote from the common theories of philosophy. All belief of matter of fact or real existence is derived merely from some object, present to the memory or senses, and a customary conjunction between that and some other object" (p.46). Philosophy should, perhaps, attempt nothing further, especially since the mental operations that produce belief "are a species of natural instincts, which no reasoning or process of the thought and understanding is able either to produce or to prevent" (pp.46–47). Hume apologizes elaborately for his "curiosity" in going on anyway to consider the nature of belief and the *"customary conjunction*, whence it is derived" (p.47). He even suggests that "readers of a different taste" may well pass over the rest of this section.

What Hume promises is moderate enough: "some explications and analogies that will give satisfaction; at least to such as love the abstract sciences, and can be entertained with speculations, which, however accurate, may still retain a degree of doubt and uncertainty" (p.47). What the *Treatise* resorts to in tight corners, the *Enquiry* offers freely: philosophy confesses its limits, promises pleasure to those who undertake it as a liberating game.[84] And the discussion of belief that follows is far less knotty and technical than the corresponding pages in the *Treatise*. Hume proceeds with all imaginable caution, recapitulating the limits of our perceptual universe, omitting his youthful arrogance and love of complication, highlighting analogies and concrete instances of a domestic sort (billiard balls, absent friends), and returning in the middle of this modified rigor to the verbal limits of his discourse.[85] Belief is undefinable but a *"description"* can be attempted in hopes of arriving "at some analogies, which may afford a more perfect explication of it" (p.49).

Hume began this section by celebrating the power of imagination, which is able to mix, compound, separate, and divide its "original stock of ideas" and "feign a train of events, with all the appearance of reality" (p.47). The undefinable recalcitrance of belief is balanced against another rendition of the power of the imagination, evoked with admiring fullness and making the *"description"* of belief itself a cryptic failure.

The imagination has the command over all its ideas, and can join and mix and vary them, in all the ways possible. It may conceive fictitious objects with all the circumstances of place and time. It may set them, in a manner, before our eyes, in their true colours, just as they might have existed. But as it is impossible that this faculty of imagination can ever, of itself, reach belief, it is evident that belief consists not in the peculiar nature or order of ideas, but in the *manner* of their conception, and in their *feeling* to the mind. I confess, that it is impossible perfectly to explain this feeling or manner of conception. We may make use of words which express something near it. But its true and proper name, as we observed before, is *belief*; which is a term that every one sufficiently understands in common life. And in philosophy, we can go no farther than assert, that *belief* is something felt by the mind, which distinguishes the ideas of the judgement from the fictions of the imagination. (P.49)

Hume describes a series of situations in which belief operates because resemblance, contiguity, and causation assist the imagination. He calls these "experiments," but they are compressed scenes from common life, resembling those in the corresponding discussion in the *Treatise* but more economical and focused. Strictly speaking, though, the experiments seem to prove nothing, since we need a prior belief in the reality of the object these relations make vivid to us. "The influence of the picture supposes, that we *believe* our friend to have once existed. Contiguity to home can never excite our ideas of home, unless we *believe* that it really exists" (pp.53–54). Custom and experience, in Hume's concluding set of scenes, are more important than the relations that bring objects to mind vividly.

What Hume labels a passage of difficult reasoning turns into another endorsement of the finality of common experience, underlining the irrelevance of rationality, not quite canceling the validity of the preceding "experiments" but making them merely part of the process whereby thought runs into its own boundaries. Belief is "only a present object and a customary transition to the idea of another object, which we have been accustomed to conjoin with the former" (p.54). This is a stark summary of "the whole operation of the mind, in all our conclusions concerning matter of fact and existence," but Hume declares it "a satisfaction to find some analogies, by which it may be explained" (p.54). We are part of nature, he says, and custom is our means of serving the ends of our species. A narrow literalizing of experience is made an affirmation of natural process.

As nature has taught us the use of our limbs, without giving us the knowledge of the muscles and nerves, by which they are actuated; so has she implanted in us an instinct, which carries forward the thought in a correspondent course to that which she has established among external objects; though we are ignorant of those powers and forces, on which this regular course and succession of objects totally depends. (P.55)

The philosophic curiosity Hume claims to serve in this section ends by merely ratifying nature and deferring to experience as an imponderable, impenetrable category. One would think such gestures superfluous, but the literary pleasures of the *Enquiries* lie precisely in the controlled irony of these delayed affirmations. Hume makes the now comically obvious failure of philosophical speculation the source of a wonder hitherto reserved for its ambitions: "Those, who delight in the discovery and contemplation of *final causes* have here ample subject to employ their wonder and admiration" (p.55). The calculated dismantling of a system for explaining, in this case, belief leads to essayistic closure and psychological symmetry. Hume and his willing reader occupy the privileged contemplative position of the abstract reasoner without violating the facts of experience, and by their passage through negative sequences like this avoid the merely affirmative superficiality of the "easy philosophy."

The delayed discovery operating in separate sections of this *Enquiry* is the organizing principle of the entire *Enquiry concerning the Principles of Morals*. As he comes to its conclusion, Hume wonders why he has tried to prove the obvious: "It may justly appear surprising that any man in so late an age, should find it requisite to prove, by elaborate reasoning, that Personal Merit consists altogether in the possession of mental qualities, *useful* or *agreeable* to the *person himself* or to *others*" (p.268). Earlier, Hume has found it difficult to separate speculation about the origin of morals from testimony to their reality. He has to stop himself, he tells us, from recommending generosity and benevolence: "These, indeed, sufficiently engage every heart, on the first apprehension of them; and it is difficult to abstain from some sally of panegyric, as often as they occur in discourse or reasoning" (p.177). Reasoning about morals is very much after the fact, merely a descriptive recognition of their powerful inevitability. It is only "in the schools" that men are at a loss about the foundation of morals in pleasure and utility; "systems and hypotheses have perverted our natural understanding, when a theory, so simple and obvious, could so long have escaped the most elaborate examination" (pp.268–269).

Hume then moves from a portrait of Cleanthes, whose praise by ordinary men encompasses the ethical categories of qualities useful and agreeable to himself and others, to an evocation of a "gloomy, hairbrained enthusiast," whose "monkish virtues" of celibacy, fasting, penance, mortification, self-denial, humility, silence, and solitude are transferred in the telling to "the catalogue of vices" (p.270). As Hume summarizes the case for the identity of morality with the useful and agreeable, he appeals to the rhetorical effect of just such a telling. To describe social virtues is to produce certain pleasurable effects in auditors. And that rhetorical proof is underlined by a rhetorical experiment he performs on himself. He concedes for a moment that he may be wrong and agrees to "swallow this absurdity" that "an object is approved of on account of its tendency to a certain end, while the end itself is totally indifferent" (p.277).

The preceding delineation or definition of Personal Merit must still retain its evidence and authority: it must still be allowed that every quality of the mind, which is *useful* or *agreeable* to the *person himself* or to *others*, communicates a pleasure to the spectator, engages his esteem, and is admitted under the honourable denomination of virtue or merit. Are not justice, fidelity, honour, veracity, allegiance, chastity, esteemed solely on account of their tendency to promote the good of society? Is not that tendency inseparable from humanity, benevolence, lenity,

generosity, gratitude, moderation, tenderness, friendship, and all the
other social virtues? Can it possibly be doubted that industry, discretion,
frugality, secrecy, order, perseverance, forethought, judgement, and this
whole class of virtues and accomplishments, of which many pages would
not contain the catalogue; can it be doubted, I say, that the tendency of
these qualities to promote the interest and happiness of their possessor,
is the sole foundation of their merit? Who can dispute that a mind,
which supports a perpetual serenity and cheerfulness, a noble dignity
and undaunted spirit, a tender affection and good-will to all around; as
it has more enjoyment within itself, is also a more animating and rejoicing spectacle, than if dejected with melancholy, tormented with anxiety,
irritated with rage, or sunk into the most abject baseness and degener-
acy? (P.277)

In spite of his aversion to dogma and his conviction that "where men are
the most sure and arrogant, they are commonly the most mistaken, and
have there given reins to passion, without that proper deliberation and
suspense, which can alone secure them from the grossest absurdities"
(p.278), Hume declares himself moved by his own eloquence, more assured "at present" by his own rhetoric than by anything he can "learn
from reasoning and argument" (p.278). Hume's delight in the force and
fullness of his moral rhetoric is an appreciation of its capacity to overrule
his own most cherished and indeed axiomatic skeptical caution.

But reflection intervenes even here. Hume wonders whether such conviction can be accepted as final. Natural philosophy has mapped the
world, "subjected to their proper laws" the heavenly bodies, and "Infinite
itself reduced to calculation," but "men still dispute concerning the foundation of their moral duties" (p.278). Rather than propose that mankind
has overlooked so obvious a notion, Hume falls back for the moment into
"diffidence and scepticism" (p.278). This move should arouse a reader's
suspicion, since Hume has not hesitated before to reveal learning's enormous blindness in the face of the obvious and the immediate. There is,
however, another part of his conclusion, and it renews Hume's conviction
by turning away from just that world of endless disputation and returning
him to a world of persuasive immediacy. Men do in fact identify personal
pleasure and utility with social advantage, and Hume's true conclusion is
a series of illustrations of the persuasiveness of enlightened self-interest.
Skepticism and diffidence yield to observations of our collective natural
preference for pleasure and advantage, tendencies that are a compelling
fact of nature rather than an abstract truth. "Truths which are *pernicious*
to society, if any such there be, will yield to errors which are salutary and
advantageous" (p.279). The argument is founded on the psychological

inevitability revealed by rhetorical elaboration: personal pleasure and utility must be good because we are always persuaded to accept them as good. Philosophical truths are exchanged for salutary errors, which are transformed into moral facts by a rhetorical appeal like the following one:

> But what philosophical truths can be more advantageous to society, than those here delivered, which represent virtue in all her genuine and most engaging charms, and make us approach her with ease, familiarity, and affection? The dismal dress falls off, with which many divines, and some philosophers, have covered her; and nothing appears but gentleness, humanity, beneficence, affability; nay, even at proper intervals, play, frolic, and gaiety. She talks not of useless austerities and rigours, suffering and self-denial. She declares that her sole purpose is to make her votaries and all mankind, during every instant of their existence, if possible, cheerful and happy; nor does she ever willingly part with any pleasure but in hopes of ample compensation in some other period of their lives. The sole trouble which she demands, is that of just calculation, and a steady preference of the greater happiness. And if any austere pretenders approach her, enemies to joy and pleasure, she either rejects them as hypocrites and deceivers; or, if she admits them in her train, they are ranked, however, among the least favoured of her votaries.
>
> And, indeed, to drop all figurative expression, what hopes can we ever have of engaging mankind to a practice which we confess full of austerity and rigour? Or what theory of morals can ever serve any useful purpose, unless it can show, by a particular detail, that all duties which it recommends, are also the true interest of each individual. The peculiar advantage of the foregoing system seems to be, that it furnishes proper mediums for that purpose. (Pp.279–280)

Hume's allegory of virtue is a pleasing representation, whose charm and desirability we all acknowledge. Moral authenticity lies in the reader's acquiescence, as Hume assumes it, in the rhetorical force of this embodiment of our pleasure and advantage, Nature as much as she is Virtue, irresistible and thereby beyond dispute. Hume replaces disputation with literary pleasure. True to his promise, he reserves actual argument about the "principles" of morality (the issue with which he began the *Enquiry*)[86] for the four appendices to the book. The *Enquiry* is what he promised: "moral discourses" which observe the ways moral language affects us and describe the circumstances in which we are moved to blame or esteem. Book III of the *Treatise* begins by establishing the principle that moral distinctions are not produced by reason but found by it. The *Enquiry*'s suppression or delay of that argument is a grand rhetorical gesture, epitomized in this amiable personification at the conclusion whereby reason finds virtue irresistible and discovers moral distinctions in its own assent to persuasive imagining.

In a letter to Andrew Millar in 1757, Hume expressed surprise at the anger his opinions provoked, since he thought he had managed a diffidence whereby his opinions were not defended "positively." "I only propose my Doubts, where I am so unhappy as not to receive the same Conviction with the rest of Mankind."[87] Such a disingenuous protest comes rather short of what Hume manages in the *Enquiries*, where skepticism is buried by an unfolding of persuasive presentation. In part, Hume twists and turns issues to exhibit his rhetorical control, his ability to extract graceful moral essays out of the awkward oppositions and problems that define traditional philosophical disputation. He makes good on his promise in "Of Essay Writing" to act as an ambassador "from the dominions of learning to those of conversation." More specifically, both *Enquiries* establish what he calls in this essay a "balance of trade" between those dominions whereby the "materials" of their commerce "must chiefly be furnished by conversation and common life: the manufacturing of them alone belongs to learning." Learning reexamines experience but descends into "the conversable world" for the "company and conversation" that render such reexamination "a proper exercise for the mind."[88] Both *Enquiries* present a continuous transaction between learning and the conversable world, but learning in the process is turned into a distinctly social exercise, a conversation even when it is a monologue of the mind. The moral world, like the scene of sense perception, proves its reality by convincing us, by establishing an indefinable force and vividness beyond argument, or rather by imagining the materials for argument. The center of Hume's thought is a moment when we convince ourselves about the world, and the *Enquiries* give primacy to that moment by deliberately and clearly putting persuasive writing before demonstrative reasoning.

Notes

INTRODUCTION

1. *Anatomy of Criticism* (Princeton: Princeton University Press, 1957), p. 350.
2. *After the New Criticism* (Chicago: University of Chicago Press, 1980), p. 25.
3. *Allegories of Reading* (New Haven and London: Yale University Press, 1979), p. 10.

1. RHETORIC, STYLE, AND PHILOSOPHICAL WRITING

1. John Locke, *An Essay Concerning Human Understanding,* ed. Peter H. Nidditch (Oxford: Clarendon Press, 1975), III. x. 34. All further references in the text are to this edition.
2. *The Works of Aristotle,* ed. W. D. Ross (Oxford: Clarendon Press, 1924), vol. XI, *Rhetorica,* trans. W. Rhys Roberts, I.2.1356b.
3. I.2.1357a.
4. I.2.1356a.
5. *The Motives of Eloquence: Literary Rhetoric in the Renaissance* (New Haven and London: Yale University Press, 1976), p. 43.
6. *Homo Ludens: A Study of the Play Element in Culture* (1938; Boston: Beacon Press, 1955), p. 115.
7. Julián Marías, *Philosophy as Dramatic Theory,* trans. James Parsons (University Park and London: Pennsylvania State University Press, 1971), p. 9.
8. *The Presence of the Word* (New Haven: Yale University Press, 1967), p. 221.
9. "Philosophy as a Kind of Writing: An Essay on Derrida," *New Literary History,* 10 (Autumn 1978), 156.
10. *Interpreting Modern Philosophy* (Princeton: Princeton University Press, 1972), p. 17.
11. A professional philosopher summarizes the situation very well when he remarks that Hume's works "seem often to be read as if they had been written for

submission to the journal *Analysis*. But to understand Hume it is necessary always to remember that he thought of himself as contributing in these works to a would-be Newtonian science of man; or failing that, to some sort of mental geography." Antony Flew, "On the Interpretation of Hume," in *Hume: A Collection of Critical Essays,* ed. V. C. Chappell (Notre Dame, Ind.: University of Notre Dame Press, 1968), p. 284.

12. *The Philosophy of Composition* (Chicago: University of Chicago Press, 1977), p. 31.

13. *Wittgenstein's Vienna* (New York: Simon and Schuster, 1973).

14. *Philosophy as Social Expression* (Chicago: University of Chicago Press, 1974), pp. 210, 154.

15. *Structures of Experience: Essays on the Affinity between Philosophy and Literature* (New York: Harper and Row, 1974), pp. 242, 240.

16. *Allegories of Reading* (New Haven and London: Yale University Press, 1979), p. 131.

17. "Criteria for Style Analysis," *Word*, 15 (1959), 155.

18. *The Aims of Interpretation* (Chicago: University of Chicago Press, 1976), pp. 67, 56, 57.

19. *Self-Consuming Artifacts: The Experience of Seventeenth-Century Literature* (1972; Berkeley: University of California Press, 1974), p. 424.

20. *Beginnings: Intention and Method* (New York: Basic Books, 1975), p. 257.

21. "The Text, the World, the Critic," in *Textual Strategies: Perspectives in Post-Structuralist Criticism*, ed. Josué V. Harari (Ithaca: Cornell University Press, 1979), p. 163.

22. Ibid.

23. *The Motives of Eloquence*, pp. 4, 6–8.

24. *Signs*, trans. Richard C. McCleary (Chicago: Northwestern University Press, 1964), p. 104.

25. For a full discussion of this question, see Robert Adolph, *The Rise of Modern Prose Style* (Cambridge, Mass.: M.I.T. Press, 1968), esp. pp. 1–25.

26. *Style: An Anti-Textbook* (New Haven: Yale University Press, 1974), p. 45. In his *Eighteenth-Century British Logic and Rhetoric* (Princeton: Princeton University Press, 1971), W. S. Howell speaks of a new rhetoric that corresponds to the new inductive logic and that grew in importance as the old method of topics and commonplaces was challenged in the textbooks published from 1662 to 1750. He points out that such revision was largely owing to the influence of Ramus, who proposed that rhetoric be restricted to style and delivery and separated from logic (pp. 79–80). Philosophical writing was faced with a special dilemma, according to Howell: it had to purge itself of the rhetorical fullness of traditional discourse wherein rhetoric and logic both treated the arts of invention and arrangement. It also had to develop another kind of rhetoric suited to the plainer tastes of the age and to the simpler preferences of its own thought, which thereby has a nicely problematic relationship to language. E. D. Hirsch says flatly that the history of English prose itself is the discovery of a readable prose that can be easily understood by a large audience. He finds between the sixteenth and the eighteenth centuries a search for a style lying somewhere between oratory and conversation. *The Philosophy of Composition*, pp. 58–59.

27. *Philosophy as Social Expression*, p. 242.

28. *On Philosophical Style* (Bloomington: Indiana University Press, 1954), p. 1.

29. "David Hume: Reasoning and Experience," in *The English Mind*, ed. Hugh Sykes Davies and George Watson (Cambridge: University Press, 1964), p. 134.

30. "On the Edge," a review of *Nietzsche: A Critical Life*, by Ronald Hayman, *The New York Review of Books*, 9 Oct. 1980, p. 26.

31. Arthur A. Luce, *The Life of George Berkeley* (London and Edinburgh: Thomas Nelson and Sons, 1949), p. 105.

32. *Philosophical Commentaries*, 405, in *The Works of George Berkeley, Bishop of Cloyne*, ed. A. A. Luce and T. E. Jessop (London: Thomas Nelson and Sons, 1949), I, 51. All further references in the text to Berkeley's works are to this edition.

33. *Enquiries concerning Human Understanding and concerning the Principles of Morals*, ed. L. A. Selby-Bigge, 3rd ed. rev. by P. H. Nidditch (Oxford: Clarendon Press, 1975), p. 79. All further reference in the text to Hume's *Enquiries* are to this edition.

34. *Of Grammatology*, trans. G. C. Spivak (1974; Baltimore: Johns Hopkins University Press, 1976), pp. 162, 160.

35. "White Mythology: Metaphor in the Text of Philosophy," *New Literary History*, 6 (Autumn 1974), 48.

36. *Gulliver's Travels*, ed. Herbert Davis (Oxford: Basil Blackwell, 1941), p. 169.

37. *The Dialogues of Plato*, trans. Benjamin Jowett, 2 vol. (New York: Random House, 1973), II, 176.

38. *A Tale of a Tub*, ed. D. Nichol Smith and A. C. Guthkelch, 2nd ed. (Oxford: Clarendon Press, 1958), pp. 288–289.

39. *An Essay on Philosophical Method* (Oxford: Clarendon Press, 1933), pp. 209, 210.

40. *What Philosophy Is* (New York: Harper, 1968), p. 146.

41. *The Life of the Mind: Thinking* (New York: Harcourt Brace Jovanovich, 1977), p. 20.

42. *Philosophy as Dramatic Theory*, p. 6.

43. Peter King, *The Life of John Locke, With Extracts from His Correspondence, Journals, and Common-place Books*, 2 vols. (London, 1830), I, 123.

44. *Locke, Berkeley, Hume* (Oxford: Clarendon Press, 1971), pp. 209, 25.

45. *The Problem of Knowledge* (1956; Harmondsworth: Penguin, 1980), p. 141.

46. *What Philosophy Is*, p. 146.

47. *A Treatise of Human Nature*, ed. L. A. Selby-Bigge, 2nd ed., rev. by P. H. Nidditch (Oxford: Clarendon Press, 1978), p. 594. All further references in the text are to this edition.

48. *The Life of the Mind*, p. 140.

49. *A History of English Thought in the Eighteenth Century*, 2 vols. (1878; New York: Barnes and Noble, 1962), I, 25.

50. *Minima Moralia: Reflections from Damaged Life*, trans. E. F. N. Jephcott (London: New Left Books, 1974), p. 80.

51. *Why Does Language Matter to Philosophy?* (Cambridge: Cambridge University Press, 1975), pp. 29, 51–52, 32.

52. *Discipline and Punish: The Birth of the Prison*, trans. Alan Sheridan (New York: Pantheon, 1977), p. 193.

53. *Possessive Individualism* (Oxford: Clarendon Press, 1962), p. 263.

54. *The Providence of Wit: Aspects of Form in Augustan Literature and the Arts* (Oxford: Clarendon Press, 1974), p. 57.

55. *The Discourse of the Mind in Eighteenth-Century Fiction* (The Hague: Mouton, 1974), p. 33.

56. *Confinement and Flight: An Essay on English Literature of the Eighteenth Century* (Berkeley and Los Angeles: University of California Press, 1977), p. 15.

57. Raymond Polin, "Locke's Conception of Freedom," in *John Locke: Problems and Perspectives*, ed. John Yolton (Cambridge: University Press, 1969), p. 17.

58. *Sensible Words: Linguistic Practice in England 1640–1785* (Baltimore and London: Johns Hopkins University Press, 1977), p. 74.

59. *Literary Meaning and Augustan Values* (Charlottesville: University Press of Virginia, 1974), p. 40.

60. *The Life and Character of . . . the Late Dr. Edw. Stillingfleet* (1710), pp. 86–87, quoted by John Yolton, *John Locke and the Way of Ideas* (London: Oxford University Press, 1956), p. 89. Yolton agrees that Locke's success in the *Essay* owed a great deal to his polished style.

61. George Saintsbury, *A History of English Prose Rhythm* (1912; Bloomington: Indiana University Press, 1965), p. 229.

62. *John Locke* (1937; Oxford: Clarendon Press, 1971), p. 49.

63. In a letter dated December 24, 1695, Molyneux, tireless flatterer that he was, assures Locke that his "Admirable Perspicuity of Writing is so clearly different from all the World, almost peculiar to your self; that in vain you expect to be conceald in any thing that comes from you." He says further that he gave "my Lord Deputy Capel" a copy of "Some Considerations of the Consequences of the Lowering of Interest, and Raising the Value of Money." "He answerd Me, The Printer presented it to him as yours, and besides (says he) All the World knows Mr Lockes Way of Writing, and if I may Gues, I believe the Paper You gave me a few days ago came from Mr Locke; Pray, did it not?" *The Correspondence of John Locke*, ed. E. S. DeBeer (Oxford: Clarendon Press, 1979), V, 492.

64. *Correspondence*, V, 596.

65. Ibid., 266.

66. *Self-Consuming Artifacts*, p. 34.

67. *Of Grammatology*, p. 162.

68. "The Essayist in His *Essay*," in *John Locke: Problems and Perspectives*, pp. 238, 255.

69. *Of Grammatology*, pp. 283, 98.

70. *Marxism and Literature* (Oxford: Oxford University Press, 1977), pp. 128–129.

71. Colie describes this very well: "Locke did not care for delimitation; he was interested in process—for him, human understanding was a lifelong process for each man, a natural condition of humanity. Some of this interest in process—this

preference, one might say, for a process-model over a mechanical model — may be related to Locke's awareness as a physician of the lifelong processes of the human body, processes which, like breathing, we undertake almost without being aware of them. It was as a doctor and scientist, too, that he looked, not at 'the mind,' nor at 'knowledge,' but at men thinking, or, at active patients busy in the process of understanding." "John Locke and the Publication of the Private," *Philological Quarterly*, 45 (1966), 32–33.

72. *The Works of George Berkeley, D.D.*, 4 vols. (Oxford: Clarendon Press, 1871), I, x.

73. *The Pound Era* (Berkeley and Los Angeles: University of California Press, 1973), p. 97.

74. Quoted by Donald Davie, *Articulate Energy: An Inquiry into the Syntax of English Poetry* (London: Routledge and Kegan Paul, 1955), p. 97.

75. Norman Kemp Smith, *The Philosophy of David Hume* (London: Macmillan, 1941), pp. 8–9.

76. David Hume, "Of Essay Writing," *Essays Moral, Political and Literary* (London: Oxford University Press, 1963), p. 568.

77. "The Hermeneutics of Literary Indeterminacy: A Dissent from the New Orthodoxy," *New Literary History*, 10 (Autumn 1978), 87.

2. LOCKE

1. Rosalie Colie calls it the "requisite modesty-trope" and refers us to Curtius' "affected modesty trope" and "things never thought before trope." "The Essayist in His *Essay*," in *John Locke: Problems and Perspectives*, p. 240.

2. Ibid., p. 247.

3. As a number of scholars have pointed out, the "Epistle" is a fair description of the actual origins of the *Essay*. Locke came to philosophical speculation, as Peter Laslett says, after he left Oxford and moved in the orbit provided by Shaftesbury, "the political, social and intellectual life of Restoration London." See *Locke's Two Treatises of Government* (1960; New York: New American Library, 1965), p. 41. The meeting of friends Locke describes took place often at Exeter House in London during Shaftesbury's lifetime. According to James Tyrrell, who was there, the subject that led Locke on to his great work was to what extent men are directed by the "principles of morality and revealed religion." See Maurice Cranston, *John Locke, a Biography* (London: Macmillan, 1957), p. 414. Rosalie Colie built an approach to Locke's writing on its origins in such private intellectual activity. In "Locke and the Publication of the Private," *Philological Quarterly*, 45 (1966), 24–45, Colie finds that Locke "became a publishing writer almost by accident," pushed toward that by his involvement during his Dutch exile in 1683 with Jean le Clerc and *Le Bibliothèque universelle* (p.29). Hans Aarsleff insists that Locke remained a private writer even when he published and that the disorder and lack of precision he exhibits come from his "private way" of writing for himself and a few friends. See "The State of Nature and the Nature of Man in Locke," in *John Locke: Problems and Perspectives*, p. 263. Aarsleff's thesis is modified by considering that Locke gave his printers the manuscript of the *Essay* in batches so that he could continue making revisions, and that the four editions

of the *Essay* printed in his lifetime were heavily if not always substantially revised. See Nidditch, Introduction to the *Essay*, pp. xvi, xix–xxxi. Locke certainly began his work in a private context, but that privacy became in due course part of his public manner as a writer.

4. *Mythologies*, trans. Annette Lavers (New York: Hill and Wang, 1972), p. 141.

5. *The Works of John Locke*, 10 vols. (London, 1823), VII, 135.

6. *Correspondence*, III, 575, 21 Feb. 1689. *Essay*, III.x.20.

7. Reviewing Macpherson's *Possessive Individualism* and defending Locke's integrity, Alan Ryan admits that in his economic writings "his attitude to the labouring poor, and even more to the unemployed, is indubitably severe." "Locke and the Dictatorship of the Bourgeoisie," *Political Studies*, 12 June 1965, 222.

8. Locke is more moderate in the *Reasonableness of Christianity*. There he defends popular religion as a suitable simplification: "This is a religion suited to vulgar capacities; and the state of mankind in this world, destined to labour and to travail . . . The greatest part of mankind have not leisure for learning and logic, and superfine distinctions of the schools. Where the hand is used to the plough and the spade, the head is seldom elevated to sublime notions, or exercised in mysterious reasoning." *Works*, VII, 157.

9. *John Locke and the Way of Ideas*, p. 116.

10. Locke speaks here only of his own "severer enquiry," not of the criticism of others. The deference and concession sprinkled throughout the *Essay* are obviously ironic and sometimes downright disingenuous. As Nidditch notes, Locke ignored his hostile critics, responding "positively and expansively mainly to the generous encouragement and polite suggestions of his friends" (p. xix). With characteristic coyness, Locke remarks in the "Epistle" to the second edition: I have not had the good luck to receive any light from those Exceptions, I have met with in print against any part of my Book, nor have, from any thing has been urg'd against it, found reason to alter my Sense, in any of the Points have been question'd" (p. 11).

11. "A Letter to the Right Reverend Edward Lord Bishop of Worcester," in *The Works of John Locke*, 3 vols. (London, 1751), I, 349.

12. Ibid., 356–357.

13. *Correspondence*, VI, 294–295, 10 Jan. 1698.

14. Maurice Mandelbaum argues that Locke's descriptions of the arbitrariness of our perceptions do not make him a skeptic. Objects have a reality consisting of an "atomic constitution" that causes us "to form the ideas we do form of them." *Philosophy, Science and Sense Perception* (Baltimore: Johns Hopkins University Press, 1964), p. 60. Kathleen Squadrito summarizes recent views of Locke that question the traditional notion of the *Essay* as implicitly skeptical: "By saying that perception and knowledge are mediated by ideas Locke may simply be saying that our observation is theory-laden. What we do see directly is determined by such factors as attention, different capacities for recognizing and classifying objects, learning, past experience with things, etc. There is no contradiction in saying that our perception is mediated by such mental aspects and saying that perception is direct." *John Locke* (Boston: G. K. Hall, 1979), p. 62.

15. Review of Nidditch's edition of the *Essay*, *Times Literary Supplement*, 9 Sept. 1975, p. 1043.

16. *Correspondence*, IV, 624, 20 Jan. 1693.

17. *Some Thoughts Concerning Education*, in *Works* (1823), IX, 177.

18. *Words into Rhythm: English Speech Rhythm in Verse and Prose* (Cambridge: Cambridge University Press, 1976), p. 126.

19. *Rhetoric of Motives* (1950; Berkeley and Los Angeles: University of California Press, 1969), p. 58.

20. *Leviathan*, ed. Michael Oakeshott (Oxford: Basil Blackwell, n.d.), I.15.p.99.

21. Peter Laslett's edition of *Locke's Two Treatises on Government*, XI,137.p.406. All further references in the text are to this edition.

22. *Leviathan*, I.13.p.82.

23. I.5.p.30.

24. I.13.p.15.

25. Peter King was struck by this. He remarks of Locke's *Journals*, "they afford a striking proof of the activity of his mind, of his industry in obtaining information, and of the accuracy of his descriptions." *The Life of John Locke*, II, 61.

26. *The Enlightenment: An Interpretation, The Science of Freedom* (New York: Random House, 1969), p. 14.

27. R. F. Jones has summarized this situation: "The position of the scientists was that the truth of ideas regarding nature was dependent upon the accuracy of language and that the advancement of science must necessarily wait upon the introduction of greater precision and clarity into the use of words." Jones says that the climax of this ambition was John Wilkins' *Essay towards a Real Character and a Philosophical Language* (1668). See "Science and Language in England of the Mid-Seventeenth Century" (1932), rpt. in *Seventeenth-Century Prose: Modern Essays in Criticism*, ed. Stanley Fish (New York: Oxford University Press, 1971), pp. 100, 102.

28. *Political Writings: Surveys from Exile*, ed. David Fernbach (New York: Random House, 1974), p. 148.

29. Macpherson, *Possessive Individualism*, pp. 162, 243–247.

30. Curiously enough, very few commentators have bothered with the obtrusive rhetorical quality of the *Second Treatise*. Theodore Redpath is an exception. He calls it "a masterpiece of rhetorical ingenuity" but expends some rather misplaced outrage on its dubious logical status as he examines its "evocative language or imagery, persuasive definitions, appeals to reverenced authority, or tendentious equivocation." "John Locke and the Rhetoric of the *Second Treatise*," in *The English Mind*, pp. 77, 55. Peter Laslett is more helpful when he redefines the *Treatise* as something other than political philosophy and Locke as "the writer of a work of intuition, insight and imagination, if not of profound originality, who was also a theorist of knowledge." Introduction to *Two Treatises*, p. 99.

31. Gordon Schochet explains Locke's premises when he notes that for him the social but nonpolitical institutions of the state of nature (the family) blend imperceptibly with civil society. Schochet's paraphrase of Locke's omissions and evasions in his theory coincides with my reading of Locke's prose: "By not always making clear the apparent differences between political and non-political societies while simultaneously contending that non-civil societies existed in the state of nature, Locke developed a conception of politics in which the transition from the state of nature to government was virtually effortless; it was, in addition, barely

perceptible." See "The Family and the Origins of the State in Locke's Political Philosophy," in *John Locke: Problems and Perspectives*, pp. 88–89.

32. *The Concept of Mind* (1949; Harmondsworth: Penguin, 1963), p. 153.

33. *The Rhetorical World of Augustan Humanism: Ethics and Imagery from Swift to Burke* (Oxford: Clarendon Press, 1965), pp. 298–299.

34. "Locke and the Dissolution of the Ego," *Modern Philology*, 52 (1955), 161.

35. "Locke's Concept of Experience," in *Locke and Berkeley: A Collection of Critical Essays*, ed. C. B. Martin and D. M. Armstrong (Garden City, N.Y.: Doubleday, 1968), p. 43.

36. Madness, for Locke, uses the "imagination" to restore the fading traces of memory, but it is an intensified and demented substitute for memory that refuses to accept the inevitable gap between the perceived world and the available world. King prints one of Locke's notes that is echoed in the *Essay*: "the ideas of memory, like painting after the life, come always short, *i.e.* want something of the original . . . But the imagination, not being tied to any pattern, but adding what colours, what ideas it pleases, to its own workmanship, making originals of its own which are usually very bright and clear in the mind, and sometimes to that degree that they make impressions as strong and as sensible as those ideas which come immediately by the senses from external objects, — so that the mind takes one for the other, and its own imagination for realities. And in this, it seems, madness consists, and not in the want of reason" (II,170–171).

37. *The Concept of Mind*, p. 153.

38. "John Locke on the Human Understanding," in Martin and Armstrong *Locke and Berkeley*, p. 19.

39. Locke quotes this passage in II.xxi.41: "*Happiness* and *Misery* are the names of two extremes, the utmost bounds whereof we know not; 'tis what *Eye hath not seen, Ear hath not heard, nor hath it entred into the Heart of Man to conceive*."

40. *Locke, Berkeley, Hume*, p. 102.

41. *John Locke and the Way of Ideas*, p. 134. This is, to be sure, a vexed question in Locke studies. Maurice Mandelbaum says that Locke did not believe we have a distinct idea of substance; it is only a supposition about it that we make rather than an idea of sense or reflection. See *Philosophy, Science and Sense Perception*, p. 34. W. VonLeyden explains that Locke adhered in one sense to the traditional notion of real essences even though he saw that our idea of such a thing was not clear. VonLeyden notes that both Stillingfleet and Berkeley thought Locke was merely bantering the idea, treating it as a fiction. And VonLeyden concedes that this is occasionally just what Locke seems to do. See "What Is a Nominal Essence the Essence Of?" in *John Locke: Problems and Perspectives*, p. 225.

42. Laslett points out that in 1681 Locke was at work on the *Essay* and the *Two Treatises*. Page 70.

43. *Sensible Words*, p. 40.

44. "The Epistemology of Metaphor," *Critical Inquiry*, 5 (Autumn 1978), 16.

45. "Locke's Distinction between Primary and Secondary Qualities," in Martin and Armstrong, *Locke and Berkeley*, p. 63.

46. "There is not so contemptible a Plant or Animal, that does not confound the most inlarged Understanding. Though the familiar use of things about us, take off our Wonder; yet it cures not our Ignorance. When we come to examine the Stones, we tread on; or the Iron we daily handle, we presently find, we know not their Make; and can give no Reason of the different Qualities we find in them" (III.vi.9).

47. ". . . yet, methinks, it is not unreasonable to propose, that Words standing for Things, which are known and distinguished by their outward shapes, should be expressed by Draughts and Prints made of them" (III.xi.25).

48. "The Epistemology of Metaphor," pp. 20, 21–22.

49. *Correspondence*, IV, 625–626, 20 Jan. 1693.

50. *Boswell's Life of Johnson*, ed. G. B. Hill and L. F. Powell, 6 vols. (Oxford: Clarendon Press, 1964), II, 82.

51. "Locke and the Problem of Personal Identity," in Martin and Armstrong, *Locke and Berkeley*, p. 176.

3. BERKELEY

1. *Discussions on Philosophy and Literature* (New York: Harper, 1860), p. 82.

2. "The Text, the World, the Critic," in *Textual Strategies: Perspectives in Post-Structuralist Criticism*, ed. Josué V. Harari (Ithaca: Cornell University Press, 1979), pp. 186–187. Said refers to Lukács' essay "On the Nature and Form of the Essay."

3. *A History of English Thought in the Eighteenth Century*, 2 vols. (1878; New York: Barnes and Noble, 1962), I, 33.

4. Gavin Ardley calls "scholastic" and "analytical" studies of Berkeley mistaken in supposing that he was "primarily a speculative metaphysician who, conjointly, nurtured religious prepossessions." Ardley stresses the unity of Berkeley's thought and personality and warns that a merely "external" criticism distorts him and misrepresents his aims. *Berkeley's Renovation of Philosophy* (The Hague: Nijhoff, 1968), pp. 60–61.

5. "On Locke's Essay on the Human Understanding," in *The Collected Works of William Hazlitt*, 12 vols., ed. A. R. Waller and Arnold Glover (London: J. M. Dent, 1904), XI, 107–108.

6. A. A. Luce, *The Dialectic of Immaterialism: An Account of the Making of Berkeley's Principles* (London: Hodder and Stoughton, 1963), pp. 15, 25.

7. *The Unconscious Origin of Berkeley's Philosophy* (London: Hogarth Press, 1953), pp. 39–40.

8. The remark occurs in *The Theory of Vision or Visual Language shewing the immediate Presence and Providence of a Deity Vindicated and Explained* (1733), Berkeley's first published work after his return from America in 1731.

9. *Characteristics of Men, Manners, Opinions, Times*, ed. John M. Robertson, 2 vols. (Indianapolis: Bobbs-Merrill, 1964), II, 282.

10. Ibid., 144.

11. Ibid., 31.

12. *The Impossible Observer: Reason and the Reader in Eighteenth-Century Prose* (Lexington: University Press of Kentucky, 1979), pp. 2–5.

13. *Philosophy and the Mirror of Nature* (Princeton: Princeton University Press, 1979), p. 144.

14. Luce points out that the book is heavily indebted to previous books on vision, especially Molyneux' *Dioptrics*. "Much that passes as his theory was not originated by him, nor by him claimed as his. That distance is not itself seen, that it is a line turned endwise to the eye, that the perception of it is an act of judgment rather than of sense, that we judge it by intermediate objects, by the comparative size of bodies, by the faintness of colour, and by the turn of the eye—all these 'Berkeleian principles' are to be found on one page of Molyneux' *Dioptrics*" (I,156–157).

15. "The Origin of Berkeley's Paradoxes," in *New Studies in Berkeley's Philosophy*, ed. Warren E. Steinkraus (New York: Holt, Rinehart and Winston, 1966), p. 42.

16. As Luce reconstructs it, Berkeley and his Kilkenny school friends visited the cave in July 1699. In a charming editorial moment, Luce notes that he has himself visited the cave and "can testify to the accuracy of Berkeley's description" (IV,243).

17. In a letter to Percival from London Berkeley described Bermuda, a place he had never seen, with similar literary verve: "It would take up too much of your Lordship's time minutely to describe the beauties of Bermuda, the summers refreshed with constant cool breezes, the winters as mild as our May, the sky as light and blue as a sapphire, the ever green pastures, the earth eternally crowned with fruits and flowers. The woods of cedars, palmettos, myrtles, oranges &c., always fresh and blooming. The beautiful situations and prospects of hills, vales, promontories, rocks, lakes and sinuses of the sea. The great variety, plenty, and perfection of fish, fowl, vegetables of all kinds, and (which is in no other of our Western Islands) the most excellent butter, beef, veal, pork, and mutton. But above all, that uninterrupted health and alacrity of spirit, which is the result of the finest weather and gentlest climate in the world, and which of all others is the most effectual cure for the cholic, as I am most certainly assured by the information of many very credible persons of all ranks who have been there" (VIII,128–129).

18. On the *Analyst* and the battle of books it provoked, see Luce's introduction, IV, 60.

19. *Berkeley* (London: Routledge and Kegan Paul, 1977), p. 79.

20. See I. C. Tipton, *Berkeley: The Philosophy of Immaterialism* (London: Methuen, 1974), p. 143.

21. "The Origin of Berkeley's Paradoxes," p. 41.

22. Pitcher, p. 135. "Perhaps the most striking advantage that Berkeley sees in his view that it is God who causes all our ideas of sense is that it moves God into the very center of our lives. It has God producing fantastically complex, conscious effects in each of our minds during every moment of our waking life."

23. "Berkeley's Two Concepts of Mind," in *Berkeley's Principles of Human Knowledge: Critical Studies*, ed. Gale W. Engle and Gabriele Taylor (Belmont, Calif. Wadsworth, 1968), p. 27.

24. *The Early Reception of Berkeley's Immaterialism, 1710–1733* (The Hague: Martinus Nijhoff, 1965), p. 80.

25. "Berkeley's Two Concepts of Mind," p. 27.

26. *Berkeley: The Philosophy of Immaterialism*, p. 72.

27. *Berkeley*, p. 224.

28. *Berkeley: the Philosophy of Immaterialism*, p. 236.

29. *The Dialectic of Immaterialism*, pp. 11, 96, 102.

30. "The forms of nature have been and are being invented by an artist, who also maintains them in life and specific functioning with a 'present exercise of art,' when and so long as he wills to do so. Berkeley the theologian thus explains Berkeley the philosopher: his philosophy seen in the light of his theology is no longer a pungent paradox but a recognition that things are made to be experienced and minds in order to experience them, and that a universe composed of these two orders of being was willed by a single Author who, having made them for one another, designed and willed connections, between them." Augusto Guzzo, "Berkeley and 'Things,'" in Steinkraus, *New Studies in Berkeley's Philosophy*, p. 83.

31. I borrow the broadened application of these terms from Hayden White's *Metahistory: The Historical Imagination in Nineteenth-Century Europe* (Baltimore: Johns Hopkins University Press, 1973).

32. "Berkeley and the Possibility of an Empirical Metaphysics," in Steinkraus, *New Studies in Berkeley's Philosophy*, pp. 17–18.

33. *The Dialectic of Immaterialism*, pp. 162–163, 165.

34. *The Order of Things: An Archaeology of the Human Sciences* (London: Tavistock, 1970), p. 78.

35. See Pitcher, *Berkeley*, p. 207. "The theory of time that so dramatically saves the day is the incredibly simple one that time is nothing more nor less than the succession of conscious willings and perceivings that occur in each mind—or, to put it in the inaccurate, but more convenient, way that Berkeley himself regularly does, the view is that time is the succession of ideas that occur in each mind."

36. *Articulate Energy: An Inquiry into the Syntax of English Poetry* (London: Routledge and Kegan Paul, 1955), p. 119.

37. *European Literature and the Latin Middle Ages*, trans. Willard R. Trask (New York: Harper and Row, 1963), p. 324.

38. "Berkeley on Other Selves: A Study in Fugue," *Philosophical Quarterly*, 4 (1954), 32.

39. *Berkeley*, pp. 132–134; and see *Principles*, sect. 25 (II,51–52).

40. Philonous in *Three Dialogues* is explicit about this method of knowing God: "Ideas are things inactive, and perceived: and spirits a sort of beings altogether different from them. I do not therefore say my soul is an idea, or like an idea. However, taking the word *idea* in a large sense, my soul may be said to furnish me with an idea, that is, an image, or likeness of God, though extremely inadequate. For all the notion I have of God, is obtained by reflecting on my own soul heightening its powers, and removing its imperfections. I have therefore, though not an inactive idea, yet in myself some sort of an active thinking image of the Deity" (II,231–232).

41. *Berkeley: The Philosophy of Immaterialism*, p. 107.

42. *The Unconscious Origin of Berkeley's Philosophy*, p. 62.

43. *The Dialectic of Immaterialism*, p. 38.

44. In *Reason, Ridicule and Religion: The Age of Enlightenment in England, 1660–1750* (Cambridge, Mass.: Harvard University Press, 1976), p. 68, John Redwood finds that Berkeley made his freethinkers too eloquent and left some readers worried that he had done harm to his own cause in *Alciphron*.

45. As Harry Bracken points out, Andrew Baxter's attack on Berkeley in his *Enquiry into the Nature of the Human Soul* (1733) was not the beginning of such criticism: "Before 1733 he had been charged with denying the reality of our sense experience, with failing to distinguish sensations from objects of sensations, with denying the substance/attribute distinction, with propounding an argument against the reality of matter which could be applied to the Self, with committing what we now call the fallacy of initial predication, and in his attack on abstract ideas, he was charged with making a proposal which 'may well set our philosophy on a new footing.'" *The Early Reception of Berkeley's Immaterialism*, p. 5.

46. "Berkeley as Religious Apologist," in Steinkraus, *New Studies in Berkeley's Philosophy*, p. 102.

47. See the second stanza of Davie's poem "The Fountain," *Collected Poems, 1950–1970* (London: Routledge and Kegan Paul; New York: Oxford University Press, 1972), p. 59:

For Berkeley this was human thought, that mounts
From bland assumptions to inquiring skies,
There glints with wit, fumes into fancies, plays
With its negations, and at last descends,
As by a law of nature, to its bowl
Of thus enlightened but still common sense.

48. *A "Letter" from an anonymous Writer to the Author of the "Minute Philosopher,"* printed as an appendix by Luce (I,277).

49. *A History of English Prose Rhythm* (1912; Bloomington, Ind.: Indiana University Press, 1965), p. 253. Saintsbury's praise of *Alciphron* occurs in *The Peace of the Augustans* (London: G. Bell and Sons, 1916), p. 259.

50. In his sermon "On Immortality" of 11 January 1707/08, Berkeley finds the Pauline evocation of that heaven "no other than this empty tho emphatical description of it" (VII,12).

51. "Berkeley's Style in *Siris*," *Cambridge Journal*, 4 (1950–51), 429.

52. Ibid., 429.

53. *Philosophical Studies* (1922; London: Routledge and Kegan Paul, 1951), pp. 18–19, 25.

54. *Writing and Difference*, trans. Alan Bass (Chicago: University of Chicago Press, 1978), p. 11.

4. HUME

1. Hume, "My Own Life," in *Essays Moral, Political and Literary* (London: Oxford University Press, 1963), pp. 607–608. All further references to Hume's *Essays* are to this edition.

2. *The Letters of David Hume*, ed. J. Y. T. Greig, 2 vols. (Oxford: Clarendon

Press, 1932), I, 16, March or April 1734. Greig accepted John Hill Burton's identification of the intended recipient of this letter as Dr. George Cheyne, but Hume's most recent biographer, Ernest Mossner, says it must have been Arbuthnot. See *The Life of David Hume* (Edinburgh: Thomas Nelson and Sons, 1954), p. 84.

3. *Literary Meaning and Augustan Values* (Charlottesville: University Press of Virginia, 1974), p. 43.

4. "Hume's Place in Philosophy," in *David Hume: A Symposium*, ed. D. F. Pears (London: Macmillan, 1963), p. 1.

5. *David Hume* (Edinburgh: Ramsay Head Press, 1976), p. 19.

6. *David Hume* (1958; New York: Dover, 1968), pp. 70, 92.

7. "Hume's Place in Philosophy," p. 1.

8. "Linguistic Analysis as Rhetorical Pattern in David Hume," in *Hume and the Enlightenment: Essays Presented to Ernest Campbell Mossner*, ed. W. B. Todd (Edinburgh: University Press, 1974), p. 80.

9. *Letters*, I, 33. The letter reflects Hume's repeated use of this opposition in the *Treatise*. As he begins Book III, he resolves to ask whether it is by means of our ideas or our impressions that "we distinguish betwixt vice and virtue, and pronounce an action blameable or praise-worthy? This will immediately cut off all loose discourses and declamations, and reduce us to something precise and exact on the present subject" (p.456).

10. "Of Eloquence," *Essays*, p. 105. W. S. Howell notes that Smith's *Lectures on Rhetoric and Belles Lettres* (1762–63) praise Demosthenes on political grounds in part, for Athenian democracy produced a freer and easier style than Roman aristocracy. See *Eighteenth-Century British Logic and Rhetoric* (Princeton: Princeton University Press, 1971), p. 570. The point appears to have been a cultural commonplace. Swift expresses the same preference in almost the same terms in "A Letter to a Young Gentleman, Lately entered into Holy Orders"; see *Irish Tracts 1720–1723*, ed. Herbert Davis (Oxford: Basil Blackwell, 1963), pp. 68–69.

11. *Essays*, p. 109.

12. Ibid., pp. 200, 196.

13. *Letters*, II, 240.

14. Ibid., I, 373.

15. Ibid., I, 32, 13 Sept. 1739.

16. Ibid., I, 33.

17. Ibid., I, 374, Jan. 1763.

18. Thomas Reid's *Inquiry and Essays*, ed. Keith Lehrer and Ronald E. Beanblossom (Indianapolis: Bobbs-Merrill, 1975), pp. 5–6, 8, 15.

19. Quoted by Mossner, *David Hume*, p. 298.

20. *Letters*, I, 375, 376, 25 Feb. 1763.

21. Ibid., I, 376, n. 4.

22. *Inquiry*, pp. 5–6.

23. Ibid., p. 7. Philosophy and Common Sense have been engaged in the preceding sentences in an "unequal contest."

24. *Inquiry*, p. 118.

25. "It is undeniable, and indeed is acknowledged by all, that when we have found two things to have been constantly conjoined in the course of nature, the

appearance of one of them is immediately followed by the conception and belief of the other. The former becomes a natural sign of the latter; and the knowledge of their constant conjunction in time past, whether got by experience or otherwise, is sufficient to make us reply with assurance upon the continuance of that conjunction." *Inquiry*, p. 96.

26. Ibid., p. 103.

27. *Essays on the Intellectual Powers*, p. 21.

28. "Hume's Place in Philosophy," pp. 9–10.

29. *The Concept of Irony*, trans. Lee M. Capel (Bloomington: University of Indiana Press, 1968), pp. 98, 235n, 152n.

30. The phrase is James Noxon's in *Hume's Philosophical Development* (Oxford: Clarendon Press, 1973), p. 22.

31. Writing from a purely philosophical perspective, A. P. Cavendish describes Hume's intellectual assumptions: "For him our understanding is limited because our imagination is limited, and our experience is limited. What is more, these limitations are intrinsic and not accidental. That is to say, it is not simply that our imagination is not so strong as it might be, and our experience is not so extensive as it might be. So long as our imagination works in the way it does, and so long as our experience is of the kind it is, the limitations Hume seeks to impose will hold." *David Hume*, p. 26.

32. "As the explication of this [the continued existence of bodies by virtue of the constancy of their appearance and their coherence] will lead me into a considerable compass of very profound reasoning; I think it proper, in order to avoid confusion, to give a short sketch or abridgement of my system, and afterwards draw out all its parts in their full compass" (p.199).

33. *Hume* (London: Routledge and Kegan Paul, 1977), p. 115.

34. *The Philosophy of David Hume* (London: Macmillan, 1941), p. 13.

35. "In believing that two events are necessarily connected we believe only something about the way the world is, and nothing about our own minds, although we believe what we do only because certain things occur in our minds. And so it can be said after all that we really do believe (albeit falsely, according to Hume) that necessity is something that 'resides' in the relations between objects or events in the objective world." *Hume*, p. 86.

36. "Hume's Theory of Mental Activity," in *Hume: A Collection of Critical Essays*, ed. V. C. Chappell (Notre Dame, Ind.: University of Notre Dame Press, 1968), p. 100.

37. "Hume and the Ethics of Belief," in *David Hume: Bicentenary Papers*, ed. G. P. Morice (Edinburgh: University Press, 1977), pp. 83, 85.

38. *Essays*, pp. 224–225.

39. "The Rationale of Hume's Literary Inquiries," in *David Hume: Many-sided Genius*, ed. Kenneth R. Merrill and Robert W. Shahan (Norman: University of Oklahoma Press, 1976), p. 105.

40. *Hume*, p. 72.

41. *Life of Johnson*, I, 439.

42. *Locke, Berkeley, Hume* (Oxford: Clarendon Press, 1971), pp. 230, 303.

43. *Hume's Philosophical Development*, p. 138.

44. *Occasional Form: Henry Fielding and the Chains of Circumstance* (Baltimore: Johns Hopkins University Press, 1975), p. 150.

45. *Letters*, I, 187, to John Stewart, Feb. 1754.

46. *Letters*, I, 25, 26, Dec. 1737.

47. *Hume's Intentions* (London: Duckworth, 1968), p. 12.

48. *Letters*, I, 27.

49. *Hume's Philosophical Development*, pp. 112, 119. As Noxon stresses elsewhere in his book, Hume was anti-Newtonian in his opposition to the exalted argument from design used by the theological Newtonians of the time (see p. 77). Hume's reservations about the reach of natural philosophy are well known, palpable in the philosophical works and memorably stated in the *History of Great Britain*: "While Newton seemed to draw off the veil from some of the mysteries of nature, he shewed at the same time the imperfections of the mechanical philosophy and thereby restored her ultimate secrets to that obscurity in which they ever did and ever will remain." Cited by Norman Kemp Smith, Introduction to Hume's *Dialogues Concerning Natural Religion* (Indianapolis: Bobbs-Merrill, n. d.), p. 33.

50. *Hume's Philosophical Development*, pp. 19–20, 75, 9.

51. "Some Misunderstandings of Hume," in Chappell, *Hume: A Collection of Critical Essays*, p. 42.

52. "David Hume: Reasoning and Experience," in *The English Mind*, ed. Hugh Sykes Davies and George Watson (Cambridge: University Press, 1964), p. 126.

53. *Letters*, I, 17, to Dr. Arbuthnot, March 1734.

54. "Hume on Personal Identity," in Chappell, *Hume: A Collection of Critical Essays*, pp. 228, 231.

55. Ibid., p. 215.

56. Ibid., p. 229.

57. *Hume's Intentions*, pp. 82–83.

58. "David Hume: His Pyrrhonism and His Critique of Pyrrhonism," in Chappell, *Hume: A Collection of Critical Essays*, p. 98.

59. *The Philosophy of David Hume*, pp. 500–501.

60. "On the Interpretation of Hume," in Chappell, *Hume: A Collection of Critical Essays*, pp. 285, 284.

61. *David Hume*, p. 39.

62. "Some Misunderstandings of Hume," p. 52.

63. Hume often speaks of the pleasures of reasoning, placing them here in "Of the Delicacy of Taste and Passion" right next to the enjoyment of poetry: "When a man is possessed of that talent, [the delicacy of sentiment] he is more happy by what pleases his taste, than by what gratifies his appetites, and receives more enjoyment from a poem, or a piece of reasoning, than the most expensive luxury can afford." *Essays*, p. 5.

64. "David Hume: Reasoning and Experience," p. 127.

65. All of Berkeley's arguments, Hume says in a footnote to the *Enquiry concerning Human Understanding*, "form the best lessons of scepticism, which are to be found either among the ancient or modern philosophers, Bayle not excepted." Of course, Hume notes, Berkeley intended them to counter skeptics and free-thinkers, but they are in reality skeptical, in "*that they admit of no answer and produce no conviction*. Their only effect is to cause that momentary amazement and irresolution and confusion, which is the result of scepticism" (p.155). That is,

Berkeley's arguments lack a properly philosophical rhetorical effect; they do not engage us in discourse or make us thoughtful.

66. *Hume's Intentions*, p. 122.

67. The reference is to Addison's *Spectator*, #412, the first in the series of essays about "the pleasures of the imagination."

68. *Minima Moralia: Reflections from Damaged Life*, trans. E. F. N. Jephcott (London: New Left Books, 1974), p. 64.

69. The interests of the moral historian he was to become sometimes sparkle in Hume's observations: "Nothing is more evident, than that any person acquires our kindness, or is expos'd to our ill-will, in proportion to the pleasure or uneasiness we receive from him, and that the passions keep pace exactly with the sensations in all their changes and variations." System coexists with acute observation, but in the next sentence a delight in moral variety takes over. "Whoever can find the means either by his services, his beauty, or his flattery, to render himself useful or agreeable to us, is sure of our affections: As on the other hand, whoever harms or displeases us never fails to excite our anger or hatred" (p.348).

70. For example, he begins with an appeal to impatience. Since it is impossible to define the will, "we shall cut off all those definitions and distinctions, with which philosophers are wont to perplex rather than clear up this question" (p.399). A catalogue of examples follows, a few pages later, to show how human regularity matches natural pattern: "a very slight and general view of the common course of human affairs" (p.401) is actually an insistent rhetorical appeal. "For is it more certain, that two flat pieces of marble will unite together, than that two young savages of different sexes will copulate?" (p.402). Hume brings on an opponent who objects at length and who commands generalizing aphorisms of his own: "Necessity is regular and certain. Human conduct is irregular and uncertain. The one, therefore, proceeds not from the other" (p.403). And Hume answers with elaborate underlining: "To this I reply" (p.403) begins an oration, complete with the pure argumentation of paradoxical examples like this: "'Tis commonly allow'd that mad-men have no liberty. But were we to judge by their actions, these have less regularity and constancy than the actions of wise-men, and consequently are farther remov'd from necessity" (p.404).

71. To his conclusion that "all inferences from experience" are the "effects of custom, not of reasoning" (p.43) Hume adds a long note denying the distinction between reason and experience. In fact, general maxims said to be the result of reason are simply less immediate than insights from experience, where "the experienced event is exactly and fully similar to that which we infer as the result of any particular situation" (p.44). What Hume calls an "unexperienced reasoner," could strictly speaking be no reasoner at all, since such a reasoner is someone we suppose "possessed of experience, in a smaller and more imperfect degree" (pp.44–45).

72. *David Hume* (New York: Twayne, 1968), pp. 50–51.

73. Consider, for example, the opening of the "Conclusion" of Book I, where Hume pauses before launching out "into those immense depths of philosophy, which lie before me" (p.263). He has narrowly escaped shipwreck in the coastal waters of epistemological controversy but "has yet the temerity to put out to sea in the same leaky weather-beaten vessel, and even carries his ambition so far as to

think of compassing the globe under these disadvantageous circumstances" (pp.263–264). Further contemplation of this prospect, however, makes him "resolve to perish on the barren rock, on which I am at present, rather than venture myself upon that boundless ocean, which runs out into immensity" (p.264).

74. *Enquiries concerning Human Understanding and concerning the Principles of Morals*, "Introduction," p. x.

75. *An Inquiry Concerning the Principles of Morals* (Indianapolis: Bobbs-Merrill, 1957), p. ix.

76. *Structures of Experience: Essays on the Affinity between Philosophy and Literature* (New York: Harper and Row, 1974), pp. 57–58.

77. "Hume's Theory of Mental Activity," pp. 99–100.

78. *Hume*, pp. 184–185.

79. *Dialogues Concerning Natural Religion*, ed. Norman Kemp Smith (1947; Indianapolis: Bobbs-Merrill, n. d.), pp.182–183. According to Kemp Smith, Hume completed a first version of the *Dialogues* in 1750–51 and made revisions before 1761 and just before his death in 1776 (p. v.). Hume wrote to Adam Smith as he revised them for the last time "that nothing can be more cautiously and more artfully written." *Letters*, II, 334, 15 Aug. 1776.

80. *Letters*, I, 158, March or April 1751.

81. Selby-Bigge's introduction to his edition of the *Enquiries* contains a useful table comparing the *Treatise* to its recasting in the later works.

82. Perhaps the best example of this occurs in section VIII of *An Enquiry concerning Human Understanding*, where Hume proposes to resolve "the long disputed question concerning liberty and necessity" by treating it as merely a verbal matter, some ambiguous expressions which have for the last two thousand years obscured the plain fact "that all men have ever agreed in the doctrine both of necessity and liberty, according to any reasonable sense, which can be put on these terms" (p.81).

83. Ernest Mossner uses it as the epigraph for his biography, *The Life of David Hume*.

84. At the end of Book II of the *Treatise*, Hume finds in "Of curiosity, or the love of Truth" that philosophy provides pleasures much like those of gaming and hunting, all three requiring some sort of conviction of utility or actual gain in the pursuit. Philosophy in the *Treatise* is a passion that encourages a belief in the possibility of final truth, just as a well-fed man will only hunt game birds and a wealthy gambler will take no pleasure in playing for nothing. In the *Enquiries*, the game of philosophy is more like chess or crossword puzzles, self-enclosed and symmetrical and providing its own internal satisfactions.

85. The notorious billiard balls are not in the *Treatise* proper but in the *Abstract* Hume published in 1740.

86. "But though this question, concerning the general principles of morals, be curious and important, it is needless for us, at present, to employ further care in our researches concerning it. For if we can be so happy, in the course of this enquiry, as to discover the true origin of morals, it will then easily appear how far either sentiment or reason enters into all determinations of this nature" (p.173).

87. *Letters*, I, 265.

88. *Essays*, pp. 569, 570, 568.

Index

1E